HANDBOOK OF ORGAN ROUTINES

Handbook of Organizational Routines

Edited by

Markus C. Becker

Professor, Strategic Organization Design Unit, Department of Marketing and Management, University of Southern Denmark

Edward Elgar

Cheltenham, UK • Northampton, MA, USA

Published by
Edward Elgar Publishing Limited
The Lypiatts
15 Lansdown Road
Cheltenham
Glos GL50 2JA
UK

Edward Elgar Publishing, Inc.
William Pratt House
9 Dewey Court
Northampton
Massachusetts 01060
USA

Paperback edition 2010

A catalogue record for this book
is available from the British Library

Library of Congress Control Number: 2008927945

MIX
Paper from
responsible sources
FSC
www.fsc.org   FSC® C021018

ISBN 978 1 84376 958 3 (cased)
      978 1 84980 051 8 (paperback)

Printed in Great Britain by Berforts Information Press Ltd

Contents

List of contributors   vii

PART I

1   The past, present and future of organizational routines:
    introduction to the *Handbook of Organizational Routines*   3
    Markus C. Becker
2   The concept of a routine   15
    Geoffrey M. Hodgson

PART II   ORGANIZATIONAL ROUTINES ACROSS
          DIFFERENT FIELDS

3   Organizational routines in political science   31
    Timothy J. McKeown
4   Routines, 'going concerns' and innovation:
    towards an evolutionary economic sociology   52
    Marc J. Ventresca and William N. Kaghan
5   Organizational routines in accounting   87
    John Burns and Robert W. Scapens
6   Problem solving and governance in the capability-based view
    of the firm: the roles and theoretical representations of
    organizational routines   107
    Giovanni Dosi, Marco Faillo and Luigi Marengo

PART III   ORGANIZATIONAL ROUTINES, SEARCH AND
           LEARNING

7   Organizational routines in evolutionary theory   125
    Thorbjørn Knudsen
8   Organizational routines and organizational learning   152
    Anne S. Miner, Michael P. Ciuchta and Yan Gong
9   Organizational routines and performance feedback   187
    Henrich R. Greve
10 Routines and routinization: an exploration of some
    micro-cognitive foundations   205
    Nathalie Lazaric

11 Staying on track: a voyage to the internal mechanisms of
   routine reproduction   228
   Martin Schulz
12 The role of teams and communities in the emergence of
   organizational routines   256
   Patrick Cohendet and Patrick Llerena

PART IV   CONDUCTING EMPIRICAL RESEARCH ON
          ORGANIZATIONAL ROUTINES

13 Issues in empirical field studies of organizational routines   281
   Brian T. Pentland and Martha S. Feldman
14 Conducting experimental research on organizational routines   301
   Alessandro Narduzzo and Massimo Warglien

Index   325

Contributors

Markus C. Becker, University of Southern Denmark, Odense, Denmark

John Burns, University of Dundee, UK

Michael P. Ciuchta, University of Wisconsin, US

Patrick Cohendet, HEC Montreal, Canada and BETA University Louis Pasteur – CNRS, Strasbourg, France

Giovanni Dosi, Sant' Anna School of Advanced Studies, Pisa, Italy

Marco Faillo, University of Trento, Italy

Martha S. Feldman, University of California, Irvine, US

Yan Gong, University of California, Irvine, US

Henrich R. Greve, INSEAD, Singapore

Geoffrey M. Hodgson, Business School, University of Hertfordshire, UK

William N. Kaghan, Santa Clara University, CA, US

Thorbjørn Knudsen, University of Southern Denmark, Odense, Denmark

Nathalie Lazaric, Centre National de Recherche Scientifique, Sophia-Antipolis, France

Patrick Llerena, BETA, University Louis Pasteur – CNRS, Strasbourg, France

Timothy J. McKeown, University of North Carolina, Chapel Hill, US

Luigi Marengo, Sant' Anna School of Advanced Studies, Pisa, Italy

Anne S. Miner, University of Wisconsin, US

Alessandro Narduzzo, Free University of Bozen-Bolzano, Italy

Brian T. Pentland, Michigan State University, US

Robert W. Scapens, University of Groningen, the Netherlands and Manchester Business School, UK

Martin Schulz, University of British Columbia, Canada

Marc J. Ventresca, Naval Postgraduate School, Monterey CA and Oxford University, UK

Massimo Warglien, Ca' Foscari University of Venice, Italy

PART I

1 The past, present and future of organizational routines: introduction to the *Handbook of Organizational Routines*

Markus C. Becker

To understand routines is to understand organizations.[1] Routines are ubiquitous in organizations, and an integral part of organizations. One is hard put to identify an organization where no routines are present. A large part of the tasks carried out in organizations, such as manufacturing, marketing and selling goods and services, are accomplished in routinized ways. This is not only true for trivial operations, such as manufacturing, but also pervades processes such as decision making, strategizing or even change and innovation. Organizational routines are the building blocks of organizations: they capture the typical ways in which organizations accomplish their tasks.

As it turns out, understanding organizational routines is not a trivial undertaking. So far, just getting an overview of the concept of organizational routines and what we know about organizational routines was quite difficult. For one, no obvious point of reference was available, the 1996 *Industrial and Corporate Change* article documenting the discussion of the Santa Fe group perhaps being the only exception (Cohen et al., 1996). The *Handbook of Organizational Routines* addresses this gap.

In this introduction, I will not attempt to describe comprehensively the present state of the research on organizational routines. As James March (1965: ix) so eloquently put it, 'no editor, and least of all a sympathetic one, should attempt to summarize that state. It is what it is; and what it is can best be discovered by reading the detailed chapters'. Rather, I want to use the occasion to sketch an overarching framework for the chapters in this volume, and highlight some threads that link them in ways that are not always obvious from the individual chapters themselves. The *Handbook* is structured around four topics, corresponding to its four sections. Each mirrors an important set of questions in the literature on organizational routines.

The concept of organizational routines

A recurrent theme in articles on organizational routines in the past was the definitional ambiguity surrounding the concept. For obvious reasons, this is no attractive feature, neither of the concept nor of the literature that deals with it. The *Handbook* bears good news on the issue. For starters, a cause of ambiguity in definitions has now become clear. On this basis, scholars have subsequently pointed out several ways to move forward. In my reading, when scholars have used the term 'organizational routine', they have referred to three different concepts: recurrent behaviour patterns, rules or procedures, and dispositions (for a detailed review of the literature, see Becker, 2004). At the same time, routines are ubiquitous in organizations, and the term has an everyday, commonsense meaning. Against this backdrop, it does not come as much of a surprise that the term 'routine' has been linked to a set of different (albeit related) concepts. What to make of it? The three concepts clearly cannot be reduced to one or the other. Rules are not behaviour, behaviour is not the same as rules, potential behaviour is not the same as actual behaviour, and so on. This might indicate that the underlying constructs the terms refer to might also be irreducible to one another. This question clearly lies beyond the scope of this introduction. It does, however, hint at the *relations* between rules, behaviour and disposition as fruitful foci of description and analysis. How do rules relate to recurrent behaviour patterns? How do dispositions relate to recurrent behaviour patterns? Answering these questions is important for understanding organizations. Acknowledging that scholars link the term 'routines' to three different concepts that are related but different holds the key to unlocking the potential of the routines concept to inform research questions on organizations. The way ahead is to consider the contribution each of those concepts, and their interactions, interrelations and interdependencies, bring to such research questions.

One more immediate question remains, however: what *does* – and should – the term 'organizational routines' refer to? In the *Handbook*, this question is tackled from two angles. In his entry, 'The concept of a routine', Geoffrey M. Hodgson approaches the question by picking up the distinction of potentiality and actuality. From this perspective, the three constructs that authors have referred to fall into two groups: recurrent behaviour patterns (actualized, realized), and rules and procedures, and dispositions (both describing potential behaviour). Using this distinction, Hodgson concludes that one term cannot usefully denote both potentiality and actuality. He argues that the term 'organizational routines' should refer to potential behaviour – causes of stable behaviour patterns – rather than to actual behaviour that has been expressed. In 'Organizational routines in evolutionary theory', Thorbjørn Knudsen considers the question from a different angle, garnering support for a similar conclusion from different quarters. He asks: 'What characteristics does the concept of organizational routines need to have in order to answer the questions it is supposed to answer?' Economic (and organizational) change is the most prominent question to which the organizational routines concept is seen to provide an answer. Famously, Nelson and Winter's (1982) idea of routines as equivalent of genes proposes one possible explanatory avenue. Precisely what characteristics, however, would the concept of routines need to have in order to fulfil the role of 'equivalent to the gene' in evolutionary theories of cultural and economic change? Importantly for the definition of routines, Knudsen's answer is that, to fulfil such a role, organizational routines need to be defined as causes of behaviour (more specifically, as dispositions), rather than behaviour patterns.[2]

Looking ahead, these insights suggest three issues on which it appears fruitful to adapt our thinking. First, to use the label 'routines' for only one of these three concepts, and other labels for the others (while not denying all three are important in explaining certain phenomena). Second, to take note of powerful arguments as to why organizational routines should refer to dispositions: amongst others, it seems that only if understood as dispositions can we expect routines to do the explanatory work that has always been their promise. Third, to unpack the potential that lies in recognizing there are three different concepts that seem to be linked. The potential is to explore (systematic) interactions between these three concepts. This could open a potential explanatory avenue for phenomena of great importance to understanding organizations, such as their stability and change. The tide is thus turning. Definitional ambiguity is giving way to clearly outlined paths for tackling important research questions on organizations.

Organizational routines across different fields
The concept of organizational routines has a number of particular features that should make it very attractive for many fields of the social sciences. The first comes out clearly if we consider the concept of organizational routines as a part of the family of concepts such as institutions, norms or conventions. All these concepts refer to the collective level. The concept of organizational routines is the most micro-level concept amongst these collective-level concepts. Thus, it seems particularly well-suited for capturing collective action below the level of the organization as a whole, such as collective action encompassing only a fraction of the organization's members as in a team or group.

The second feature of the organizational routines concept that sets it apart from other, collective-level concepts is to relate the individual level to the collective level. Organizational routines capture stable structures in collective action that emerge from the interrelating of individual action. Such individual action can itself be patterned in stable ways, as expressed by the individual-level concept of habit. Habits can be building blocks of organizational routines. This idea can be found in the works of, for instance, Dewey (Cohen, 2007), but also other pragmatist authors such as C.S. Peirce. The feature of relating the individual level to the collective level has another powerful implication: it means that, by nature, the concept of organizational routine is neither over- nor undersocialized, to use Granovetterian terminology (Granovetter, 1985). Precisely because the concept of organizational routines *relates* individual to collective behaviour, abstracting from individual action that is intertwined into collective patterns of action would leave out an important part of what organizational routines are supposed to capture. It would result in omitting an important part of organizational routines. The same would result from attempting to reduce the pattern of interlocked actions of individuals to the individual level only. In so doing, one would lose sight of the pattern (and of its performance implications). Furthermore, there is an even stronger reason why the organizational routines concept is neither over- nor undersocialized. To interlock individual action seems to require orienting one's actions towards others. The empirical studies of organizational routines by Karl Weick and co-workers (Weick, 1990; Weick and Roberts, 1993) forcefully establish the importance of orienting oneself towards triggers and cues by other team members, in order to generate a smooth and well-functioning routine that will remain stable even under extreme pressure.[3] The interlocking of individual actions into collective-level routines seems crucial. Trying to reduce organizational routines exclusively to the collective or the individual level would sideline one of its crucial characteristics.

In this context, it is interesting to note that the concept of organizational routines can be seen as a concept of order. Going back to Weber, the concept of order refers to 'a prescription for how to act, that is "exemplary" or "obligatory" ' (Weber, 1978: 311, cf. Knudsen and Swedberg, 2007: 16).[4] Many other concepts of order exist, such as institution, convention, norm, tradition, folkways or mores. All of them have been applied to the sphere of the economy (even the notion of folkways: see Ellsworth's (1952) 'factory folkways'). There are many differences between these concepts, and to consider them is beyond the scope of this chapter. What is similar across all these concepts of order is that they generate more or less stable links between situations and behavioural options. When facing a particular situation, the actor is likely to choose a particular behavioural option. In this respect, orders have a similar effect to what James March (1994) calls the 'logic of appropriateness'. It answers the question, 'What does a person such as I, or an organization such as this, do in a situation such as this?' Such appropriateness also generates more or less stable links between situations and behavioural options.[5] All concepts of order guide actors towards more or less stable links between situations and behavioural options.

Institutions, conventions, norms, traditions, folkways and mores do so in different ways, for instance through sanctions (in the case of norms). Orders all increase the probability that actors will respond to a certain (trigger in a) situation with a particular action, rather than other actions. Concepts of order link situations to behaviour. By so doing, they structure individual behaviour.

Orders play important roles in all fields of the social sciences. The concept of organizational routines has not received much attention outside the field of, broadly speaking, management and business, and economics. One reason is that each field of the social sciences has a 'primary' concept of order that has absorbed most of the fields' attention, such as institutions in sociology. It certainly makes sense to focus on a concept of order that is aligned with the level of analysis of the field. Organizational routines allow us to capture order below the level of the organization and, thus, to describe building blocks of structured behaviour that the organization's behaviour is made up of.

Organizations are omnipresent in modern society (Simon, 1991). They pervade (almost) all aspects of social life, and all fields of the social sciences. Adding additional analytical power on the organizational level should be in the interest of theories in all fields of the social sciences. The chapters in this section take stock of the reception of the concept of organizational routines in a number of fields of the social sciences.

In his chapter, 'Organizational routines in political science', Timothy McKeown presents an overview of the political science literature, which shares an interest in phenomena such as administrative organizations and bureaucracies with the literature interested in organizational routines. As he explains, the political science literature has used the notion of organizational routines for analysing issues such as bureaucracies, administration and government conduct. He describes the historical trajectory of studies of routines within political science, tracing the interpretations of routines as patterned behaviour and as rules and how they have allowed us to analyse problems in political science. McKeown's article identifies docking points and potential synergies between political science and studies of organizations. In doing so, he goes beyond identifying obvious points of contact such as bureaucratic formalization and points to areas of fruitful cooperation between the fields.

Sociology is, of course, another discipline that should have a strong shared interest in organizational routines, yet, for many non-sociologists, it is not easy to leverage the sociology literature for adding to their understanding of organizational routines. In the article 'Routines, 'going concerns' and innovation: towards an evolutionary economic sociology', Marc Ventresca and William Kaghan build a bridge. In their chapter, they guide non-sociologists through micro- and macro-sociological approaches, carefully pointing out how they can be linked up with the concept of organizational routines and the literature on it. They review work from organizational and economic sociology that focuses on the relationship between routines and organizational and institutional innovation. In their article, Ventresca and Kaghan identify docking points between the management literature on organizational routines and the sociological literature and foster transfer of ideas between the two fields. Moreover, they outline a sociological view of routines that relates organizational stability to organizational change and that forms the basis for a 'theory of the innovative firm', and identify some elements of an evolutionary economic sociology.

John Burns and Robert Scapens's chapter on 'Organizational routines in accounting' describes how scholars within the accounting discipline have developed an understanding of its subject through conceptualizing accounting routines, and how accounting might contribute towards developing our understanding of organizational routines literature. In accounting, formalized rules obviously have a particularly important role. Linking back to the relation between rules, behaviour patterns and dispositions mentioned at the beginning, accounting therefore presents a particularly good occasion for research on the interaction between rules and behaviour patterns. Burns and Scapens offer an insightful discussion of this interaction. Let me point out a curious coincidence that perhaps is more than just accidental: their analysis of the transmission of routines in the specific context of accounting bears an interesting resemblance to recent conceptual work on evolutionary theory in the social realm (Knudsen, 2002: 450). The authors have arrived at this argument by different routes (empirical description in accounting and theoretical argument) and, apparently, without being aware of each other's work. This is an encouraging sign because it signals convergence between empirical research in specific fields and conceptual research anchored in disciplinary arguments.

Organizational routines are often seen in connection with competences and capabilities, usually considered the building blocks of the latter (Dosi et al., 2000). Largely because of this connection, organizational routines also have a role in the strategy literature. The chapter on 'Problem solving and governance in the capability-based view of the firm: the roles and theoretical representation of organizational routines', by Giovanni Dosi, Marco Faillo and Luigi Marengo provides a detailed overview of the relationship between the notion of organizational routines and the capability-based view of the firm, a particular instance of the resource-based view of strategy (Barney, 1991; Peteraf, 1993). A special focus in that overview is on the double function of routines as both problem-solving arrangements and governance devices, and on recent efforts to formalize the processes of search and organizational adaptation, in which routines emerge and are stabilized. The chapter provides an overview of such efforts, including NK models (Kauffman, 1993). By broaching the topic of search, the chapter provides a link to the following section, on 'Organizational routines, search and learning'.

Organizational routines, search and learning
Part III turns to some of the key issues that organizational routines can help understand better. Some readers might be surprised to see organizational routines associated with 'dynamic' topics such as search and learning. Are organizational routines not linked, rather, to stability or rigidity? The answer is 'yes and no'. Yes, because organizational routines can be sources of stability in organizations (Schulz, this volume). No, because, at the same time, organizational routines can *also* be sources of organizational change, for instance, through learning and search. In a series of articles, Martha Feldman (2000; 2003; Feldman and Pentland, 2003) recently explained how organizational routines are endogenous drivers of organizational change (see also Knudsen, this volume). Learning and search are some of the key processes by which such change is generated (Miner et al., this volume; Greve, this volume). Organizational routines have crucial roles in these processes. Part III is devoted to identifying the role of organizational routines in learning, search and adaptation processes, thereby tightening our grasp of when and how organizational routines can drive change. Keeping in mind that organizational routines can be the source both of stability and of change, it should be clear why the topics dealt with in Part III are crucial: to understand when and how organizational routines fuel stability, and when and how they fuel change.

The analytical power of organizational routines in understanding incremental organizational change represents one of the most important potentials of the organizational routines concept. Martha Feldman (2000; 2003; Feldman and Pentland, 2003) changed the way we understand routines when she explained how organizational routines can be endogenous drivers of organizational change – a far cry from the idea of organizational routines as the opposite of organizational change that is so widely diffused. If one accepts this idea, the chapters in this section open the door to coming to grips with understanding the role of organizational routines in bringing about organizational change.

While the other entries in this section focus on one particular instance of change, Thorbjørn Knudsen's chapter on 'Organizational routines in evolutionary theory' considers the role of organizational routines in evolutionary theories of cultural and economic change. He identifies features of organizational routines that account for their role in such theories, and characteristics that every evolving unit needs to have in an evolutionary theory. Nelson and Winter's (1982) notion of 'routines as genes' has turned out to be most inspiring to many scholars. It has also turned out difficult to understand, and not easily applied in further research. For the first time, Knudsen's chapter presents a full-fledged analysis of the role of routines in evolutionary theories of cultural and economic change, a helpful endeavour for all who grapple with applying Nelson and Winter's (1982) inspiring idea.

In their chapter, 'Organizational routines and organizational learning', Anne S. Miner, Michael Ciuchta and Yan Gong provide an overarching framework that demonstrates how organizational learning processes that involve routines can encapsulate many of the sub-processes described elsewhere in this part of the *Handbook*. Numerous empirical findings that substantiate the model are presented. The authors first note that routines can form the basis of organizational memory, thus providing a source of stability in organizations discussed by Schulz (this volume). Miner et al. then establish that a variation–selection–retention model can be used to account for both deliberate and emergent learning processes involving routines. Notably, the performance feedback learning processes discussed by Greve (this volume) are a special case of the selection process found within the broader variation–selection–retention perspective. The authors also note that, although much empirical research has viewed routines as stable with the change in the mix of routines as evidence of organizational learning, more attention is now being directed towards the concept that change in routines themselves can be engines of learning (Miner, Ciuchta and Gong, this volume). This more contemporary understanding of the role that routines play in organizational learning provides needed insights into the emergence of routines (Lazaric, this volume). Lastly, the authors tackle an understudied organizational process by exploring how specific routines can be deployed to generate learning.

In the management literature, search processes are amongst the most important explanations of change (Cyert and March, 1963). In such processes, performance feedback plays a crucial role. Measured against an aspiration level, it triggers search when results are below the aspiration level (in case of slack, extra resources trigger search). In the entry 'Organizational routines and performance feedback', Henrich Greve analyses the role of routines in this important step of search processes and, thus, the role of routines in what is the perhaps most widely diffused explanation of organizational change. Many papers on search have focused on *either* the macro or micro level. In his chapter, Greve treads more or less unchartered territory in exploring the meso level. Moreover, he covers the multi-level nature of performance feedback effects on routines, that is, performance feedback operating on the organization, on work groups in the organization, and on individuals, with differing goals and consequences.

The objective of Nathalie Lazaric's chapter on 'Routines and routinization: an exploration of some micro-cognitive foundations' is to provide a framework for examining changes occurring *within* organizational routines. For doing so, she casts light on the cognitive micro foundations of routines in order to understand the drivers and triggers of the routinization process. Establishing the link between organizational routines and procedural memory (Cohen and Bacdayan, 1994), she then explores how individual and collective memorization occurs, in order to grasp how knowledge can be converted into routines.

'Staying on track: a voyage to the internal mechanisms of routine reproduction', by Martin Schulz, focuses on the stability of routines and its sources. Organizational routines are sources of stability and, thus, core concepts in theories of social and economic order. What mechanism endogenous to routines generates such stability? If their stabilizing effect could be reduced to external forces, we would not need a concept of routine. Schulz reviews mechanisms that address how prior actions select consecutive action, and how the mechanisms coevolve with routines. The mechanisms cover, amongst others, habitualization, priming, institutionalization, value infusion, formalization, artefacts, calculation and competency traps.

The chapter on 'The role of teams and communities in the emergence of organizational routines', by Patrick Cohendet and Patrick Llerena, considers how routines emerge. The authors elaborate on the well-established feature of context-dependency of organizational routines, exploring teams and communities as two different contexts in which routines emerge and develop. In so doing, they also cast light on two aspects that have often received less attention than deemed appropriate, that is, the nature of the group of agents involved in the routine (cf. Feldman, 2000), and the cognitive, motivational and incentive aspects of organizational routines (cf. Coriat and Dosi, 1998).

Conducting empirical research on organizational routines
The final Part shifts to considering how to apply the concept of organizational routines in empirical research. Empirical research will play an important role in casting light on organizational phenomena. So far, however, employing the concept of organizational routines in empirical research has turned out to be somewhat difficult. Qualitative studies have lacked cumulativeness, partly due to different definitions of organizational routines that authors have used. Moreover, different definitions have often led to different operationalizations (for instance in surveys). The authors of the two chapters in this part share their rich experience on how to carry out

empirical research on organizational routines. This final part covers qualitative, quantitative and experimental methods, providing inputs on all the drawers in the methodological toolbox.

In 'Issues in empirical field studies of organizational routines', Brian Pentland and Martha Feldman cover qualitative and quantitative methods for research on organizational routines. Focusing on the two tasks of identification and comparison, they elaborate on a set of issues involved in these two tasks. They also offer practical advice, based on their own empirical research. Regarding identification, they discuss ostensive and performative aspects of routines, as well as artefacts (such as written standard operating procedures), their relationship and how to identify each in practice. As regards comparison, they discuss details of quantitative methods for comparing the similarity of behaviour sequences, an issue pioneered by one of the authors.

In the chapter on 'Conducting experimental research on organizational routines', Alessandro Narduzzo and Massimo Warglien review experimental research related to the concepts of routine and routinization, and explore some opportunities for dialogue with the recent work in experimental economics and behavioural game theory. In so doing, they identify some features of organizational routines that are amenable to experimental inquiry, focusing on issues of procedural memory, how routines are retrieved, the implications of routinization for information search, suboptimality and path dependency. They argue that many experimental game settings provide interesting grounds for the emergence of routinized behaviour, even though the classical paradigm within which experiments on learning in games are developed seems too narrow for understanding the development of routines. They suggest how experimental practices on games might be oriented to further the dialogue between experimental research, and point out what insights there are in behavioural game theory for students of routines.

Conclusion and outlook

As a research topic, organizational routines have quite particular features. They are ubiquitous, everyone has an intuitive idea of what they are, and they seem taken for granted and difficult to trace in empirical research. Moreover, when we want to use the concept, it often turns out more difficult than expected. It would be a mistake, however, to resign and leave off at this point. Much progress on clarifying the concept of routines, and how it can be used in empirical research, has been made over the last couple of years. Different methodologies for empirical research on organizational routines have been pioneered, described and tested. They cover quantitative, qualitative and experimental methods. By now, templates are increasingly available – and being applied – for carrying out quantitative, qualitative and experimental research on organizational routines. This is a big step forward. An increasing number of empirical studies on organizational phenomena, applying organization routines as an analytical lens, are now carried out. The results are starting to cumulate (for instance, articles applying Pentland-style sequence analysis). More elaborate methodologies are being developed and consolidated. At the same time, the concept has also been sharpened. Another encouraging sign is worth noting: for making advances in understanding empirical phenomena, it seems helpful to draw both on empirical research and on research firmly rooted in conceptual frameworks in the scientific disciplines. This also holds for advancing research on organizations (Heath and Sitkin, 2001). It is encouraging to see this is feasible and actually being done in the case of organizational routines. We have actually broached the task of drawing on underlying disciplinary knowledge in doing research on organizations by using the concept of organizational routines. In this light, the fact that much still remains to be done signals there is much unused potential still to be reaped. These are all promising signs that bode well for the potential of applying the concept of organizational routines in research on understanding organizations.

Notes

1. Thanks to Thorbjørn Knudsen, Anne Miner, Nils Stieglitz and Francesco Zirpoli for helpful comments on earlier versions of this draft. This introduction has also benefited from discussions of related topics with Michael Cohen, Brian Pentland and Richard Swedberg. All remaining errors and omissions are my own. Support from the Agence Nationale de Recherche, France, is gratefully acknowledged ('Jeunes Chercheuses et Jeunes Chercheurs' program, grant no. JC05-44029).
2. The careful reader will note that authors of the different chapters use different interpretations of the term 'organizational routines'. In all chapters, authors clearly identify their definitions in order to help the reader. The variety of interpretations of the term reflects the current state of the field. It is one thing to argue what should be and another to actually reach that state. As pointed out in this introduction, there are promising signs of convergence.
3. The notion of 'mindfulness' that empirical research on organizational routines such as Weick's has identified provides a bridge to the 'orientation towards others' in Weber. 'Mindfulness' points to attention, and 'orientation' to how it is directed or on what it is focused. Links to the 'focus of attention' in the Behavioral Theory of the Firm are obvious.
4. In the sphere of the (capitalist) economy, the concept of order refers to a 'general prescription for how to act in the sphere of the economy, with the purpose of making a profit' (Knudsen and Swedberg, 2007: 16).
5. The stability of such links can be usefully described as conditional probability (Knudsen, this volume).

References

Barney, Jay (1991), 'Firm resources and sustained competitive advantage', *Journal of Management*, **17**(1), 99–120.

Becker, Markus C. (2004), 'Organizational routines: a review of the literature', *Industrial and Corporate Change*, **13**(4), 643–77.

Cohen, Michael D. (2007), 'Reading Dewey: reflections on the study of routine', *Organization Studies*, **28**(5), 773–86.

Cohen, Michael and Paul Bacdayan (1994), 'Organizational routines are stored as procedural memory: evidence from a laboratory study', *Organization Science*, **5**(4), 554–68.

Cohen, Michael D., Roger Burkhart, Giovanni Dosi, Massimo Egidi, Luigi Marengo, Massimo Warglien and Sidney G. Winter (1996), 'Routines and other recurring action patterns of organizations: contemporary research issues', *Industrial and Corporate Change*, **5**(3), 653–98.

Coriat, Benjamin and Giovanni Dosi (1998), 'Learning how to govern and learning how to solve problems: on the co-evolution of competences, conflicts and organizational routines', in Alfred D. Chandler, Jr., Peter Hagström and Örjan Sölvell (eds), *The Dynamic Firm. The Role of Technology, Strategy, Organization and Regions*, Oxford: Oxford University Press, pp. 103–133.

Cyert, Richard M. and James G. March (1963/1992), *A Behavioral Theory of the Firm*, 2nd edn, Oxford: Blackwell.

Dosi, Giovanni, Richard R. Nelson and Sidney G. Winter (2000), 'Introduction: the nature and dynamics of organizational capabilities' in Giovanni Dosi, Richard R. Nelson and Sidney G. Winter (eds), *The Nature and Dynamics of Organizational Capabilities*, Oxford: Oxford University Press, pp. 1–22.

Ellsworth, John S. (1952), *Factory Folkways – A Study of Institutional Structure and Change*, New Haven, CT: Yale University Press.

Feldman, Martha S. (2000), 'Organizational routines as a source of continuous change', *Organization Science*, **11**(6), 611–29.

Feldman, Martha S. (2003), 'A performative perspective on stability and change in organizational routines', *Industrial and Corporate Change*, **12**(4), 727–52.

Feldman, Martha S. and Brian T. Pentland (2003), 'Reconceptualizing organizational routines as a source of flexibility and change', *Administrative Science Quarterly*, **48**(1), 94–118.

Granovetter, Mark (1985),' 'Economic action and social structure: the problem of embeddedness', *American Journal of Sociology*, **9**(3), 481–510.

Heath, Chip and Sim B. Sitkin (2001), 'Big-B versus big-O: what is organizational about organizational behavior?', *Journal of Organizational Behavior*, **22**, 43–58.

Kauffman, S.A. (1993), *The Origins of Order*, New York: Oxford University Press.

Knudsen, Thorbjørn (2002), 'Economic selection theory', *Journal of Evolutionary Economics*, **12**, 443–70.

Knudsen, Thorbjørn and Richard Swedberg (2007), 'Capitalist entrepreneurship: making profit through the unmaking of economic orders', paper presented at the Conference on Capitalism and Entrepreneurship, Center for the Study of Economy and Society, Cornell University, 28–29 September.

March, James G. (1965), 'Introduction', in James G. March (ed.), *Handbook of Organizations*, Chicago, IL: Rand McNally, pp. ix–xvi.

March, James G. (1994), *A Primer on Decision Making – How Decisions Happen*, New York: The Free Press.

Nelson, Richard R. and Sidney G. Winter (1982), *An Evolutionary Theory of Economic Change*, Cambridge, MA: Harvard University Press.

Peteraf, Margaret A. (1993), 'The cornerstone of competitive advantage: a resource-based view', *Strategic Management Journal*, **14**, 179–88.

Simon, Herbert A. (1991), 'Organizations and markets', *Journal of Economic Perspectives*, **5**(2), 25–44.

Weber, Max (1978), *Economy and Society*, Guenther Roth and Claus Wittich (eds), Berkeley and Los Angeles: University of California Press.

Weick, Karl E. (1990), 'The vulnerable system: an analysis of the Tenerife air disaster', *Journal of Management*, **16**(3), 571–93.

Weick, Karl E. and Roberts, Karlene H. (1993), 'Collective mind in organizations: heedful interrelating on flight decks', *Administrative Science Quarterly*, **38**, 357–81.

2 The concept of a routine
Geoffrey M. Hodgson

The significance of routines in modern, learning, innovating economies is widely appreciated.[1] Routines are vital to all organizations. Hence it is important to understand both how they can be built and how they can be changed. Such an appreciation is important, for analyzing how the business world works, for understanding how knowledge is retained and transferred, for the development of business strategy, and for the creation of policies to encourage more beneficial business practices.

Detailed empirical investigation is essential in this regard, but detailed taxonomic studies based on empirical evidence are relatively rare. One reason why empirical investigations have so far remained rather limited is that the conceptual specification of a routine remains hazy. Greater conceptual precision is a vital precondition of fruitful empirical enquiry.

The aim of this chapter is to help refine and define the concept of the routine, by citing relevant insights from philosophy, social theory and psychology, and by focusing on some milestone contributions in this area. The chapter is divided into four sections. The first section addresses the analogous and component concept of habit, with a view to making a distinction between habits and routines. The second section explores the metaphor of 'routines as genes' and argues that routines must be treated as capacities or dispositions, rather than behaviours. The third section considers the mechanics of routine persistence and replication in more detail, by briefly discussing some important theoretical and empirical studies in the area. The fourth section concludes the chapter.

1   Habits as the basis and individual analogue of routines

For two reasons, to understand the concept of a routine we need to appreciate the idea of a habit. First, routines operate through the triggering of individual habits. Second, routines are the organizational analogue of individual habits. So the analysis starts here with the habit concept.

Like 'routine', the word 'habit' exists in common parlance and is taken to mean a variety of things. Both words need to be defined more precisely for scientific usage. Even in scientific circles, and especially since the rise of behaviourist psychology after the First World War, there has been some ambiguity in the definition of habit. The concept of habit was central to the pragmatist philosophy and institutional economics of the early twentieth century. It is useful to return to the meaning of the term employed then, especially as this earlier usage is now enjoying a revival.

Pragmatist philosophers and institutional economists such as Thorstein Veblen (1919) regarded habit as an acquired proclivity or capacity, which may or may not be actually expressed in current behaviour (Hodgson, 2004). Repeated behaviour is important in establishing a habit. But habit and behaviour are not the same. If we acquire a habit we do not necessarily use it all the time. It is a propensity to behave in a particular way in a particular class of situations.

The pragmatist philosopher and psychologist William James (1892, p. 143) proclaimed: 'Habit is thus the enormous fly-wheel of society, its most precious conservative agent.' Similarly, the pragmatist sociologists William Thomas and Florian Znaniecki (1920, p. 1851) criticized 'the indistinct use of the term "habit" to indicate any uniformities of behavior. . . . A habit . . . is the tendency to repeat the same act in similar material conditions'. Also treating habit as a propensity, William McDougall (1908, p. 37) wrote of 'acquired habits of thought and action' as 'springs of action' and saw 'habit as a source of impulse or motive power'. Elsewhere, in his defences against the behaviourist invasion in psychology, McDougall (1924) explicitly emphasized the conceptual difference between dispositions and behaviour. As the pragmatist philosopher and psychologist John Dewey (1922, p. 42) put it: 'The essence of habit is an acquired predisposition to *ways* or modes of response.' The use of habit is largely unconscious. Habits are submerged repertoires of potential behaviour; they can be triggered or reinforced by an appropriate stimulus or context.[2]

As the pragmatist philosopher Charles Sanders Peirce (1878, p. 294) declared, the 'essence of belief is the establishment of habit'. Accordingly, habit is not the negation of deliberation, but its necessary foundation. Reasons and beliefs are often the rationalizations of deep-seated feelings and emotions that spring from habits that are laid down by repeated behaviours. This interplay of behaviour, habit, emotion and rationalization helps to explain the normative power of custom in human society. Hence 'custom reconciles us to everything' – as Edmund Burke wrote – and customary rules can acquire the force of moral authority. In turn, these moral norms help to further reinforce the institution in question.

Habits are socially acquired, not genetically transmitted. By accepting the foundational role of habit in sustaining rule-following behaviour, we can begin to build an alternative ontology of institutions and routines, in which we avoid the conceptual problems of an account based primarily on intentionality. This is not to deny the importance of intentionality, but to regard it as a consequence as much as a cause, and to place it in the broader context of other, non-deliberative behaviours.

Importantly, all learning, and the attainment of all skills, depends on the acquisition of habits. Knowledge and skills involve the capacity to address a complex problem and to identify rapidly the means of dealing with it. Experience and intuition are crucial here, and these must be grounded in acquired habits of thought or behaviour that dispose the agent to identify the crucial aspects of or responses to the problem. All skills, from knowledge of mathematics through competence with languages to ability with a musical instrument, depend on habits. Habits are the necessary means of avoiding full reflection over every detail, so that the more deliberative levels of the mind are freed up for more strategic issues. If all details were necessarily the subject of conscious deliberation, then the mind would be overwhelmed and paralysed by minutiae.

We may briefly consider two possible types of mechanism by which habit may be replicated from person to person.[3] The first is by incentive or constraint. These can provide reasons to acquire specific customs, follow particular traffic conventions and use specific linguistic terms. In these cases, because others are acting in a particular way, we can have powerful incentives to behave accordingly. In doing so, we too build up habits associated with these behaviours. The behaviours are reproduced and also the habits giving rise to them are replicated.

Another possible mechanism is imitation. Imitation need not be fully conscious, and it will also involve some 'tacit learning' (Polanyi, 1967; Reber, 1993; Knudsen, 2002). Perhaps imitation can occur even without strong incentives, on the grounds that the propensity to imitate is instinctive, and this instinct has itself evolved for efficacious reasons among social creatures (James, 1892; Veblen, 1899; Campbell, 1975; Boyd and Richerson, 1985; Simon, 1990; Tomasello, 2000). However, an imitation instinct would require an existing set of common behaviours in the group, otherwise an emerging propensity to imitate might not have a selection advantage. For instinctive imitation to take off, common behaviours may have to emerge for other reasons. Furthermore, if imitation is more than mimicry, then the rules and understandings associated with it also have to be transmitted. Imitation is more problematic than it appears. Nevertheless, there are provisional grounds to consider a partially instinctive propensity to imitate as a strong element in the complex social glue, and hence a force behind the replication of habits.

Having established the concept of habit, and for reasons that should become clearer below, we are now in a stronger position to turn to the concept of a routine. In the following section it will be explained how routines play a similar role for organizations that habits play for individuals.

2   Routines as organizational genes

In everyday parlance the word 'routine' is used loosely to refer to repeated sequences of behaviour, by individuals as well as by organizations. However, when Richard Nelson and Sidney Winter (1982) used the concept in their seminal work on economic and organizational evolution, and repeated the metaphor of 'routines as genes', they suggested a more specific and technical meaning for the term. It is important to clarify and refine this technical meaning.

A consensus has now emerged that routines relate to groups or organizations, whereas habits relate to individuals (Cohen et al., 1996; Dosi et al., 2000). Individuals have habits; groups have routines. Routines are the organizational analogue of habits. But routines do not simply refer to habits that are shared by many individuals in an organization or group. Routines are not themselves habits: they are organizational meta-habits, existing on a substrate of habituated individuals in a social structure. Routines are one ontological layer above habits themselves.

Having established the analogy between habits and routines, in the next section the causal connection between the two will be examined in more detail. It is first necessary to address an important question concerning the nature of routines: are they organizational dispositions or organizational behaviours?

Some confusion persists on this question. In their 1982 book, Nelson and Winter sometimes treat routines as dispositions, but otherwise described them as behaviours. For example, Nelson and Winter (1982, p. 15) write: 'It is that most of what is *regular and predictable* about business behavior is plausibly subsumed under the heading "routine" '. But they go on in the same sentence to describe routines as 'dispositions . . . that shape the approach of the firm' to problems. Routines are also treated as 'organizational memory', which refers more to capabilities than to behaviour.

Another passage introduces the useful analogy between a routine and a computer program, but repeats the same confusion. Nelson and Winter (1982, p. 97) see a 'routine' as being like a computer 'program', referring thereby 'to a repetitive pattern of activity in an entire organization' as well as to skills or capacities. But there is a difference between a computer program and the computer's output or behaviour. The computer program is a rule-based system, with a generative coding that, along with other inputs, determines the computer's output or behaviour. Nelson and Winter conflate generative and dispositional factors such as the computer program with outputs such as 'repetitive pattern of activity' or 'performance'.

Nelson and Winter (1982) refer repeatedly to 'routines as genes'. This is another useful analogy, but, of course, routines are very different from genes. Routines do not replicate biologically and they are much less enduring. All analogies are inexact in some respects and must be handled with care, as Nelson and Winter are fully aware. The gene analogy usefully points to routines as relatively durable carriers of information through shorter periods of time, with the algorithmic capacity to generate particular outcomes in given circumstances. Routines are like genes in the sense that they are both generative, rule-like structures and potentialities. However, routines (like genes) cannot be both generative structures and outcomes of such structures. This point is not about the appropriateness or otherwise of biological analogies, but about the clear meanings of words and their ontological references.

Winter (1995, pp. 149–50) distinguishes between a 'routine in operation at a particular site . . . a web of coordinating relationships connecting specific resources' and the 'routine *per se* – the abstract activity pattern'. But the one term 'routine' cannot apply to both the 'web of coordinating relationships' and the 'activity pattern' that is the outcome of the coordinating structure and its environmental triggers; it cannot usefully denote both potentiality and actuality. It has to denote one or the other, but not both.

At root there is a philosophical problem here, which is worthy of brief discussion. Basically, the essence of what an entity *is* cannot be entirely appraised in terms of what an entity *does*. If we make this confusion, then we wrongly imply that, when the entity interrupts its characteristic activity, it ceases to exist. Birds fly. But what defines a bird is the (existing or past) *capacity* to fly, not flying itself. If a bird were wrongly defined as a flying animal, then any bird sitting on a branch or pecking on the ground would cease to be a bird.

Accordingly routines are not behaviour; they are stored behavioural capacities or capabilities. Consider a firm in which all employees and managers work between 9am and 5pm only. During this working day a number of organizational routines can be energized. At other times the firm is inactive. But the routines do not all disappear at 5pm, to reappear mysteriously the next day. The routines-as-capacities remain, as long as the individuals have the capacity and disposition to work again together in the same context. Subject to this condition, the routines can be triggered the next day by appropriate stimuli.

Aristotle made the central philosophical point here, more than 2300 years ago. In his *Metaphysics*, Aristotle (1956, pp. 227–8) criticized Eucleides of Megara (a disciple of Socrates) and his school

who maintain that a thing *can act* only when it *is acting*. But the paradoxes attending this view are not far to seek. . . . Now if a man cannot have an art without having at some time learned it, and cannot later be without it unless he has lost it, are we to suppose that the moment he stops building he has lost his art? If so, how will he have recovered it if he immediately resumes building? The same is true of inanimate objects. . . . The Megaric view, in fact, does away with all change. On their theory that which stands will *always* stand, that which sits will *always* sit; . . . Since we cannot admit this view . . . we must obviously draw a distinction between potentiality and actuality.

An enduringly relevant point here is that definitions or ontologies that are based on behaviour cannot cope with instances where the behaviour changes or ceases. But the capacity to produce the original characteristic behaviour remains, and this capacity, not the outcome, defines the essence of the entity. Although ancient, this point is not arcane; it is widely utilized in modern realist philosophy of science. Central to most strands of modern realist philosophy is the distinction between the *potential* and the *actual*, between dispositions and outcomes, where in each case the former are more fundamental than the latter.

Science is about the discovery of causal laws or principles. Causes are not events; they are generative mechanisms that can under specific conditions give rise to specific events. For example, a force impinging on an object does not always make that object move. The outcome also depends on friction, countervailing forces, and other factors. Causes relate to potentialities; they are not necessarily realized in outcomes. As Veblen (1919, p. 89) put it: 'The laws of nature are . . . of the nature of a propensity.' Hence there must be a distinction between an observed empirical regularity and any causal law that lies behind it. Similarly there must be a distinction between the capacities and behaviours of an entity.[4]

In biology, genes and genotypes are wholly potentialities; they are not behaviours. In the socioeconomic domain, the closest things to genotypes are the generative rule-like structures inherent in ingrained individual habits and in organizational routines. Habits and routines are thus understood as conditional, rule-like potentialities or dispositions, rather than behaviour as such. The key distinction in the socioeconomic sphere is between habits and routines as dispositions, on the one hand, and manifest behaviour, on the other hand.

In this light, any emphasis on the allegedly *predictable* character of routines is misplaced. Predictions relate to outcomes or events, not to causal laws, rules or generative structures. The moderately dependable feature of a routine, rule or computer program is not one of predictability but of durability. Routines (or rules or computer programs) are usually conditional on other inputs or events. As a result any predictability does not stem from the routine alone but from the predictability of these other inputs. For example, a firm may have a fixed mark-up pricing routine of adding 20 per cent to the unit cost of its products. If costs were capricious and highly variable, as they might be under some circumstances, then the resulting price would be equally unreliable. The relatively enduring and persistent quality of a routine is not its outcome but its generative, rule-like structure.

While a consensus has been established that a routine is an organizational rather than an individual phenomenon, some confusion remains on the above points, and this has led to some conceptual and empirical difficulties.[5] Some of these difficulties can be overcome by consistently treating a routine as an organizational capacity and generative structure, analogous to biological genes or computer programs, but having distinctive features of their own.

To their credit, both Nelson and Winter are now more inclined to describe the routine in terms of a capacity. Nelson and Winter (2002, p. 30) write: 'we treat *organizational routine* as the organizational analogue of individual skill'. A similar attitude is evident elsewhere. Barbara Levitt and James March (1988, p. 320) write: 'The generic term "routines" includes the forms, rules, procedures, conventions, strategies, and technologies around which organizations are constructed and through which they operate.' Another useful definition of a routine as a potentiality or capability, rather than behaviour, is found in the discussion in Cohen et al. (1996, p. 683) 'A routine is an executable *capability* for repeated performance in some *context* that [has] been *learned* by an organization in response to *selective pressures.*'

A routine is here defined as a generative structure or capacity within an organization. *Routines are organizational dispositions to energize conditional patterns of behaviour within an organized group of individuals, involving sequential responses to cues.* The next section raises the general questions of how routines work within organizations and how they carry information.

3 How do routines carry information?

The analysis of how routines endure and replicate is enormous and incomplete (Hodgson, 2003). At present, our general understanding is limited, and progress depends largely on the accumulation of detailed case studies. As Winter (1990, p. 270) notes, so far 'little attention has been paid to the mechanism by which whatever-it-is-called is transmitted' and to its 'replication mechanism'. For Winter (1990, p. 294n.) this amounts to a regrettable 'vagueness on a key issue'. As Winter (1990, pp. 270–75) insisted: 'The question of what is "inherited" and how the inheritance mechanisms work is, however, . . . central and . . . far from definitive resolution . . . To develop the routines as genes approach fully, the problem of inheritance mechanisms needs to be dealt with convincingly.'

To understand how routines work it is necessary to consider how any tacit or other information associated with a routine is preserved and replicated

A very useful study in this regard is by Michael Cohen and Paul Bacdayan (1994). They use the distinction in psychology between procedural and other, more cognitive, forms of memory, such as semantic, episodic or declarative memory. As psychologists Endel Tulving and Daniel Schacter (1990, p. 301) put it:

> The domain of procedural memory is behavior, whereas that of semantic and episodic memory is cognition or thought. Cognitive memory systems have the capability of modeling the external world – that is, of storing representations of objects, events, and relations among them – whereas procedural memory does not have this capacity.

Procedural memory is triggered by preceding events and stimuli. It typically leads to behavioural responses and has a major tacit component. It is potential action that is energized by social or other cues. 'Procedural knowledge is less subject to decay, less explicitly accessible, and less easy to transfer to novel circumstances' (Cohen and Bacdayan, 1994, p. 557).

Routines depend upon a structured group of individuals, each with habits of a particular kind, where many of these habits depend upon procedural memory. The behavioural cues by some members of a structured assembly of habituated individuals trigger specific habits in others. Hence various individual habits sustain each other in an interlocking structure of reciprocating individual behaviours. Together these behaviours take on collective qualities associated with teams. But both individuals and structures are involved throughout. The organization or group provides a structured social and physical environment for each individual, including rules and norms of behaviour, of both the explicit and the informal kind. This environment is made up of the other individuals, the relations between them and the technological and physical artefacts that they may use in their interactions. This social and physical environment enables, stimulates and channels individual activities, which in turn can help trigger the behaviour of others, produce or modify some artefacts, and help to change or replicate parts of this social and physical environment.

Partly because of procedural memory, organizations can have important additional properties and capacities that are not possessed by individuals, taken severally. The organization provides the social and physical environment that is necessary to enable specific activities, cue individual habits and deploy individual memories. If one person leaves the organization and is replaced by another, then the new recruit may have to learn the habits that are required to maintain specific routines. Just as the human body has a life in addition to its constituent cells, the organization thus has a life in addition to its members. The organizational whole is greater than the sum of the properties of its individual members, taken severally. The additional properties of the whole stem from the structured relations and causal inter-actions between the individuals involved (Blitz, 1992; Hodgson, 2004; Weissman, 2000).

A routine derives from the capacity of an organization to provide con-ditions to energize a series of conditional, interlocking, sequential behav-iours among several individuals within the organization. Cohen and Bacdayan (1994, p. 557) write: 'The routine of a group can be viewed as the concatenation of such procedurally stored actions, each primed by and priming the actions of others.' This statement captures the dependence of routines on procedural memory, but is somewhat ambiguous concerning the genotypic or phenotypic status of a routine.

As argued above, routines are not behaviour; they are stored behavioural capacities or capabilities. These capacities involve knowledge and memory. They involve organizational structures and individual habits which, when triggered, lead to sequential behaviours. But this does not mean that a routine can be fully codified. Routines are not necessarily nominal, codified or officially approved procedures. Routines generally rely on informal and tacit knowledge, and this fact is clearly relevant for understanding their replication.

The temporal durability of routines and the way that they can embody knowledge 'forgotten' by individuals is illustrated by an anecdote related by Elting Morison (1966). A time-and-motion expert was studying film footage of Second World War motorized artillery crews. He was puzzled by a recurring three-second pause just before the guns were fired. An old soldier also watching the film suddenly realized that the three-second pause had originated from the earlier era in which the guns were drawn by horses, and the horses had to be held and calmed in the seconds just before the guns went off. Despite its eventual redundancy, this part of the routine had sur-vived the transition from horse-driven to motorized artillery. Part of the knowledge held in a routine can become obsolete, yet still be reproduced, like the examples of 'rudimentary organs' discussed by Charles Darwin (1859, pp. 450–58).

Just as habits replicate from individual to individual, routines replicate from group to group and from organization to organization. In studies of technological diffusion, organization studies, and the strategic manage-ment literature there is some discussion of the diffusion or replication of routines (DiMaggio and Powell, 1983; Hannan and Freeman, 1984, 1989; Zucker, 1987; Levitt and March, 1988; Stinchcombe, 1990; Rogers, 1995; Szulanski, 1996, 2000; Lazaric and Denis, 2001; Aldrich and Martinez, 2003; Becker and Lazaric, 2003). Prominent mechanisms for the replication of routines involve the movement of employees from organiza-tion to organization, or independent experts or consultants that help to transfer knowledge and experience gained in one context to another. The above authors cite case studies involving the transfer of technologies, management procedures, corporate multidivisional structures, accounting conventions and much else. What is central to these transfers is the replication of practices and organizational relationships. What is generally critical is the capacity of the receiving organization to accommodate and utilize these practices and relationships in the context of its own ingrained culture of habits and beliefs.

In some respects the replication of routines may be more difficult than the replication of habits from individual to individual. Take the mechanism of imitation. Among individuals, any evolved capacity to imitate others must involve the ability to sense the more significant actions, and the tacit rules and meanings associated with behaviour. This capacity would have evolved over millions of years. By contrast, complex organizations are extremely recent in human history. Many organizations may have evolved only limited capacities to discern and prioritize the important rules and meanings. It is likely that replication through imitation is even more difficult with (and at the level of) organizations than it is with individuals.

Nevertheless, as noted in the organization studies literature, many examples of successful routine replication exist. They typically involve the combination of codifiable information and instructions with extensive personal example, advice and contact, where the receiving organization has sufficient plasticity to usefully absorb and accommodate the routine. Sometimes routines are spread as a result of laws or rules that emanate from a third organization, such as the state or an association of employers. Otherwise the replication of routines can occur as the result of the strategy of its receiving organization, or it can result from lower-level contact, stimulation and imitation. Routines replicate, and they do so on a substrate of organized and habituated individuals.

There is an important and ongoing debate concerning the degree of durability of routines. Michael Hannan and John Freeman (1989) are leading proponents of the view that the capacity to change routines within organizations is relatively limited, and that changes in the population of routines within industries or societies largely comes about through the survival or extinction of specific organizations, and the consequent persistence or disappearance of the routines they carry, rather than through modifications in the routines themselves. This is an important area of ongoing enquiry.[6]

This raises theoretical and empirical questions concerning how routines are selected and the structures they require in order to survive. One approach is to establish in this context the general distinction between a 'replicator' and an 'interactor', as found in the philosophy of evolutionary systems (Hull, 1988). It is beyond the scope of this chapter to go into details, but the key points can be summarized in brief. In a general and meaningful sense, routines may be regarded as replicators, because when routines are copied they satisfy the necessary basic criteria of causation, similarity and information transfer (Godfrey-Smith, 2000; Sperber, 2000; Hodgson, 2003). What then are the corresponding interactors? David Hull (1988, p. 408) defines an interactor as 'an entity that directly interacts as a cohesive whole with its environment in such a way that this interaction *causes* replication to be differential'. The term 'cohesive whole' indicates that its components stick together and remain united. This must mean at least that all the components depend critically on the survival of the whole, and that to some degree the components depend on the survival of each other. Refining this definition still further, Geoffrey Hodgson and Thorbjørn Knudsen (2004) argue that a firm may be regarded as an inter-actor, and consequently as a 'vehicle' for its inherent habits and routines. The fate of a routine is often dependent on the fate of its host firm. It should be pointed out, however, that although this type of evolutionary approach has a long history (Hodgson, 2004), at least in its present form and context it is in the early stages of its development, and many out-standing conceptual problems remain to be resolved.

4   Conclusion

This chapter has explored the concept of a routine in fundamental terms, using insights from philosophy, psychology and social theory. A routine is here defined as a generative structure or capacity within an organization. *By definition, routines are organizational dispositions to energize conditional patterns of behaviour within an organized group of individuals, involving sequential responses to cues.* There are important philosophical reasons, endorsed by modern philosophy of science, why routines should be defined as organizational dispositions or capacities, rather than behaviour as such.

Just as habits relate to individuals, routines relate to organizations. Both are socially transmitted dispositions, formed through repeated behaviours. Routines themselves are structures of interlocking individual habits. But routines are more than mere aggregations of habits, because they also depend on the emergent properties of organization itself, emanating from structured causal relations and interactions between individuals.

One of the reasons why the study of routines is important for the study of business practice is that they are repositories and carriers of knowledge and skill. The routine is often the means through which individual skills are triggered and energized. One psychological mechanism that is important here is procedural memory, which means that some powers of recall can be enhanced when triggered by cues provided by others. In this manner the routine as a whole becomes more than the sum of the capacities of the individuals involved, taken severally.

Without going into details, this chapter has pointed to a further agenda of conceptual enquiry, inspired by evolutionary principles taken from the modern philosophy of biology. In theoretical, conceptual and empirical terms, the study of routines offers an exciting agenda for future research.

Notes

1. Thanks are due to Markus Becker for useful comments on an earlier version of this chapter.
2. The conception of a habit as a propensity or disposition is also found in modern works such as Camic (1986), Margolis (1994), Murphy (1994), Kilpinen (2000) and others.
3. See the more extensive discussion in Hodgson and Knudsen (unpublished).
4. For realist accounts upholding a distinction between generative mechanisms or causal powers, on the one hand, and outcomes or events, on the other, see for example Bhaskar (1975), Harré and Madden (1975), Popper (1990).
5. For discussions of some of these difficulties see Cohen et al. (1996), Lazaric (2000) and Becker (2001).
6. Usher and Evans (1996) provide a useful review of this literature, with further evidence. However, it has been argued elsewhere that their characterization of this debate as between 'Darwinian' and 'Lamarckian' concepts of change is at best highly misleading (Hodgson and Knudsen, 2006).

References

Aldrich, Howard E. and Martha Martinez (2003), 'Entrepreneurship as social construction: a multi-level evolutionary approach', in Z.C. Acs and David B. Audretsch (eds), *Handbook of Entrepreneurial Research*, Boston: Kluwer, pp. 359–99.

Aristotle (1956), *Metaphysics*, edited and translated by John Warrington with an introduction by W. David Ross, London: Dent.

Becker, Markus C. (2001), 'The role of routines in organisations: an empirical and taxonomic investigation', PhD thesis, University of Cambridge.

Becker, Markus C. and Nathalie Lazaric (2003), 'The influence of knowledge in the replication of routines', *Économie appliquée*, **56**(3), September, 65–94.

Bhaskar, Roy (1975), *A Realist Theory of Science*, 1st edn, Leeds: Leeds Books.

Blitz, David (1992), *Emergent Evolution: Qualitative Novelty and the Levels of Reality*, Dordrecht: Kluwer.

Boyd, Robert and Peter J. Richerson (1985), *Culture and the Evolutionary Process*, Chicago, IL: University of Chicago Press.

Camic, Charles (1986), 'The matter of habit', *American Journal of Sociology*, **91**(5), March, 1039–87.

Campbell, Donald T. (1975), 'On the conflicts between biological and social evolution and between psychology and moral tradition', *American Psychologist*, **30**(12), December, 1103–26.

Cohen, Michael D. and Paul Bacdayan (1994), 'Organizational routines are stored as procedural memory – evidence from a laboratory study', *Organization Science*, **5**(4), November, 554–68.

Cohen, Michael D., Roger Burkhart, Giovanni Dosi, Massimo Egidi, Luigi Marengo, Massimo Warglien and Sidney Winter (1996), 'Routines and other recurring action patterns of organizations: contemporary research issues', *Industrial and Corporate Change*, **5**(3), 653–98.

Darwin, Charles R. (1859), *On the Origin of Species by Means of Natural Selection, or the Preservation of Favoured Races in the Struggle for Life*, 1st edn, London: Murray.

Dewey, John (1922), *Human Nature and Conduct: An Introduction to Social Psychology*, 1st edn, New York: Holt.

DiMaggio, Paul J. and Walter W. Powell (1983), 'The iron cage revisited: institutional isomorphism and collective rationality in organizational fields', *American Sociological Review*, **48**(2), April, 147–60.

Dosi, Giovanni, Richard R. Nelson and Sidney G. Winter (2000), 'Introduction: the nature and dynamics of organizational capabilities' in Giovanni Dosi, Richard R. Nelson and Sidney G. Winter (eds), *The Nature and Dynamics of Organizational Capabilities*, Oxford: Oxford University Press, pp. 1–22.

Godfrey-Smith, Peter (2000), 'The replicator in retrospect', *Biology and Philosophy*, **15**, 403–23.

Hannan, Michael T. and John Freeman (1984), 'Structural inertia and organizational change', *American Sociological Review*, **49**(2), April, 149–64.

Hannan, Michael T. and John Freeman (1989), *Organizational Ecology*, Cambridge, MA: Harvard University Press.

Harré, Rom and Edward H. Madden (1975), *Causal Powers: A Theory of Natural Necessity*, Oxford: Basil Blackwell.

Hodgson, Geoffrey M. (2003), 'The mystery of the routine: the Darwinian destiny of *An Evolutionary Theory of Economic Change*', *Revue Économique*, **54**(2), March, 355–84.

Hodgson, Geoffrey M. (2004), *The Evolution of Institutional Economics: Agency, Structure and Darwinism in American Institutionalism*, London and New York: Routledge.

Hodgson, Geoffrey M. and Thorbjørn Knudsen (2004), 'The firm as an interactor: firms as vehicles for habits and routines', *Journal of Evolutionary Economics*, **14**(3), July, 281–307.

Hodgson, Geoffrey M. and Thorbjørn Knudsen (2006), 'Dismantling Lamarckism: why descriptions of socio-economic evolution as Lamarckism are misleading', *Journal of Evolutionary Economics*, **16**(4), October, 343–66.

Hodgson, Geoffrey M. and Thorbjørn Knudsen (unpublished), 'The replication of habits', unpublished mimeo.

Hull, David L. (1988), *Science as a Process: An Evolutionary Account of the Social and Conceptual Development of Science*, Chicago, IL: University of Chicago Press.

James, William (1892), *Psychology: Briefer Course*, New York and London: Holt and Macmillan.

Kilpinen, Erkki (2000), 'The enormous fly-wheel of society: pragmatism's habitual conception of action and social theory', University of Helsinki, Helsinki.

Knudsen, Thorbjørn (2002), 'The significance of tacit knowledge in the evolution of human language', *Selection*, **3**(1), 93–112.

Lazaric, Nathalie (2000), 'The role of routines, rules and habits in collective learning: some epistemological and ontological considerations', *European Journal of Economic and Social Systems*, **14**(2), 157–71.

Lazaric, Nathalie and Blandine Denis (2001), 'How and why routines change: some lessons from the articulation of knowledge with ISO 9002 implementation in the food industry', *Économies et Sociétés*, Série *Dynamique technoloqique et organisation*, **6**(4), 585–611.

Levitt, Barbara and James G. March (1988), 'Organizational learning', *Annual Review of Sociology*, **14**, 319–40.

Margolis, Howard (1994), *Paradigms and Barriers: How Habits of Mind Govern Scientific Beliefs*, Chicago, IL: University of Chicago Press.

McDougall, William (1908), *An Introduction to Social Psychology*, 1st edn, London: Methuen.

McDougall, William (1924), 'Can sociology and social psychology dispense with instincts?', *American Journal of Sociology*, **29**(6), May, 657–73.

Morison, Elting E. (1966), *Men, Machines and Modern Times*, Cambridge, MA: MIT Press.

Murphy, James Bernard (1994), 'The kinds of order in society', in Philip Mirowski (ed.), *Natural Images in Economic Thought: 'Markets Read in Tooth and Claw'*, Cambridge and New York: Cambridge University Press, pp. 536–82.

Nelson, Richard R. and Sidney G. Winter (1982), *An Evolutionary Theory of Economic Change*, Cambridge, MA: Harvard University Press.

Nelson, Richard R. and Sidney G. Winter (2002), 'Evolutionary theorizing in economics', *Journal of Economic Perspectives*, **16**(2), Spring, 23–46.

Peirce, Charles Sanders (1878), 'How to make our ideas clear', *Popular Science Monthly*, **12**, January, 286–302.
Polanyi, Michael (1967), *The Tacit Dimension*, London: Routledge and Kegan Paul.
Popper, Karl R. (1990), *A World of Propensities*, Bristol: Thoemmes.
Reber, Arthur S. (1993), *Implicit Learning and Tacit Knowledge: An Essay on the Cognitive Unconscious*, Oxford and New York: Oxford University Press.
Rogers, Everett M. (1995), *Diffusion of Innovations*, 3rd edn, New York: Free Press.
Simon, Herbert A. (1990), 'A mechanism for social selection and successful altruism', *Science*, **250**, 21 December, 1665–8.
Sperber, Dan (2000), 'An objection to the memetic approach to culture', in Robert Aunger (ed.), *Darwinizing Culture: The Status of Memetics as a Science*, Oxford and New York: Oxford University Press, pp. 162–73.
Stinchcombe, Arthur L. (1990), *Information and Organizations*, Berkeley, CA: University of California Press.
Szulanski, Gabriel (1996), 'Exploring internal stickiness: impediments to the transfer of best practice within the firm', *Strategic Management Journal*, **17**, Winter Special Issue, 27–43.
Szulanski, Gabriel (2000), 'Appropriability and the challenge of scope: Banc One routinizes replication', in Giovanni Dosi, Richard R. Nelson and Sidney G. Winter (eds), *The Nature and Dynamics of Organizational Capabilities*, Oxford: Oxford University Press, pp. 69–98.
Thomas, William and Florian Znaniecki (1920), *The Polish Peasant in Europe and America*, vol. 2, New York: Octagon.
Tomasello, Michael (2000), *The Cultural Origins of Human Cognition*, Cambridge, MA: Harvard University Press.
Tulving, Endel and Daniel L. Schacter (1990), 'Priming and human memory systems', *Science*, **247**, 4940, 19 January, 301–6.
Usher, John M. and Martin G. Evans (1996), 'Life and death along gasoline alley: Darwinian and Lamarckian processes in a differentiating population', *Academy of Management Journal*, **39**(5), October, 1428–66.
Veblen, Thorstein B. (1899), *The Theory of the Leisure Class: An Economic Study in the Evolution of Institutions*, New York: Macmillan.
Veblen, Thorstein B. (1919), *The Place of Science in Modern Civilization and Other Essays*, New York: Huebsch.
Weissman, David (2000), *A Social Ontology*, New Haven, CT: Yale University Press.
Winter, Sidney G., Jr (1990), 'Survival, selection, and inheritance in evolutionary theories of organization', in Jitendra V. Singh (ed.), *Organizational Evolution: New Directions*, London: Sage, pp. 269–97.
Winter, Sidney G. Jr (1995), 'Four Rs of profitability: rents, resources, routines, and replication', in Cynthia A. Montgomery (ed.), *Resource-Based and Evolutionary Theories of the Firm: Towards a Synthesis*, Boston: Kluwer, pp. 147–78.
Zucker, Lynne G. (1987), 'Institutional theories of organization', *Annual Review of Sociology*, **13**, 443–64.

PART II

ORGANIZATIONAL ROUTINES ACROSS DIFFERENT FIELDS

3 Organizational routines in political science
Timothy J. McKeown

Introduction

A student of routines in organizations might easily suppose that this topic is a central concern of political science. Fundamentally, political science is concerned with what governments do, and what they do usually is embodied in the laws or regulations that they adopt. These laws and regulations are typically created by formal organizations: legislatures, administrative agencies, military services, or international organizations. They regulate the conduct of other organizations as well as their own. Treating routines in organizations as formal rules governing a micropolitical system is a simple extension of this perspective.

Just as organization theorists long ago realized that many of the rules that matter in organizations are not in the rulebook, political scientists, especially those who study international politics and diplomacy, have recognized that informal norms govern the conduct of governments. They typically view these norms as patterns of behavior that could be described as following a rule, but not necessarily a rule that is visible to participants in the political systems being studied. Stephen Krasner's (1982) definition of international regimes as 'principles, norms, rules and decision-making procedures around which actor expectations converge' is a well known statement that deliberately ignores the distinction between formal and informal to stress the importance of patterns of behavior based on convergent expectations. Thus, the dual perspectives on the nature of organizational routines that are found in other disciplines are also found in political science.

In what follows I first discuss how the study of routines in political science has evolved, and note some of the reasons for its currently having a far less central place in the discipline than it did two generations ago. I then briefly discuss several political science research programs that have close parallels to research performed in other disciplines, before turning to three research programs that are more distinctive and linked less often to the study of routines: efforts to develop a theory of types of international law; studies of bureaucratic politics in foreign policy bureaucracies and the relation between their organizational routines and organizational political processes, and the creation, modification, and diffusion of norms of proper international conduct. The first two of these exemplify the long-standing interest

31

of the discipline in the impact of formal rules, while the third reflects an interest in treating rules as patterns of cooperation that emerge out of individual self-interested behavior, but also constrain that behavior.

The historical trajectory of studies of routines within political science
The assumption that political science ought to have a great deal to say about organizational routines is seemingly confirmed by surveying the literature on this topic. From the work of Simon and March to more recent writing by Cohen and Feldman, important contributions to the study of organizational routines have been made by political scientists. But these path-breaking individuals find most of the audience for their work outside their own discipline. Within contemporary political science, the study of organizational phenomena of any sort is a neglected topic (Bendor's (2003) verdict on the place of Herbert Simon within political science – cited but seldom followed – can easily be generalized to the way the discipline regards all of organization theory). The study of organizational routines is an important part of only a few research programs within the discipline, and there is scant evidence of any trends in research activity that would lead one to be optimistic that this will soon change.

The reasons for this general disciplinary lack of interest are worth noting, partly because they speak to challenges that many other students of organizational routines face. First, organizational routines are relatively time-consuming to study, compared to downloading a dataset of economic data or election returns. Documenting the micro-processes of even a single organization may take months of observation. Second, the world view within which questions about improving the functioning of organizations (especially public agencies) is a central concern has been in eclipse in political science for decades. The mid-twentieth century expansion of the role of government in the developed world was associated with the development of organization theory and public administration. It has given way to a period of stasis or retrenchment in the public sector, and keeping the existing state apparatus running smoothly is generally seen as being at most a matter of normal science, not an opportunity for path-breaking work. Third, within the United States the long-standing and deeply rooted intellectual distinction between politics and administration has meant that questions of organization and management are all too easily relegated by American political science to the intellectual margins. As argued by one of the founders of American political science (Wilson, 1887):

> The field of administration is a field of business. It is removed from the hurry and strife of politics; it at most points stands apart even from the debatable ground of constitutional study. It is a part of political life only as the methods

of the counting house are a part of the life of society; only as machinery is part of the manufactured product.

Over the last seventy years public administration and policy analysis programs in the United States have broken away from political science departments and formed separate departments and even separate schools. When they departed, most of the people in the discipline who were interested in how organizations work went with them. Even before World War II, prominent American theorists of public administration were describing their field of study as separate from political science. Although they conceded that historically and formally public administration is a branch of political science, 'this aspect [was] not emphasized' (Waldo, 1948, p. 22). Finally, the long period in American political science in which qualitative research and case studies were viewed as unscientific and hence not worthy activities for scholars who wished to be tenured at research-oriented universities cast into eclipse those research programs whose empirical foundation relied upon qualitative rather than quantitative data, that did not view hypothesis testing as a central activity, and that required long periods of observation of a single organization (never mind how rich the record of behavior in that case).

In spite of these formidable difficulties, the study of organizational routines persists within political science. Some of these research areas overlap considerably with mainstream organization theory. The literature on the causes and consequences of 'red tape' – rules and procedures in excess of what is optimal (Buchanan, 1975; Kaufman, 1977; Rosenfeld, 1984; Bozeman et al., 1992; Lan and Rainey, 1992; Bozeman and Scott, 1996; Pandey and Scott, 2002; Turaga and Bozeman, 2005) overlaps considerably with work on bureaucratic formalization. Research on street-level bureaucrats (Meyers et al., 1998; Headrick et al., 2002; Favarel-Garrigues, 2002; Bovens and Zouridis, 2002; Hill, 2003) published in political science, public administration or policy analysis journals also is closely tied to a larger cross-disciplinary conversation with sociologists, social workers, and city planners. The question of how teachers, social workers, police and firefighters implement rule-based policies in environments where they are not subject to close supervision and face various pressures to deviate from those policies is also reminiscent of research on foremen and other low-level supervisory personnel in businesses and how they balance conflicting demands from the workers they supervise and the superiors to whom they report.

Very little research has systematically investigated how top-level policy changes translate into changes in standard operating procedures guiding the work of lower-level government agency employees (Hooton, 1995).

More has been written on the persistence or alteration of national administrative practices as a result of the process of European integration (Spanou, 1998; Bulmer and Burch, 1998; Howlett, 2003; Laegreid et al., 2004). This literature has been inspired by the finding that typically high-level policy convergence within the EU nations has been significantly greater than convergence at the level of 'machinery', that is, 'governmental structures and procedure' and it seeks to confirm and refine this judgment, and then to account for this development. Andrew Jordan's (2003) verdict, that the impact of Europeanization on day-by-day administrative activity only seems limited because the question has not been examined empirically at anywhere near the depth required, is quite plausible. However, the studies in this vein are of limited interest to a student of routines in organizations because they generally do not describe these organizations in terms of their routines, and they typically paint with a rather broad brush.

Analytical studies of international law

Other research programs within political science are less well connected to studies of organizational routines, but offer insights that might be helpful in studying routines. Analytic studies of international law are one of them.[1] This research program arose out of the marriage of the long-standing disciplinary interest in the causes and effects of formal rules with the techniques, assumptions and objectives of the social sciences. It is important because it raises several issues of interest to students of routines as rule-governed behavior:

1. Why would governments make agreements formal, when they often seem able to rely on informal ones?
2. Why would governments sometimes prefer vague to specific rules – or to no rules at all?
3. Why would governments comply with rules when there is no enforcement mechanism to ensure compliance?

This literature is helpful in presenting a considerably richer typology of types of rules than the familiar formal–informal distinction, and then beginning to develop a theory that links situational factors to the nature of the laws found in each situation. It then begins to sketch how law might evolve as experience accumulates. The degree of 'hardness' (or 'softness') of law varies along three dimensions: the degree of obligation imposed, the precision with which proper and improper conduct is specified, and the extent to which enforcement of the law is delegated to an explicitly identified body (Abbot and Snidal, 2000). International law seldom conforms to the 'hard' ideal of strong obligation, precise delimitation, and explicit delegation to a body with monitoring and enforcement powers, and a deviation on one dimension need not imply a deviation on others. Interested readers who wish for an introduction to this research should consult Lipson (1991), the summer, 2000 special issue of the journal *International Organization* on legalization, the comment by Finnemore and Toope (2001) and the rejoinder by Goldstein et al. (2001) to gain a sense of the main issues.

Bureaucratic politics

Discussion of how contemporary political science understands organizational routines must contend with the immense impact of Allison's (1971) two models of bureaucratic politics. Allison's original account of the Cuban missile crisis had been cited over 1300 times by mid-2004. Model II, the organizational process model, at its heart is an account of organizational action as a routine-driven process. It has received considerably less attention than Model III, the governmental politics model, which focuses on politicking among high-level officials involved in inter-agency bargaining. (A good summary of current understandings of bureaucratic politics is Preston and 't Hart (1999).) A second edition of the book (Allison and Zelikow, 1999) broadens the theoretical focus of Model II from routines to a longer menu of organizational concepts (the 'organizational process' paradigm has been renamed the 'organizational behavior' paradigm). However, the 'dominant inference pattern' still focuses on the inertia in organizational activities that is imparted by the organizational reliance on routines.

Allison's conception of how organizational routines shape foreign policy did not change from 1971 to 1999:

> Governments perceive problems through organizational sensors. Governments define alternatives and estimate consequences as their component organizations process information; governments act as these organizations enact routines. Governmental behavior can therefore be understood ... less as deliberate choices and more as outputs of large organizations functioning according to standard patterns of behavior ... To perform complex routines, the behavior of large numbers of individuals must be coordinated. Coordination requires standard operating procedures, rules according to which things are done. ... At any given time, a government consists of existing organizations, each with a fixed set of standard operating procedures and programs. (Allison, 1971, pp. 67–8, or Allison and Zelikow, 1999, pp. 143–4)

However, his treatment of the constraining effects of standard operating procedures softened in the second edition. His position evolved from 'Existing organizational routines for employing present physical capabilities constitute the range of effective choice open to government leaders confronted with any problem.' (Allison, 1971, p. 79), to

> Existing organizational capabilities influence government choice. The existence of an organization with special capacities for doing something increases the probability that its output/action/option will be chosen by the leadership of the organization and the government. (Allison and Zelikow, 1999, pp. 176–7)

This change accommodates critics of the first edition (Welch, 1992; Bendor and Hammond, 1992) who had noted that the theoretical basis for inferring organizational rigidity merely because of a reliance on routines was weak, and that empirically the evidence for rigidity based on reliance on routines was not persuasive in this case.

In the aftermath of *Essence of Decision* a number of analysts, including Allison, argued that organizational routines shape the bargaining games that are played within and between government agencies by constraining top decision makers' menu of options. 'Organizational routines play a critical role in the political bargaining process by setting the terms of the political debate' (Barnet ([1972] 1973, pp. 79–80). In a series of publications (Allison and Halperin, 1972; Halperin and Kanter, 1973; Halperin, 1974) Allison, Morton Halperin and Arnold Kanter sought to integrate Model II and Model III frameworks by identifying the ways in which various routines shape the conduct of the organizational bargaining and politicking that are the central features of Model III.

1. Information for making decisions is gathered and processed according to routines.
2. Routines determine what middle and lower-level officials will be involved in decision making on any given issue.
3. Actions for which routines exist, have been tested, and have been taught to organization members are 'live' options in a way that other actions are not.
4. Routines determine how decisions are implemented.
5. Because routines are influential in shaping decisions, organizational participants sometimes act to influence routines as a way of influencing decisions.

Morton Halperin broadened the discussion of routines by arguing that precedent and habit account for a substantial proportion of organizational behavior that is apparently driven by routines:

> Once things have happened, no matter how accidentally, they will be regarded as manifestations of an unchangeable Higher Reason. For every argument inside government that some jerry-built bureaucratic arrangement should be changed, there are usually twenty arguments to show that it rests on God's own Logic, and that tampering with it will bring down the heavens. (Halperin, 1974, p. 106, quoting Frankel, 1968, p. 5)

Levy (1986) examined a thesis, common among diplomatic and military historians, that the war plans of the European powers contributed to the outbreak of World War I by locking them into a rigid schedule of mobilization. Once begun, mobilization plans could not easily be altered in real time and news of the mobilization would leak, causing other governments to begin mobilizing as well. Thus, even if governments wanted to step back from the abyss, they would face a strategic situation in which their unilateral restraint might be tantamount to receiving the 'sucker's' payoff in a Prisoners' Dilemma game. If a government wished to alter its mobilization plans at the last minute it would be unable to do so and only chaos would result.

Most of Levy's commentary points to the interactions between existing plans and other variables, rather than the main effect of the plans themselves, as the potent causal agents. For example, the interaction of Austrian diplomatic strategy, the war plans of the Austrian army, and the policy of granting harvest furloughs to troops to help in their home villages created a situation where the Austrian government could not apply coercive pressure against Serbia early in the crisis, before all the other European capitals had become fully engaged by events in the Balkans. This probably doomed any attempt to localize the dispute with the Serbian government.

Levy noted several other ways by which the baleful effect of rigid plans was aggravated by other factors. Beliefs about the nature of the conflict – that the offense had a big advantage over the defense; that a time lag in mobilization could be disastrous; that initial mobilization could be conducted in secret; that war was inevitable, that the worst case analysis should govern military decisions, that the damage to prestige incurred by backing down after mobilizing would be unacceptably expensive – all fed the desire to use force. A domestic political balance between the military and other branches of government favoring the former meant that challenges to military plans, either before the crisis when they could have been revised or during the crisis when revision would have been difficult, were unlikely to succeed and hence unlikely to occur. Perceptual rigidity was aggravated by the acute stress levels brought about by the crisis – this too inhibited search for and consideration of alternatives. In addition, civilian ignorance of the content of war plans meant that they were in no position to second-guess the military's judgment, and the lack of non-military plans to deal with the crisis meant that those who had doubts about the wisdom of the military's plans were in no position to offer a well developed alternative (Betts, 1977, p. 155).

Parker and Stern (2002) discuss the importance of standard operating procedures in the events of 11 September 2001. They observe that the US North American Air Defense (NORAD) Command had no procedures in place for responding to a hijacking of a civilian air-liner within the United

States (it had conducted drills on how to deal with a hijacked airliner entering US airspace). NORAD apparently lacked a secure direct telephone extension to the Federal Aviation Agency, the regulatory agency for civil aviation in the United States. Someone who believes that organizational routines grow out of precedent or are mutations of familiar procedures and that organizations generally cannot perform well when they are required to adapt quickly would not be surprised by the performance of US air defence systems on that day.

Parker and Stern also note that al-Qaeda's success that day rested partly on their learning some of the standard operating procedures that US airline pilots were taught to follow in the event of a hijacking, and their exploitation of this knowledge to win easier control of the aircraft. They apparently secured quick cooperation from aircrews and passengers by promising them that, if they cooperated, the hijackers would not hurt them. Because aircrews had been instructed to follow hijackers' demands and let police forces or other outside agents deal with the hijacking, they were ill-prepared to deal with the situation that they faced that morning.

McKeown (2001) revisited the Cuban missile crisis to exploit the extensive declassification of government documents on both the US and Soviet sides. The more complete record now available suggests that the organizational processes implied by Carnegie School arguments about satisficing and moving aspiration levels and problem-induced search do not explain US government conduct well. First, although decision makers agreed on the magnitude of the threat and the possibility that it might be faced, the effort to prepare political plans for dealing with Soviet missiles in Cuba did not bear fruit before October 1962. Second, dissatisfaction with blockade as a response to prospective Soviet missile deployments was general, but it did not spur the development of alternative courses of action. Third, when plans for an air strike were developed, they did not significantly constrain US action, because the plans were continuously revised in response to changing conditions and the directives of top leadership. Finally, the air strike planning shaped US actions, not by limiting US responses, but by becoming a vehicle for the Joint Chiefs of Staff to promote their favored options of air strike and invasion. Ironically, their strategic behavior created a situation where civilian leaders became less rather than more likely to use force.

The theoretical perspective suggested by these new findings is that plans and routines are important not merely because they constrain the range of organizational action, but because they are assets or liabilities in the bargaining and contention that takes place within the government. Models such as those presented by Cyert and March (1963) treat organizational decision making as problem solving under bounded rationality. However, problem solving takes place within an organizational political system in which the assigning of credit and blame affects political influence and is affected by it. Sagan (1993) makes this point with regard to the analysis of accidents in handling nuclear weapons, but it generalizes to other organizational activities easily. When the problems to be solved are nested within larger political conflicts and enduring rivalries within the organization, problem definition, search, and the formulation of proposed solutions are all colored by the larger political context within which they take place. This concept of politics is sufficiently broad that it encompasses sub-unit parochialism within organizations in general.

Kuperman (2001) attempted to uncover the existence and effect of organizational rules regulating the response of the Israeli government to terrorist attacks by observing the response of the Israeli government to these attacks over an extended period. (An earlier example of the same strategy of inquiry is Rhodes' (1994) examination of US naval procurement). He used observations of the characteristics of the terrorist attack to predict the nature of the Israeli government response, then analysed the responses with a statistical model. Such an approach can show that observed behavior is consistent with some postulated decision rule, and compare the statistical goodness of fit of a variety of postulated rules, so long as they generate behaviorally distinctive implications. It thus fits within the less prevalent routines-as-patterned-behavior approach exemplified by Krasner (1982). However, such an approach is ill-suited for resolving the precise nature of the source of the observed coherence in the actions of the Israeli government. One could, for example, argue that the coherence arises because Israeli government leaders adopted a particular strategy for responding to terrorism, and that the use of the strategy was stable over the period in which the government was observed. Without information on internal government decision processes, there is often no clear basis for rejecting the hypothesis that coherence arises from strategic choice rather than the constraining effect of organizational routines.

A research agenda for bureaucratic politics and routines
What research agenda does this literature imply?

1. Our knowledge of how top-level officials respond to the standard operating procedures is suggestive but limited, and not extensively theorized. We know, for example, that US presidents have devised a wide variety of management styles designed to cope with the problems they encounter in attempting to receive high-quality information from their national security bureaucracies and secure the timely and accurate implementation of their decisions (George, 1980). We do not have

comparable studies of how other high-level officials deal with their agency's standard operating procedures.

2. Although Allison (1971, pp. 94–5) and many who have followed him have noted that routines can be quite flexible and may be modified or overridden, political scientists are unable to say much about when this is most or least likely to happen in the organizations that they study. We generally lack information about the births and early lives of routines. Feldman's (2000) point that we have generally not studied the role of agency in creating and changing routines is well taken. The only point about the creation and changing of routines for which we have some evidence is that routines are most rapidly modified when top-level officials focus their attention on them and call for changes. Indeed, Allison (1971, p. 89) seems to anticipate this point when he notes that what most agencies do at any given moment is determined by their routines, not by the directions of political leadership. Implicitly, the task of managing these agencies in real time is so forbidding that top leadership could not do it even if it tried. However, when an issue is sufficiently important, and top-level decision makers do focus on it, then routines are sometimes shown to be unimportant barriers. In the case of the US military planning process during the Cuban missile crisis, the level of top-level attention was intense (what journalists might term presidential 'micro-management'), and the corresponding rapidity with which plans were changed was dramatic (McKeown, 2001).

3. Why can the President not delegate this capacity to redirect organizations to subordinates with the same degree of success? There is a well known literature (Neustadt, 1960, and successors) that notes that even Presidential attempts to alter organizational routines under non-crisis conditions often do not succeed. Sometimes the explanation for apparently rigid bureaucracies is found to lie in the behaviour of Congress or interest groups – elements of the bureaucratic task environment so important that it is not unreasonable to speak of bureaucracies being subject to multiple principals. Sometimes the complex of agency, Congressional committee and interest group is so tightly linked and so impervious to outside pressures that analysts have termed them 'iron triangles' (Adams, [1981] 1984; Vernon, et al., 1991). Under what conditions might such iron triangles arise, either in governmental or non-governmental settings?

4. Where agency behavior appears to be rigid, is that due to organizational factors, or is the source found in the situation confronting the organization? Levy's (1986) point that war plans may appear to be rigid simply because military necessity leaves few or no alternatives can readily be generalized. Thompson (1980) makes the same point when

discussing how the lack of options available to US presidents at various points in the Vietnam War was due, not to organizational rigidity, but simply to the fact that prior choices had foreclosed options that once had been available. They had done so allegedly by altering the expectations of audiences in ways that locked the US government into escalation after escalation.

5. The literature on the relations of routines to organizational change (Miner, 1991; Adler et al., 1999; Feldman 2000, 2003) could be exploited by political scientists to investigate what organizational characteristics are associated with rapid and successful change in routines in governmental organizations, but doing so will require more attention to the systematic measurement of routines and changes in routines (Pentland, 2003a, 2003b).

6. Do seemingly rigid routines simply mask political stalemate? If routines represent an outcome of an Allison Model III-style bargaining process, they are the expression of a 'truce' existing at the moment when the routines were codified (Becker, 2004; see also Nelson and Winter, 1982, pp. 108–9 and Coriat and Dosi, 1998). If changing the routine would disadvantage the coalition that adopted the routine, and that coalition is still in power, Model III would lead one to expect that the routine will not be replaced. Here the stickiness of routines arises not from bounded rationality and problem complexity, or from search costs, but from political stability. Unfortunately, political scientists have generally not explored the relationship between routines in organizations and political struggles within the same organizations.

7. Political science needs better metrics of 'routine-ness'. With the exception of the literature on red tape, political scientists generally have not attempted to devise methods of describing or measuring the extent and nature of the set of organizational routines. There is no counterpart within the discipline to Pentland's (2003a, 2003b) effort to develop suitable measures. While the work on types of international law outlines some distinctions and definitions that might prove useful, it has not inspired a body of systematic empirical work.

8. Political science has neglected the failure of routines (Weick, 1990, 1993). Sagan's (1993) work on accidents with nuclear weapons systems has been attentive to the need to understand just how routines may break down, the consequences of those breakdowns, and how they might be prevented, but much more remains to be done.

International norms and the interorganizational transmission of rules
Among analysts of international norms, only Goertz (2003) seems intent on connecting the study of norms to standard operating procedures or routines.

Within the study of international politics recent decades have witnessed a revival of interest in the role of law and norms as effective regulators of the conduct of national governments. The fundamental motivation for this interest is a long-standing observation: national governments obey international law routinely, but the enforcement mechanisms for this law are often weak or even non-existent International law is often promulgated by international organizations, an organizational form that has received little attention within mainstream organization theory. Rather than compelling national governments or other organizations to obey their rulings, they are 'missionaries' to (Barnett and Finnemore, 1999) or 'teachers' of (Keck and Sikkink, 1998, p. 34) national governments.

Broadly speaking, there are two approaches to explaining this phenomenon. On one side are theorists who view adherence to international law as an equilibrium outcome of a repeated game (Goldsmith and Posner, 2000). What appears to be customary law is merely a stable pattern of collusive play. From that perspective, calling such a pattern 'customary law' or a 'regime' merely conceals the sharp difference between rule observance in a world where courts and law enforcement are available to deal with violations and the world of international politics, where these features are usually absent. Norms are stable sets of strategies, nothing more.

Bendor and Swistak (2001) exemplify this approach by using evolutionary game theory to explain the development of norms. A key theorem of theirs is that 'In a repeated game of enforceable cooperation in which the future is sufficiently important, a uniformly stable state with social strategies can support any strictly positive degree of . . . cooperation.' A 'social' strategy is one that takes into account the behavior of a third party, not just the behavior of the party with whom one is currently interacting. Any set of strategies that yield payoffs to players that surpass those obtained under complete defection is 'supported', that is, can persist indefinitely under given conditions. Thus, as the authors note, the 'strong functionalist thesis that the outcomes are Pareto optimal does not hold'. Such a situation is one of multiple equilibria, and within the confines of game theory, there is no obvious way to select a unique equilibrium. However, another mechanism identified by Bendor and Swistak offers a basis for believing that more deeply cooperative strategy sets will, in the long run, prevail: more efficient (that is, more cooperative) strategies require smaller frequencies in the population in order to stabilize in a group. They also establish that strategies that are normatively nice (do not defect first, and punish third parties that do) and retaliatory require the smallest minimal frequency in order to be uniformly stable. These findings provide some basis for treating norms as the product of rational choice.

Unfortunately, this theoretical accomplishment might not be useful to the empirically or the practically minded. If among a given set of strategies there is no single strategy that dominates in terms of normative niceness and retaliatory propensity, then from within the confines of their framework there is no basis for selecting one strategy set as especially likely to emerge over the long run. Even when such a strategy exists, their result guarantees only that it will persist in numbers sufficient to survive – not that it necessarily will take over the entire system and displace all other strategies. Thus, there is considerable scope for mechanisms outside of game theory to play a role in selecting which strategy set (or norm) comes to be dominant.

Swaine (2002) contends that the Goldsmith-Posner position 'places the interests of states front and center, but makes little headway in explaining state adherence to existing legal institutions, other than to suggest that they comprise some form of "organized hypocrisy"' (p. 592).

Why then even bother to label such practices 'international law'? Perhaps one could appeal to the oft-recognized point that law, by virtue of its impersonality, tends to mask differences in social position as it is seemingly applied uniformly and impartially to all parties. However, this does not dispose of situations where national governments act as if they take the law seriously, even when it is manifestly against their interests to do so. Jones (2002, pp. 122–32) cites a particularly apt instance of this – Nazi Germany's acquiescence to international laws pertaining to the treatment of ethnic minorities in Upper Silesia, in the face of a strong German government desire to apply a punitive policy to Jews. Hypocrisy arguments also presume that some parties can be fooled and that it is worthwhile to take the trouble to fool them – thus, they cannot apply to a perfect information world.

A second criticism by Swaine, one that echoes Bendor and Swistak, is that stories about customary law as equilibrium typically do not address why one particular equilibrium out of many becomes the preferred solution. One way in which norms can be integrated into the game-theoretic explanation is by treating them as a means for creating 'focal points' (Garrett and Weingast, 1993; Goldstein and Keohane, 1993, p. 12) that induce convergent expectations and behavior favoring one equilibrium over others. Some rationalist authors also point at the usefulness of norms for establishing and stabilizing cooperation (Axelrod, 1986; Gehring, 1994). Swaine (2002, p. 599) mentions another consideration: to understand which particular equilibrium will emerge, one must understand how the choice of equilibrium in one arena is constrained by equilibria chosen in other arenas – that is, how customary law can accommodate some innovations far more easily than others. A game that is solved by one solution cannot create contradictory expectations to those arising from a similar game. Thus, the expansion of customary international law faces some consistency constraints (or, as a legal scholar might say, it is constrained by precedent). Moreover, the value of a predictable world may be so high that agents find it worthwhile to expend the effort to resolve legal questions via procedures that are to some degree insulated from considerations of 'power'. In this way the consistency and coherence of law as a whole can be better preserved.

At a minimum, any two provisions of international law have one similarity relation: they are both law, and as such any behavior that deviates from the law in one domain may be viewed as implying some chance that a deviation will be observed in the other domain as well. As Swaine and many others have noted, the costs of having one's reputation for law-abiding behavior engaged by voluntarily taking up the burden of complying with an international law is a commitment mechanism – a way of showing to others that one will pay costs if one abandons the legal standard just taken up. 'To maintain custom, it is only necessary that a group of nations invest their reputations in a nontrivial number of rules' (Swaine, 2002, p. 617). Those governments are also free to withhold their commitment – and their reputations – from cooperation in other arenas, where, for example, they might want to maintain credibility as the zealous defenders of their national interests.

One can conceive of the various provisions of international law as being situated in an attribute space such that provisions that are close to one another are termed similar, while those that are distant are dissimilar. For example, one might have a reputation for being unwilling to adhere closely to one type of law, human rights law, for example, while being more prepared to adhere to a different body of law, such as the law of international trade. Without a conception of whether two laws are 'near' or 'far' from one another, we have no way of understanding whether or how a reputation for law-abiding behavior might be segmented.

What determines the outcome when an exponent of a novel norm attempts to incorporate that norm into an existing set of norms? Acharya (2004) paints a picture of the norm adoption process that is an implicitly rule utilitarian account. Although it may be desirable to extend or modify a system of norms in response to pressures from outside forces, such an action is constrained by the desire to make new norms congruent with existing ones. If a community is faced with the dilemma of adopting a novel norm that is incongruent with its existing norms, or else suffering some deterioration in its relations with the larger world due to its failure to adopt, then local agents are hypothesized by Acharya to 'reconstruct foreign norms to ensure the norms fit with the agents' cognitive priors and identities. . . . Localization, not wholesale acceptance or rejection, settles most cases of normative contestation'. Acharya then compares the impact of two transnational norms on the Association of Southeast Asian Nations (ASEAN), showing that the variation in the norms' acceptance, indicated by the changes they produced in the goals and institutional apparatuses of the regional group, could be explained by the differential ability of local agents to reconstruct the norms to ensure a better fit with prior local norms, and the potential of the localized norm to enhance the appeal of some of their prior beliefs and institutions.

Standing apart from rational choice accounts are those who suggest that a 'logic of appropriateness' (March and Olsen, 1998) leads to a fundamentally different explanatory mechanism than that postulated by rational choice theories. Governments are seen as rule-governed agents. They are simultaneously 'socialized' into acceptance of two sets of norms (Boekle et al., 1999):

> *Transnational socialization* describes a process whereby government decision-makers internalize international norms, i.e. value-based expectations of appropriate behavior that are shared by states. *Societal socialization* refers to a process whereby government decision-makers internalize societal norms, i.e. value-based expectations of appropriate behavior that are shared by the citizens of their state.

Socialization should not be viewed as a one-way process in which the person being socialized passively absorbs norms. Rather, the person being socialized may modify the norm in the light of her previous beliefs (Schimmelfennig, 1994, p. 339). Moreover, socialization is not a once-and-for-all process but rather is continuous, as agents constantly face new decision-making situations and hence must learn new responses or reinterpret those that they have already internalized (Parsons, 1951, p. 208).

Acceptance of norms is seen as being driven by the fit between the norms and the subject's self-identity; that by identifying certain goals as legitimate, norms shape and even can become motives. Norms do not merely constrain or regulate, but sometimes *constitute* interests. 'Norms legitimize goals and thus define actors' interests' (Klotz, 1995, p. 26).

Farrell (1998) offers an account of Irish military planning in 1940–41 for defending against an invasion by Great Britain that supposedly illustrates the potency of transnational norms in the face of the conflicting pull of practical interests. Faced with overwhelming British conventional military superiority, Irish military planners nonetheless continued to plan for a conventional defense of their country rather than relying on the same guerilla tactics that had secured Irish independence from Britain. Farrell argues that implementation on such a plan would have been suicidal, and that the Irish had experience with an alternative that had delivered success in the past and that they knew how to carry out. Why then would they rely on conventional defense? His answer is that Irish army officers identified themselves as professional soldiers, that their definition of professional conduct was taken from the British Army – not exactly their friends, but certainly the army with which they had had the most contact – and that, following the British army view, 'guerrilla warfare was not the business of professional armies'.

There is, however, an alternative explanation for the lack of realism in Irish army planning. Clarke (1999) suggests that governments forced to plan for situations that are both quite unlikely and beyond their capacity to manage will engage in 'fantasy planning' – the content of the plans is essentially irrelevant, but planning is a reassuring social ritual, intended to reassure the citizenry that government is acting effectively to protect them. If the realism of a plan is not a relevant consideration, then there is no good reason not to use planning as an opportunity to affirm one's professional values. The case is therefore not nearly as sharp a challenge to conventional interest-based accounts as might be supposed.

Drezner (2000) explores what happens when organizations that are imprinted with novel policy ideas have to compete with other organizations in order to survive. His basic conclusion is that

> Agencies that are insulated from other bureaucracies have a better chance of surviving, but are unlikely to influence the broad contours of policy. The reverse is also true; embedded agencies have a much lower chance of keeping their ideational mission intact, but if they do survive, their odds of thriving are greater.

A research agenda for international norms and organizational routines

The international norms research program faces a number of challenges.

1. Parallel to the challenge posed by the distinction between strategies and routines, we must clarify the difference, if any, between collusive equilibria and informal norms, and how they can be distinguished in practice. If a norm prescribes behavior that results in an equilibrium outcome, then, as long as the situation is stable, there is no distinction between the two. One would have to search for distinct behavioral traces of a system of norms at those moments before equilibrium has been established, when it has broken down, or when a political entrepreneur attempts to shift a system from one equilibrium (and accompanying set of norms) to another.
2. If the diffusion of norms is a process marked by teaching and learning, then what are the reinforcements and how are they administered? Often arguments about the importance of norms are framed as if they

provided a competing explanation to ones rooted in the concepts of interests and power. Norm-based accounts do indeed differ from accounts that treat preferences as fixed and exogenous, but to treat preferences as partly endogenous does not amount to a claim that preferences do not matter. Likewise, learning is a process in which a reinforcement schedule shapes what is learned and how quickly. To the extent that material goods are reinforcers, no account of the learning of norms can be entirely divorced from a consideration of how these material goods are distributed. 'To overlook how state power and organizational missionaries work in tandem and the ways in which international organization officials channel and shape states' exercise of power is to disregard a fundamental feature of value diffusion' (Barnett and Finnemore, 1999). Herrmann and Shannon (2001) extend these observations by noting that the effects of norm-sending interventions are mediated by subjects' perceptions. This is not a particularly novel point about learning processes, but it is one that should receive more attention in this context.

3. Our empirical foundation for arguments about norm transmission and diffusion tends to be sketches of processes rather than highly detailed accounts. This is partly because participant-observation as a research technique generally cannot be used owing to security restrictions that national governments and international organizations impose on the policy-making process. Techniques for exploiting the material that is available – declassified documents, public documents, oral histories, journalistic accounts, etc. – could be improved by making their exploitation more systematic.

4. Arguments about norm diffusion have not yet presented methods to resolve situations where conflicting norms are sent, or a norm that is sent evokes conflicting norms in reply (Boekle et al., 1999). While some do not see this as problematic, arguing that fuzzy logic is used to deal with such situations (Goertz, 2003, pp. 110–14), we really do not know enough to adjudicate such a disagreement.

Conclusions

Although organizational routines have not been a central research concern of political science, a number of research streams in the discipline do make a contribution to understanding them. The central concerns of the discipline – how laws are made, and their effects – speak to a perspective on organizations that sees them as collections of rules. A central insight of political science – that any process of rule making for a social system is filled by individuals whose goals usually weight parochial benefits more heavily than systemic welfare – suggests at the least an attentiveness to the way in which any rule-making system is strategically exploited by those who populate it.

Note

1. The term 'analytic' refers to studies that seek to explain why and how laws are adopted, and their effects on the behavior of national governments. This work stands apart from the much older prescriptive literature on international law.

References

Abbott, Kenneth W. and Duncan Snidal (2000), 'Hard and soft law in international governance', *International Organization*, **54**(3), 421–56.

Acharya, A. (2004), 'How ideas spread: whose norms matter? Norm localization and institutional change in Asian regionalism', *International Organization*, **58**(2), 239–75.

Adams, Gordon ([1981] 1984), *The Politics of Defense Contracting: The Iron Triangle*, New Brunswick, NJ: Transaction Books.

Adler, P.S., B. Goldoftas and D.I. Levine (1999), 'Flexibility versus efficiency? A case study of model changeovers in the Toyota production system', *Organization Science*, **10**, 43–67.

Allison, Graham T. (1971), *Essence of Decision: Explaining the Cuban Missile Crisis*, Boston, MA: Little, Brown.

Allison, Graham T. and Morton H. Halperin (1972), 'Bureaucratic politics: a paradigm and some policy implications', in Raymond Tanter and Richard H. Ullman (eds), *Theory and Policy in International Relations*, Princeton, NJ: Princeton University Press, pp. 40–79.

Allison, Graham T. and Philip Zelikow (1999), *Essence of Decision: Explaining the Cuban Missile Crisis*, 2nd edn, New York: Longman.

Axelrod, Robert M. (1986), 'An evolutionary approach to norms', *American Political Science Review*, **80**(4), 1095–1111.

Barnet, Richard J. ([1972](1973)), *Roots of War: The Men and Institutions behind US Foreign Policy*, New York: Penguin Books.

Barnett, Michael N. and Martha Finnemore (1999), 'The politics, power, and pathologies of international organizations', *International Organization*, **53**(4).

Becker, Markus C. (2004), 'Organizational routines: a review of the literature', *Industrial and Corporate Change*, **13**(4), 643–77.

Bendor, J. (2003), 'Herbert A. Simon: Political scientist', *Annual Review of Political Science*, **6**, 433–71.

Bendor, J. and Thomas H. Hammond (1992), 'Rethinking Allison's models', *American Political Science Review*, **86**(2), 301–22.

Bendor, J. and P. Swistak (2001), 'The evolution of norms', *American Journal of Sociology*, **106**(6), 1493–1545.

Betts, Richard K. (1977), '*Soldiers, Statesmen, and Cold War Crises*', Cambridge, MA: Harvard University Press.

Boekle, Henning, Volker Rittberger and Wolfgang Wagner (1999), 'Norms and foreign policy: constructivist foreign policy theory', Center for International Relations/Peace and Conflict Studies, Institute for Political Science, University of Tübingen. (Found at http://www.uni-tuebingen.de/uni/spi/ab2menu.htm).

Bovens, M. and D. Zouridis (2002), 'From street-level to system-level bureaucracies: how information and communication technology is transforming administrative discretion and constitutional control', *Public Administration Review*, **62**(2), 174–84.

Bozeman, Barry and Patrick Scott (1996), 'Bureaucratic red tape and formalization: untangling conceptual knots', *American Review of Public Administration*, **26**(1), 1–17.

Bozeman, Barry, Pamela N. Reed and Patrick Scott (1992), 'Red tape and task delays in public and private organisations', *Administration and Society*, **24**(3), 290–322.

Buchanan, B. (1975), 'Red tape and the service ethic: some unexpected differences between public and private managers', *Administration and Society*, **6**(4), 423–44.

Bulmer, S. and M. Burch (1998), 'Organising for Europe', *Public Administration*, **76**, 601–28.

Clarke, Lee (1999), *Mission Improbable: Using Fantasy Documents to Tame Disaster*, Chicago, IL: University of Chicago Press.

Coriat, B. and G. Dosi (1998), 'Learning how to govern and learning how to solve problems', in A.D.J. Chandler, P. Hadstroem and O. Soevell (eds), *The Role of Technology, Strategy, Organization, and Regions*, Oxford: Oxford University Press.

Cyert, Richard M. and James G. March (1963), *A Behavioral Theory of the Firm*, Englewood Cliffs, NJ: Prentice-Hall.

Drezner, Daniel W. (2000), 'Ideas, bureaucratic politics, and the crafting of foreign policy', *American Journal of Political Science*, **44**(4).

Farrell, T. (1998), 'Professionalization and suicidal defence planning by the Irish Army, 1921–1941', *Journal of Strategic Studies*, **21**(3), 67–85.

Favarel-Garrigues, G. (2002), 'Soviet policemen and the carrying out of penal policies (1965–1986)', *Revue d'Histoire Moderne et Contemporaine*, **49**(2), 54–77.

Feldman, Martha S. (2000), 'Organizational change as a source of continuous change', *Organization Science*, **11**(6), 611–29.

Feldman, Martha S. (2003), 'A performative perspective on stability and change in organizational routines', *Industrial and Corporate Change*, **12**, 727–52.

Finnemore, Martha and Stephen J. Toope (2001), 'Alternatives to "legalization": richer views of law and politics', *International Organization*, **55**(3),741–56.

Frankel, Charles (1968), *High on Foggy Bottom: An Outsider's Inside View of the Government*, New York: Harper & Row.

Garrett, Geoffrey and Barry R. Weingast (1993), 'Ideas, interests, and institutions. Constructing the European Community's internal market', in Judith Goldstein and Robert O. Keohane (eds), *Ideas and Foreign Policy. Beliefs, Institutions, and Political Change*, Ithaca, NY: Cornell University Press, pp. 173–206.

Gehring, Thomas (1994), 'Der Beitrag von Institutionen zur Förderung der internationalen Zusammenarbeit. Lehren aus der institutionellen Struktur der Europäischen Gemeinschaft, *Zeitschrift für Internationale Beziehungen*, **1**(2), 211–42.

George, Alexander L. (1980), *Presidential Decisionmaking in Foreign Policy: The Effective Use of Information and Advice*, Boulder, CO: Westview Press.

Goertz, Gary (2003), *International Norms and Decision Making: A Punctuated Equilibrium Model*, Lanham, MD: Rowman & Littlefield.

Goldsmith, J.L. and Eric A. Posner (2000), 'Understanding the resemblance between modern and traditional customary international law', *Virginia Journal of International Law*, **40**, 639–72.

Goldstein, Judith and Robert O. Keohane (eds) (1993), *Ideas and Foreign Policy: Beliefs, Institutions, and Political Change*, Ithaca, NY: Cornell University Press.

Goldstein, Judith, Miles Kahler, Robert O. Keohane and Anne-Marie Slaughter (2001), 'Response to Finnemore and Toope', *International Organization*, **55**(3).

Halperin, Morton H. (1974), *Bureaucratic Politics and Foreign Policy*, Washington, DC: The Brookings Institution.

Halperin, Morton H. and Arnold Kanter (1973), 'The bureaucratic perspective: a preliminary framework', in M.H. Halperin and A. Kanter (eds), *Readings in American Foreign Policy – A Bureaucratic Perspective*, Boston, MA: Little, Brown.

Headrick, B., G. Serra and J. Twombly (2002), 'Enforcement and oversight – using congressional oversight to shape OSHA bureaucratic behavior', *American Politics Research*, **30**(6), 608–29.

Herrmann, Richard K. and Vaughn P. Shannon (2001), 'Defending international norms: the role of obligation, material interest, and perception in decision making', *International Organization*, **55**(3).

Hill, H.C. (2003), 'Understanding implementation: street-level bureaucrats' resources for reform', *Journal of Public Administration Research and Theory*, **13**(3), 265–82.

Hooton, Cornell G. (1995), 'Policy adoption and the redefinition of operating procedures: comparison cases at UMTA', *Governance*, **8**(1), 78–111.

Howlett, M. (2003), 'Administrative styles and the limits of administrative reform: a neo-institutional analysis of administrative culture', *Canadian Public Administration – Administration Publique du Canada*, **46**(4), 471–94.

Jones, Dorothy V. (2002), *Toward a Just World: The Critical Years in the Search for International Justice*, Chicago, IL and London: University of Chicago Press.

Jordan, Andrew (2003), 'The Europeanization of national government and policy: a departmental perspective', *British Journal of Political Science*, **33**, 261–82.

Kaufman, Herbert (1977), *Red Tape: Its Origins, Uses, and Abuses*, Washington, DC: The Brookings Institution.

Keck, Margaret E. and Kathryn Sikkink (eds) (1998), *Activists Beyond Borders: Advocacy Networks in International Politics*, Ithaca, NY: Cornell University Press.

Klotz, Audie (1995), *Norms in International Relations: The Struggle Against Apartheid*, Ithaca, NY: Cornell University Press.

Krasner, Stephen D. (1982), 'Structural causes and regime consequences – regimes as intervening variables', *International Organization*, **36**(2), 185–205.

Kuperman, Ranan D. (2001), 'Rules of military retaliation and their practice by the state of Israel', *International Interactions*, **27**, 297–326.

Laegreid, Per, Runolfur S. Steinthorsson and Baldur Thorhallsson (2004), 'Europeanization of central government administration in the Nordic states', *Journal of Common Market Studies*, **42**, 347–69.

Lan, Zhiyong and Hal G. Rainey (1992), 'Goals, rules, and effectiveness in public, private and hybrid organizations', *Journal of Public Administration Research and Theory*, **2**(1), 5–28.

Levy, Jack S. (1986), 'Organizational routines and the causes of war', *International Studies Quarterly*, **30**(2), 193–22.

Lipson, Charles (1991), 'Why are some international agreements informal?', *International Organization*, **45**(4), 495–538.

March, James G. and Johan P. Olsen (1998), 'The institutional dynamics of international political orders', *International Organization*, **52**(4), 943–69.

McKeown, Timothy J. (2001), 'Plans and routines, bureaucratic bargaining and the Cuban missile crisis', *Journal of Politics*, **63**(4), 1163–90.

Meyers, Marcia K., Bonnie Glaser and Karin MacDonald (1998), 'On the front lines of welfare delivery: are workers implementing policy reforms?', *Journal of Policy Analysis and Management*, **17**(1), 1–22.

Miner, A.S. (1991), 'Organizational evolution and the social ecology of jobs', *American Sociological Review*, **56**, 772–85.

Nelson, Richard R. and Sidney G. Winter (1982), *An Evolutionary Theory of Economic Change*, Cambridge, MA: Belknap Press and Harvard University Press.

Neustadt, Richard E. (1960), *Presidential Power: The Politics of Leadership*, New York: Wiley.

Pandey, Sanjay K. and Patrick G. Scott (2002), 'Red tape: a review and assessment of concepts and measures', *Journal of Public Administration Research and Theory*, **12**(4), 553–81.

Parker, C.F. and E.K. Stern (2002), 'Blindsided? September 11 and the origins of strategic surprise', *Political Psychology*, **23**(3), 601–30.

Parsons, Talcott (1951), *The Social System*, London: Routledge & Kegan Paul.

Pentland, B.T. (2003a), 'Conceptualizing and measuring variety in the execution of organizational work processes', *Management Science*, **49**, 857–70.

Pentland, B.T. (2003b), 'Sequential variety in work processes', *Organizational Studies*, **14**, 528–40.

Preston, Thomas and Paul 't Hart (1999), 'Understanding and evaluating bureaucratic politics: the nexus between political leaders and advisory systems', *Political Psychology*, **20**(1), 49–98.

Rhodes, E. (1994), 'Do bureaucratic politics matter? Some disconfirming findings from the case of the US Navy', *World Politics*, **47**, 1–41.

Rosenfeld, R.A. (1984), 'An expansion and application of Kaufman's model of red tape: the case of community development block grants', *The Western Political Quarterly*, **37**, 603–20.

Sagan, Scott D. (1993), *The Limits of Safety: Organizations, Accidents, and Nuclear Weapons*, Princeton, NJ: Princeton University Press.

Schimmelfennig, Frank (1994), 'Internationale Sozialisation neuer Staaten. Heuristische Überlegungen zu einem Forschungsdesiderat', *Zeitschrift für Internationale Beziehungen*, **1**(2), 335–55.

Spanou, C. (1998), 'European integration in administrative terms: a framework for analysis and the Greek case', *Journal of European Public Policy*, **5**(3), 467–84.

Swaine, Edward T. (2002), 'Rational custom (customary international law)', *Duke Law Journal*, **52**(3), 559–69.

Thompson, James C. (1980), *Rolling Thunder: Understanding Policy and Program Failure*, Chapel Hill, NC: The University of North Carolina Press.

Turaga, Rama M.R. and Barry Bozeman (2005), 'Red tape and public managers' decision making', *The American Review of Public Administration*, **35**(4), 363–79.

Vernon, Raymond, Deborah L. Spar and Glenn Tobin (1991), *Iron Triangles and Revolving Doors: Cases in US Foreign Economic Policymaking*, New York: Praeger.

Waldo, Dwight (1948), *The Administrative State: A Study of the Political Theory of American Public Administration*, New York: The Ronald Press Company.

Weick, Karl E. (1990), 'The vulnerable system: an analysis of the Tenerife air disaster', *Journal of Management*, **16**, 571–93.

Weick, Karl E. (1993), 'The collapse of sensemaking in organizations: the Mann-Gulch disaster', *Administrative Science Quarterly*, **38**, 628–52.

Welch, David A. (1992), 'The organizational process and bureaucratic politics paradigms: retrospect and prospect', *International Security*, **17**(2), 112–46.

Wilson, Woodrow (1887), *Study of Administration*, New York: Academy of Political Science. (Found at http://teachingamericanhistory.org/library/index.asp?document=465).

4   Routines, 'going concerns' and innovation: towards an evolutionary economic sociology
Marc J. Ventresca and William N. Kaghan

Introduction: opening up the dynamics of routines

The language of routines in much strategy and organization theory research today is grounded in ideas that live between the Carnegie tradition's approach to organizational behavior and institutions (Cyert and March, 1962; March and Olsen, 1979; Cohen and Levinthal, 1990; March and Simon, 1993) and neo-Schumpeterian evolutionary economics (Nelson and Winter, 1982). This view treats routines (rather than individuals[1]) as the basic unit of organizational action, foregrounds programmed activity and gives primacy to selection and retention mechanisms operating over time as central to understanding processes of organizational stability, learning, adaptation, and decline. Current research explores how and to what degree routines build into broader organizational competencies and affect organizational adaptation.

The broad contemporary move in the study of organization routines highlights concern with explaining organizational and institutional innovation, a move in which traditional views of routines as 'habitual/inertial' and stable encounter difficulty. The gift of an evolutionary economics is to enjoin researchers to explore 'creative' aspects in the variation of routines and to be wary of assuming equilibrium conditions at both micro and more macro levels. In short, this work served to develop more fully the intuitions of Schumpeter's ([1934] 1983, [1942] 1975) imagery of 'creative destruction'. In current research, these arguments emphasize how understanding the nature of the adaptation of organizational routines is critical to understanding how firms survive and possibly thrive (or decline and die) in competitive environments, and that modifying organizational routines is a primary lever through which managers attempt to enact organizational change (Teece et al., 1997; Zollo and Winter, 2002).

Though this work has been fruitful, it is also plagued by some recurring conceptual and analytic limits (Carlile, 2002; Edmondson et al., 2001; Feldman and Pentland, 2003). We aim to extend current approaches in the study of organizational routines by reviewing available work from organizational and economic sociology that focuses on the relationship between routines and organizational and institutional innovation. This work shifts and refocuses the analytic issues and offers solutions to some of the plaguing problems by developing a process institutionalism that is sensitive to contextual dynamics. In the process, we outline some elements of an evolutionary *economic sociology* that recognizes routines as social conventions and accomplishments, in (often complex, contested) contexts and that serves as the foundation for a 'theory of the innovative firm'. In place of Schumpeter's imagery of 'creative destruction' we substitute Everett Hughes's (1971c) imagery of 'disorganization and reorganization' in the context of a 'society of organizations' (Perrow, 1991).

Organizational sociologists and others who study work and occupations have long been interested in the routines of working life (Becker, 1982; Hughes, 1971a; Strauss, 1993) as well as critical moments when routines cross boundaries, encounter difficulties or collapse altogether (Abbott, 1997; Bechky, 2003; Carlile, 2002; Rudolph and Repenning, 2002; Weick, 1993). From a microsociological perspective, routines are viewed not as elementary, 'black-boxed' units of analysis but rather as ongoing social accomplishments that are embedded in broader and more persistent patterns of activity and meaning that make everyday work life simultaneously 'commonsensical', 'inertial', 'dynamic' and 'fragile'. This approach to routines, common in sociological and institutional studies of work and occupations (Abbott, 1989, 1993; Meyerson and Scully, 1995; Strauss, 1988), has recently been developed anew in management research (Kellogg et al., 2006; Obstfeld, 2005; Pentland and Feldman, 2005). In particular, these management researchers have expanded on Nelson and Winter's contention (1982, chap. 5) that organizational routines not only constrain variation and maintain stability but are also a source of variation and organizational change.

From a macrosociological perspective, in recent decades the Weberian tradition has come to view organized and large-scale innovation as a process accomplishment that is achieved in an institutional environment that both encourages innovation and rewards 'successful' innovators.[2] In this regard, much recent work on the institutional environment of innovation puts considerable emphasis on the role of transposition of context (Latour, 1987; Westney, 1987), the distributed and systemic nature of innovation (Heimer and Stinchcombe, 1999; Star, 1989; Stinchcombe, 1990, chap. 5; T. Hughes, 1992), the work that occurs to make innovation both recognizable and 'doable' in social and cognitive terms (Carlile, 2002; Fine, 1996, 2006; Fujimura, 1987; Hargadon and Douglas, 2001), and the role of collective, often professional or industry control in the dynamics of organizational routines (Kaghan, 2000; Lacey, 2006; Washington and Ventresca, 2004). In this view, institutional (e.g. markets, governments, religious and educational establishments) and organizational (e.g. bureaucracies or partnerships) environments shape the enactment of organizational routines and, in turn, evolve through variations generated through the regular enactment (both directed and undirected) of routines and the field-wide retention of selected routines.

This processual institutionalism conduces to empirical work in an evolutionary economic sociology, in which the dynamics surrounding organizational routines understood as a particular type of social convention are a key locus of variation, selection, and retention or, more broadly, innovation (i.e. – at least partially – directed evolution). We foreground the virtues of this perspective for developing a sociological 'theory of the innovative firm' that will advance the study of management, organization and institutional innovation that complements and extends a Schumpeterian appreciation of the processes of creative destruction. In this view, people both as individuals and in their group activities are viewed as purposeful and pragmatic within the bounds set by cognitive capacities and the environmental resources on which they can draw. People recognize and deal with material, technological and institutional constraints in largely conventional (rather than formally rational) ways while occasionally making 'intelligent' attempts to 'change the rules of the game' to their advantage with sometimes unanticipated consequences (Hallett, 2007).

We structure our argument as follows. In the first section, we introduce the concepts of organizations as 'going concerns' (Hughes, 1971b) and 'loosely-coupled systems' (Weick, 1979) as central concepts for a sociological view of routines that relates organizational stability and organizational change and that forms the basis for a 'theory of the innovative firm'. In the second section, we connect this processual institutional view of organizational stability and change to organizational routines by focusing on the microsociology of conventions. We treat organizational routines as a particular type of social convention characteristic of particular social settings, organizations, that are influenced by systems of meaning and social practices characteristic of the organizational fields in which they operate. Organizational routines are a major locus of variation in organizational activity. We focus attention on the mutability of social conventions and the ways in which they may be expected to adapt and spread over time. In the third section, we shift focus to look at how organizational routines are selected and retained in the environment, revisiting in selective ways the macrosociology of the modern economic institutions (i.e. industries and markets) in which 'going concerns' operate. We draw particular attention to the importance of bureaucratic processes, managerial work, and their relation to organizational stability and change. We underscore the importance of resisting efforts to separate analytically (whether by initial assumption or by research design) the performance of routine activity from the supporting social structures and meanings (Stinchcombe, 2002). In the final section, we review fundamental findings about organizational routines and organizational sociology and point to some implications for research methods and research design, to contribute to a more productive research conversation about organizational strategy and innovation.

Organizations as going concerns and loosely coupled systems: towards a sociological theory of the innovative firm

In 'Going concerns: the study of American institutions', Everett Hughes (1971b, p. 53) describes the difficulty of studying modern institutions where innovation and institutional change are the norm:

> Since a common feature of definitions of institutions is that they are clusters of conventions, the obvious things to put into a list (of institutions) are those phenomena that are beyond dispute conventional, the things that have a place in the more established public statements of how we do things (strongly tinged with the notion that these are the right way to do things). But if we close our lists there, we miss the main and most fascinating part of the sociologists' work, which is to understand how social values and collective arrangements are made and unmade: how things arise and how they change. To make progress with our job, we need to give full and comparative attention to the not-yets, the didn't quite-make-its, the not quite respectable, the unremarked and the openly 'anti' goings-on in our society (as well as the more noticed and respectable).

Hughes also argues that though large formal organizations and professional associations are examples of innovative and adaptive modern social forms, he is wary of using terms like 'organization' or 'association'. In his view, such terms convey an image of large, legitimate/respectable social groups that are well-integrated, optimally functional, and have well-understood boundaries that reliably demarcate insiders and outsiders. This connotation tends to obscure poorly articulated change processes, the porous boundaries across which change processes flow, and the heterogeneous structures on which change processes work. In short, they neglect the provisional and messy features of organized activity. Instead, Hughes and colleagues use the term 'going concern' to convey a large association or network of people linked together in some collective line of action.[3] People manage to 'do things together' (Becker, 1986a) by drawing on some pragmatic (i.e. substantively rational) cluster of conventions that provide some level of stability and predictability while allowing for some possibility of change in response to changing circumstances. In short, a going concern is an inhabited institution (Hallett and Ventresca, 2006) in which interaction processes are linked to social structure through social conventions.

Hughes's concept of a going concern is an extension of the ecological approach to urban sociology of Robert Park and the first Chicago School of Sociology (Park, 1952; Chapoulie, 1996) and the interactionist social psychology of American pragmatists (Strauss, 1959; Blumer, 1969). This ecological approach views occupations as akin to neighborhoods in an urban environment and workplaces as similar to 'downtown' areas in a city, the environments in which members of these different occupations interact on a daily basis. Furthermore, just as in urban ecologies some neighborhoods have high status and some neighborhoods have low status, in workplaces, some occupations (e.g. the professions) have relatively high status and other occupations (e.g. blue collar work of various sorts) have relatively low status (Becker et al., 1961; Hughes, 1971d; see also Gladwell, 2000).

The 'social worlds/arenas' framework[4] (Becker, 1982; Clarke, 1991; Strauss, 1993) generalizes this sociological tradition to focus particular attention on the processes that underpin both stability and change in both organizations and organizational fields. A social world is an empirically identifiable network of people 'doing (purposeful) things together' (either collaborating or competing) through a cluster of interdependent conventions and/or routines at some particular point in time which has a history and a future. From an 'objective' perspective, the social conventions that underpin social worlds tend to be stable or inertial (for reasons outlined in the next section.) From a 'subjective perspective', social conventions tend to be meaningful, sensible and taken-for-granted. Arenas, on the other hand, are realms in which conventions are in the process of being negotiated in the course of everyday work (again either collaborative or competitive) and possibly deconstructed and reconstructed over time (Hughes, 1971c; Strauss, 1978). An arena can be relatively small (e.g. a product development project or a small business) or relatively large (e.g. an emerging industry).

In the social worlds/arenas framework, a going concern is simultaneously a social world with characteristic conventions and an arena in which those conventions and the larger structures in which they are embedded are contested. Moreover, a large going concern (such as a business firm or other types of organization such as a university or government agency) is typically constructed from smaller interlinked social worlds such as functional departments or product divisions (Clarke, 1991). As such, a large going concern like a global business firm is both a provisional, adaptable and negotiated order and a locally robust but globally fragile structure.

In this respect, the concept of an organization as a going concern has much in common with the image of organizations as loosely-coupled systems (Weick, 1979) and organized anarchies – organizations characterized by problematic preferences, unclear technologies, and fluid participation

(Cohen et al., 1972; Cohen and March, 1974). By focusing more directly on the nature of managerial activities and the problems of organization design, these two central organization theory concepts help to fill out the structural imagery of formal organizations as going concerns. The idea of 'coupling', and loose coupling in particular, came to organization theory through work on problems of bureaucratic leadership, organizational change and reform in educational institutions. Cohen, March and colleagues (1972, 1974; see also Heimer and Stinchcombe, 1999) focused on how decisions happen in organizations, reshaping standard views of both decision process and leadership in administrative hierarchies to argue that many (public) organizations are usefully understood as 'organizational anarchies'. Weick (1979) formalized the loose coupling concept as a system description, with a social psychology of activity, to challenge then prevailing images of an organization as a set of densely linked elements held together by technical interdependencies and formal control structures. The imagery of loose coupling challenged the assumption that organizations operated with intentional plans, clear means–end goals, responsiveness, and direct coordination. Moreover, it incorporated the then novel idea of broader environments that interpenetrated organizations, further challenging the analytic integrity of a unit-level bureaucratic organization.[5]

The loose coupling concept envisions organized activity as a system that consists of sets of interconnected and interdependent functional units that vary in the degree of coupling. This variation in patterns of coupling accounts for various critical features of the system. Loose coupling here suggests that, despite being interconnected, the system elements can develop and act autonomously to some extent, and that a loosely-coupled system may well be more robust than a more tightly-coupled system. Here, control, flexibility, and coordinated action work both through the modularity of the system (e.g. the division of labor) and the manner in which activities within these modules are performed and how these intramodular activities are tied to the activities of the other modules of the system and the system as a whole. In particular, though tightly-coupled systems may be efficient systems in relatively stable environments, loosely-coupled systems are often more robust, adaptable, and effective in the face of equivocality (high volatility and ambiguity).[6] The concept of a going concern suggests that an organization survives based on the 'fitness' of its organizational routines and combinations of organizational routines (i.e. capabilities) (March and Olsen, 1979; Zollo and Winter, 1999) and its ability to adapt or reconfigure capabilities to fit changing circumstances in a fashion that makes 'sense' to the participants (Weick, 2001).[7]

In sum, the particular attraction of the going concern concept as the basis for a 'theory of the innovative firm' is that it is explicitly dynamic and is grounded in an ecological and evolutionary view of social/ economic/ organizational stability and change. By viewing going concerns as 'clusters of conventions', the concept leads to studying the dynamics of organizational routines in the context of ongoing organizational action. In a complementary manner, loosely-coupled systems are composed of hundreds and possibly thousands of interconnected and interdependent organizational routines and sub-routines. These sub-routines are often relatively tightly coupled in comparison to the system as a whole. However, even in loosely-coupled systems, the system can both enable and constrain action within sub-systems and changes within sub-systems may exert stresses on the system as a whole. The concept of a loosely coupled system emphasizes the role that evolving and interdependent organizational routines play in overall system adaptation.

Conventions and the microsociology of organizational routines
In the previous section, we defined going concerns as 'clusters of conventions' but did not provide a definition or discussion of what a convention was and how conventions were related to organizational routines. Markus Becker (2004), in a comprehensive review of research on organizational routines in organizational and evolutionary economics, notes that one prevailing definition views an organizational routine as a 'recurrent pattern of collective activity'. At a general level, this definition of a 'routine' works well for our approach, with two adjustments. First, we propose use of the term 'social convention' rather than 'routine'. Second, we would elaborate and define a social convention as 'a recurrent (and observable) pattern of collective activity *performed in accord with some mutually meaningful (and generally unobservable) template for contextually specific (i.e. situational) interaction*'. This definitional modification points to four things about Becker's discussion and the manner in which the term 'organizational routines' is deployed in much of the existing routines literature that we explore here.

First, as researchers well-grounded in organizational/evolutionary economics recognize, but organizational sociologists may not, organizational routines in the organizational/evolutionary/institutional economics research tradition are viewed as a key element in a dynamic/evolutionary theory of the business firm operating in a capitalist economy. Rather than focusing on equilibrium conditions (as in neoclassical theories), the key contribution here is to focus on disequilibrium conditions and how organizations and organizational routines change in response to changing market conditions. More particularly, organizational routines are critical for understanding Schumpeterian processes of creative destruction that underpin economic change (Nelson, 2005).

Second, though evolutionary economics is proposed as a remedy to the perceived limitations/weaknesses of the traditional neoclassical theory of the firm and traditional macroeconomic theories of economic growth, the behavioural assumptions concerning the people participating in the routines (i.e. patterns of collective activity) have the decidedly rational (albeit bounded) character characteristic of game theory or bounded rationality approaches (Kreps, 1990; Foss, 2001).[8] Though evolutionary economics does subtly shift the focus from the independent choices of individual actors to the ongoing and jointly purposeful activities of a group of actors and takes institutions seriously, research in this tradition has tended to treat the 'methodological individualism' of economics as unproblematic.

These points highlight that much of the recent literature on organizational routines in the area of strategic management, though (properly) cast as a critique of the traditional neoclassical economics literature, still reflects assumptions characteristic of a more economics-oriented than a sociological sensibility (Hirsch et al., 1987). The thrust of these critiques represents an attempt to provide a more satisfactory explanation of organizational transformations and product and process innovation in response to changing circumstances that move beyond simplified views of the 'production possibilities frontier' (e.g. Varian, 1987) and assumptions of general equilibrium.

Two additional observations are also important. The first observation would be that the study of 'recurrent patterns of collective activity' (i.e. 'conventions') has, from its earliest days as a discipline, been a core concern of general sociology (and the sociology of organizations, occupations and work more particularly) and that the rational choice approach has only recently begun to have (still limited) impact in sociological research (Kiser, 1999). These rational choice approaches join with established interactionist, network-based/structuralist, institutionalist and systems/functions-based views, which all have well-developed frameworks for studying 'recurrent patterns of collective activity'. In particular, the behavioral assumptions (and particularly assumptions of the social/cultural capacity and group orientation of human beings) between rational choice approaches and other sociological approaches are quite distinct.

Second, and more importantly, though sociologists have always been interested in patterns of collective activity, dominant approaches in organizational sociology have tended to have a macrostructural orientation and paid less attention to the finer grained microstructures such as routines or to the relationship between routines and organizational evolution. For example, the institutional stream of organizational sociology has focused most closely on the impact of extra-organizational sources of authority and systems of meaning in organized fields of activity (Bourdieu, 1977,

1990; DiMaggio and Powell, 1983; Lacey, 2006). In contrast, resource dependence theorists (Pfeffer and Salancik, [1978] 2003) have focused more explicitly on how struggles among organizations for control over resources is used to maintain equilibrium but may help to generate organizational change. Organizational ecologists (Carroll and Hannan, 2000), on the other hand, have assumed that individual organizations have difficulty adapting their structures (i.e. structural inertia) in response to changing environmental conditions and have used this insight to help explain patterns of organizational births and deaths. Though some researchers have tried to synthesize the findings of one or the other of these macrostructural approaches with the neo-Schumpeterian evolutionary economics of Nelson and Winter (Aldrich and Ruef, 2006), these efforts have, unlike evolutionary economics, only rarely (and relatively recently) focused on microstructures like routines.

However, where macrostructurally-oriented organizational sociologists have had some difficulty focusing on organizational routines as a unit of analysis, some economic sociologists have become increasingly interested in the relationship between social conventions and economic action. Biggart and Beamish (2003, p. 444) argue that *conventions* are a powerful way of accounting for social and market order, defining conventions as understandings that organize and coordinate activity in predictable ways. They define conventions as 'shared templates for interpreting situations and planning courses of action in mutually comprehensible ways that involve social accountability . . . [and] thus are a means of economic coordination between actors that are inherently collective, social, and even moral in nature'. Howard Becker (1986b) uses this view of conventions to outline an interactionist/ecological perspective on the concept of culture and contrasts this view with more holistic and essentialist views of culture. Where holistic/essentialist conceptions focus on culture as the norms and values characteristic of a distinctive society or large social collective (e.g. Maori culture, Japanese culture, or American culture), Becker views culture as a collection of social conventions where social conventions are the mechanisms used by group members to organize and enact specific collective activities.

Becker's classic account of how a dance band might be organized to play at a traditional local Friday night gig exemplifies this view of culture as a set of interrelated social conventions (1986b, pp. 10–11). Audience and band members have similar expectations about how they will jointly perform in a particular sort of situation, a Friday night dance. The audience who attends these dances expects the band to play conventional dance music and the band that is assembled for a particular dance can generally put together a reasonable collection of conventional tunes that are appropriate for the event. Becker points out that what a casual observer might not realize is that the band often assembles at the last minute from a set of experienced 'dance musicians' who know the conventional tunes, know how to play together well enough to satisfy the audience that they have been hired to entertain, and may or may not have played together before. The dance event is an example of a situation where the consumers (i.e. the audience) of the dance music have conventional expectations, or a template, and the producers of the dance music (i.e. the dance musicians) follow 'routines' that allow them to perform so as to meet these expectations without much forethought or planning. And the conventions and expectations held by both producers and consumers make possible a range of innovation amidst familiarity. A game of pick-up basketball on a playground would work via similar routines, expectation templates, and rules, where a particular context or situation is matched with a set of resources that can be and are easily mobilized to produce a particular kind of performance or event.

The basic stability of social conventions stems from well-understood premises. First, people have limited cognitive (and physical) capacities which constrain their ability to participate in patterned and goal-directed collective activities. It is costly in resources to create new social conventions to govern interaction in particular situations when established conventions work perfectly well (Becker, 1995). Second, interaction processes are time-dependent in the sense that, in particular situations, a slow response is essentially equivalent to no response and a conventional response is preferable to a poorly-considered unconventional response in terms of keeping an interaction process going (Eisenhardt and Bourgeois, 1988; Orlikowski and Yates, 2002). Finally, over time, individuals tend to become not only habituated but emotionally committed to (i.e. identify with) particular social conventions and associated patterns of thought that make it very difficult for them to act contrary to social conventions (Becker, 1970a; Selznick [1957] 1984). Another way to state this is that people become socialized into a particular set of conventions in much the same way that people learn their native language.

However, the Hughesian social worlds tradition pushes past the simple association of conventions with social stability and social order by emphasizing that social conventions (i.e. 'templates for interaction'), though resistant to change, always allow some room for 'organized' or 'planned' variation in specific performances (Becker, 1995, 2000), in the colloquial, improvization (Barrett, 1998; Orlikowski, 1996). In a particular situation, performances will be enacted and accounted for in accord with a well-established convention. However, in the course of enacting a convention, some level of variation in the actual execution of elements of a convention is to be expected and may be built into the social convention. That is, the performances of a social convention may be relatively orchestrated or standardized so that variation across performances is reduced or they may remain open to improvization so that variation across performances is increased. In turn, these small variations may, over time, affect processes of interaction within communities. Previously coupled communities may become decoupled through processes of segmentation. Previously uncoupled communities may become linked through processes of intersection (either deliberate or emergent). As new communities emerge, old conventions may disappear and new conventions are discovered or invented. In this way, social conventions mediate between social stability and social change and can be seen to vary from place to place and evolve over time (Strauss, 1993; Hallett and Ventresca, 2006).

The recognition of the role of social conventions in both stability and change resonates in diverse, contemporary streams of sociologically-influenced management research at all levels of analysis. At a micro level, studies of sensemaking (Weick, 1979, 1995) build around the evolution of 'interacts in the face of equivocality'. That is, people attempt to minimize equivocality (i.e. ambiguity) in interaction but have the cognitive resources to actively address equivocality if they encounter it in particular situations (Weick, 1995). Feldman and Pentland (2003), Pentland (1995), Feldman (2000), Pentland and Feldman (2005) extend this contribution, linking directly insights from sensemaking research, the Carnegie tradition, and evolutionary economics to focus attention on how organizational routines provide a mechanism for organizational change. Other researchers who, like Becker, view organizational culture as a cluster of interrelated conventions have, in studying the role of provisional and situated identities in organizational culture, refocused the organizational culture literature, spurring new theory and methods that engaged 'culture' with the social psychology of conflict as well as the social psychology of order (Martin, 1992). This work can be usefully adapted to analyzing cultural stability and cultural change in organizations on a spectrum from relatively tightly-coupled (integrated) to relatively modular (differentiated) to relatively loosely-coupled (fragmented). Furthermore, many studies highlight the central role that professional management, because of its considerable formal authority, plays in 'shaping' organizational culture and their role in establishing (or disestablishing) workplace conventions (Kunda, 1992; Meyerson, 1994, 1998).

At a more meso level, social network research has always emphasized that social action is situated in, in fact, conditioned by, the structure of social networks, e.g., relative tie strength, kinds of ties (Podolny and Page, 1998). However, in recent years, organizational researchers in this area have paid increasing attention to the complementary nature of network structure and the enactment of conventions within networks (Heimer, 1992; Mutch et al., 2006; Uzzi and Lancaster, 2003). Similarly, much recent work on large-scale sociotechnical systems has highlighted the multidimensionality of organizations (Monge and Contractor, 2003), the sociotechnical nature of the workplace, and the interdependence of technological infrastructure and social conventions in providing the stage on which routine workplace interactions take place (Thomas, 1994; Barley, 1996; MacKenzie, 1996; Star and Ruhleder, 1996; Bowker and Star, 1999; Orlikowski, 2000; Kaghan and Bowker, 2001).

Finally, at a more macro-level, 'institutionalists' in economic and organizational sociology focus on organizational fields (i.e. populations and communities of organizations) and on the development and maintenance of field-level conventions that are used to build structures that tie together participants in very large (but relatively loosely-coupled) networks such as markets, industries (and trade associations), and strategic alliances (Brown, 1978; Orrù et al., 1997; Callon, 1998; Podolny 2001; Thevenot, 2001; Garud et al., 2002). This stream of research serves to reinforce the idea that 'going concerns' do not operate in a vacuum but respond to (and possibly attempt to shape) the environment (full of other going concerns) in which they operate. We address this issue in more depth in the following section.

Organizational routines, managerial work and the macrosociology of capitalism

So far, we have argued that organizational routines are usefully viewed as a type of social convention and that social conventions are situated in specific contexts such as organizations or villages or cities and allow for complex coordination (both collaborative and competitive) among individuals and social groups. In this section, we explore the value of linking the 'routines as conventions' perspective outlined in the previous section with macrosociological investigations of bureaucratic and professional management institutions within capitalist political economies. Central to our discussion is Weber's scholarly legacy on bureaucracy and rationalist modern institutional orders (Collins, 1986; Perrow, 1986; Clegg, 1995; Swedberg, 1998; Lounsbury and Carberry, 2005). In particular, we review possible intersections between the Weberian tradition and the ecological approaches of Hughes and the complementary perspectives in organizational sociology that we have discussed above. We show how Hughes' concept of a 'going concern' and the extended concepts of social worlds/arenas as a dynamic and evolving cluster of social conventions can be reconciled with Weber's view of the modern Western institutional order grounded in rational (and specifically formally rational) authority.[9] From this integrated Hughesian/Weberian perspective, we view organizational routines as social conventions with a decidedly rational orientation and formal organizations as institutions characterized by 'clusters of rationalized social conventions' (i.e. organizational routines) that are distinct from social conventions and institutions found in 'pre-modern' societies (e.g. the traditional small 'closed' societies studied by cultural anthropologists) and which may be superseded by new sets of conventions and institutions in post-modern societies (e.g. cyberculture).

Weber argued that, to understand individual behavior and collective patterns of action, it is necessary to understand not only the local context but also the particular institutions in which the action is situated. In particular, he asserted that there are two crucial elements associated with any particular set of institutional arrangements. The first element is the 'objective' functionality of institutional arrangements, i.e. the way in which institutional arrangements enable and constrain the actors operating in the environment and the manner in which these arrangements differ from place to place and develop and change over time (Stinchcombe, 1986). The second element is the 'subjective' legitimacy of the institutional arrangements, i.e. what actors believe about the rightness, fitness, or legitimacy of a particular set of institutional arrangements (Weber, 1978). From an objective point of view, Weber observed that there are many 'functional' arrangements in the sense of arrangements that have allowed social systems to survive and reproduce themselves and that these arrangements were subject to change over time. From a subjective point of view, Weber asserted that people are both individually and collectively purposeful (i.e. substantively rational) in their behavior but are enabled and constrained by the particular institutional order that they operate in and tend to commit themselves to working within or working against that particular institutional order because that is the institutional order that they understand and to which they relate.

Though Weber was interested in understanding the full range of institutions found in societies around the world and throughout history, he was particularly interested in explaining the distinctiveness of the institutional order of modern Western capitalist society (Heilbroner, 1986; Fligstein, 2001), In particular, Weber emphasized that, in comparison to earlier and competing civilizations, modern Western (i.e. bourgeois/capitalist) society tended to be highly rationalized and to be more dependent on formal rules, structures, and professional expertise for coordinating and controlling interaction.

Though Weber's writing on bureaucracy and the 'rational' institutional environment of the modern West is richly suggestive, the limits of Weber's discussion have been highlighted by subsequent historical developments (e.g. globalization and computerization) and debates over his theoretical legacy in several streams of research (including but not restricted to organizational/management research). In particular, Weber's work on bureaucracy was initially interpreted for the English-language audience by structural–functional sociologists (Parsons, 1937; Merton, 1957) who made strong assumptions about social equilibrium and social order that hindered the development of more evolutionary perspectives. To the extent that interpretations of Weber's corpus have been dominated by organizational sociologists with a structural–functional/equilibrium orientation, these difficulties of accounting for evolution and change have been accentuated (Brown, 1978). This customary framing of Weber's writings on the general characteristics of institutional environments has presented several challenges for researchers who want to incorporate the concept of organizational routines as a source of change into a Weberian perspective. In the remainder of this section, we briefly touch on these challenges and suggest how they may be resolved in a more processual and ecologically focused Weberian conception of 'evolutionary economic sociology'.

First, from an 'objective' perspective, it is important to note that Weber's original picture of bureaucracy tends to highlight management structures and the role of administrators in organizations and neglect the structure of other work activities and the role of occupational expertise and professionalization in governing organizational action. This strong focus on administration and administrative routines has tended to be retained in Weberian-style organizational research and the role of other occupational groups (and non-managerial professionals in particular) is often played down (Barley, 1996). To the extent that organizations and organizational routines are shaped through the interplay of multiple occupational groups and several competing professional groups including but not restricted to professional administrators (Abbott, 1988a; Lounsbury and Kaghan, 2001), this strong focus on administration may mask some important (and non-managerial) aspects of organizational routines (Becker, 1970b; Mintzberg and Waters, 1985).

Relatedly, Weber's original discussion of bureaucracy concentrates on formalized and rationalized social structures (Brown, 1978) but pays little attention to the underlying technological infrastructures of work or the manner in which social structure and technological infrastructure are interdependent (Callon, 1992; Kaghan and Bowker, 2001). Organizational researchers (e.g. those associated with the sociotechnical systems tradition of the Tavistock School), many evolutionary economists (who draw on Schumpeter and through Schumpeter on Marx), and most researchers in the sociology of science and technology have developed the theories of highly interdependent social and technical (i.e. sociotechnical) systems to redress this. In this extended view, formal bureaucracies and standard administrative practices become one of a larger set (e.g. rationalized legal systems, large-scale research and development operations, technology-enhanced production and distribution systems, etc.) that promote what Latour (1987) has termed 'action-at-a-distance' (i.e. the ability of modern organizations to act in a highly coordinated and controlled fashion over great distances and for extended periods of time (Yates, 1989).[10] Rather than talking only about bureaucracies, it may be more fruitful to talk about technocracies constructed out of material technologies (e.g. automobiles, airplanes, computers) and 'symbolic' technologies (e.g. legal systems, organizational and management structures) and employing technical experts (including but not restricted to professional managers) to run these systems. Organizational routines arise and develop in these contexts (Lacey, 2006).

Second, from a more 'subjective' standpoint, it is essential to remember that Weber emphasized that the concrete institutional arrangements found in any particular historical context (including the modern era) are grounded in some combination of Weber's three ideal typical forms of legitimate authority: charismatic, traditional, legal-rational.[11] This highlights the point that organizational routines are likely to be grounded in some combination of charismatic, traditional, and rational authority and the nature of these combinations is likely to be contested over time.

Relatedly, it is important to understand Weber's concepts of formal and substantive rationality and how they relate to organizational routines. For Weber, formal rationality means that people behave in a formally logical way in accord with formalized (and universal) first principles. Formal rationality is at the heart of 'rational' forms of authority. Substantive rationality, on the other hand, means that people behave in an adaptive way so as to make out in the environment in which they are working and living. In an environment in which institutions are rationalized on the basis of 'first principles', people can be expected to think and behave more or less in a formally rational way (constrained as the theory of 'bounded rationality' contends by individual and collective cognitive limitations.) However, though people may tend to behave in a formally rational way most of the time, substantive rationality suggests that people may behave in a way that seems inconsistent with rational principles (and consistent with charismatic or traditional principles) if there is an adaptive advantage to behaving in that way. It also suggests, in line with many other streams of sociological thought, that 'first principles' may be contested and (socially) reconstructed over time and that human behavior may be more malleable and culturally conditioned than allowed for in formal rational choice theories such as those found in neoclassical microeconomics.

Finally, Weber's corpus is primarily historical comparative in intent and (in contrast to Marx) only weakly and indirectly developmental or evolutionary in the sense of explaining how new institutional arrangements arise, develop, and survive (or fail to survive) over time. Most notable in Weber's work is his linking the Protestant work ethic with the rational spirit of capitalism and his 'prediction' (made in the first decades of the twentieth century) that society was in the process of becoming fully rationalized (i.e. an 'iron cage', where structures persist once meaning is exhausted) in a formal sense.

In short, in the Weberian tradition, routines have been treated as set pieces, the artifacts of rationalized bureaucracies, rather than a central analytic focus or a mechanism by which activity is accomplished. However, as we argued in the previous two sections, other sociological traditions such as symbolic interactionism and the ecological institutionalism of Robert Park and Everett Hughes, and the social ecology of Amos Hawley and the organizational ecology of Hannan and Freeman are much more strongly evolutionary in outlook. To the extent that the concept of organizational routines is central to the theory of evolutionary economics posited by Nelson and Winter, viewing Weberian institutionalism from an evolutionary and more processualist perspective is important for a sociological view of the innovative firm.

Towards an evolutionary economic sociology

In the previous sections, we have outlined a sociological perspective that synthesizes insights from the Hughesian tradition in the sociology of work and occupations with the Weberian tradition on organizational and institutional sociology in which organizational routines have a central analytical role. We label this Hughesian–Weberian perspective 'evolutionary economic sociology'. We have also provided a brief overview of schools of thought in organization and management theory that complement this perspective. In this section, we compare 'evolutionary economic sociology' with evolutionary economics (in the Nelson and Winter tradition) in terms of their approaches to organizations, organizational routines, organizational environments and organizational innovation, and briefly explore some of the methodological implications of encouraging a more nuanced dialogue between evolutionary economic sociology and evolutionary economics. (See Table 4.1.)

To review, in their seminal book, *An Evolutionary Theory of Economic Change*, Nelson and Winter (1982) outline a paradigm for studying business firms and organizational and economic change that is at dramatic variance from the standard paradigm of neoclassical economics. Where neoclassical economics is concerned with well-defined choice sets, efficiency, and market equilibrium, the evolutionary economics of Nelson and Winter assumes the bounded rationality of economic actors, the importance of tacit knowledge, imperfect information as the normal state of affairs, and firms as

Table 4.1   Assumptions in economics and economic sociology

Assumptions	Neoclassical economics	Evolutionary economics	Evolutionary economic sociology	Structural–functional sociology
Primary unit of analysis	Individuals and firms	Organizational routines	Group and network conventions	Social system
Cognitive capacity	Unbounded	Bounded	Bounded	Unbounded
Human nature	Individualistic	Individualistic	Socialized	Socialized
Economic institutions	Independent of social institutions	Independent of social institutions	Interdependent with social institutions	Interdependent with social institutions
State of the environment	Equilibrium	Disequilibrium	Disequilibrium	Equilibrium
Routines/conventions	Artifacts of optimizing choice	Variable and subject to selective pressures	Both generative and inertial	Static, constraining and stable
Firms and organizations	Treated as a single acting unit	Modular systems characterized by dynamic capabilities	Clusters of loosely-coupled informal and formal conventions	Treated as a single hierarchic unit
Methodological tendencies	Formal models of equilibrium states	Mixed formal and appreciative theory and quantitative and qualitative methods with more emphasis on model development	Mixed formal and appreciative theory and quantitative and qualitative methods with more emphasis on contextual grounding and thick (theoretically-informed) description	Middle-range/appreciative theories of equilibrium states

laboratories that produce variations in organizational routines that are sub-sequently selected for in the market. From an evolutionary perspective, the ability of firms to generate or adopt new and favorable organizational routines is, despite the costs involved, as important to firm survival and firm growth (and, collectively, economic growth) as producing the optimal amount of a product at minimal cost (Becker, 2004).

Subsequent research in strategic management and organizational learning has developed a rich stew of concepts and frameworks that draw on these basic ideas. With Nelson and Winter's strong grounding in a Schumpeterian view of competition and its focus on innovation and change as the key to maintaining a sustainable competitive advantage, communication with a broader population of researchers who identify themselves under the umbrella of the 'resource-based view of the firm' (Barney et al., 2001) has been relatively easy and relatively productive. Like evolutionary economics, the resource-based view of the firm is an 'economics-oriented' paradigm that departs in important ways from the standard neoclassical theory of the firm. Perhaps the richest product of this interaction has been the attempt to understand the relationship between the concept of organizational routines as dealt with in evolutionary economics and the concept of organizational capabilities as dealt with in the resource-based view of the firm and more specifically with the concept of dynamic capabilities and their relation to firm adaptation (Teece et al., 1997; Zollo and Winter, 1999, 2002; Eisenhardt and Martin, 2000).

Though requiring a bit more work, we believe that it is also possible to better articulate the relationship between evolutionary economics (as represented by Nelson and Winter and the resource-based view of the firm) and an evolutionary economic sociology and a view of organizational routines as social conventions (i.e. a Hughesian/neo-Weberian perspective). In particular, we believe that the concept of a 'going concern' and the concept of 'dynamic capabilities' offer a valuable point of contact. A 'going concern' is centrally concerned with the manner in which organizations adapt to their environments but remains very aware of how difficult and risky adaptation is likely to be. Dynamic capabilities, as developed by organizational economists, are precisely the kinds of qualities that would provide mechanisms for the persistence of 'going concerns'. Furthermore, to the extent that dynamic capabilities can be viewed as the capacity to manipulate or influence 'clusters of conventions' that are subject to modification over time, it is relatively easy to picture the relationship between dynamic capabilities and organizational routines (Zollo and Winter, 1999). Comparing these two concepts provides a good opportunity to build bridges between organizational sociology and organizational economics that will both allow research domains greater understanding of each other and provide more opportunities for productive interchange of ideas (Kaghan and Phillips, 1998). The key aspect of both concepts is their insistence on accounting for the ongoing performance and the evolution of 'recurrent collective patterns of action' within particular contexts in a manner that links micro and macro perspectives.

Nevertheless, there are some important differences in theoretical outlook and methodological emphases between evolutionary economics and evolutionary economic sociology that reflect their treatment of organizational routines. Evolutionary economics has traditionally resonated with Simon's 'object-oriented' view of the 'architecture of complexity' (1969) in which complex social structures such as organizations are rationally designed and modularized with formal, explicit, and well-defined boundaries between the organizational modules and a well-defined boundary between the organization and its environment (Schilling, 2000). Though some organizational and evolutionary economists have moved away from this perspective to some extent (Koppl and Langlois, 2001), evolutionary economic sociology more explicitly attempts to 'denaturalize' these processes and open 'black boxes' (i.e. well-bounded modules). (See Table 4.2.)

Evolutionary economic sociology acknowledges that attempts are often made to impose a formal and modular structure on a 'going concern' (e.g. Brown, 1978; Callon, 1998) but argues that these 'formal structures' must still be implemented and reconciled with less formal but thoroughly

Table 4.2 *Evolutionary mechanisms in evolutionary economics and evolutionary economic sociology*

	Evolutionary economics	Evolutionary economic sociology
Variation	Modelled as a stochastic process	Random variation in enactment of routines Improvisation Transposition of context (translation to new contexts) Collision of social worlds (intersection) Directed innovation
Selection	Market selection based on satisfying demand through superior organization of resources	Market selection Hierarchical choice Negotiation and standard setting
Retention	Development of imitable 'best practices'	Development of imitable best practices Administrative fiat Legitimization of norms Segmentation and boundary formation Establishment of standard discourses

routinized informal conventions. Ultimately any implementation – if successful (i.e. survivable and self-supporting) – results in a substantively rational but socially constructed organizational structure (Stinchcombe, 2002; Townley, 2002). Organizational 'structure' as an institution is a cluster of interrelated social conventions or organizational routines that may or may not be formally standardized. Rather than assuming that formally rational designs are implemented as planned, a 'going concern' perspective takes design implementation (and organizational change) as an empirical question in which the efficacy of formally rational design is variable and the congruence between formal and substantive rationality is not taken for granted.

Relatedly, evolutionary economics and evolutionary economic sociology tend to differ in their approach to the question of rationality and culture. Evolutionary economics stresses the formal (but bounded) rationality of individuals and of professional managers and the nature of selection (i.e. rational choice) in the market. Evolutionary economic sociologists make fewer assumptions about formal rationality and focus more on processes of sensemaking (Weick, 1995) and the relationship between culture, cognition, and collective action (Martin, 1992). That said, organizational sociologists have also tended to pay less attention to the capitalist market as an arena for change which is central to Schumpeterian views such as those of Nelson and Winter. Evolutionary economic sociologists should strive to return to the concerns of classical sociological thinkers such as Weber, Durkheim, and Marx with economic institutions (Stern and Barley, 1996; Callon, 1998).

Methodologically, organizational and economic sociologists have been less focused than organizational and evolutionary economists on creating the sort of highly abstracted representations that are necessary for mathematical models and statistical analysis. Conversely, organizational and evolutionary economists have been less focused than organizational economic sociologists on producing 'thick' (i.e. theoretically-informed) descriptions of organizational routines that can be used for comparative case analysis and developing 'grounded' theories of the middle range. That said, encouraging a dialogue between organizational economics and organizational sociology also represents an opportunity to explore more mixed-method approaches that draw equally on the 'dirty hands' fieldwork of sociologists (and anthropologists) and the 'clean models' of economists (Abbott, 1988b; Bechky, 2006; M. Becker, 2005; Black et al., 2004; Hirsch et al., 1987; Kaghan et al., 1999, Weick, 1999) and enrich appreciative theory, formal theory, and empirical research (Nelson and Winter, 1982, pp. 45–8). In line with this basic outlook, in the remainder of this section, we explore what this might mean in terms of rethinking 'organizational ethnography' and (to borrow the words of Andrew Abbott) 'transcending general linear reality' in quantitative research to support an evolutionary economic sociology.

The integrated evolutionary economic sociology framework that we outlined in the previous sections was prefigured in several seminal book-length organizational ethnographies[12] that were produced in the 1950s and early 1960s but have been largely neglected since the 1960s. These book-length ethnographies work as canonical texts for an evolutionary economic sociology. Taken together, they map out core concerns of this framework and point to the distinct analytic commitments. Among these organizational ethnographies, we focus special attention on *Men Who Manage* (1959) by Melville Dalton, *Patterns of Industrial Bureaucracy* (1954) by Alvin Gouldner, *Psychiatric Ideologies and Institutions* (1964) by Anselm Strauss and others, *The Management of Innovation* (1961) by Tom Burns and G.M. Stalker, and *The Bureaucratic Phenomenon* (1964) by Michel Crozier. In the following few paragraphs, we provide an outline of the major themes found in these works and how these themes have been extended in more recent field-based participant–observer research.[13]

Dalton was a student of Everett Hughes and was the first scholar to apply a 'going concerns' sensibility (though he did not label it as we have) to the study of organizations and management. Where we have focused primarily on innovation, Dalton focused on the process of supervising routine operations and on the relationship between the formal and informal structure of management hierarchies. His discussion of management processes prefigures much of the discussion of Cyert and March (1962) on organizational decision making and provides empirical observations germane to Cohen, March and Olsen's 'Garbage Can Model' of organizations (1972). Martha Feldman (1989) in *Order Without Design: Information Production and Policy Making* builds on March's research to describe the work in a government agency in which policy analysis reports are produced but have little influence on policy making. William Kaghan (2000), in 'Harnessing a Public Conglomerate: Technology Transfer Managers and the Entrepreneurial University', extended Dalton's research on the role of formal and informal structures in firms to the investigation of the construction of 'deals' between universities and firms around the transfer of university-generated inventions.

Gouldner's book, undertaken to extend early Weberian organization theories, focuses attention on the difficulties that arise in 'imposing' formally rational procedures in a workplace with little reference to the conventional work practices of 'non-managers'. Gouldner also introduces the theme of the importance of wider environments that shape organizational routines: in *Patterns of Industrial Bureaucracy* he pays attention to how societal and community change, the provision of rationalized and 'scientifically-certified' management practices, and new kinds of social accountability impinged on local work places and work practices (Hallett and Ventresca, 2006). John

Weeks (2003), in *Unpopular Culture: Ritual of Complaint in a British Bank*, picks up on many of the themes pioneered by Gouldner in his account of fine-grained distinctions in work routines, convention, and vocabularies for 'complaint' in a large bureaucracy.

Strauss and his co-authors (1964) provide three important insights about the dynamics of occupational jurisdictions. First, they emphasize that there is often competition for dominance in a workplace among different 'ideologies' (in their cases, among psychiatrists with different paradigms on the nature of psychiatric illness and treatment). Furthermore, the dominant professions (doctors in this case) are linked to other occupations (e.g. nurses and medical technicians) in institutionalized (i.e. routinized) patterns of work and, though dominant professions have the authority to lead, they can rarely fully dictate the routines that can be followed. Other occupations often have the power to resist direction that they consider unreasonable. Finally, by studying psychiatric hospitals (before the rise of 'managed' medicine), they emphasize that the management tasks of coordination and control are not the exclusive province of professional administrators. Strauss and colleagues gave us the term 'negotiated order' to capture this set of insights. A negotiated order is arbitrary, though not random, built up from the interactions of local actors, stable at any single point in time but adaptable over time. Andrew Abbott in *The System of Professions* (1988a) pushed forward these ideas and engaged them with a broader historical/cultural analysis of shifting jurisdictions among occupations and professions and an explicit research strategy for the study of this sort of ecological evolution. Stephen Barley's (1986, 1996) work on technicians and the occupational struggles that emerge out of the introduction of new technologies in the workplace also fits squarely in this thematic stream.

Burns and Stalker introduced the idea that management style varied depending on the purpose of the work. For routine production, a mechanized and highly orchestrated set of conventions/organizational routines were likely to be appropriate. For product or process development work, a set of conventions and a management style that provided more room for improvisation were likely to be more appropriate. Several more recent ethnographies have done much to enrich various aspects of Burns and Stalker's work. Lucy Suchman's (1987) *Plans and Situated Actions* can be viewed as a complement to Burns and Stalker that takes into account human interaction with technologies and technological infrastructure. Robert J. Thomas's (1994) *What Machines Can't Do* helped to extend Burns and Stalker's insights to the actual implementation of innovations. Diane Vaughan's (1996) *The Challenger Launch Decision: Risky Technology, Culture, and Deviance at NASA* illustrates how Burns and Stalker's categories may be difficult to separate in a large-scale sociotechnical project like the Space Shuttle. Joan Fujimura's (1996), *Crafting Science: A Sociohistory of the Quest for the Genetics of Cancer* provides a picture of the social worlds/arenas in which large-scale innovation efforts are carried out. Finally, Stephen Barley and Gideon Kunda's (2004) *Gurus, Hired Guns, and Warm Bodies: Itinerant Experts in the Knowledge Economy* provides great insight into how the organization of innovation has changed since Burns and Stalker first published their book, with particular emphasis on how organizations contract with 'temporary experts' to complete specific projects.

We end with Crozier's work because Crozier emphasized that, despite all the complications and qualifications laid out by Dalton, March, Gouldner, Strauss, and Burns and Stalker, Weber's basic instinct that bureaucratic hierarchies and formal rules provided powerful (but imperfect) tools for 'going concerns' that were, however modified in structure and variable in terms of process, an essential element of modern organizations. In this respect, Chester Barnard's (1938) *The Functions of the Executive* can be read as a powerful account of the work of senior managers by a reflective practitioner (Schon, 1983) that complements Crozier's work. Philip Selznick's (1957) *Leadership in Administration: A Sociological Interpretation* presents a Weberian view of what is demanded of executives that head large bureaucracies. Arthur Stinchcombe's (1990) *Information and Organizations* re-examines a number of classic ethnographic and historical works in organizational studies to unpack how bureaucratic structures have been (and may continue to be) valuable mechanisms for organizing work in large-scale 'going concerns' generally and 'innovative firms' in particular.

We end this section by noting that although evolutionary economic sociology places great emphasis on the continued importance of both ethnographic and historical research that takes situational/locational and historical contexts seriously, it should also recognize that fieldwork alone is not adequate for uncovering all aspects of these processes. In this regard, a number of researchers have spent considerable energy attempting to find qualitative, quantitative and 'mixed' methods to consolidate and generalize their findings and advance a range of methodologically diverse research (Obstfeld, 2005; Ragin, 1994; Uzzi and Lancaster, 2003). These general efforts are consistent with a perspective that is ecological and focuses on 'going concerns' in which social conventions or organizational routines are central analytic concerns.

We end by noting that Nelson and Winter's discussion of 'appreciative theory', 'formal theory' and 'empirical research' can be applied to sociological approaches to the study of organizational routines. In the previous paragraphs, we drew attention to the close relationship between empirical qualitative research and 'appreciative' theory and further noted that sociologists would likely view 'appreciative theory' and 'grounded theory' as essentially synonymous. Developing a truly robust set of 'mixed methods' that could be used by both economists and sociologists would likely involve more reflection on this observation. In addition, it is also important to recognize that the possible links between formal sociological theory and the strongly qualitative traditions such as the Chicago School have been underexplored (Abbott, 1988b; White, 1992; Pentland, 1995, Monge and Contractor, 2003) and hold much promise. These efforts may also provide points of contact between evolutionary economic and organizational sociology and organizational evolutionary and organizational economics.

Conclusion

Routines, through their use by Nelson and Winter as a critical element for a neo-Schumpeterian evolutionary economics, have become part of the crowded conceptual toolkit of the contemporary 'knowledge-based' and 'resource-based' views of strategy and innovation. Along with capabilities, learning and the rest, this promising view of strategy has provided a more dynamic and emergent view of strategy, structure and organizational change than that found in the work of Chandler, Porter, Williamson and others who shaped the modern economics-oriented tradition in strategy research. In this chapter, we have developed a framework for evolutionary economic sociology that focuses on routines, not as minimal units of analysis, but rather as social accomplishments, regularly and persistently embedded in broader patterns of activity and 'held' in the activities of numerous sense-making actors. We have further proposed using the concept of a 'going concern' as the basis for a sociological 'theory of the innovative firm'.

We argue that 'routines-as-conventions' understood in an evolutionary economic sociology framework resolves theoretical tensions in the prevailing approaches, proffers the basis for work on organizational and institutional innovation, and provides unanticipated ways to inform conversations on business strategy and organizational design. This view of routines is developed explicitly but unevenly in both classic and contemporary sociological and institutional studies of organizations. We use this chapter to foreground the virtues of this approach, and we contrast the sociological view of routines – along with studies of work, occupations, and organizations – with the evolutionary economics view as exemplified by Nelson and Winter. Here our point is to join with Nelson and Winter and those in the evolutionary economics tradition to enrich another generation of research in the areas of organizational learning, knowledge, and innovation.

The attention to knowledge and practices, along with other resources, usefully refocuses analysts on specific work, occupations, and organizational processes, and away from linear and reified abstractions like Porter's 'five forces'. We look instead to work on the dissolution and reconfiguration of routines/conventions within organizations (i.e. a specific type of going concern characterized by professional administrative hierarchies) and broader organizational fields (i.e. a specific type of social world populated by interacting organizations). We attend to the ways in which collective action is enacted with reference both to local, context-sensitive conventions and through more global systems of meaning that articulate and propel activity across entire fields. We argue that new directions in the study and application of organizational routines viewed as a particular type of social convention focused on facilitating innovation are promising. In developing this approach, we drew heavily on the processual institutionalism or social worlds/arenas approach (Becker, 1982; Strauss, 1993). This perspective has been developed most fully in the sociology of work and occupations and emphasizes the role that 'socially aware' actors take in pragmatically enacting 'scripted' patterns of interaction, making and giving meaning to their interactions, and sometimes modifying these patterns of activity and the natural environments and technological infrastructures in which new patterns are enacted.[14]

We end this chapter with a brief reflection on 'research routines' in sociology and economics. One major difficulty with discussing a concept like organizational routines in a way that is meaningful to both sociologists and economists is that either the concept is removed from and examined outside of the institutional context in which it is deployed or that a particular 'default' context is taken for granted and left unstated. That is, even if economists and sociologists agree to use the same term and settle on a common definition of organizational routines (e.g. recurrent patterns of collective activity in an organizational context), the concept does not stand alone. Rather it is deployed by sociologists and economists in more comprehensive theoretical frameworks where the exact sense of the concept is colored by its relationship to other concepts in the theoretical framework (Mauws and Phillips, 1995). Furthermore, concepts are operationalized in different ways and evidence is collected using a variety of methods or procedures which may not be fully consistent. All of these factors are a crucial aspect of the way economic or sociological 'puzzles' (Kuhn, 1970) get solved. As these 'contextual' differences mount, barriers to productive communication and interaction (similar to what Kuhn meant by incommensurability) arise and distinct research communities emerge (Kaghan and Phillips, 1998).

As these barriers grow higher, the temptation just to communicate with others in your 'research neighborhood' and conduct 'stovepipe' research is great. That said, the mere fact that different schools of thought can agree on a common term with a common definition (or find synonyms that share a common definition) provides an opportunity to build bridges and surmount barriers so that a productive exchange of ideas can occur. This chapter represents an attempt to explore both how the concept of organizational routines can be used to reinvigorate sociological explorations of organizational and institutional innovation and economic change and as a mechanism for more productively translating between economic and sociological perspectives and developing a more nuanced appreciation of the respective strengths and limitations of economic and sociological approaches and how they might complement and reinforce each other.

Acknowledgements

We thank Howard Becker, Geof Bowker, Lynn Eden, Martha Feldman, David Obstfeld, Brian Pentland, Rodney Lacey, Mike Lounsbury, Ann Vogel, Meng Zhao, and colleagues in the Innovation Leadership Working Group for useful conversations and comments on draft versions of the chapter. Markus Becker provided careful editorial guidance for us, and was extraordinarily helpful and accommodating in the gestation of this work.

Notes

1. We make the distinction between routines and individuals for two reasons. First we want to highlight the fact that, in our discussion, the fundamental structural unit of analysis is the group rather than the individual. That is, we lean toward 'methodological groupism' or 'methodological networkism' rather 'methodological individualism'. The 'proper' way to study the relationship between macrostructures and microstructures and how they relate to the subjective understandings and behaviors of individuals has a very long history in Sociology (Bourdieu, 1977, 1990; Douglas, 1986; Giddens, 1984; Granovetter, 1985; Weber, 1978) and discussing this literature in any depth would be well beyond the scope of this chapter. Our 'methodological groupism' is quite different in focus from the sort of 'methodological individualism' that underpins 'rational choice' perspectives. We discuss this point in rather more detail in a subsequent section and will discuss some aspects of how the two perspectives might be reconciled in the final section of this chapter. In addition, we made the distinction between routines and individuals to emphasize that our interest was in collective action (and the shared understandings that facilitate collective action) rather than in individual choice (and the self-motivations that may undermine collective action).

2. Clearly this is also true of the neo-Schumpeterian tradition (Nelson, 1977, 1990). However, sociological studies of innovation that resonate with the Weberian tradition tend to be more sensitive to what Rogers (1995, pp. 100–106) terms 'pro-innovation' bias as it manifests itself in this particular institutional environment (Latour, 1993; Winner, 1986).

3. The term 'line of action' is central in the work of Hughes's Chicago School colleague, Herbert Blumer (1969) as well as in the work of students and colleagues of Blumer and Hughes (Fine, 1995). The term 'line of action' is meant to convey a coherent path of collective action as it develops over time.

4. Similar frameworks have been developed by other sociologists grappling with common concerns, marked by difference of emphasis: Bourdieu's logic of practice and his concept of habitus (1977, 1990) can be viewed as occurring within specific social worlds. In Giddens' concept of structuration (1984), social conventions mediate between everyday action and relatively obdurate institutions. However, both because of the close

association between the social worlds' approach and the sociology of work and occupations and the more evolutionary flavor of the Chicago tradition, we organize our discussion in the idiom of social worlds.

5. Similar to the social worlds/arenas extension of the concept of a 'going concern', Meyer and Rowan (1977, 1978) reinforced the concept of organizations as loosely-coupled systems, by arguing that many of the formal structures of organizations incorporate broader cultural rules, what they term 'rationalized myths' in the Durkheimian sense of accounts that provide meaning and rationales for activity. They argued that educational bureaucracies as exemplars of loosely-coupled organizations characterized by weak ties, ritualized (i.e. highly conventional) activity, inconsistent responses, and segmentation with regard to plural external environments: organizations buffer 'formal structures from the uncertainties of daily operations by becoming loosely coupled, building gaps between their formal structures and actual work activities' (Meyer and Rowan, 1977, pp. 340–41). However, Meyer and Rowan (1978) propose that loose coupling is less the outcome of strategic action, more a mechanism by which 'rationalized building blocks' of organization elements are recombined and bundled into categorically-correct forms. This argument recognizes that activity is present and that 'rationalized myths' and 'societal charters' provide the recipes for assembly of elementary forms in the organizational landscape. Though this perspective does not explicitly address innovation as strategic action, it does serve as a useful corrective to fads and fashions in strategic management that are narrowly focused on strategic action (Abrahamson, 1991).

6. Simon's (1969) discussion of the 'architecture of complexity' and much of the research literature on modularity that was inspired by his work (Garud et al., 2002) is grounded in a more specific view of coupling in which there is tight coupling within modules and 'loose' (or, more accurately, narrow and specific) coupling between modules. What Simon does not explicitly deal with is high volatility, ambiguity, or innovation. However, a full discussion of this topic is well beyond the scope of this chapter.

7. These capabilities are often shaped by the administrative activities of professional managers but managerial activities are only one (and not necessarily the most important) factor in balancing stability and change. In fact, in this view, it is theoretically possible for a firm to survive (even thrive) with relatively poorly developed formalized managerial/administrative capabilities.

8. This point could also be made about Cyert and March's work, *A Behavioral Theory of the Firm* (1962) with the proviso that Cyert and March look at the firm as a decision-making unit and that Nelson and Winter are more concerned with the firm as a unit of production.

9. We are not unique in proposing a rapproachment between Hughes and Weber. Brown (1978) is a stimulating agenda statement, and many social theorists have engaged this challenge: Giddens (1984), Bourdieu (1977, 1990), Collins (1988), Strauss (1993), Latour (1987, 1993) and Callon (1998), who are concerned with the 'structure–action' problem and with connecting the macrosociological and microsociological imaginations.

10. Recent work on 'global microstructures' (Knorr Cetina and Bruegger, 2002) and 'performative economics' (MacKenzie and Millo, 2003) that build on concepts of 'macrostructuring' (Callon and Latour, 1981) along with research focused on institutional entrepreneurship (Garud et al., 2002; Greenwood and Suddaby, 2006) have pushed forward ideas about the interconnection between global structures and globally coordinated local activities.

11. Modern capitalist institutions may be considered 'rational' when compared to non-Western and/or non-modern institutions but modern institutions remain dependent on traditional and charismatic forms of authority in subtle and significant ways. In addition, the nature of these combinations may change from place to place and over time. For example, Weber argued that charismatic authority tends to be a transient phenomenon and that charismatic institutions are typically transformed into traditional arrangements (e.g. in a prophetic religion) or into rational arrangements (e.g. in an entrepreneurial firm) over time. Furthermore, as Weberians have argued, rational arrangements may become 'inertial' or 'ritualized' (i.e. become traditional) and traditional

arrangements may become 'rationalized' (i.e. explained – usually post-hoc – in terms of formal principles) (Meyer and Rowan, 1977).

12. 'Ethnography' as a genre particularly associated with cultural anthropology can convey some misleading impressions for the work in organizational ethnography. Many classic ethnographies such as those of Malinowski, Boas, Evans-Pritchard and Kroeber tend to be 'ethno-eccentric' (Hughes, 1971d) in the sense that they focused on providing comprehensive accounts of small non-Western cultures that were 'eccentric' and difficult to understand from a Western perspective. A common assumption in this work was that 'cultures' were stable and resistant to change (i.e. reliably reproduced their structures from generation to generation and resisted ongoing dynamics of creative destruction). Cultural anthropologists are today less likely to make these assumptions (Banks, 2003; Marcus, 1995) and are much more focused on explaining patterns of cultural diffusion, segmentation, and change across the globe (Maurer, 2005; Perry and Maurer, 2003). Czarniawska (1997) coined the term 'ergonography' (i.e. a description/analysis of a workplace culture) in place of the term 'organizational ethnography' because organizations happen to be places in which different 'ethnic cultures' and 'occupational cultures' are likely to meet. We think that the term 'ergonography' is preferable to 'organizational ethnography' but follow prevailing convention with the term 'ethnography'.

13. We emphasize that our discussion is meant to be suggestive rather than comprehensive. A comprehensive account of the relevant research literature is well beyond the scope of this chapter.

14. Renate Meyer (2006, p. 727) points out how this perspective grounds agency in social and historical contexts and, thus provides a microfoundational alternative to the 'methodological individualism' of rational choice approaches without giving up the Weberian legacy. In this context, it is important to note that this focus on the individual as analytical reference category for social research neither entails a specific ontological or epistemological perspective, nor deny the social character of structures and institutions or make economic rationality the ultimate logic underlying action.

References

Abbott, Andrew (1988a), *The System of Professions: An Essay on the Division of Expert Labour*, Chicago, IL: University of Chicago Press.

Abbott, Andrew (1988b), 'Transcending general linear reality', *Sociological Theory*, **6**, 169–86.

Abbott, Andrew (1989), 'The new occupational structure: what are the questions?', *Work and Occupations*, **16**(3), 273–91.

Abbott, Andrew (1993), 'The sociology of work and occupations', *Annual Review of Sociology*, **19**, 187–209.

Abbott, Andrew (1997), 'On the concept of turning point', *Comparative Social Research*, **16**, 85–105.

Abrahamson, Eric (1991), 'Management fads and fashions: the diffusion and rejection of innovations', *Academy of Management Review*, **16**, 586–612.

Aldrich, Howard and Martin Ruef (2006), *Organizations Evolving*, 2nd edn, Thousand Oaks, CA: Sage.

Banks, Marcus (2003), 'Indian Jainism as social practice at the end of the twentieth century', in Olle Qvarnström (ed.), *Jainism and early Buddhism: Essays in Honour of Professor P.S. Jaini*, Fremont, CA: Asian Humanities Press.

Barley, Stephen R. (1986), 'Technology as an occasion for structuring: evidence from observations of CT scanners and the social order of radiology departments', *Administrative Science Quarterly*, **31**, 78–108.

Barley, Stephen R. (1996), 'Technicians in the workplace: ethnographic evidence for bringing work into organization studies', *Administrative Science Quarterly*, **41**, 404–41.

Barley, Stephen R. and Gideon Kunda (2004), *Gurus, Hired Guns, and Warm Bodies: Itinerant Experts in the Knowledge Economy*, Princeton, NJ: Princeton University Press.

Barnard, Chester I. (1938), *The Functions of the Executive*, Cambridge, MA: Harvard University Press.

Barney, Jay B. and William G. Ouchi (eds) (1986), *Organizational Economics*, San Francisco, CA: Jossey-Bass Publishers.
Barney, Jay, Michael Wright and Douglas J. Ketchen (2001), 'The resource-based view of the firm: ten years after 1991', *Journal of Management*, **27**, 625–41.
Barrett, Frank J. (1998), 'Creativity and improvisation in jazz and organizations: implications for organizational learning', *Organization Science*, **9**(5), 605–22.
Bechky, Beth A. (2003), 'Object lessons: workplace artifacts as representations of occupational jurisdiction', *American Journal of Sociology*, **109**, 720–52.
Bechky, Beth A. (2006), 'Analyzing artifacts: material methods for understanding identity, status, and knowledge in organizational life', forthcoming in David Barry and Hans Hansen (eds), *Sage Handbook of the New and Emerging in Management and Organization*, Thousand Oaks, CA: Sage Publications.
Becker, Howard S. (1970a), 'Notes on the concept of commitment,' in Howard S. Becker, *Sociological Work*, New Brunswick, NJ: Transaction Books, pp. 261–74.
Becker, Howard S. (1970b), 'Whose side are we on?', in Howard S. Becker, *Sociological Work*, New Brunswick, NJ: Transaction Books, pp. 123–34.
Becker, Howard S. (1982), *Art Worlds*, Berkeley, CA: University of California Press.
Becker, Howard S. (1986a), *Doing Things Together: Selected Essays*, Evanston, IL: Northwestern University Press.
Becker, Howard S. (1986b), 'Culture: a sociological view', in Howard S. Becker, *Doing Things Together: Selected Essays*, Evanston, IL: Northwestern University Press, pp. 7–17.
Becker, Howard S. (1995), 'The power of inertia', *Qualitative Sociology*, **18**, 301–9.
Becker, Howard S. (2000), 'The etiquette of improvisation', *Mind, Culture, and Activity*, **7**(3), 171–6.
Becker, Howard S., Blanche Geer, Everett C. Hughes and Anselm L. Strauss (1961), *Boys in White: Student Culture in Medical School*, Chicago, IL: University of Chicago Press.
Becker, Markus C. (2004), 'Organizational routines: a review of the literature', *Industrial and Corporate Change*, **13**(4), 643–77.
Becker, Markus C. (2005), 'A framework for applying organizational routines in empirical research: linking antecedents, characteristics and performance outcomes of recurrent interaction patterns', *Industrial and Corporate Change*, **14**(5), 817–46.
Biggart, Nicole W. and Thomas D. Beamish (2003), 'The economic sociology of conventions: habit, custom, practice, and routine in market order', *Annual Review of Sociology*, **29**, 443–64.
Black, Laura J., Paul Carlile and Nelson Repenning (2004), 'A dynamic theory of expertise and occupational boundaries in new technology implementation: building on Barley's study of CT-scanning', *Administrative Science Quarterly*, **49**(4), 572–607.
Blumer, Herbert (1969), *Symbolic Interactionism*, Berkeley, CA: University of California Press.
Bourdieu, Pierre (1977), *Outline of a Theory of Practice*, translated by Richard Nice, Cambridge, UK: Cambridge University Press.
Bourdieu, Pierre (1990), *The Logic of Practice*, translated by Richard Nice, Stanford, CA: Stanford University Press.
Bowker, Geoffrey C. and S. Leigh Star (1999), *Sorting Things Out: Classification and Its Consequences*, Cambridge, MA: MIT Press.
Brown, Richard Harvey (1978), 'Bureaucracy as praxis: towards a political phenomenology of formal organizations, *Administrative Science Quarterly*, **23**, 365–82.
Burns, Tom and G.M. Stalker (1961), *The Management of Innovation*, London: Tavistock Publications.
Callon, Michel (1992), 'The dynamics of techno-economic networks', in Rod Coombs, Paolo Saviotti, and Vivien Walsh (eds), *Technological Change and Company Strategies*, London: Academic Press Ltd, pp. 72–102.
Callon, Michel (1998), 'Actor–network theory – the market test', in John Law and John Hassard (eds), *Actor Network Theory and After*, Cambridge, MA: Blackwell, pp. 181–95.
Callon, Michel and Bruno Latour (1981) 'Unscrewing the big Leviathan: how actors macrostructure reality and how sociologists help them to do so', in Karin Knorr Cetina and Aaron Cicourel (eds), *Advances in Social Theory and Methodology: Toward an Integration of Micro and Macro-Sociologies*, London: Routledge & Kegan Paul.

Carlile, Paul R. (2002), 'A pragmatic view of knowledge and boundaries: boundary objects in new product development', *Organization Science*, **13**(4), 442–55.

Carroll, Glenn R. and Michael T. Hannan (2000), *The Demography of Corporations and Industries*, Princeton, NJ: Princeton University Press.

Chapoulie, Jean-Michel (1996), 'Everett Hughes and the Chicago tradition', *Sociological Theory*, **14**(1), 3–29.

Clarke, Adele E. (1991), 'Social worlds/arenas theory as organizational theory', in David R. Maines (ed.), *Social Organization and Social Process: Essays in Honor of Anselm Strauss*, New York: Aldine De Gruyter.

Clegg, Stewart (1995), 'Of values and occasional irony: Max Weber in the context of the sociology of organizations', in Samuel B. Bachrach, Pasquale Gagliardi and Bryan Mundel (eds), *Research in the Sociology of Organizations: Studies of Organizations in the European Tradition*, Greenwich, CT: JAI Press, pp. 1–46.

Cohen, Michael D. and James G. March (1974), *Leadership and Ambiguity: The American College President*, New York: McGraw-Hill.

Cohen, Michael D., James G. March and Johan Olsen (1972), 'A garbage can model of organization choice', *Administrative Science Quarterly*, **17**, 1–25.

Cohen, Wesley and Daniel A. Levinthal (1990), 'Absorptive capacity: a new perspective on learning and innovation', *Administrative Science Quarterly*, **35**, 128–52.

Collins, Randall (1986), *Weberian Sociological Theory*, Cambridge, UK: Cambridge University Press.

Collins, Randall (1988), *Theoretical Sociology*, San Diego, CA: Harcourt, Brace, Jovanovich.

Crozier, Michel (1964), *The Bureaucratic Phenomenon*, Chicago, IL: University of Chicago Press.

Cyert, Richard M. and James G. March (1962), *A Behavioral Theory of the Firm*, Englewood Cliffs, NJ: Prentice-Hall.

Czarniawska, Barbara (1997), *Narrating the Organization: Dramas of Institutional Identity*, Chicago, IL: University of Chicago Press.

Dalton, Melville (1959), *Men Who Manage: Fusions of Feeling and Theory in Administration*, New York: Wiley.

DiMaggio, Paul J. and Walter W. Powell (1983), 'The iron cage revisited: institutional isomorphism and collective rationality in organizational fields', *American Sociological Review*, **48**, 147–60.

Douglas, Mary (1986), *How Institutions Think*, Syracuse, NY: Syracuse University Press.

Edmondson, Amy C., R. Bohmer and Gary P. Pisano (2001), 'Disrupted routines: team learning and new technology adaptation,' *Administrative Science Quarterly*, **46**, 685–716.

Eisenhardt, Kathleen M. and Jay L. Bourgeois (1988), 'Politics of strategic decision making in high-velocity environments: towards a mid-range theory', *Academy of Management Journal*, **31**, 737–70.

Eisenhardt, Kathleen M. and Jeffrey A. Martin (2000), 'Dynamic capabilities: what are they?', *Strategic Management Journal*, **21**(10–11), 1105–21.

Feldman, Martha S. (1989), *Order Without Design: Information Production and Policy Making*, Stanford, CA: Stanford University Press.

Feldman, Martha S. (2000), 'Organizational routines as a source of continuous change', *Organization Science*, **11**, 611–29.

Feldman, Martha S. and Brian T. Pentland (2003), 'Reconceptualizing organizational routines as a source of flexibility and change', *Administrative Science Quarterly*, **48**, 94–118.

Fine, Gary A. (1995), *The Second Chicago School: The Development of a Post-War American Sociology*, Chicago, IL: University of Chicago Press.

Fine, Gary A. (1996), *Kitchens: The Culture of Restaurant Work*, Berkeley, CA: University of California Press.

Fine, Gary A. (2006), 'Ground truth: verification games in operational meteorology', *Journal of Contemporary Ethnography*, **35**, 3–23.

Fligstein, Neil (2001), *The Architecture of Markets: An Economic Sociology of Twenty-First Century Capitalist Societies*, Princeton, NJ: Princeton University Press.

Foss, Nicholai J. (2001), 'Bounded rationality in the economics of organization: present use and (some) future uses', *Journal of Management and Governance*, **5**, 401–25.

Fujimura, Joan H. (1987), 'Constructing doable problems in cancer research: articulating alignment', *Social Studies of Science*, **17**, 257–93.

Fujimura, Joan H. (1996), *Crafting Science: A Sociohistory of the Quest for the Genetics of Cancer*, Cambridge, MA: Harvard University Press.

Garud, Raghu, Sanjay Jain and Arun Kumaraswamy (2002), 'Institutional entrepreneurship in the sponsorship of common technological standards: the case of Sun Microsystems and Java', *Academy of Management Journal*, **45**, 196–214.

Garud, Raghu, Arun Kumaraswamy and Richard N. Langlois (eds) (2002), *Managing in the Modular Age: Architectures, Networks, and Organizations*, Oxford, UK: Blackwell.

Giddens, Anthony (1984), *The Constitution of Society: Outline of the Theory of Structuration*, Berkeley, CA: University of California Press.

Gladwell, Malcolm (2000), 'Designs for working: why your bosses want to turn your new office into Greenwich Village', *The New Yorker*, **75**(11 December), 60–70.

Gouldner, Alvin W. (1954), *Patterns of Industrial Bureaucracy*, Glencoe, IL: Free Press.

Granovetter, Mark (1985), 'Economic action and social structure: the problem of embeddedness', *American Journal of Sociology*, **91**, 481–510.

Greenwood, Royston and Roy Suddaby (2006), 'Institutional entrepreneurship in mature fields: the big five accounting firms', *Academy of Management Journal*, **49**(1), 27–48.

Hallett, Timothy P. (2007), 'Institutional recoupling and turmoil in an urban elementary school', working paper, University of Indiana.

Hallett, Timothy P. and Marc J. Ventresca (2006), 'Inhabited institutions: social interaction and organizational forms in Gouldner's *Patterns of Industrial Bureaucracy*', *Theory & Society*, **35**, 213–36.

Hargadon, Andrew B. and Yellowlees Douglas (2001), 'When innovations meet institutions: Edison and the design of the electric light', *Administrative Science Quarterly*, **46**(3), 476–503.

Heilbroner, Robert L. (1986), *The Nature and Logic of Capitalism*, New York: WW Norton & Co.

Heimer, Carol A. (1992), 'Doing your job and helping your friends: universalistic norms about obligations to particular others in networks', in Nitin Nohria and Robert G. Eccles (eds), *Networks and Organizations: Structure, Form, and Action*, Boston, MA: Harvard Business School Press, pp. 143–64.

Heimer, Carol A. and Arthur L. Stinchcombe (1999), 'Remodeling the garbage can: implications of the origins of items in decision streams', in Morton Egeberg and Per Lægreid (eds), *Organizing Political Institutions: Essays for Johan P. Olsen*, Scandinavian University Press, pp. 25–57.

Hirsch, Paul M., Stuart Michaels and Ray Friedman (1987), ' "Dirty hands" versus "clean models": is sociology in danger of being seduced by economics?', *Theory and Society*, **16**, 317–36.

Hughes, Everett C. (1971a), *The Sociological Eye: Selected Papers*, Chicago, IL: Aldine-Atherton.

Hughes, Everett C. (1971b), 'Going concerns: the study of American institutions', in Everett C. Hughes, *The Sociological Eye: Selected Papers*, Chicago, IL: Aldine-Atherton, pp. 52–64.

Hughes, Everett C. (1971c), 'Disorganization and reorganization', in Everett C. Hughes, *The Sociological Eye: Selected Papers*, Chicago, IL: Aldine-Atherton, pp. 65–72.

Hughes, Everett C. (1971d), 'Ethnocentric sociology', in Everett C. Hughes, *The Sociological Eye: Selected Papers*, Chicago, IL: Aldine-Atherton, pp. 473–7.

Hughes, Everett C. (1971e), 'the humble and the proud: the comparative study of occupations', in Everett C. Hughes, *The Sociological Eye: Selected Papers*, Chicago: Aldine-Atherton, pp. 417–27.

Hughes, Thomas P. (1992), 'The dynamics of technical change: salients, critical problems, and industrial revolutions', in Giovanni Dosi, Renato Gianetti and Pierangelo Maria Toninelli (eds), *Technology and Enterprise in an Historical Perspective*, Oxford: Clarendon Press, pp. 97–118.

Kaghan, William N. (2000), 'Harnessing a public conglomerate: technology transfer managers and the entrepreneurial university', in Jennifer Croissant and Sal Restivo (eds), *Degrees of Compromise: Industrial Interests and Academic Values*, Albany, NY: SUNY Press, pp. 77–100.

Kaghan, William N. and Geoffrey C. Bowker (2001), 'Out of the machine age? Complexity, sociotechnical systems and Actor Network Theory', *Journal of Engineering and Technology Management*, **18** (3&4), 253–70.

Kaghan, William N. and Nelson Phillips (1998), 'Building the Tower of Babel: communities of practice and paradigmatic pluralism in organization studies', *Organization*, **5**(2), 191–215.

Kaghan, William N., Anselm L. Strauss, Steve R. Barley, MaryYoko Brannen and Robert J. Thomas (1999), 'The practice and uses of field research in the 21st century organization', *Journal of Management Inquiry*, **8**(1), 67–81.

Kellogg, Katherine C., Wanda J. Orlikowski and Joanne Yates (2006), 'Life in the trading zone: structuring coordination across boundaries in the postbureaucratic organization', *Organization Science*, **17**(1), 22–44.

Kiser, Edgar V. (1999), 'Comparing varieties of agency theory in economics, political science, and sociology: an illustration from state policy implementation', *Sociological Theory*, **17**(2), 146–70.

Knorr Cetina, Karin and Urs Bruegger (2002), 'Global microstructures: the virtual societies of financial markets', *American Journal of Sociology*, **107**(4), 905–50.

Koppl, Roger and Richard N. Langlois (2001), 'Organizations and language games', *Journal of Management and Governance*, **5**, 287–305.

Kreps, David M. (1990), *A Course in Microeconomic Theory*, Princeton, NJ: Princeton University Press.

Kuhn, Thomas S. (1970), *The Structure of Scientific Revolutions*, Chicago, IL: University of Chicago Press.

Kunda, Gideon (1992), *Engineering Culture*, Philadelphia, PA: Temple University Press.

Lacey, Rodney (2006), 'Control and authority in the organization of aviation safety: issues and lessons from the professionalization of risk and prevention', working paper, University of California, Irvine.

Latour, Bruno (1987), *Science in Action*, Cambridge, MA: Harvard University Press.

Latour, Bruno (1993), *We Have Never Been Modern*, Cambridge, MA: Harvard University Press.

Lounsbury, Michael and Edward J. Carberry (2005), 'From king to court jester? Weber's fall from grace in organization theory', *Organization Studies*, **26**(4), 501–25.

Lounsbury, Michael and William N. Kaghan (2001), 'Organizations, occupations and the structuration of work', in Steven P. Vallas (ed.), *Research in the Sociology of Work*, **10**, New York: JAI Press, pp. 25–50.

MacKenzie, Donald A. (1996), *Knowing Machines: Essays on Technological Change*, Cambridge, MA: The MIT Press.

MacKenzie, Donald A. and Yuval Millo (2003), 'Constructing a market, performing theory: the historical sociology of a financial derivatives exchange', *American Journal of Sociology*, **109**(1), 107–45.

March, James G. (1989), *Rediscovering Institutions: The Organizational Basis of Politics*, New York: The Free Press.

March, James G. and Johan P. Olsen (1979), *Ambiguity and Choice in Organizations*, 2nd edn, Bergen, Norway: Universitetsforlaget.

March, James G. and Herbert A. Simon (1993), *Organizations*, 2nd edn, Cambridge, MA: Blackwell.

Marcus, George E. (1995), 'Ethnography in/of the world system: the emergence of multi-sited ethnography', *Annual Review of Anthropology*, **24**, 95–117.

Martin, Joanne (1992), *Cultures in Organizations: Three Perspectives*, New York: Oxford University Press.

Maurer, Bill (2005), *Mutual Life, Limited: Islamic Banking, Alternative Currencies, Lateral Reason*, Princeton, NJ: Princeton University Press.

Mauws, M.K. and N. Phillips (1995), 'Understanding language games', *Organization Science*, **6**, 322–34.

Merton, Robert K. (1957), *Social Theory and Social Structure*, Glencoe, IL: Free Press.

Meyer, John W. and Brian Rowan (1977), 'Institutionalized organizations: formal structure as myth and ceremony', *American Journal of Sociology*, **83**, 340–63.

Meyer, John W. and Brian Rowan (1978), 'The structure of educational organizations', in Marshall W. Meyer and Associates, (eds), *Environments and Organizations*, New York: Jossey-Bass, pp. 78–109.

Meyer, Renate (2006), 'Visiting relatives: current developments in the new sociology of knowledge', *Organization*, **13**(5), 725–38.

Meyerson, Debra (1994), 'Stress in institutions: the cultural production of ambiguity and burnout', *Administrative Science Quarterly*, **39**, 628–53.

Meyerson, Debra (1998), 'Feeling stressed and burned out: a feminist reading and revision of stress-based emotions', *Organization Science*, **9**, 103–18.

Meyerson, Debra and Maureen Scully (1995), 'Tempered radicalism and the politics of ambivalence and change', *Organization Science*, **6**, 585–600.

Mintzberg, Henry and John Waters (1985), 'Of strategies, deliberate and emergent', *Strategic Management Journal*, **6**, 257–72.

Monge, Peter R. and Noshir S. Contractor (2003), *Theories of Communication Networks*, New York: Oxford University Press.

Mutch, Alistair, Rick Delbridge and Marc J. Ventresca (2006), 'Situating organizational action: the relational sociology of organizations', *Organization*, **13**(6), 607–25.

Nelson, Richard R. (1977), *The Moon and the Ghetto*, New York: Norton.

Nelson, Richard R. (1990), 'Capitalism as an engine of progress', *Research Policy*, **19**, 193–214.

Nelson, Richard R. (2005), 'Physical and social technologies and their evolution', in Richard R. Nelson, *Technology, Institutions, and Economic Growth*, Cambridge, MA: Harvard University Press.

Nelson, Richard R. and Sidney G. Winter (1982), *An Evolutionary Theory of Economic Change*, Cambridge, MA: Belknap Press/Harvard University Press.

Obstfeld, David (2005), 'Social networks, the *tertius iungens* orientation, and involvement in innovation', *Administrative Science Quarterly*, **50**, 100–130.

Orlikowski, Wanda J. (1996) 'Improvising organizational transformation over time: a situated change perspective', *Information Systems Research*, **7**, 63–92.

Orlikowski, Wanda J. (2000), 'Using technology and constituting structures: a practice lens for studying technology in organizations', *Organizational Science*, **11**, 404–28.

Orlikowski, Wanda J. and Joanne Yates (2002), 'It's about time: temporal structuring in organizations', *Organization Science*, **13**(6), 684–700.

Orrù, Marco, Nicole W. Biggart and Gary G. Hamilton (1997), *The Economic Organization of East Asian Capitalism*, Thousand Oaks, CA: Sage

Park, Robert E. (1952), *Human Communities*, Everett Hughes, et al. (eds), Glencoe, IL: The Free Press.

Parsons, Talcott (1937), *The Structure of Social Action*, New York: McGraw-Hill.

Pentland, Brian T. (1995), 'Grammatical models of organizational processes', *Organization Science*, **6**, 541–56.

Pentland, Brian T. and Martha S. Feldman (2005), 'Organizational routines as units of analysis', *Industrial and Corporate Change*, **14**(5), 793–815.

Perrow, Charles (1986), *Complex Organizations: A Critical Essay*, 3rd edn, New York: Random House.

Perrow, Charles (1991), 'A society of organizations', *Theory and Society*, **20**(6), 725–62.

Perry, Richard Warren and Bill Maurer (eds) (2003), *Globalization Under Construction: Governmentality, Law and Identity*, Minneapolis, MN: University of Minnesota Press.

Pfeffer, Jeffrey and Gerald R. Salancik (1978), *The External Control of Organizations: A Resource Dependence Perspective*, New York: Harper & Row; (2003) (Stanford Business Classics edition), Stanford, CA: Stanford University Press.

Podolny, Joel M. (2001), 'Networks as the pipes and prisms of the market', *American Journal of Sociology*, **107**(1), 33–60.

Podolny, Joel M. and Karen L. Page (1998), 'Network forms of organization', *Annual Review of Sociology*, **24**, 57–76.

Ragin, Charles C. (1994), *Constructing Social Research*, Thousand Oaks, CA: Pine Forge Press.

Rogers, Everett M. (1995), *Diffusion of Innovations*, 4th edn, New York: Free Press.

Rudolph, Jenny and Nelson Repenning (2002), 'Disaster dynamics: understanding the role of stress and interruptions in organizational collapse', *Administrative Science Quarterly*, **47**, 1–30.

Schilling, Melissa A. (2000), 'Toward a general modular systems theory and its application to interfirm product modularity', *Academy of Management Review*, **25**(2), 312–34.

Schon, Donald A. (1983) *The Reflective Practitioner: How Professionals Think In Action*, New York: Basic Books.

Schumpeter, Joseph A. (1934), *The Theory of Economic Development*, Cambridge, MA: Harvard University Press; (1983), New Brunswick, NJ: Transaction Publishers.

Schumpeter, Joseph A. (1942), *Capitalism, Socialism, and Democracy*, New York: Harper and Bros; (1975) (Harper Colophon Edition), New York: Harper & Row.

Selznick, Philip (1957), *Leadership in Administration: A Sociological Interpretation*, New York: Harper & Row; (1984) Berkeley, CA: University of California Press.

Simon, Herbert A. (1969), 'The architecture of complexity', in Herbert A. Simon, *The Sciences of the Artificial*, Cambridge, MA: The MIT Press, pp. 183–215.

Star, S. Leigh (1989), 'The structure of ill-structured solutions: boundary objects and heterogeneous distributed problem solving', in Les Gasser and Michael Huhns (eds), *Distributed Artificial Intelligence*, vol. 2, San Francisco, CA: Morgan Kaufmann Publishers Inc., pp. 37–54.

Star, S. Leigh and Karen Ruhleder (1996), 'Steps toward an ecology of infrastructure: design and access for large information spaces', *Information Systems Research*, **7**, 111–34.

Stern, Robert N. and Stephen R. Barley (1996), 'Organizations and social systems: organization theory's neglected mandate', *Administrative Science Quarterly*, **41**, 146–62.

Stinchcombe, Arthur L. (1986), 'Rationality and social structure', in Arthur L. Stinchcombe, *Stratification and Organization: Selected Papers*, Cambridge, UK: Cambridge University Press.

Stinchcombe, Arthur L. (1990), *Information and Organizations*, Berkeley, CA: University of California Press.

Stinchcombe, Arthur L. (2002), 'New sociological foundations for organization microtheory: a postscript', in Michael Lounsbury and Marc J. Ventresca (eds), *Social Structure and Organizations Revisited*, **19**, Oxford, UK: JAI Press/Elsevier Science.

Strauss, Anselm L. (1959), *Mirrors and Masks: The Search for Identity*, Glencoe, IL: The Free Press.

Strauss, Anselm L. (1978), *Negotiations: Varieties, Contexts, Processes, and Social Order*, San Francisco, CA: Jossey-Bass.

Strauss, Anselm L. (1988), 'The articulation of project work: an organizational process', *Sociological Quarterly*, **29**, 163–78.

Strauss, Anselm L. (1993), *Continual Permutations of Action*, New York: Aldine de Gruyter.

Strauss, Anselm L., Rue Bucher, Danuta Ehrlich, Leonard Schatzman and Melvin Sabshin (1964), *Psychiatric Ideologies and Institutions*, New York: The Free Press.

Suchman, Lucy A. (1987), *Plans and Situated Actions: The Problem of Human–Machine Communication*, Cambridge, UK: Cambridge University Press.

Swedberg, Richard (1998), *Max Weber and the Idea of Economic Sociology*, Princeton, NJ: Princeton University Press.

Teece, David J., Gary Pisano and Amy Shuen (1997), 'Dynamic capabilities and strategic management', *Strategic Management Journal*, **18**(7), 509–33.

Thevenot, Laurent (2001), 'Organized complexity: conventions of coordination and the composition of economic arrangements', *European Journal of Social Theory*, **4**(4), 405–25.

Thomas, Robert J. (1994), *What Machines Can't Do: Politics and Technology in Industrial Enterprise*, Berkeley: University of California Press.

Townley, Barbara (2002), 'The role of competing rationalities in institutional change', *Academy of Management Journal*, **45**(1), 163–79.

Uzzi Brian and Ryon Lancaster (2003), 'Relational embeddedness and learning: the case of bank loan managers and their clients', *Management Science*, **49**(4), 383–99.

Varian, Hal R. (1987), *Intermediate Microeconomics*, New York: W.W. Norton & Company.

Vaughan, Diane (1996), *The Challenger Launch Decision: Risky Technology, Culture, and Deviance at NASA*, Chicago, IL: University of Chicago Press.

Washington, Marvin and Marc J. Ventresca (2004), 'How organizations change: the role of institutional support mechanisms in the incorporation of higher education visibility strategies, 1874–1995', *Organization Science*, **15**(1), 82–97.

Weber, Max (1978), *Economy and Society: An Outline of Interpretive Sociology*, Guenter Roth and Claus Wittich (eds), Berkeley, CA: University of California Press.

Weeks, John R. (2003), *Unpopular Culture: The Ritual of Complaint in a British Bank*, Chicago, IL: University of Chicago Press.

Weick, Karl E. (1979), 'Educational organizations as loosely coupled systems', *Administrative Science Quarterly*, **21**, 1–19.

Weick, Karl E. (1993), 'The collapse of sensemaking in organizations: the Mann Gulch disaster', *Administrative Science Quarterly*, **38**, 628–52.

Weick, Karl E. (1995), *Sensemaking in Organizations*, Thousand Oaks, CA: Sage Publications.

Weick, Karl E. (1999), 'Theory construction as disciplined reflexivity: tradeoffs in the 90s', *Academy of Management Review*, **24**(4), 797–806.

Weick, Karl E. (2001), *Making Sense of the Organization*, Madden, MA: Blackwell Publishers.

Westney, D. Eleanor (1987), *Imitation and Innovation: The Transfer of Western Organizational Patterns to Japan*, Cambridge, MA: Harvard University Press.

White, Harrison C. (1992), *Identity and Control: A Structural Theory of Social Action*, Princeton, NJ: Princeton University Press.

Winner, Langdon (1986), *The Whale and the Reactor: a Search for the Limits of High Technology*, Chicago, IL: University of Chicago Press.

Yates, Joanne (1989), *Control Through Communication: The Rise of System in American Management*, Baltimore, MD: Johns Hopkins University Press.

Zollo, Maurizio and Sidney G. Winter (1999), 'From organizational routines to dynamic capabilities', *Organization Science*, **13**(3), 339–51.

Zollo, Maurizio and Sidney G. Winter (2002), 'Deliberate learning and the evolution of dynamic capabilities', *Organization Science*, **13**(3), 339–51.

5 Organizational routines in accounting
John Burns and Robert W. Scapens

Introduction

> One area of firm behavior that plainly is governed by a highly structured set of routines is accounting. Like other routines of real organizations, accounting procedures have the important characteristic that they can be applied on the basis of information actually available in real situations. (Nelson and Winter, 1982, pp. 410–11)

This chapter discusses recent research within the accounting discipline that endeavours to highlight the routinised nature of its subject. The following aims to provide the reader with insight into how certain scholars within the accounting discipline have developed an understanding of its subject through conceptualisation of accounting routines but also, more generally, how accounting might claim to contribute towards development of the broader organisational routines literature.

At the outset we define these routines as accounting procedures in use – for example, costing and budgeting procedures (Burns and Scapens, 2000, p. 7). Rules represent the formalised statement of such procedures – e.g., a budgeting manual, and are normally changed only at discrete intervals, whereas accounting routines have the potential to be in a cumulative process of change as they continue to be reproduced. Thus accounting procedures in use (routines) may not actually replicate the accounting systems (rule) as set out in the procedures manual (Roberts and Scapens, 1985). Thus, in this respect, our definition is consistent with the view that accounting routines can be 'effortful accomplishments' (Feldman and Pentland, 2003) and, over time, can change and involve adaptive and creative behaviour (Becker, 2004, p. 649).

The section below establishes definitions, and context, to the term 'accounting'. Following that, we summarise recent research that has attempted both to conceptualise and empirically investigate the dynamics of accounting routines in real organisations. As we shall elaborate later in our chapter, such research is particularly informed by institutional theories with mainly economics and sociological roots. Our discussion then highlights some of the properties of accounting routines; finally, we discuss how the accounting routines literature contributes to a broader understanding of organisational change.

Accounting

It would seem appropriate to define what we actually mean by 'accounting' since its interpretation can vary considerably, and because it is quite often an oversimplified term. To most, accounting probably connotes glossy reports that organisations make available at least once a year ('the year-end accounts') and which are scrutinised by such interested groups as shareholders, investors and market analysts.

However, accounting, both as an organisational practice and as an academic discipline, covers much more. The annual 'glossy reports', referred to above, apply to a very specific aspect of organisational accounting, namely, financial accounting.[1] And we could consider how the process by which an organisation produces its annual (bi-annual and/or quarterly) financial reports is significantly infused with routines. However, in this chapter at least, we shall concentrate on the routines implicated in an organisation's *management* accounting, which is also where most of the extant routines-focused accounting research situates itself.

Management accounting denotes the part of an organisation's accounting procedures that deal with providing the information needed to inform managerial decision making.[2] Such information will normally constitute an important part of the basis from which managers make decisions in respect of planning, control, performance evaluation and more. The technology for this information is the accounting system, which draws on a variety of organisation-specific data captured at source (i.e., invoices, order forms, etc.). But, also, these accounting systems are normally accompanied by a variety of management accounting techniques which enable managers to derive useful information from the core data. Such techniques include budgets, costing techniques, capital appraisal, performance measurement, and more.

Orthodoxy in management accounting research portrays its subject as information systems and a raft of techniques that faithfully represent the economic reality of organisations and, in turn, which present business managers with information that informs rational optimising decisions (Scapens, 1994). Indeed, the bulk of traditional management accounting techniques are premised in assumptions pertaining to neoclassical economic theory, including those assumptions of rationality and optimisation (Scapens and Arnold, 1986). The majority of management accounting textbooks, as well as most accounting programmes in higher education, also maintain such undertones.

However, some scholars, particularly amongst European universities, have pursued a broader understanding of the significance, role(s) and dynamics of management accounting beyond a purely technical remit (Ryan et al., 2002, chapter 4). More specifically, such researchers have explored management accounting within its broader social, economic, political, organisational and institutional contexts – the contributions of whom include a plethora of both theoretical development and empirical investigation (Berry et al., 1985; Miller, 1994).

Over the last three decades, there has been impressive growth, and variety, in so-called 'non-orthodox' management accounting research.[3] Such works are unified in their attempts to explore accounting in its broader contexts, and move beyond accounting as merely a technical source of rational optimising decisions. This said, across these various non-orthodox approaches there are also key differences – for instance, in their respective key foci, intellectual roots, methodological underpinnings, research methods, and more. A concise review of such literature is beyond the remit of this chapter.[4] However, we shall focus predominantly on a particular strand of non-orthodoxy within the management accounting literature that in recent years has specifically endeavoured to conceptualise its subject as routinised organisational phenomena – i.e., an *institutional* perspective on management accounting (Burns and Scapens, 2000; Burns, 2000; Soin et al., 2002; Johansson and Baldvinsdottir, 2003; Busco, 2003).[5]

An institutional perspective starts with a belief that social practices, including accounting, are not natural phenomena but socially constructed and that, in turn, such constructs are shaped by social actions (Macintosh and Scapens, 1990). Moreover, there is an assumption that, because most accounting procedures are largely routine (Nelson and Winter, 1982, pp. 410–11), they have potential over time to underpin settled patterns of organisational action and thought (Burns and Scapens, 2000).

Normally, an institutional study of accounting would be interpretive, involving detailed case studies that attempt to locate accounting practices in their historical as well as economic, social and organisational contexts. Researchers, in general, adopt a holistic orientation by which accounting is studied as part of a unified social system, and a picture of the system's wholeness can be built up (Ryan et al., 2002, p. 87). Their work sets out to interpret accounting as social practice, and the resulting deeper understanding should in turn enable accounting practitioners and other business actors to cope with the day-to-day demands of their jobs (Burns et al., 2003). We shall now describe some of the core elements of an institutional view of accounting.

An institutional perspective of accounting

Well it is, you see, how things evolve. I suppose in the academic world it's all clear cut. But it isn't really, you know. When you come down here, it's all a hell of a big mish-mash, all inter-related influences. It's not clear cut and logical. It looks completely illogical, but that is how it happens. And I'm not sure we're no

> different from any other outfit. And you'll go back and say 'what a load of idiots'. But that's how it happens.

The above quotation encapsulates an accountant's view of how accounting practices had developed in his organisation, acknowledging the diversity of influences that shape intraorganisational practices. Looked at from outside his organisation the process might appear irrational, but this would be to ignore the interplay of many disparate influences. Nevertheless, it is difficult to see the process in terms of the application of economic rationality that informs the development of so-called 'optimal' techniques in most accounting textbooks.

If we recognise the complexities of organisational life, as portrayed in the above quotation, we have to ask how coordination and relative stability is actually achieved in organisations. Why, in practice, do we not see more chaos, tension and conflict (Nelson and Winter, 1982; Coriat and Dosi, 1998)? Because, we argue, in most organisations coordination is achieved through the interplay of rules, routines and shared assumptions concerning the nature of an organisation's activities (Stene, 1940; Nelson and Winter, 1982; March and Olsen, 1989; Segelod, 1997; Becker, 2004). The following section now attempts to illustrate how the rules, routines and shared assumptions embedded in accounting contribute towards such traits in an organisation. First, we discuss and define the nature of accounting rules and routines.

Accounting rules and routines
Rules are necessary (though not necessarily sufficient) to coordinate and give coherence to the actions of groups and/or individuals (Scapens, 1994). Rule-based behaviour can result from an explicit assessment of available alternatives, and selected rules subsequently followed to avoid any difficulties and costs of undertaking such assessments on every occasion. Moreover, by repeatedly following rules, behaviour can become programmatic and based increasingly on tacit knowledge that individuals acquire through reflexive monitoring and experience. Such rule-based behaviour can be described as a routine, or 'the habits of a group' (Burns and Scapens, 2000, p. 6).

In the process of routinisation, previously formulated rules can be modified, as the individuals or groups involved locate mutually acceptable ways of implementing them. For example, a new budgeting procedure could be defined as a set of rules, written down in a budgeting manual. These rules would, for instance, be formulated when one organisation (i.e., subsidiary) is acquired by another (i.e., parent), and the latter's standard budgeting procedures are 'imposed' on the former.

However, as the new rules (i.e., budgeting procedures) are implemented, modifications are possible, either deliberate or subconscious. For instance, deliberate change can emerge out of resistance within the acquired organisation, whereas subconscious change can occur when, for example, there is a misunderstanding of the new rules. Nevertheless, as budgeting procedures are re-enacted, routines will emerge, and these routines will be repeated over time and 'passed on' to others within the organisation (Nelson and Winter, 1982). In this context, rules are established and, through their implementation, routines will emerge.

The dynamic relationship between accounting rule and routine can, however, be reversed. For instance, in various types of organisational activity routines can emerge which either have deviated from the original rules, or were never explicitly formalised into a set of rules. Thus, informal procedures (e.g., 'back-of-the-fag-packet' budget calculations made by individuals or groups at particular intervals) can develop as routines alongside more formal procedures (i.e., budgeting manuals). And so, in such cases, the emergent routines will normally be formalized in the procedures manual, hence comprising a (reverse) process that moves from routine to rule. In particular an organization would normally do this to avoid new knowledge being lost if key staff leave; to facilitate the training of new staff; and/or to exercise control over further modification.

To summarise, rules are the formalised statements of accounting procedures, whereas routines are the accounting procedures actually used. In the context of budgeting, for instance, rules comprise the budgeting system as set out in the budgeting manual, whereas routines are the budgeting procedures actually in use. Clearly, there will be relationships between rules and routines, but it is important not to confuse the two, as an accounting system in use will not always accurately mirror the system described in the procedures manual.

Actions and institutions

In order to complete our brief overview of an institutional perspective of accounting we should also define 'institutions', which we view as shared and taken-for-granted assumptions that identify categories of human actors and their appropriate activities and relationships (Barley and Tolbert, 1997 – modified slightly in Burns and Scapens, 2000). As such, they are the taken-for-granted assumptions which inform and shape the actions of the groups of individuals who comprise the organisation – they define the expected patterns of behaviour and simply 'the way things are' (Burns and Scapens, 2000).

In our discussion above, we defined the procedures in budget manuals as rules, and the budgeting procedures in use as routines. A step further: if budgets are institutionalised in an organisation they are said to be a generally accepted way things are done (Burns, 1997). For instance, evidence shows the continuing predominance of budgeting systems within organisations (Burns and Yazdifar, 2001) despite multiple calls to go 'beyond budgeting' (Hope and Fraser, 1999). In fact, we would argue that it is partly because budgeting is an institutionalised feature of most businesses that attempts to move away from routinised budgeting procedures as the main tool of organisational planning have encountered much resistance.

The accounting literature boasts numerous examples of case studies in which the underlying assumptions about the nature of the business and the activities of its managers are expressed in terms of the 'language' of accounting (see, for instance, Roberts and Scapens, 1990; Dent, 1991; Burns, 1997). As such, accounting is portrayed as an important constituent of the institutions that underpin and inform the prevalent organizational rules and routines, and it is those rules and routines which, in turn, influence (shape and re-shape) the day-to-day activities of the managers and workers (Roberts and Scapens, 1990). That said, and as Roberts and Scapens (1990) in particular demonstrate, there are numerous other rules and routines which shape managers' day-to-day activities. In Roberts and Scapens' case, prevalent organisational rules and routines were shaped by institutions that reflected volume-related concerns over production and sales in a UK manufacturing organisation. Although accounting routines existed and were reproduced over time, they were generally viewed in the organisation as being of little relevance to the managers, and something of interest only to the accountants. In contrast, Burns (1997) described a case study of a small UK-based chemicals manufacturer where the entire institutional basis of that organisation was dominated by, and embedded in, accounting rules and routines.

The relationship between rules, routines and institutions, and the day-to-day actions of managers, is shown diagrammatically in Figure 5.1 (reproduced from Burns et al., 2003). Institutions are shown at the top of the diagram, and reflected (line a) in the rules and routines of the organisation. As described above, there is interaction between rules and routines on an ongoing basis. But it is these rules and routines which shape (line b) the actions of the members of the organisation, thereby achieving coordination and relative stability. Line b is shown as a solid line because there is a direct connection between the rules and routines and the actions. The actions are themselves the enactment of the rules and routines. However, line a is shown as a broad dotted line, because institutions are normally general, and the connection (to rules and routines) is more abstract and indirect.

But how do rules, routines, and institutions come to be widely shared in an organisation? The process is illustrated diagrammatically in Figure 5.2. Here, the horizontal lines (representing institutions and actions) each have

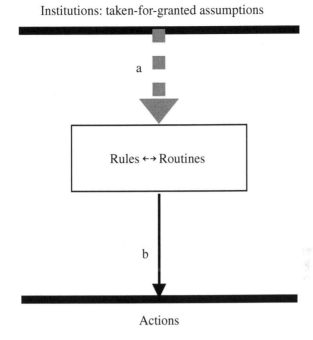

Institutions: taken-for-granted assumptions

Rules ←→ Routines

a

b

Actions

Figure 5.1   The relationship between roles, routines, institutions and day-to-day actions in an organisation

a time dimension. Rules are established, normally with the assistance of actors' power and political mobilisation, are repeatedly enacted and routines thereby created. Line c thus represents the reproduction of rules and routines over time, i.e., repeated use in practice. Over a much longer period of time, the rules and routines become taken-for-granted or institutionalised, represented by line d (a broad dotted line because the process is gradual and indirect).

Finally, it should be stressed that rules are not always necessarily enacted as they were originally intended. Unanticipated consequences can evolve, as new emerging routines give rise to tensions between different managers. Over time, however, such tensions can be accommodated within the emerging routines, as managers find mutually acceptable ways of working with the new rules and routines (Nelson and Winter, 1982; Feldman, 2000).

Accounting routines: some properties

Rules, routines and institutions (as conveyed in Figure 5.1), including those embedded in accounting, contribute to the creation of coordination and

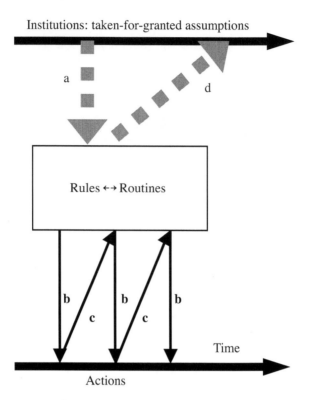

*Figure 5.2   How rules, routines and institutions come to be widely shared
in an organisation*

stability in organisations (Hodgson, 1993; Becker, 2004). Some authors
have attributed this to the potential for routines to establish 'truce' in organisational settings (Nelson and Winter, 1982; Burns, 2000). First, routines
enable members of an organisation to make sense of the complexities that
characterise organisational life. They inform individuals about what is
expected of them, and enable them to understand and even predict the
actions of others. Accounting routines are explicitly intended to guide participants towards acceptable ways to carry out their duties, and such
routines become reinforced by their reproduction. For instance, some managers would 'just know' to prepare a 'payback calculation' as part of their
capital expenditure proposal, because 'payback' is the normal, accepted
and expected procedure.

Second, rules, routines and institutions comprise an organisation's
know-how. This know-how evolves over time and can be 'passed on' to new
recruits: thereby, organisational know-how is maintained over long periods

in spite of people leaving an organisation (Nelson and Winter, 1982). As such, organisational know-how cannot be reduced to the knowledge of individuals per se; rather, it is the organisation's rules, routines and institutions that comprise such know-how. Accounting information (e.g., costs, profit or losses, budgets, cash-flow) supplements the knowledge which informs participants' interpretation of business situations – an interpretation that constitutes much more than merely a portrayal of 'economic reality'. We now elaborate on some of these and other properties of accounting routines.

Enabling and constraining routines

Although change can occur (see below), accounting routines are generally stable phenomena. An implicit assumption is that accounting routines provide an overall framework for predicting possible outcomes of the management processes. There is, however, a chance of unintended failure in the accuracy or composition of such information that would invalidate such an assumption.

This would suggest that intraorganisational action and thought is enabled by the institutionalisation of intent in accounting routines (Scapens, 1994). In other words, accounting routines provide a coherent basis from which organisational actors can make sense, and predict the consequence of, their actions and the action of others (Macintosh and Scapens, 1990; Simon, 1947; Thornton, 1979). And, thus, accounting routines define an organisation's 'domain of economic processes' (Miller, 1994, p. 4) by providing a means through which economic processes are made visible.

However, there also exists a constraining element – namely that routines define what is deemed acceptable and proper behaviour in an organisation (Becker and Knudsen, 2005). Accounting routines thus create boundaries for, and structure, action and thought in organisations. In turn, this then has potential to assist reduction of the complex, dynamic and usually unpredictable business world to a simpler and comprehensible form by creating norms of calculation.

Budgeting procedures are an example of accounting routines that constrain organisational activity (Cyert and March, 1963). Rules and routines associated with the budgeting process define in advance a set of fixed commitments and expectations within an organisation. Although flexibility may be possible within a budget, its overall framework provides an important control device through which organisations operate, evaluate performance and/or alter programmes. Thus, in conclusion, accounting routines can both constrain and enable the management process via their ongoing and frequently unquestioned use.

Meanings and routines

Accounting routines continually shape the meanings that organisational
actors attach to business phenomena, by influencing the cognitive structures that enable people to make sense of their complex business world.
They frame meanings identified with such terms as 'budget', 'profit' and
'costs' (Preston, 1995), and these meanings reproduce over time and are
understood in terms of the institutionalised rules and routines which define
their calculation. Thus, in this sense, accounting procedures often represent
much more than their adopters bargain for – i.e., they can underpin action
and thoughts as well as act as decision-making aids (Swieringa and Weick,
1987).

Individuals and/or groups within the same organisation can hold
different meanings for the same thing – for example, consider the term
'cost'. In most organisations there are multiple costs incurred in day-to-day
operations, and there are also the costs used in external financial reports.
These may differ within or between organisations – e.g. historical cost,
current cost, marginal cost, replacement cost, expected cost, and more. The
meaning of cost (or other accounting terms) is institutionally defined and
reflects experience of such terms – e.g., the meaning that an engineer
attaches to 'cost' will normally differ from that of an accountant. Having
said this, we should not construe this as a problem, since meanings assist
interpretations.

The importance of accounting routines for shaping meanings brings to
the fore a question of whether it is the institutionalisation of 'accounts'
rather than 'accounting' practices per se which is the more prominent issue.
For example, accounts portray and carry news of 'bad' profits which, in
turn, send warning signals within and outside an organisation, because
such accounts have been interpreted as reflecting poor performance. But
such interpretations can be misleading and might overlook other important
factors. For instance, 'bad profits' might be due to low productivity or poor
quality rather than due necessarily to high costs. The importance of
accounting routines in this sense cannot be overstated, because, if emerging perceptions identify high costs with poor results, this could likely lead
to a shedding of labour and/or other detrimental implications.

Continuing this line of thinking, a further interesting issue is how dominant frames of meaning within organisations might change. So, for instance,
how and why might an organisation's predominant focus on production-
related goals shift to an economic focus, whereby more emphasis is then
placed on accounting (in particular, financial measurement) routines? Jagd
(1995) cites one organisation where he observed a shift from 'a dominant
production frame of meaning' to 'a dominant economic frame of meaning'.
While the former was dominant in this organisation, production-related

success (e.g., in terms of yields, throughput, etc.) constituted the primary goal for all business activity. And, in such a context, accounting was deemed mainly to be a technical instrument for enabling production. Moreover, the accounting process did not interfere with the production process (Scapens and Roberts, 1993). In later years, however, an economic frame of meaning became dominant. Activities thus became more focused on economic success, defined by such accounting terms as 'lower costs' and 'higher profits', and with subtle distinctions differentiating one frame of meaning from the other.

There are several reasons why such change can occur, although management might not necessarily be aware of the change process. One example is when change evolves from managers' perceived failure of existing dominant frames as targets are continually not met (Seo and Creed, 2002). An important factor in such instances would be the lessons learnt from past experiences as well as observations made of other organisations, whose frames of meaning are regarded as being successful. For example, one could think in terms of the efforts by UK and US organisations during the 1980s and 1990s to emulate Japanese and German management practices in a bid to emulate the latter's success in world markets (Currie, 1995).

Know-how and decision-making routines
As mentioned above, accounting routines reinforce organisational know-how or 'memory' (Nelson and Winter, 1982), thereby enabling actors to cope with the inherent uncertainties of day-to-day organisational life, defining organisational capabilities and helping actors to make sense of their own, and others' actions: 'the routinization of activity in an organization constitutes the most important form of storage of the organization's specific operational knowledge [. . .] organizations *remember by doing*' (Nelson and Winter, 1982, p. 99, emphasis in original).

Once accounting routines have become an institutionalised part of day-to-day organisational activity, their ongoing use reinforces know-how. They assist in the transmission of know-how from one person to another (e.g., manager to junior), or one organisation to another (e.g., parent to subsidiary) in a role that is analogous to the biological gene (Nelson and Winter, 1982).

The recurrent use of accounting systems and techniques thus acts as a carrier of organisational knowledge (Cyert and March, 1963), although there will usually be limits to the extent of transferability (Szulanski and Winter, 2002). In particular, it has been argued that routines are strong repositories for tacit knowledge (Nelson and Winter, 1982; Cohen and Bacdayan, 1994; Becker, 2004). For instance, as mentioned above, actors who regularly engage in budgeting procedures 'just know' that such practice is both acceptable and expected. Similarly, actors in many organisations 'just know' that 'payback calculations' constitute the appropriate tool for capital expenditure requests. Such knowledge is embedded in the rules that underpin them, and the knowledge of what is deemed appropriate is passed on through reproduction of such rules in the form of accounting routines (Burns, 1997).

Finally, accounting routines also assist decision-making in organisations. Day-to-day organisational life involves complex and often ambiguous decisions, made at all levels. Whether it is workers deciding if the machinery is running effectively, or executives formulating the next five years' strategy, decision-making is central to all organisations. And, some decisions are undertaken as a matter of routine because contexts are broadly similar to those which decision makers have previously experienced. Much of the decision-making that we observe in organisations reflects the routine way in which people do what they believe they are supposed to do, and following appropriate rules (Cyert and March, 1963; Betsch et al., 1998). In this vein, Scapens (1994) argued that accounting routines provide more of an 'institutional basis' for decision making rather than merely information for decision making, as others have stressed how routines contribute towards the ability of actors to choose a particular course of action under conditions of uncertainty (Munby et al., 2003). Where business decisions involve new and unfamiliar situations, organisational actors cope by drawing from the know-how which accounting routines underpin (Thornton, 1979), thus providing them with a frame of reference for decision making. And, as some have argued, having the ability to fall back on recurring situations normally helps in the sense of economising on the time necessary to make decisions about non-routine situations (Reason, 1990; Ashmos et al., 1998; Betsch et al., 1998).

Ceremonial accounting routines
Finally we consider potential ceremonial properties of accounting routines, with particular reference to financial measurement routines. Ceremonial behaviour discriminates between individuals or groups, and preserves existing power structures (Tool, 1993). And, once institutionalised in organisations, financial measurement routines indeed have potential to not serve the interests of all people or situations. Humphrey and Olson (1995), for example, questioned whether orthodox accounting techniques, rooted in neoclassical economic assumptions of rationality and optimisation, are appropriate for public sector organisations, on the basis of (1) their provision of a public service, and (2) the complexity and possible conflict in their multiple goals. An emphasis on financial ('efficiency') measurement routines, argued Humphrey and Olson, imported from private sector

organisations and practices, can convey inconsistencies with public sector 'effectiveness criteria', thus driving dysfunctional behaviour.

Miller (1990) also highlighted that problems can arise when business actors continually draw upon financial measurement routines which may have been useful and successful at some point in time, rather than being receptive to and actually seeking alternative paradigms. For instance, an organisation might formulate its strategy primarily on the basis of indicators and calculation routines that prioritise expected financial returns, but this may be at the expense of considering alternative and strategic indicators such as product quality, customer satisfaction and/or employee satisfaction.

Traditionally, Western private enterprises would adopt financial measurement routines in an unquestioned manner as the primary basis for measuring business 'success' (Merino, 1993). Moreover, short-term profitability can dominate such alternative goals as long-term growth and strategic value: Johnson and Kaplan (1987) famously dubbed such features in Westernised organisations as 'short-termism' facilitated by a 'financial accounting mentality'. However, there are alternative approaches to the fulfilment of business success – for instance, by focusing primarily on product quality and customer service, thereby reinforcing a loyalty that in turn might generate economic benefits in the long run.

Accounting change

In this section we now describe recent work within the accounting literature that has attempted to further our understanding of accounting and, more broadly, organisational change (Burns and Scapens, forthcoming). Importantly, such efforts build on the institutional perspective described above.

The accounting change literature has been vibrant in recent years (Quattrone and Hopper, 2001), not least because accounting itself is in the throes of significant change but also because accounting normally situates itself at the hub of broader organisational change. The accounting literature is laden with detailed case studies of organisations that have recently implemented change in their accounting systems, techniques, and even changing roles for accountants (for an overview, see Burns and Vaivio, 2001).

By definition, routines tend to change infrequently, although their reproduction should be viewed as processual and recurring over time (Becker, 2004). Their organisational embeddedness demands for actors to continue to cooperate in general, to know their jobs, to understand which routines are required, and to know when to carry them out (Hill et al., 1990). Much of this reproduction in routines constitutes a mixture of imitation and replication of previously enacted routines, although this does not preclude routines being imported from elsewhere (Nelson and Winter, 1982).

Despite the regularities that accounting and other organisational routines bring, they *can* nevertheless change – for instance, as old routines break down or adjust, and new routines appear in modified forms to their predecessors (Feldman, 2000, 2003). Indeed, some scholars have argued that accounting can itself be a primary instrument of change within organisations (Boland, 1979; Dent, 1991), some deliberate and some non-deliberate.

Consider a hypothetical example of intraorganisational change whereby newly-appointed senior managers demand new accounting information to monitor their activities. This would represent a change in organisational rules – more specifically, a change in the nature of accounting systems. Taken a stage further, as these new systems (rules) are implemented, new accounting procedures (routines) will emerge. These new accounting procedures must be re-enacted alongside the numerous other organisational routines already recurring. And, importantly, these new accounting procedures will be shaped by existing institutions – i.e., taken-for-granted assumptions concerning the nature of organisational activities and relationships between the various organisational members.

New intentional accounting systems (rules) can be modified, as acceptable alternatives (re-)negotiated. However, what is deemed acceptable here will be influenced by the meanings and norms embedded in recurring routines and institutions, and also by the relative power of individual actors and groups.

Emergent new routines can be difficult to predict; however, they are not arbitrary and usually can be explained. The adoption of a new budgeting system, for example, can be intentional (even 'rational') and, in a business organisation, will normally reflect overall concerns for economic efficiency and cost control. But there can be other (possibly external) influences. For example, when a subsidiary organisation has a new management team put in place by its parent organisation, that management team will be infused with (taken-for-granted) assumptions constituting the nature of its parent company's business. The same management team will also be influenced by broader assumptions such as 'best-practice' and professional-oriented recommendations, and even by the latest business fads. As such, although the selection of a new accounting system can be attributed to efficiency-based criterion, it need not be 'optimal' in the neoclassical economic sense. However, the selection will be context- and path-dependent, in the sense that it will be shaped by existing routines and institutions (Levitt and March, 1988; David, 1997; Becker, 2004).

If, over time, new and emergent routines become widely accepted in an organisation, so that they become the unquestionable form of management control, then they can be said to be institutionalised. And, as such, they are more than a set of routine procedures required by senior management. That is, they are an inherent feature of the management control process, and thus represent an important part of the expected nature of organisational behaviour, as well as defining relations between the various groups within the organisation. The new systems and practices will thus strongly influence day-to-day organisational activity and are likely to be quite resistant to any potential challenge.

These processes of intraorganisational change, described above, can be interpreted in Nelson's (1995) terms as representing and incorporating (1) change over time; (2) both random elements (e.g., the working out of mutually acceptable methods of working) and systematic mechanisms (e.g., selection of the new 'efficient' system); and (3) inertial forces which underpin continuity over time. Thus, rather than implying a Panglossian argument that only the fittest survive and optimal solutions eventually emerge, we are arguing that change processes are shaped by a combination of random, systematic and inertial forces (Nelson and Winter, 1982), which together create the context out of which new practices can emerge. And we add further that processes of intraorganisational change are embedded in more complexity than the rational selection of optimal systems (rules) and practices (routines) – they are inherently path-dependent (Cohen et al., 1996).

Intraorganisational change can also be 'revolutionary', meaning that it entails radical changes to existing routines, and involves fundamental challenges against prevailing institutions (Soin et al., 2002). Nevertheless, such change processes will still be influenced, to some extent, by existing routines and institutions, and, as such, the change process remains path-dependent. Revolutionary change is likely to emerge from major extra-organisational change events (e.g., takeovers, economic recessions or market collapses). However, an organisation's response to such events will largely be determined by its existing institutional context.

Burns et al. (2003) explored the management accounting systems in two different operating units of the same multinational organisation. Importantly, they describe how one operating unit was embedded in production-oriented rules, routines and taken-for-granted assumptions, whereas the other was accounting-oriented. They ask a hypothetical question: would we expect the two operating units to react in the same way to the implementation of a new accounting system, say an activity-based costing system? The authors argued that there would likely be more resistance in the first operating unit, and, in so doing, they were assuming that past history and embedded experience would have an impact on the response to organisational (in this case, accounting) change.

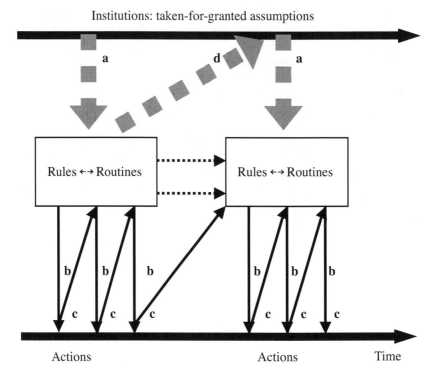

Institutions: taken-for-granted assumptions

Figure 5.3   The introduction of new rules and potential resistance to change

Further, Burns et al. (2003) argued that, if the assumptions underlying such change are inconsistent with embedded and taken-for-granted assumptions in the organisation, there will be a likelihood of conflict and resistance. In other words, since the institutions in the first operating unit were predominantly production/sales-oriented, a major accounting change (grounded in new accounting rules and routines) will likely give rise to resistance. In the second operating unit, however, because the managers' assumptions and routine activities were largely accounting-oriented, they were more likely to accept accounting change. We illustrate this diagrammatically in Figure 5.3. The right-hand box in the figure represents the new rules and routines which are introduced into the organisation (e.g., a new costing system). These new rules and routines will be understood by the organisational members in terms of past actions, existing rules and routines, and also in terms of their taken-for-granted assumptions about their business (i.e. their institutions).

Burns et al. (2003) present several additional case studies of accounting change implementation, and identify each case as being either 'successful' or 'unsuccessful' according to the extent to which the intentions of the change programme are mostly accomplished and, in keeping with this view, whether or not the change process involved minimal resistance or conflict. In a similar vein, Burns (2000) described a case study of the unsuccessful implementation of very basic accounting procedures within the product development department of a small UK-based chemicals manufacturer. The principal reason why the change programme failed, he argued, was that the new routines which emerged were too 'mechanical' and failed to shift the dominant 'chemistry ways of thinking' within that department towards the intended 'financial results-orientation'. Thus, new accounting-based rules and routines conflicted with, and failed to replace, the chemistry-orientation in that department, and this existing institutional platform was found to be paramount in terms of the (unsuccessful) outcome of the change programme.

An important message to emerge from such research is that change management requires thorough understanding of an organisation's institutional context, especially organisational routines and taken-for-granted assumptions (Burns and Scapens, forthcoming). Moreover, this encompasses a great deal more than simply knowledge of any formal systems (rules). It requires understanding of the prevalent habits and routines of an organisation's individuals and groups, as well as the underpinning assumptions which are taken for granted in day-to-day activity (Becker et al., 2005). Recent research has shown the potential for accounting to make such embedded organisational features more visible (Burns and Baldvinsdottir, 2005).

Concluding remarks

Our chapter represents a brief insight into how some scholars of accounting have recently endeavoured to provide insight into their subject as a largely routines-based organisational practice that can eventually underpin institutionalised action and thought. Although this interpretation is but a small part of the literature in this area, and is certainly not the only way that accounting is presented, our intention was to share such insights with like-minded scholars who endeavour to place greater emphasis in their scholarly work on the importance of theorising and empirically investigating routines.

Notes

1. Or financial reporting.
2. In its earlier days, management accountants were primarily concerned with calculating and managing an organisation's (product) costs. Indeed, the forerunner of management accounting was usually labelled 'cost accounting' and its practitioners were called 'cost accountants'.

3. Such is the growth in this literature, it is questionable whether our 'non-orthodox' labelling is appropriate. However, the point is that the vast majority of accounting textbooks and accounting programmes in (particularly US) universities remain premised in their century-old neoclassical roots.
4. For an overview, see Chapter 4 in Ryan et al. (2002). The journals where non-orthodox accounting research has flourished in recent decades include *Management Accounting Research, Accounting, Organizations and Society, Critical Perspectives in Accounting* and *Accounting, Auditing and Accountability Journal.*
5. Earlier works also highlighted the routinised nature of accounting (Roberts and Scapens, 1990; Dent, 1991; Mouritsen, 1994; Scapens, 1994).

References

Ashmos, D., D. Duchon and R. McDaniel (1998), 'Participation in strategic decision making: the role of organisational predisposition and issue interpretation', *Decision Sciences*, **29**, 25–51.

Barley, S.R. and P.S. Tolbert (1997), 'Institutionalization and structuration: studying the links between action and institutions', *Organization Studies*, **18**(1), 93–117.

Becker, M.C. (2004), 'Organizational routines: a review of the literature', *Industrial and Corporate Change*, **13**(4), 643–77.

Becker, M.C. and T. Knudsen (2005), 'The role of routines in reducing pervasive uncertainty', *Journal of Business Research*, **58**, 746–7.

Becker, M.C., N. Lazaric, R. Nelson and S. Winter (2005), 'Applying organizational routines in understanding organizational change', *Industrial and Corporate Change*, **14**(5), 775–91.

Berry, A., T. Capps, D. Cooper, P. Ferguson, T. Hopper and A. Lowe (1985), 'Management accounting in an Area of the NCB: rationales of management accounting practices in a public enterprise', *Accounting, Organizations and Society*, **10**(1), 3–28.

Betsch, T., K. Fiedler. and J. Brinkmann (1998), 'Behavioral routines in decision making: the effects of novelty in task presentation and time pressure on routine maintenance and deviation', *European Journal of Psychology*, **28**, 861–78.

Boland, L.A. (1979), 'Knowledge and the role of institutions in economic theory', *Journal of Economic Issues*, **13**(4), 957–72.

Burns, J. (1997), 'The institutionalization of accounting routines', in K. Vagneur, C. Wilkinson and A.J. Berry (eds), *Beyond Constraint: Exploring the Management Control Paradox*, Sheffield: Management Control Association, pp. 217–34.

Burns, J. (2000), 'The dynamics of accounting change: inter-play between new practices, routines, institutions, power and politics', *Accounting, Auditing and Accountability Journal*, **13**(5), 566–96.

Burns, J. and G. Baldvinsdottir (2005), 'An institutional perspective of accountants' new roles – the interplay of contradictions and praxis', *European Accounting Review*, **14**(4), 725–57.

Burns, J. and R.W. Scapens (2000), 'Conceptualizing management accounting change: an Institutional Framework', *Management Accounting Research*, **11**(1), 3–25.

Burns, J. and R.W. Scapens (forthcoming), 'Conceptualizing intra-organizational change: an institutional framework', in K. Nielsen and C.A. Koch (eds), *Institutional Change, Values and Learning*, Cheltenham, UK and Northampton, MA, USA: Edward Elgar.

Burns, J. and J. Vaivio (2001), 'Management accounting change', *Management Accounting Research*, **12**(4), 389–402.

Burns, J. and H. Yazdifar (2001), 'Trick or treats', *Financial Management*, March, 33–5.

Burns, J., M. Ezzamel and R.W. Scapens (2003), *The Challenge of Management Accounting Change: Behavioural and Cultural Aspects of Change Management*, Oxford: Elsevier/CIMA publishing.

Busco, C. (2003), 'The role of performance measurement systems within processes of (un)learning and change', PhD thesis, University of Manchester.

Cohen, M. and P. Bacdayan (1994), 'Organisational routines are stored as procedural memory: evidence from a laboratory study', *Organisation Science*, **5**, 554–68.

Cohen, M.D., R. Burkhart, G. Dosi, M. Egidi, L. Marengo, M. Warglien and S. Winter (1996), 'Routines and other recurring action patterns of organisations: contemporary research issues', *Industrial and Corporate Change*, **5**, 653–98.

Coriat, B. and G. Dosi (1998), 'Learning how to govern and learning how to solve problems: on the co-evolution of competencies, conflicts and organisational routines', in A.D.J. Chandler, P. Hadstroem and O. Soelvell (eds), *The Role of Technology, Strategy, Organisation and Regions*, Oxford: Oxford University Press.

Currie, W. (1995), 'A comparative analysis of management accounting in Japan, USA/UK and West Germany', in D. Ashton et al. (eds), *Issues in Management Accounting*, London: Prentice-Hall, pp. 321–46.

Cyert, R. and J. March (1963), *A Behavioural Theory of the Firm*, Englewood Cliffs, NJ: Prentice-Hall.

David, P.A. (1997), 'Path dependence and the quest for historical economics: one more chorus of the ballad of QWERTY', Discussion Papers in Economic and Social History no.20, University of Oxford.

Dent, J. (1991), 'Management accounting and organizational cultures: a field survey of the emergence of a new organizational reality', *Accounting, Organizations and Society*, **16**(8), 705–32.

Feldman, M.S. (2000), 'Organisational routines as a source of continuous change', *Organisation Science*, **11**, 611–29.

Feldman, M.S. (2003), 'A performative perspective on stability and change in organizational routines', *Industrial and Corporate Change*, **12**, 727–52.

Feldman, M.S. and B.T. Pentland (2003), 'Reconceptualizing organizational routines as a source of flexibility and change', *Administrative Science Quarterly*, **48**, 94–118.

Hill, C., P. Hwang and W.C. Kim (1990), 'An eclectic theory of the choice of international entry mode', *Strategic Management Journal*, **11**, 117–28.

Hodgson, G.M. (1993), *Economics and Evolution*, Cambridge: Polity Press.

Hope, J. and R. Fraser (1999), 'Beyond budgeting: building a new management model for the information age', *Management Accounting* (UK), January, 16–21.

Humphrey, C. and O. Olson (1995), ' "Caught in the Act": public services disappearing in the world of "Accountable" Management?', in D. Ashton et al. (eds), *Issues in Management Accounting*, London: Prentice-Hall, pp. 347–70.

Jagd, S. (1995), 'Management accounting and the reproduction and transformation of organisational frames of meaning', working paper presented at EIASM workshop, Brussels, September.

Johansson, I-L. and G. Baldvinsdottir (2003), 'Accounting for trust: some empirical evidence', *Management Accounting Research*, **14**(3), 219–34.

Johnson, H. and R. Kaplan (1987), *Relevance Lost: The Rise and Fall of Management Accounting*, Boston, MA: Harvard University Press.

Levitt, B. and J. March (1988), 'Organisational learning', *Annual Review of Sociology*, **14**, 319–40.

Macintosh, N. and R. Scapens (1990), 'Structuration theory in management accounting', *Accounting, Organizations and Society*, **15**(5), 455–77.

March, J.G. and J.P. Olsen (1989), *Rediscovering Institutions – The Organisational Basis of Politics*, New York: The Free Press.

Merino, B. (1993), 'An analysis of the development of accounting knowledge: a pragmatic approach', *Accounting, Organizations and Society*, **18**(2/3), 163–85.

Miller, P. (1990), 'On the interactions between accounting and the state', *Accounting, Organizations and Society*, **15**(4), 315–38.

Miller, P. (1994), 'Accounting as social and institutional practice: an introduction', in A. Hopwood and P. Miller (eds), *Accounting as Social and Institutional Practice*, Cambridge: Cambridge University Press.

Mouritsen, J. (1994), 'Rationality, institutions and decision making: reflections on March and Olsen's rediscovering institutions', *Accounting, Organizations and Society*, **19**(2), 193–211.

Munby, H., J. Versnel, N.L. Hutchinson, P. Chin and D.H. Berg (2003), 'Workplace learning and the metacognitive functions of routines', *Journal of Workplace Learning*, **15**, 94–104.

Nelson, R. (1995), 'Recent evolutionary theorizing about economic change', *Journal of Economic Literature*, **33**, 48–90.

Nelson, R. and S. Winter (1982), *An Evolutionary Theory of Economic Change*, Cambridge, MA: Harvard University Press.

Preston, A. (1995), 'Budgeting, creativity and culture', in D. Ashton et al. (eds), *Issues in Management Accounting*, London: Prentice-Hall, pp. 273–97.

Quattrone, P. and T. Hopper (2001), 'What does organizational change mean? Speculations on a taken-for-granted category', *Management Accounting Research*, **12**(4), 403–35.

Reason, J. (1990), *Human Error*, Cambridge: Cambridge University Press.

Roberts, J. and R.W. Scapens (1985), 'Accounting systems and systems of accountability: understanding accounting practices in their organisational contexts', *Accounting, Organizations and Society*, **10**(4), 443–56.

Roberts, J. and R.W. Scapens (1990), 'Accounting as discipline', in D. Cooper and T. Hopper (eds), *Critical Accounts*, London: Macmillan Press, pp. 107–25.

Ryan, R., R.W. Scapens and M. Theobald (2002), *Research Method and Methodology in Finance and Accounting*, 2nd edn, London: Thomson publishing.

Scapens, R.W. (1994), 'Never mind the gap: towards an institutional perspective of management accounting practices', *Management Accounting Research*, **5**(3/4), 301–21.

Scapens, R.W. and J. Arnold (1986), 'Economics and management accounting research', in M. Bromwich and A. Hopwood (eds), *Research and Current Issues in Management Accounting*, London: Pitman, pp. 78–102.

Scapens, R.W. and J. Roberts (1993), 'Accounting and control: a case study of resistance to accounting change', *Management Accounting Research*, **4**(1), 1–32.

Segelod, E. (1997), 'The content and role of the investment manual – a research note', *Management Accounting Research*, **8**, 221–31.

Seo, M-G. and W.E.D. Creed (2002), 'Institutional contradictions, praxis and institutional change: a dialectical perspective', *Academy of Management Review*, **2**, 222–47.

Simon, H.A. (1947), *Administrative Behaviour*, New York: The Free Press.

Soin, K., W. Seal and J. Cullen (2002), 'ABC and organizational change: an institutional perspective', *Management Accounting Research*, **13**(2), 249–71.

Stene, E.O. (1940), 'Public administration: an approach to a science of administration', *American Political Science Review*, **34**, 1124–37.

Swieringa, R. and K. Weick (1987), 'Management accounting and action', *Accounting, Organizations and Society*, **12**(3), 293–308.

Szulanski, G. and S. Winter (2002), 'Getting it right the second time', *Harvard Business Review*, **80**, 62–71.

Thornton, D. (1979), 'Information and institutions in the capital market', *Accounting, Organizations and Society*, **4**(3), 211–33.

Tool, M. (1993), 'The theory of instrumental value: extensions, clarifications', in M. Tool (ed.), *Institutional Economics*, Boston & London: Kluwer Publishers, pp. 119–59.

6 Problem solving and governance in the capability-based view of the firm: the roles and theoretical representations of organizational routines

Giovanni Dosi, Marco Faillo and Luigi Marengo

This chapter will first discuss the relationship between the notion of organizational routines and the capability-based view of the firm. Next, we address their double function both as problem-solving arrangements and as governance devices. Third, we review some recent efforts to formalize the processes of search and organizational adaptation, leading to routines themselves.[1]

1 The capability-based view of the firm

Business organizations are *behavioural entities*[2] which embody specific and rather inertial compromises between different functions like (i) resource allocation; (ii) information processing; (iii) efforts elicitation; (iv) coordination (largely through non-price devices) among multiple cognitive and 'physical' tasks; (v) governance of competing claims upon the total generated surplus; (vi) experimentation and learning.[3] In turn, these different organizational 'functions' yield also multiple coexisting levels of interaction amongst organizational members.

Clearly, a thorough understanding of what organizations are and how they operate ought to take on board the analysis of all these mechanisms of interaction. The current literature still falls well short of such an objective. However, over the last four decades one has witnessed multiple endeavours enriching our understanding of the nature of economic organizations.

As is discussed at greater length in Dosi et al. (2003),[4] quite diverse interpretative efforts range between two extreme archetypes. On the one hand, the dominant strand of contemporary analysis interprets the nature of organizations assuming sophisticated, fully rational and self-seeking agents whose behaviours are viewed as directed by market forces. Only in those settings in which, owing to failures of information and contract incompleteness, markets are less effective in this task, are organizations called for as surrogates for such imperfections. Organizational behaviour is assumed to be essentially strategic, in the game-theoretic sense, and the focus is on the governance of incentives. Competence issues regarding the way in which an organization performs its characteristic 'output' actions, and how well it does it, are fully censored. As an extreme characterization, given the 'right' incentives, any firm can make microprocessors as well as Intel, or bioengineering as well as Genetech.

Conversely, at the opposite extreme, a small – but not negligible and growing – minority of the economics profession places its 'foundations' of the nature of economic organizations in their *problem-solving features*, in turn nested in ubiquitous forms of human 'bounded rationality', grossly imperfect processes of learning and diverse mechanisms of social distribution of 'cognitive labour'. The root of this approach can be found in the works of Herbert Simon, James March, Alfred Chandler and Richard Nelson and Sidney Winter.[5]

Contrary to the 'incentive view', the 'capability-based' or 'problem-solving',[6] view of economic organizations just assumes *weak incentive compatibility* to begin with (see Dosi and Marengo, 1995), in the sense that there exists some selection pressure which generates a connection between performance and rewards, and then focus on the analysis of how individual actions combine to solve specific problems efficiently.

The problem-solving activities of the firm can be conceived as combinations of physical and cognitive acts, within a procedure, leading to the achievement of a specific outcome. Its internal organization determines the distribution of the informational inputs across specific task units and, as such, the division of cognitive labour. In particular, firms possess the operational competencies associated with their own problem-solving procedures, i.e. organizational capabilities.

Specificity in organizational capabilities plays a key role within this framework and these are assumed to be the source of the observation of persistent differences amongst firms in terms of their inner structures, behaviours and performances (see Coriat and Dosi, 1998; Dosi et al., 2000; Dosi et al., 2003; Nelson, 1991). Capabilities are the expression of knowledge and problem-solving repertoires that enable firms to produce specific goods and services and that shape their destiny in terms of profitability, growth and probability of survival, for example.

2   Organizational routines and capabilities
Organizational routines are a major building block of organizational capabilities, with a repetitive and context-dependent nature. Adopting routines as units of analysis can help in understanding the firms' capabilities, even though it would not suffice to identify the latter simply as hierarchies of routines. A marketing competence, for example, might require a customer database, which is a contextual requisite of some of the

organizational routines supporting the competence, but not a routine itself (Dosi et al., 2003).

Let us refer to the general definition of routines provided in Cohen et al. (1996):[7] 'A routine is an executable *capability* for repeated performance in some *context* that has been *learned* by an organization in response to *selective* pressure' (Cohen et al., 1996, p. 683). The first key term, *capability* (used in Cohen et al., 1996, in a much narrower sense than our foregoing definition of organizational capabilities) is meant as the capacity to generate an action pattern that has been stored in localized or distributed form within the organization. As Nelson and Winter (1982) suggested, this capacity entails the ability to know what action pattern to perform and when to perform it. This implies that organizational members must be able to receive and interpret inputs generated, within a specific *context*, both by humans and by non-human devices. Inputs may include, for example, formal orders for a superior, informal suggestions, descriptions of the situation, the activation of another action pattern by other members, a particular date on the calendar or a particular time on the clock (Nelson and Winter, 1982, pp. 100–102). While the ability to receive inputs could be independent of the specific organizational context, the ability to recognize and interpret messages and inputs – as well as to generate appropriate messages and inputs – and to recall the appropriate pattern of action, is part of the knowledge and problem-solving repertoire that the single member *learns* within the organization.

This view of routines as stored and collectively shared problem-solving skills has been fruitfully adopted in both theoretical and empirical research on the origin, development and change of organizational capabilities: see, for example, in the recent literature, Jones and Craven (2001), Narduzzo et al. (2000), Pavitt (2002), Zollo and Winter (2002), At the same time, growing effort has gone also into the formal representation of processes of search, recombination and reinforcement of the sequence of elementary operations yielding particular problem-solving procedures. That is, one has finally begun to formally represent the processes of emergence of organizational routines themselves (see below).

3 Problem-solving capability and governance structure

In any case, routines emerge and are implemented in organizations composed of a plurality of individuals who might have conflicting interests. Certainly, a 'firm can be understood in terms of hierarchy of practised routines, which define lower-order organizational skills and how these skills are coordinated, and higher-order decision procedures for choosing what is to be done at a lower level (Nelson, 1994, pp. 234–5). This hierarchy, however, also entails mechanisms of exercise of authority and governance of the admissible behaviours by which individual members can pursue their interests. This is indeed acknowledged by Nelson and Winter (1982), who suggest that routines can be seen also as truces amongst potentially conflicting interests: 'there is a truce between the supervisor and those supervised at every level in the organizational hierarchy: the usual amount of work gets done, reprimands and compliments are delivered with the usual frequency, and no demands are presented for major modifications in the terms of the relationship' (Nelson and Winter, 1982, p. 110).

However, this complementary nature of routines has so far been relatively neglected in that literature broadly inspired by evolutionary ideas, with some exploratory exceptions. For example, in Coriat and Dosi (1998) one begins to address two possible roles of organizational routines as problem-solving and as governance devices, describing the emergence of two well-known paradigms of corporate organization, namely, first, the American 'Tayloristic' (and 'Fordist') corporation and, second, the Japanese 'Ohnistic' (or Toyotist) one. Indeed each of the two paradigms can be conceived as a particular redefinition of the nature and distribution of knowledge within the organization, which is matched by equally specific mechanisms of incentive governance and power exercises.

The transition from the 'Victorian' firm to the Tayloristic organization entailed the shift from the 'inside contractor' regime, characterized by a limited possibility of control by the owner upon the contractors' works, to an organizational form in which the definition of organizational procedures is concentrated in the Department of Planning. Such a fundamental change was deeply intertwined with the redefinition of the nature of productive knowledge and of its distribution within the organization. The *time and motion studies*, which can be considered one of Taylor's major contributions to production management, have been the prerequisite for the codification of tacit productive knowledge, previously embodied within specific skilled workers' experience, which was transformed into a set of elementary procedures and routines. This codification, in turn, has been the condition for a change in control of such knowledge – also sanctioned by the introduction of specific incentive governance mechanisms, such as a piece-wage system and direct visual control – and of the consequent reduction of contractual power of skilled workers, which represented one of the major limits to effort elicitation in the prototypical nineteenth-century firm.

The second paradigm, 'Ohnism', can be considered as the result of the need to achieve productivity gains without the possibility of exploiting the economies of scale which were at the basis of the 'Fordist' revolution. In this case, tasks that Taylorism recommended to take apart are aggregated in single work stations. In particular, task fragmentation is maintained, but jobs are broken down into components defined as the smallest combination of acts that can be transferred from one worker to another; thus both flexibility in the production process and control of workers' knowledge are guaranteed. Control over workers' activities is obtained by means of processes like 'management by eyes' and 'auto-activation', based on a workshop organized in such a way that everything is made visible to everyone. In this context the worker plays a key role in determining not only the working pace but also the quality of the outcome, having, for example, the possibility to detect anomalies (by identifying faulty products or discrepancies between plans and actual progress of production) and to stop the line. Knowledge of the whole work process, autonomy and problem-solving capacity allow workers to respond both to rapid changes in customer demands and to unexpected problems in the productive process. On the incentive side, what matters is the link between operating skills and the ability to coordinate and communicate with colleagues: '[in the Japanese firm] operating units are expected to be engaged in mutually coordinating their task as well. Exclusive attention to the efficient performance of a particular operating task in isolation may not contribute to overall efficiency' (Aoki, 1990, p. 11). Promotions are based on a merit criterion which captures a broadly defined set of problem-solving and relational capabilities.

What is important to note is that the emergence and subsequent persistence of the two (Taylorist/Fordist and 'Toyotist') paradigms, identified also by the characteristic sets of routines, rules, information flows and 'lines of command', can be explained in terms of coevolution of patterns of knowledge distribution and mechanisms of control and coordination. In both cases, the introduction of a new set of problem-solving routines corresponded to the adoption of new forms of incentive governance.

4   Toward a formal representation of the capability-based view of the firm
Can one formalize the notion of a problem-solving organization embodying at least some of the above characteristics? Several recent contributions have tried to do precisely that, mostly focusing upon the relationship between the division of cognitive labour and search process in some problem-solving space (Dosi et al., 2002, 2003; Ethiraj and Levinthal, 2004; Gavetti and Levinthal, 2000; Marengo and Dosi, 2005; Marengo et al., 2000; Rivkin and Siggelkow, 2002, 2003).[8]

The central point of departure is the assumption that economic organizations can be conceived as repositories of problem-solving knowledge, in turn an idea well in tune with the Simonian analysis of organizational problem-solving (Simon, 1962, 1981). After all, managing an organization, designing and producing cars or software packages, discovering a new drug, etc. can been seen as complicated problems whose 'solutions' comprise a large number of cognitive and physical acts, and which imply the coordination of large combinatorial spaces of components.

At one end, components which make up an artifact can assume a number of alternative states: so, for example, in the case of the production of a car, one combines different characteristics of the engine, alternative designs, different materials etc. Conversely, an innovative search may be straightforwardly represented in the form of a combination of multiple 'cognitive acts' eventually yielding the solution of the problem at hand, e.g. the discovery of a new molecule with the required characteristics, a reasonable and coherent software package, etc. Note that in both the foregoing examples the existence of strong interdependencies among the components – which often are only partially understood by the agents involved – implies that the effect on the system's performance of changes in the state of a single component depends on the values assumed by the other ones. An implication is also that, in this kind of problem, it is impossible to optimize the system by optimizing each single component. Let us explore the implications of this view for organizational analysis. Straightforwardly, one can conceive economic organizations as bundles of routines, procedures and rules characterized by strong interrelations which often are opaque even to *all* organizational members, *including those in charge of its management*. Notice first that the partial 'opaqueness' of the mappings between actions and outcomes is quite in tune with the 'garbage can' interpretation of organizational dynamics (Cohen et al., 1972). Second, it is well corroborated by plenty of evidence regarding widespread difficulty in *replication* and *transfers* of incumbent organizational arrangements and problem solving procedures (Szulanski and Winter, 2002; Winter and Szulanski, 1998; Zander and Kogut, 1995). Third, an obvious implication of such opaque interrelatedness is also that the introduction of a new routine which has proved superior in another situation might have negative effects on the performance of the organization if other interrelated components are not appropriately co-adapted (Marengo and Dosi, 2005; Marengo et al., 2000).

4.1   Formal representations of problem-solving dynamics

A path-breaking source of inspiration for modelling problem-solving procedures goes back to H. Simon's work (cf. Simon, 1981, among others). As paradoxical as it might sound nowadays, our main objection to Simon's contributions to 'bounded rationality' is that it generally continued to involve some assumption of *procedural coherence* in both problem-solving protocols and the underlying selection among them. More recent contributions implying much less 'procedural rationality' borrow some formal instruments from both 'distributed computation' and evolutionary biology, including those by Kauffman (see, among others, Kauffman, 1993).

Kauffman's 'NK-model' describes evolving entities, conceived as complex structures, characterized by non-linear interaction among their many elements. Although the original object of analysis was populations of organisms, the formal structure of his model allows for various applications in other domains.

In Kauffman's model, a system can be described by a string of N loci which refers to the set of elements ($i=1 \ldots N$) that also define its dimension. For each element i, there exist A_i possible states (alleles in biology). The set of all possible configurations (strings) of the system's elements $A_1 \times A_2 \times \ldots A_N$ is called the *possibility space* of a system. A fitness function F: $A_1 \times A_2 \times \ldots A_N \rightarrow [0,1]$ assigns a real number to each possible configuration as a measure of its relative performance. The attribution of fitness values to all possible configurations defines the *fitness landscape* of the system. This landscape can be explored in the search for the configuration with the maximum fitness value, moving from one configuration (a point in the fitness landscape) to another through changes in the value of one (or more) element(s). This 'adaptive walk' ends when a configuration is reached which has no immediate neighbour with better fitness.

The K-value refers to the number of 'epistatic' relations among elements (the structure of the system). The existence of these relations implies that the contribution of one element to the overall fitness of the system is dependent both upon its own state and upon the state of K other elements. In the case, for example, of a system characterized by K=4, the contribution of each element to the system's performance depends on the value assumed by four other elements to which it is interrelated. Two limit cases of complexity can be distinguished: *minimum complexity* when $K=0$ and *maximum complexity* when $K=N-1$.

Consider, for example, a system characterized by $N=3$, $A_i=[0,1]$ and $K=0$. Following Kauffman, we draw the fitness values of elements for the two possible states randomly from a uniform distribution between 0 and 1. The fitness of the string as a whole is then defined as the mean value of the fitness values of elements:

$$F = \frac{\sum_{i=1}^{N} f_i}{N}.$$

Suppose now the string is modified by means of a simple random one-bit mutation transforming it into a neighbouring string which differs only by one bit. A fitness value is computed for the new string. Now we can introduce a selection process by which fitness-improving mutations are retained while fitness-reducing ones are discarded. In this way we define a path in the fitness landscape which, starting from an initial string, 'climbs' toward higher fitness values until no further improving mutation is possible.

Kauffman shows that, in the case of $K=0$, i.e. when the contribution of each element to the system's fitness is independent of the values assumed by other elements, the resulting fitness landscape has only one optimum. In this context, similar configurations will have similar fitness values (the system will be highly correlated) and changes in one element have little impact on the overall fitness. Therefore one bit mutation with the selection of the fitter configuration can quickly reach the global optimum from every starting point. As K grows, similar configurations may have very different fitness values and the landscape will become rugged and less correlated. In this case even small changes in a configuration can have a great impact on the overall fitness. This results in an exponentially growing number of local peaks. The search process becomes strongly path-dependent and random mutation with selection does not necessarily lead to optimality.

Following Simon (1981), Marengo and Dosi (2005) focus on strategies for the reduction of problem complexity through a division of problem-solving labour, that results in the decomposition of large and complex problems into smaller sub-problems which can be solved independently. The basic assumption is that solving a given problem requires the coordination of many 'atomic' elements or actions or pieces of knowledge, which we can generically call 'components', each of which can assume some number of alternative states. The one-bit mutation algorithm at the basis of Kauffman's NK model can be conceived as a particular case in which the problem is fully decomposed and the search process is fully decentralized: each sub-problem consists of a single component and is solved independently of the others. As showed by Kauffmann (1993), this algorithm allows us to reach only the local optimum whose basin of attraction[9] contains the initial configuration, but on the other hand it reaches such a local optimum quickly and enjoys therefore an advantage whenever speed of adaptation is important. This also implies that the global optimum can be reached only from a limited and well specified set of starting points. In contrast, there is the case of no decomposition at all, or total centralization, corresponding to a strategy in which all the components (bits) are simultaneously mutated. In this case the global optimum can be reached from any starting point, through a much slower exploration of all the possible configurations.

Note that the effectiveness of the decomposition, in terms of system optimization, is strongly affected by the existence of interdependences among the components of the problem: separating interdependent components and then solving each sub-problem independently will prevent overall optimization. Note also that, as pointed out by Simon, because of the opaqueness of the interrelations between components, optimal decomposition – a division of labour that separate into sub-problems only the components that are independent from each other – cannot be achieved by bounded rational agents that normally are bound to adopt near-decompositions, trying to put together within the same sub-problem only those components whose interdependences are believed to be important for the performance of the system. But near-decompositions involve trade-off between complexity and optimality: a finer decomposition scheme makes search faster, but the exploration of a smaller portion of the search space increases the probability of separating interdependent components and consequently reduces the likelihood to generate and then select an optimal solution.

This approach can be a very fruitful perspective from which to tackle the analysis of organizations: different organizational forms implement different decomposition heuristics and might be characterized by different representations of the problem and therefore present different properties in terms of the effectiveness and efficiency of the derived search processes (see Marengo et al. (2005) for a theoretical discussion of the topic).

The application of these ideas to organizational design leads to the comparison, in terms of relative performance, between less than optimal decompositions and finer than optimal decompositions. One of the main conclusions is that the adoption of a finer than optimal decomposition scheme might have an advantage in terms of speed of adaptation, even if it usually implies a cost in terms of sub-optimality (impossibility to reach global optima). Coarser decompositions have a higher probability of leading to the global optimum, but only in the long run. As a consequence, the presence of strong selective pressure could favour the adoption of organizational structures with a more than optimal degree of decentralization. This is particularly true for 'modular' problems, characterized by the existence of strong interrelationships within sub-problems and weak interdependencies between sub-problems.

4.2 Modelling the coupling mechanisms between capabilities and governance

Marengo and Dosi (2005), as well as most contributions of this *genre*, while concentrating on the problem-solving features of organizational dynamics, censor any incentive compatibility issue, a theoretical inclination that, as noted above, is quite typical within the capability-based framework.

Nothing, however, prevents this type of analysis going beyond the exclusive focus on firms as *loci* of coordination and as *loci* of creation, implementation, storage and diffusion of productive knowledge,[10] and explicitly taking on board the issues of incentive governance and control discussed qualitatively in Coriat and Dosi (1998). Formal attempts in this direction include Dosi et al. (2002, 2003) which explore some admittedly 'reduced form' of conflict of interests, power and control over agents' decisions within the analytical framework of Marengo and Dosi (2005) and Marengo et al. (2000) and to discuss the interaction between problem representation and incentive mechanisms. In particular, the double role of problem representation is stressed: on the one hand it defines the 'cognitive' structure of the problem and the consequent decomposition scheme which is adopted (definition of teams as subsets or blocks of components); on the other hand, it has important consequences for a reward mechanism based on the distinction between organization's (system) and team's (block) performance as it defines what the organization conceives as a team subject to performance evaluation and incentives.

The analysis starts by considering the conflicts of interest among problem-solving teams generated by the adoption of team-level incentive mechanisms. While under a global reward scheme an alternative (a particular configuration of a sub-problem's components) is selected if it improves the overall organization's performance, with a team-level reward mechanism a would-be alternative is accepted if it enhances the performance of the unit, even if it degrades the overall organization's performance. It can be shown that, if the organization's representation of the problem is not correct (it does not correspond to the 'true' structure of the problem in terms of interrelations among components), the adoption of a global reward scheme allows the organization to reach a global optimum. But what is more interesting is that, even if the representation of the problem is not correct, the adoption of a team-level reward structure tends, in the long run, to produce performances that are similar to the global reward one. Thus goal conflicts prevent organization to remain absorbed in local optima and act as substitute for a correct representation of the problem (Dosi et al., 2003, p. 427).

Power is introduced by allowing one team (a block in the decomposition scheme) to stop the mutation of any other blocks that decrease its own performance (veto power). The evidence suggests that, under specific conditions, the adoption of such a mechanism leads to good solutions. In particular, a team-reward scheme with veto power is superior to the global reward structure when the organizational representation of the problem is based on a finer decomposition than the 'true' one and the latter is not too complex. This is due to the fact that veto power interrupts the cycling among possible solutions generated by a team-based reward structure, preserving the advantages in terms of greater search effort which are typical of this reward mechanism.

A principal–agent-like model of interaction is reproduced, considering the case of control over the decisions of other organizational members by a principal, the residual claimant of the total payoff, who can 'order' others to keep performing a given action or to switch to a different one. This activity is considered to have a cost which depends on the span of control, i.e. the dimension of each sub-unit, and it is higher when the principal wants to induce a change in the agent's action than when he wants to elicit the same behaviour (the principal's profit is defined as the total output of the organization minus the 'elicitation cost'). When actions are interdependent, the control function, as any other problem-solving activity, cannot be entirely decomposed. Thus the interaction between a cognitive dimension and a control dimension has to be considered. The effects on total performance and the principal's profit are analysed considering four different cases: right, almost right, wrong and minimal (one-component units) perceived decomposition by agents, with reference to different decompositions of the underlying problem and the 'correctness' of the decomposition itself.

Obviously, if the organizational decomposition is the 'true' one, perfectly knowledgeable agents not facing any incentive-compatibility problem would make costly control redundant. However, interestingly, when the organization has a wrong representation of the problem space (and in particular underestimates the span of interdependencies), agents subject to costly control may generate a better performance then the one produced by perfectly 'cooperative' agents.

Finally Dosi et al. (2003) analyse more explicitly the double role of problem representation. The work examines, in particular, by means of a simulation model, the relations between cognitive decompositions and operational decompositions. The former establish search heuristics and targets, whereas the latter implement search processes driven by those targets. The exercise shows that, if cognitive decompositions are correct, then it is efficient to have maximum division of labour at the operational level, as this increases speed and accuracy of adaptation to targets. On the contrary, if cognitive decompositions do not correspond to the 'true' ones, coarser division of labour at the operational level ensures less accurate but prompt adaptations to the imperfectly set targets.

5 From search processes to organizational routines

How do the processes of search discussed in the foregoing sections relate to organizational routines? Ultimately, the search dynamics described in section four are stylized representations of the *generative processes* of routines themselves. Or, putting it differently, organizational routines can be seen as the metastable[11] outcomes of processes of search and adaptation in both domains of problem solving and of governance of intraorganizational conflicting interests.

Clearly, the approximate stability of routinized patterns of behaviour represents as such one of their advantages, as effective ways of storing and reproducing organizational knowledge, as an implementation of 'truces' and as a source of predictability of intraorganizational behaviours. The other side of the same coin is their inevitable inertial nature which might easily reproduce over time behavioural patterns well beyond the times of their possible efficiency.

Indeed, a fundamental mechanism of 'de-locking' might reside in the imperfect alignment of the different functions mentioned at the beginning of this chapter. Thus, far–reaching changes in the overall organizational structure and behaviours might be triggered by the accumulation of possibly small adjustments and variations over single dimensions.

Given the ubiquitous presence of interdependencies among the multiple cognitive and organizational constituents of organizational routines, small adjustments might ultimately lead to major organizational changes. In this respect see, among others, the example discussed in Lazaric and Denis (2005), on the indirect effects of the introduction of quality management tools in an organization. This is indeed isomorphic to what Levinthal has called 'the slow pace of rapid technological change' (Levinthal, 1998).

An equally interesting issue concerns the search for new technologies, new problem-solving arrangements, etc. The conjecture, having its roots in Schumpeter (1950) and analysed in more detail in Nelson and Winter (1982), is that search itself is partly driven by sorts of 'meta-routines' which provide some order and predictability to exploratory activities and reproduce over time search knowledge and skills. All them are part of what Teece et al. (1997, 2000) have called the *dynamic capabilities* of an organization (for more on this, see also Dosi et al., 2000). This, however, is a distinct chapter of organizational analysis.

Notes

1. The work significantly draws upon other works of the authors, in particular, Dosi, Faillo and Marengo (2003), Coriat and Dosi (1998) and Cohen et al. (1996) to which the reader is referred for further details.
2. We borrow this expression from Kreps (1990).
3. This categorisztion refines a similar one suggested in Coriat and Dosi (1998).
4. See also Dosi and Marengo (2000).
5. See Chandler (1977), Cyert and March (1963), March and Simon (1993), Nelson and Winter (1982).
6. We use 'capability- view' and 'problem solving view' as synonyms. As will become clear in the next pages, capabilities are conceived as aimed at solving problems, from producing a car to discovering a new drug or artifact.

7. For a recent and exhaustive review of the literature on organizational routines, see Becker (2004), while a few contributions to the analysis of routines can be found in the Special Section on this topic of *Industrial and Corporate Change*, **14**(5), 2005.
8. These models are representative of a wider family of adaptive learning models. In comparison to other modeling styles, for instance those based upon neural networks, genetic algorithms, reinforcement learning and other similar learning algorithms, these models tend to 'black-box' the learning algorithm itself and concentrate on the selection environments, in order to provide general properties of adaptive processes which apply to wide families of learning algorithms, irrespective of the actual algorithmic details.
9. A basin of attraction of a particular configuration: x^j is defined as the set of all configurations from which x^j can be reached.
10. A more complete 'co-evolutionary' picture is discussed by Dosi (1995). Organizations are assumed to be characterized by six correlated dimensions: the distribution of formal authority; the distribution of power; the incentive structure; the structure of information flows; the distribution of knowledge; and competence. In this context organization dynamics can be conceived as a process of adaptation and selection according to multiple, and possibly conflicting, objectives.
11. '[Metastable ......] in the sense that, while persisting on a time scale longer than processes generating them, they disappear ultimately with probability one' (Dosi and Winter, 2002, p. 338).

References

Aoki, M. (1990), 'Toward an economic model of the Japanese firm', *Journal of Economic Literature*, **XXVIII** (March), 1–27.
Becker, M. (2004), 'Organizational routines: a review of the literature', *Industrial and Corporate Change*, **13**(4), 643–78.
Chandler, A. (1977), *The Visible Hand: the Managerial Revolution in American Business*, Cambridge, MA: Harvard University Press.
Chandler, A., P. Hagström and Ö. Sölvell, (eds) (1998), *The Dynamic Firm*, Oxford/New York: Oxford University Press.
Cohen, M., J.G. March and J.P. Olsen (1972), 'A garbage can model of organizational choice', *Administrative Science Quarterly*, **17**(1), 1–25.
Cohen, M., R. Burkhart, G. Dosi, M. Egidi, L. Marengo, M. Warglien and S. Winter (1996), 'Routines and other recurring action patterns of organizations: contemporary research issue', *Industrial and Corporate Change*, **5**(3), 653–99.
Coriat, B. and G. Dosi (1998), 'Learning how to govern and learning how to solve problems: on the co-evolution of competences, conflicts and organizational routines', in Chandler et al. (1998).
Cyert, R.M. and J.G. March (1963), *A Behavioral Theory of the Firm*, Cambridge: Blackwell.
Dosi, G. (1995), 'Hierarchies, markets and power: some foundational issues on the nature of contemporary economic organization', *Industrial and Corporate Change*, **4**(1), 1–19.
Dosi, G., M. Faillo and L. Marengo (2003), 'Organizational capabilities, patterns of knowledge accumulation and governance structures: an introduction', *LEM Working Papers* N.11/03, *Sant'Anna School of Advanced Studies*, Pisa.
Dosi, G., D. Levinthal and L. Marengo (2002), 'The uneasy organizational matching between distribution of knowledge, division of labor and incentive governance', *LEM Working Papers* N. 26/02, *Sant'Anna School of Advanced Studies*, Pisa.
Dosi, G., D. Levinthal and L. Marengo (2003), 'Bridging contested terrain. Linking incentive-based and learning perspectives on organizational evolution', *Industrial and Corporate Change*, **12**(1), 413–36.
Dosi, G. and L. Marengo (1995), 'Toward a theory of organizational competencies', in R.W. England (ed.), *Evolutionary Concepts in Contemporary Economics*, Ann Arbor, MI: Michigan University Press, pp. 157–78.

Dosi, G. and L. Marengo (2000), 'On the tangled discourse between transaction cost economics and competence-based views of the firm', in N. Foss and V. Mahnke (eds), *Competence, Governance and Entrepreneurship*, Oxford: Oxford University Press.

Dosi, G., R. Nelson and S.G. Winter (eds) (2000), *The Nature and Dynamic of Organizational Capabilities*, Oxford: Oxford University Press.

Dosi, G. and S.G. Winter (2002), 'Interpreting economic change: evolution, structures and games', in M. Augier and J.G. March (eds), *The Economics of Choice, Change and Organization: Essays in Memory of Richard M. Cyert*, Cheltenham, UK and Northampton, MA, USA: Edward Elgar.

Ethiraj, S. and D. Levinthal (2004), 'Modularity and innovation in complex systems', *Management Science*, **50**(2), 159–73.

Gavetti, G. and D. Levinthal (2000), 'Looking forward and looking backward: cognitive and experimental search', *Administrative Science Quarterly*, **45**, 113–37.

Jones, O. and M. Craven (2001), 'Beyond the routine: innovation management and the teaching company scheme', *Technovation*, **21**, 267–79.

Kauffman, S.A. (1993), *The Origins of Order*, Oxford: Oxford University Press.

Kreps, D.M. (1990), 'Corporate culture and economic theory', in J.E. Alt and K.A. Shepsle (eds), *Perspectives on Positive Political Economy*, Cambridge: Cambridge University Press.

Lazaric, N. and B. Denis (2005), 'Routinization and memorization of tasks inside a workshop: an illustration through a case study', *Industrial and Corporate Change*, **14**(5), 873–96.

Levinthal, D. (1998), 'The slow pace of rapid technological change: gradualism and punctuation in technological change', *Industrial and Corporate Change*, **7**(2), 217–47.

March, J.G. and H.A. Simon (1993), *Organizations*, 2nd edn, New York: Wiley.

Marengo, L. and G. Dosi (2005), 'Decentralization and market mechanisms in collective problem solving', *Journal of Economic Behavior and Organization*, **58**(2), 303–26.

Marengo, L., G. Dosi, P. Legrenzi and C. Pasquali (2000), 'The structure of problem-solving knowledge and the structure of organizations', *Industrial and Corporate Change*, **9**, 757–88.

Marengo, L., C. Pasquali and M. Valente (2005), 'Decomposability and modulariy of economic interactions', in W. Callebaut and D. Rasskin-Gutman (eds), *Modularity: Understanding the Development and Evolution of Complex Natural Systems*, Cambridge, MA: MIT Press, The Vienna Series in Theoretical Biology, pp. 835–97.

Narduzzo, A., E. Rocco and M. Warglien (2000), 'Talking about routines in the field', in Dosi, Nelson and Winter (2000).

Nelson, R. (1991), 'Why do firms differ and how does it matter?', *Strategic Management Journal*, **12**, 61–74.

Nelson, R. (1994), 'The role of firm differences in an evolutionary theory of technical advance', in L. Magnusson (ed.), *Evolutionary and Neo-Schumpeterian Approaches to Economics*, Boston, MA: Kluwer, pp. 234–55.

Nelson, R. and S. Winter (1982), *An Evolutionary Theory of Economic Change*, Cambridge, MA: Belknap Harvard Press.

Pavitt, K. (2002), 'Innovating routines in the business firm: what corporate task should they accomplish?', *Industrial and Corporate Change*, **11**(1), 117–33.

Rivkin, J.W. and N. Siggelkow (2002), 'Organizational sticking points on NK landscapes', *Complexity*, **7**(5), 31–43.

Rivkin, J.W. and N. Siggelkow (2003), 'Balancing search and stability: interdependencies among elements of organizational design', *Management Science*, **49**, 290–311.

Schumpeter, J.A. (1950), *Capitalism, Socialism and Democracy*, New York: Harper.

Simon, H.A. (1962), 'The architecture of complexity', *Proceedings of the American Philosophical Society*, **106**, 467–82.

Simon, H.A. (1981), *The Science of Artificial*, 2nd edn, Cambridge, MA: MIT Press.

Szulanski, G. and S.G. Winter (2002), 'Getting it right the second time', *Harvard Business Review*, **80**, 62–9.

Teece, D.J., G. Pisano and A. Shuen (1997), 'Dynamic capabilities and strategic management', *Strategic Management Journal*, **18**, 509–33; a revised version is published in Dosi, Nelson and Winter (2000).

Winter, S.G. and G. Szulanski, (1998), 'Replication as strategy', *Organizational Science*, **12**(6), 730–43.

Zander, U. and B. Kogut (1995), 'Knowledge and the speed of transfer and imitation of organizational capabilities: an empirical test', *Organization Science*, **6**(1), 76–92.

Zollo, M. and S.G. Winter (2002), 'Deliberate learning and the evolution of dynamic capability', *Organization Science*, **13**(3), 339–51.

PART III

ORGANIZATIONAL ROUTINES, SEARCH AND LEARNING

7 Organizational routines in evolutionary theory[1]

Thorbjørn Knudsen

1 Introduction

Habits and routines are basic elements of evolutionary theories of cultural and economic change in most of the disciplines and fields within and bordering the social sciences, including cultural studies, economics, sociology, psychology, organization studies, and management. It is important to understand why this is the case. Accordingly, the present chapter aims to consider why the nature and function of individual habits and organizational routines render them basic elements of evolutionary theory in the social sciences.

A review of a very broad empirical literature identifies three essential features that are common to all kinds of habits and routines in social populations.[2] Habits and routines are persistent, they multiply, and they contain ready-made solutions to frequently occurring problems.[3] It is these three features of habits and routines that account for their role in evolutionary theory.

Evolutionary theory is useful in providing a causal explanation of an observed history, such as the origins, change and character of firms, markets and other economic organizations. Even though the content of particular evolutionary theories of cultural and economic change is very different, there is a shared overlap (Aldrich, 1999; Hodgson and Knudsen, 2005a; Winter, 1987). All of these theories include three core principles: variation, selection and information transfer (inheritance). Indeed, these three core Darwinian principles appear to be common to all selection processes.

Only recently, a generalized concept of selection has emerged to complement variation and information transfer as a general principle of evolution. This generalized concept of selection follows from a mathematical definition, offered by George Price (1995), which can be applied both to natural and to social phenomena. Three forms of selection, that are all consistent with Price's (1995) definition, commonly occur at the social level: subset selection, diffusion and generative selection (Hodgson and Knudsen, 2005b).

Subset selection is a process in which there is differential elimination of entities. A common instance of subset selection at the social level is the elimination of relatively inefficient firms through bankruptcy (Aldrich, 1999). Diffusion occurs with the generation and differential adoption of new entities. Such processes are common in economic and organizational evolution (Aldrich, 1999; Greve, 2002; Miner and Raghavan, 1999), including the differential adoption of new cultural ways, farming methods, aircraft designs and medical practices (Nelson, Peterhansl and Sampat, 2004; Rogers, 1983; Vincenti, 1994). Subset selection and diffusion are complementary processes. For example, bankrupt firms exit an industry and are replaced with new entrants whose properties partly come from imitation of existing firms (Nelson and Winter, 1982).

Generative selection is different from both subset selection and diffusion because it involves replication, the transfer of information between a source and a copy. Generative selection is a process in which differential replication is caused by the environmental interaction of an entity called an *interactor*. The interactor of particular interest to evolutionary theories of cultural and economic change is the social organization. In some cases, interaction among social organizations causes differential replication of organizational routines (Hodgson and Knudsen, 2005b; Winter, 2003).

Habits and routines contain encoded instructions for behaviour or thought. When this information is passed on, habits and routines can function as *replicators*. This is the case when routines are revised in response to contextual cues, such as changing tastes in product markets. Replication concerns the relationship between a copy and a source. In many cases, habits are easily copied, such as the habit of greeting customers when they enter a shop. There is not much difficulty in developing and repeating the intended behaviour. Even more effortless copying seems to be involved in the unintended spread and repetition of many gestures and linguistic terms.

In the replication of organizational routines, however, reliable replication is much more critical because routines are built from habits whose functions are coordinated. A routine involves the coordination of habits among a group of people such that an orchestrated sequence of actions emerges. An organization member acquires a disposition to engage in a particular behaviour in response to a particular cue from another organization member. For example, the coordination of behaviour in a production line can be routinized such that the completion of one action (e.g. assembly) reliably triggers a disposition in the next worker to engage in a particular behaviour (e.g. apply coating). Routines are more complex than habits, therefore more information must be transferred when routines are copied.

Replication of routines happens because social organizations tend to copy well-established routines with a proven track-record (Miner and Raghavan, 1999; Nelson and Winter, 1982; Romanelli, 1999; Winter, 2003, 2005; Warglien, 2002). A social organization also replicates its own routines when it expands (Galunic and Weeks, 2002; Nelson and Winter, 1982; Metcalfe, 1998). Even when new routines are developed, prior routines tend to determine the feasible range of behavioural options that the organization can adopt (Cohen and Levinthal, 1990). Social organizations tend to revise prior routines rather than developing entirely new routines from scratch. That is, a significant portion of the prior routines of a social organization must be carried forward (replication of own routines), in order to support the development of new routines.

The remainder of the chapter proceeds as follows. Section two considers the nature and function of habits and routines. Section three examines the role of habits and routines in evolutionary theory. Evolutionary theories of cultural and economic change usually turn on the principles of variation, selection and information transfer. Variation and information transfer are concepts that readily capture cultural and economic phenomena. However, a critical issue is to adequately capture selection processes in cultural and economic evolution, which is therefore considered in more detail. In particular, the concepts of an interactor and a replicator are introduced to characterize the relation between social organizations (interactors) and routines (replicators) in selection processes. Section four briefly considers how prominent theories of organizational evolution capture what we know about habits and routines, and section five concludes.

2   The nature and function of habits and routines

Evolutionary theories of economic change build on a fundamental postulate that organizational behaviour is routinized (Aldrich, 1999; Nelson and Winter, 1982; Winter, 1971, 2005). Organizations have dispositions to engage in particular activities in response to particular contextual cues. This postulate has now become firmly rooted in the claim that individual behaviour is habituated. Habits are the fundamental, individual-level building blocks from which organizational routines emerge. Organizational routines are composed of individual habits that are orchestrated such that the execution of one habit triggers the next. In this way, subtasks can be bundled to accomplish efficient work procedures involving a group of people (Pentland and Rueter, 1994; Zollo and Winter, 2002).

Additionally, habits also have broader functions in supporting individual behaviour. Habits can be described as individual-level dispositions to engage in a particular behaviour in response to stable contextual cues. Recent advances in psychological research support this claim (Aarts and Dijksterhuis, 2000; Verplanken et al., 1997; Wood and Neal, 2007).

A habit is here defined as an individual-level disposition to behave or think in a particular way in a particular class of situations.[4] Habits are dispositions. This characterization of habits is consistent with a definition of habits that has recently re-emerged in psychological research (Wood and Neal, 2007). It is also consistent with a common definition of disposition concepts in formal logic as the assignment from a set of possible events to a subset of actual events (Malzkorn, 2001). Thus, a habit can be viewed as a subset of actual behaviours (thoughts) realized from a larger set of possible behaviours (thoughts) in a particular class of situations.[5] This translates into a useful description of habits as conditional probabilities, i.e. the probability that a particular behaviour will occur in response to a stable contextual cue.

Habits and routines characterize a very large chunk of the empirical reality in business organizations and, more broadly, in social life. Habits and routines pervade everyday life to such an extent that it may be difficult, even upon reflection, to comprehend their presence and influence. Some examples of common habits mentioned in various literatures include nail-biting habits, drug habits, purchasing habits, eating habits, lifestyle habits, reading habits, work habits and moral habits. Many daily activities are performed habitually in the sense that they are enacted almost daily and usually in the same location (Wood and Neal, 2007). This regularity in behaviour promotes a smooth, efficient handling of tasks without giving much thought to what one is doing (Aarts and Dijksterhuis, 2000; Hawkins and Hoch, 1992; Verplanken et al., 1997; Wood and Neal, 2007).

According to recent psychological research, habits represent repetition-induced shifts in the control of behaviour: cognitive mechanisms guiding behaviour shift from thought about intentions to an automatic mode where behaviours are triggered by stable contextual cues (Aarts and Dijksterhuis, 2000; Wood and Neal, 2007; Yin et al., 2004). As a habit becomes established, even complex sequences of behaviour can be smoothly executed in a near automatic way (Wood and Neal, 2007). This could apply to purchasing habits (Grunert, 1996; Hawkins and Hoch, 1992), travel mode choices (Aarts and Dijksterhuis, 2000; Verplanken et al., 1997) and a wealth of bodily habits.

As defined here, the actual repeated response to a contextual cue, e.g. the actual repeated purchase of fast-food or the actual repeated actions involved in a paint job, are behaviours. These behaviours might well be rooted in habits, in which case the disposition to purchase fast-food or the disposition to move the paint brush in a particular way, each in particular circumstances, count as habits.

Habits are defined as dispositions rather than sets of behaviours or thoughts (Hodgson, 2003; Hodgson and Knudsen, 2004a, 2004b). A habit is a disposition, which may, or may not, be expressed in current behaviour or thought. Only in the presence of an appropriate stimulus or context will a habit give rise to behaviour or thought. A habit is triggered by a cue; it is not necessarily used all the time. In the absence of the cue that triggers a particular habit, it may lie unused for a long time without withering away. A habit of buckling up or purchasing fast-food is not necessarily exercised every day. However, habits may become rusty if they are not exercised on a regular basis. Delays in habit exercise can, in conjunction with weak incentives and instability in the context of behaviour, lead to the erosion of established habits and undermine the formation of new habits.

The degree to which a particular subset of actual behaviours is repeated within a stable context provides a straightforward definition of the strength of a habit (Aarts and Dijksterhuis, 2000; Verplanken et al., 1997; Wood and Neal, 2007). The inverse of habit strength is the sequential variety of behaviours, recently suggested as a promising measure of organizational work processes (Pentland, 2003).[6] Both the stability of the context of behaviour and intentions are important determinants of habit strength. Strong habits reflect frequent repetition within a stable context whereas weak habits reflect infrequent repetition, unstable contexts, or both (Aarts and Dijksterhuis, 2000; Wood and Neal, 2007; Yin et al., 2004). Intentions might increase habit strength (Aarts et al., 1999). For example, Postrel and Rumelt (1996) describe how the presence of a daughter motivated a shift in the habit of buckling up: 'After many years the habit of fastening seatbelts was established, and he did not revert to his old ways' (Postrel and Rumelt, 1996, p. 83).

Habits can only be observed when they are exercised. If an individual's behaviour is observed and a notable regularity, a pattern, is discovered, this points to a habit, or a bundle of habits, as the source of the observed pattern. When thoughts are patterned, as evidenced in the similarity of the mental models invoked in problem-solving tasks, it also points to the influence of a habit. Without habit, behaviour and thought would be erratic.[7]

The development of habits

We are not born with habits and routines; they emerge in social life. Both empirical research (Aarts and Dijksterhuis, 2000; Arnould, 1989; Cohen and Bacdayan, 1994; Wood and Neal, 2007; Yin et al., 2004) and simulation studies (Hodgson and Knudsen, 2004a) show that repetition is the immediate, proximal cause of habit formation. When behaviour is repeated in the face of a particular situation, a persistent habit gradually emerges. If a similar situation is met in the future, the habit in question is energized. Repetition is a proximal cause of the formation of habits, but why do individuals repeat behaviours and thoughts?

A broad explanation involves constraints and incentives. Constraints in the environment can enforce repetition. If only one route is open for the driver of a car for a long period of time, there will be repetition. In consequence, a disposition to use this route in the future can emerge. Also inborn constraints are likely to promote repetition of both behaviour and thought. Because of inborn constraints, the human capacity to process and analyse information is rather limited. Therefore, individuals acquire habits to guide choice.

Problem solving is initially controlled by intentions (Wood and Neal, 2007). When the individual finds a satisfactory answer to a problem that frequently arises, there is a tendency to repeat the behaviour or thought. This procedure economizes on limited cognitive resources (Simon, 1955). Gradually, with each repetition, the individual forms a disposition to express the same behaviour or thought in response to the requirements of a particular environment. With repetition, the control of behaviour shifts from cognitive mechanisms to an automatic mode (Aarts & Dijksterhuis, 2000; Arnould, 1989; Grunert, 1996; Verplanken et al., 1997; Wood & Neal, 2007). When habits have been firmly established, they tend to persist because the control of behaviour is beyond conscious interference.

A further implication of limited human capacity to process information is that decision makers satisfice. Search for alternatives will stop when the first reasonable solution has been found (Simon, 1955). A common corollary is that you 'should not change a winning team'. This formulation of satisficing is a cornerstone in evolutionary thinking on organizations (Nelson & Winter, 1982; Winter, 1971, 2003, 2005). It suggests that firms *begin* searching for new alternatives only when a significant problem appears. When things are going well, the current way of doing things is repeated (March & Simon, 1958; March, 1988; Greve, 2003; Winter, 2003, 2005). Thus, satisficing promotes reinforcement of habits and routines in good times and the disruption of habits and routines in bad times. A (perceived) failure to meet targets at higher organizational levels can be contagious in disrupting routines also at lower levels (Perlow, 1999).

Incentives are important in habit formation, complementing the role of constraints. Not only do individuals acquire habits to guide choice, they also develop automatic behaviour to avoid pitfalls and to overcome resistance to behaviour that would otherwise be distasteful (Postrel & Rumelt, 1996). In both cases, a critical aspect of habit formation is that delayed rewards provide weak incentives for the repetition of behaviour (Postrel & Rumelt, 1996). By contrast, immediate rewards reinforce the repetition of behaviour or thought. In simple reinforcement learning, organization members find solution paths on the basis of sequences of immediate rewards (Sutton and Barto, 2000). With a stable context of rewards, organization members will then repeatedly follow these solution paths and build up a disposition to do so in the future. Self-imposed constraints can help overcome weak incentives in the absence of immediate rewards. They promote the construction of solution paths on the basis of well-rehearsed habits, e.g. prepare a memo after each customer call even though one is only rewarded when the contract is signed.

Habits are not developed in isolation; they emerge in social life. In human life, common social constraints and incentives reinforce particular behaviours. When deviants are severely punished, there is an incentive to imitate opinion leaders and majorities. When outcomes are uncertain, there is an incentive to imitate successful individuals. Yet other habits are imitated without much awareness. Gestures, linguistic terms (old chap, yo!) and many other habits can be contagious. As we imitate others within a stable context, we repeat particular behaviours and gradually build up habits. In a similar way, routines get transmitted among organizations through interorganizational imitation (Miner and Raghavan, 1999; Romanelli, 1999).

Organizational routines

The difference between habits and routines lies in the level of analysis. Whereas habits pertain to individual dispositions, routines are organizational-level dispositions, which comprise the collective set of habits in a sequence of interlocking, reciprocally-triggered actions in response to particular cues (Cohen and Bacdayan, 1994; Dosi et al., 2000; Feldman and Pentland, 2003; Hodgson and Knudsen, 2004a, 2004b; Pentland and Rueter, 1994).[8] *A routine is here defined as a sequence of individual habits, with the execution of one habit triggering the next, such that a group of people acquires a common disposition to behave or think in a particular way in a particular class of situations.*

Whenever a football team attacks, Arnold kicks the ball high and the rest of the team rushes ahead to favourable target positions. Whenever the interview of a job candidate ends, the secretary, Bob, prepares a summary review. Whenever Chris completes the assembly of a piece of furniture, Dick takes over and applies coating. In all of these cases, individual habits give rise to behaviour or thought in response to particular cues provided by other individuals.

The definition of a routine as an organization-level disposition is firmly rooted in the human individual. That is, individual habits are the microfoundations of organizational routines. However, a routine remains a useful organization-level concept because the way individuals interact gives rise to complementarities so that a routine cannot be reduced to individual contributions. There is a recursive relation between routines and individual habits. An emergent routine will influence the way individuals interact, which in turn changes the routine. Such a process of circular positive feedback in the formation of traffic conventions was modelled in Hodgson and

Knudsen (2004a). Even though the formation of a traffic convention influenced individuals, there were no mysterious social forces or types of causality involved in this model. Individual habits, individual behaviour and individual cognition were the sole causes at work. Similarly, a routine, as defined here, originates in causes that can be traced to the human individual.[9] Routines are *driven* solely by individual habituations, although enabled by a particular organizational context.

The central function of habits and routines is identical. It is to store ready-made solutions to problems that frequently arise. The difference lies in the level of analysis. Habits contain private knowledge, whereas routines contain knowledge that is common to a group of people. The habitual eating of fast-food alone in your office is private, whereas the routine of kick and rush football is common to a particular team of players. Routines emerge at the organizational level through repeated interaction among multiple actors (Cohen and Bacdayan, 1994; Dosi et al., 2000; Feldman & Pentland, 2003; Hodgson and Knudsen, 2004b; Nelson and Winter, 1982; Pentland and Rueter, 1994). Individuals cooperate in response to problems that are faced by their organization. Organization members coordinate their activities, and their behaviours and expressions of thought provide cues, which can trigger particular behaviours and thoughts of other organization members (Feldman and Pentland, 2003; Pentland and Rueter, 1994).

Not only do routines emerge through interaction among individuals, but they also structure organizational behaviour (Cohen and Bacdayan, 1994; Hodgson and Knudsen, 2004b, 2004c; Pentland and Rueter, 1994). Coordination of individual habits is of the essence in the formation of organizational routines (Winter, 2005). Routines promote coordination, which is a particularly important property when organizations face uncertain task environments (Becker and Knudsen, 2004; Cohen and Bacdayan, 1994; Hodgson and Knudsen, 2004a). The need to achieve tight coordination among a group of people adds a further level of error control and reliability to organizational routines as compared with habits.

However, in order to pass on routines, the mechanisms that secure coordination among agents must also be conveyed. For this reason, we would expect that some organizational routines – where coordination is accomplished through numerous well-rehearsed behavioural cues – can be very difficult to pass on, even with the help of language. Workgroups and management teams often have distinct routines that are not easily transferred to new organizations even in the case of mergers and acquisitions (Aldrich, 1999; Argote et al., 1990; Finkelstein and Haleblian, 2002).

Organizational routines can easily be disrupted by inattentive managers, and they appear difficult to transfer from one organization to the next

(Aldrich, 1999; Argote et al., 1990; Finkelstein and Haleblian, 2002). The flip side of this observation is that routines, once firmly established, will have a tendency to be self-reinforcing because they involve coordination among a group of people (Nelson and Winter, 1982; Winter, 2005). A work-group typically coordinates individual behaviours such that the completion of one action reliably triggers a disposition in the next worker to engage in a new behaviour. Deviants will disrupt the smooth execution of work processes. To avoid punishment or replacement, organization members have strong incentives to carefully repeat successful ways of doing things. Routines will tend to promote an efficient execution of tasks, and they will tend to be very stable once they are established (a curse in turbulent environments).

Three essential properties of habits and routines
Three essential properties are common to all kinds of habits and routines in social populations: they are persistent, they multiply, and they contain ready-made solutions to common, recurrent problems. First, habits and routines are persistent. This property has been established in empirical studies in historical, diffusion, psychological and organizational research. For example, historical research shows that habits and routines transplanted from England to North America during the great migrations around the beginning of the seventeenth century persist even into the present day (Fischer, 1989). Diffusion research shows, right from the first empirical studies, that it can take years, even decades, before new habits and routines replace old ones (Rogers, 1983; Attewell, 1992). Medical research shows that both unhealthy and healthy habits are persistent (Macready, 1999). Psychological research further uncovers the underlying mechanisms (repetition-induced shifts in the control of behaviour) that explain the persistence of habits and routines (Wood and Neal, 2007). Organizational research confirms the general picture. Routines in business organizations are often very persistent, even to an extent that they promote inertia (Baum and Amburgey, 2002; Benner and Tushman, 2002; Hannan and Freeman, 1989).

Second, habits and routines multiply as they spread in social populations (Attewell, 1992; Fischer, 1989; Greve, 2002; Miner and Raghavan, 1999; Rogers, 1983). Some habits, including gestures and many bodily habits, proliferate as if they were copied without much reflection or conscious resolve. Other habits are conveyed through education, involving instruction, feedback and example. Yet others spread by the sway of social status and authority. Habits further disseminate indirectly as a consequence of adopting new technologies, such as automated dishwashers and Internet connections in private homes. Routines spread in a similar way in business organizations (Attewell, 1992). A wide range of habits and routines spread in social populations and a wide range of mechanisms are involved.

Third, habits and routines contain ready-made solutions to common problems in a stable context, a claim supported in a large body of empirical studies (Aldrich, 1999; Cohen and Bacdayan, 1994; Wood and Neal, 2007).[10] This insight has grown out of the behavioural theory of choice (Simon, 1955; March and Simon, 1958; Cyert and March, 1963), advancing the view that decision makers are endowed with a limited capacity to both gather information about alternatives and evaluate the consequences of these alternatives. This view became one of the central pillars upon which the evolutionary economics research programme was erected (Nelson and Winter, 1982).

In the presence of bounded rationality, there is an advantage in developing habits and routines that contain ready-made, satisfactory solutions to problems confronting individuals. Habits and routines contain encoded suboptimal instructions for behaviour or thought that are expressed when similar situations arise (Verplanken et al., 1997). In addition to limits on rationality, a further source of suboptimality in habits and routines is that they contain frozen solutions to problems within a context that might require new solutions.

Such problem-solving habits and routines can be further refined or replaced if their consequences are not found to be entirely satisfactory as judged by their carriers (March, 1988; Nelson and Winter, 1982). Evolutionary theories of cultural and economic change thus emphasize a backward-looking logic according to which habits and routines are retained, refined or replaced in response to their (perceived) consequences (March, 1988; March et al., 2000; Nelson and Winter, 1982). A population of habits changes as some existing habits are refined or discarded, while others are adopted or generated *de novo*. That is, a population of habits adapts to its environment through selection processes involving differential elimination of habits (subset selection) combined with differential adoption of new habits (diffusion) and differential replication of habits (generative selection).

3   The role of habits and routines in evolutionary theory

The evolutionary theories considered here are widely accepted as illuminating and useful explanations of cultural and economic change. The nature and function of habits and routines make them basic elements of such theories. Examples include *evolutionary theories of economic, organizational, and technical change* (Aldrich, 1999; Bowles, 2004; Bergstrom, 2002; Hannan and Freeman, 1989; Hayek, 1988; Hodgson, 1993; Knudsen, 2002a; Levinthal, 1997; Nelson and Winter, 1982; Metcalfe, 1998; Mokyr,

1990; Samuelson, 1997; van de Ven and Poole, 1995; Vromen, 1995; Witt, 2003) and *evolutionary theories of cultural change* (Boyd and Richerson, 1985; Durham, 1991; Knudsen, 2002b; Mead, 1964).[11] Such theories have a long pedigree (Hodgson, 1993, 2004; Richards, 1987) and are today frequently used in most of the disciplines and fields within and bordering the social sciences.

Evolutionary theories are useful in providing a causal explanation of an observed history, such as the origins, change and character of human culture – e.g. language, art and technology – that happens as an adjustment to various social and environmental factors. Within a more narrow perspective, evolutionary theories are useful in providing a causal explanation of the origins, change and character of interesting features of economic organizations – e.g. organizational structures, administrative procedures and allocations of property rights – as a result of adjustment to specific economic factors. Even though the particular content of evolutionary theories of cultural and economic change is very different, there is a shared overlap. All of these theories include three core principles: variation, selection and information transfer.

Three core principles: variation, selection and information transfer
The empirical evidence bearing on cultural and economic change speaks clearly in favour of the existence of processes involving variation, selection and information transfer. Even so, the applicability of these concepts in social populations has been the source of much dispute.[12] One line of argument is that evolutionary theory is inappropriate as an explanation for cultural and economic phenomena (Rosenberg, 1994). A less dismissive line of argument views variation, inheritance (information transfer) and selection as biological concepts and suggests we should drop one or the other (e.g. Witt (2004) plays down the role of selection). These arguments are important reminders that biological analogies should not be used slavishly or unquestioningly to explain cultural and economic change (Hull et al., 2001; Witt, 2003, 2004).

However, in addition to being at odds with the empirical evidence, both lines of argument dispute the large number of academic studies that, across a very wide range of fields within the social sciences, find an evolutionary approach appropriate and useful. Upon closer inspection, such evolutionary theories of cultural and economic change usually turn on the principles of variation, selection and information transfer.

There are abundant and readily observable variations, both in social populations (e.g. in norms, tastes and preferences) and in populations of business organizations (e.g. in business models, organizational structures and product offerings). Even though most variations are short-lived, an indication of selection processes at work, the persistence of some variations points to the transfer of information, even across many human generations.

Selection processes in cultural and economic evolution
Price's (1995) influential definition of selection includes three forms of selection that occur at the social level: subset selection, diffusion and generative selection. Subset selection involves the elimination of members of a population. In its cleanest form, such as the death of animals or the bankruptcy of firms, subset selection involves elimination through extinction (Hodgson and Knudsen, 2005b). Diffusion processes are also common in economic and organizational evolution. They include the differential adoption of new cultural ways, farming methods, aircraft designs, medical practices and ways of doing business (Nelson et al., 2004; Rogers, 1983; Vincenti, 1994). Subset selection and diffusion are complementary processes. For example, bankrupt firms exit an industry and are replaced with new entrants whose properties partly come from imitation of existing firms (Nelson and Winter, 1982).

Subset selection and diffusion are both very different from the concept of generative selection. The concept of generative selection that follows from its general mathematical definition (Price, 1995; Frank, 1998; Hofbauer and Sigmund, 1998; Knudsen, 2004) can be described verbally in the following way: selection involves an anterior set of entities, each interacting with their environment and somehow being transformed into a posterior set, where all members of the posterior set are sufficiently similar to some members of the anterior set, and where the resulting frequencies of posterior entities depend upon their properties in the environmental context.[13] Through generative selection, a set of entities, a population, will gradually adapt in response to an environmental factor (or a complex of environmental factors).

The mathematical definition of selection introduces the concept of fitness. Fitness is a useful simplification that allows powerful analyses of population change by transforming the processes of replication and interaction into a mathematical idiom. Fitness is defined as the mapping between amounts of a population property at two time steps. A difference in fitness is a difference in the frequency of a population property between two points in time. This fitness concept is an abstract technical measure; it has no empirical definition (de Jong, 1994). Fitness omits any detailed consideration of development, interaction and replication. It is the task of the researcher to specify the relation between development, interaction and replication and to identify the components that best capture this relation within the particular empirical domain of interest. The empirical fitness components clearly differ from cultural evolution to biological evolution and they differ within particular domains of biological evolution and cultural evolution.

A very common idea of economic selection is the change that happens because some firms enter an industry and other firms are eliminated because of bankruptcy. This is an example of the elimination of firms through subset selection combined with the appearance of new entities through diffusion. Such exit and entry can give rise to a change in the average value of a population property, for example the size of firms, the vertical span of organizational structures and the content of administrative procedures. If the change in such population properties happens because of selection, these properties must remain stable. We will then see a significant covariance between fitness and the property in question. In order to provide a sharp (causal) explanation, the underlying empirical sources of fitness must be identified. Considering organizational structures, we must, for example, explain why firms with hierarchical structures exit (rather than change their structure) and why firms with flat structures enter.

Obviously, a change in a population property can also occur because of error in the transfer of information, in processes where an entity develops, or as a result of individual experimentation. Firms and other social organizations can alter their organizational structures and, in principle, any other feature. The properties of biological entities change because of error in the transfer of genetic information and are co-determined by the influence of environmental factors during stages of development. Both conceptually and empirically, the change caused by selection must be sharply distinguished from such change that happens when information is transferred, in processes where an entity develops, or as a result of individual experimentation. Such transmission and innovation effects alter the property of individual entities when the population is held constant. In contrast, selection effects alter the composition of the population, but hold constant the properties of the individual entities.

Evolutionary theories are useful in explaining cultural and economic change in a population whose properties (such as routines) remain fairly stable (Nelson & Winter, 1982; Winter, 1971). As we have seen, a plethora of empirical studies support the claim that organizational routines are fundamental sources of persistence in various organizational features. Therefore selection can operate on a population of business organizations by gradually changing their routines in response to an environmental factor.

Even though subset selection, diffusion and generative selection are all encompassed by the general mathematical definition developed by Price (1995), there is an important difference that sets generative selection apart from the other two. Only generative selection can accommodate an explanation of how new variation is created. In contrast, subset selection removes variation and diffusion relies on unexplained sources that somehow create new variation. Since some cultural and economic selection processes have remarkable endurance, the most likely *explanation* is that they are instances of generative selection involving a coupled process of interaction and replication. Such a process can, in principle, generate the variation necessary to continue indefinitely. This is good reason to consider generative selection involving replicating habits and routines in more detail.

Generative selection involving replicating habits and routines
In generative selection, the environmental interaction of an entity causes differential replication. Habits and routines are persistent containers of encoded instructions for behaviour or thought. When this information is passed on to a new copy, habits and routines function as replicators if they are causally involved in producing a new copy that is similar to the old in all relevant respects (Aunger, 2002; Godfrey-Smith, 2000; Sperber, 2000).[14] This is often the case (Hodgson and Knudsen, 2004b, 2004c). Genes are paradigm examples of replicators, but also other things, such as habits and routines in cultural and economic evolution, can be replicators. The qualities that make up good replicators are longevity, fecundity and copying fidelity (Dawkins, 1976).

Clearly, in regard to copying fidelity – understood as the reliable transfer of information contained in replicators – habits and routines are much inferior to genes. In particular, for routines, with portions of the behavioural disposition stored in different persons, having varying histories and incentives, the notion of copying a routine's representation with anything like the fidelity of genetic copying seems improbable. Also in regard to longevity – understood as the persistence of information contained in replicators – habits and routines are much inferior to genes. But habits and routines have degrees of persistence and copying fidelity that are sufficient to warrant their status as replicators in economic evolution (Hodgson and Knudsen, 2004b; Metcalfe, 1998; Winter and Szulanski, 2001).

When the lifestyle habits of opinion leaders or the work habits of farmers are differentially replicated, these people function as interactors. More generally, an interactor is an entity that interacts as a cohesive whole with its environment in a way that causes differential replication (Hull, 1990). The human individual is obviously an interactor in social life. Notably, interaction among human individuals involves more than biological attributes. Human individuals adopt social roles (e.g. friend, foe, thief) that are part of meaningful social interaction. Above the level of the human individual there is a case for regarding firms and similarly cohesive organizations as interactors (Hodgson and Knudsen, 2004b).

The designation of routines as replicators and firms as interactors helps characterize the correspondence between a firm and its routines in selection processes. The interaction of business firms (competition, cooperation, coordination) causes an adjustment of the frequencies in a distribution of routines (Nelson and Winter, 1982) in response to demands of the business environment. That is, a firm interacts as a cohesive whole with its environment in a way that causes differential replication of its routines. In consequence, some firms shrink and others grow (Metcalfe, 1998; Nelson and Winter, 1982; Winter, 1971).

The concepts of a replicator and interactor are placeholders for real entities engaging in particular kinds of coupled processes. These concepts cannot and should not adequately describe what a biological entity such as a dog, or a social entity such as a firm, is. Their role is to characterize generative selection processes. Generative selection involves repeated cycles of replication, variation and environmental interaction so structured that the environmental interaction causes replication to be differential (Hull et al., 2001).

In cultural and economic change, the differential replication of habits and routines appears to be an important phenomenon. Recently, it has been worked out how both observable and unobservable habits (habits of thought) replicate (Hodgson and Knudsen, 2004b, 2004c). Two core processes of information transfer are involved. First, the replication of a habit involves the transfer of a rudimentary habit from one human individual to the next. Second, the replication of a habit involves the transfer of *developmental capacity*, i.e., the capacity to develop a rudimentary habit so it becomes an established disposition that reliably gives rise to behaviour whenever the cue in question is present.

Considering the replication of organizational routines, the developmental aspect becomes more critical. Routines involve a group of people whose individual habits are building blocks that support a stable pattern of interlocking, reciprocally triggered sequences of behaviours or thoughts (Cohen and Bacdayan, 1994). When routines are replicated, the transfer of information includes the transfer of a capacity to develop a bundle of individual habits into established dispositions that reliably promotes behaviour or thought in response to particular cues. The cues in question are the behaviours or thoughts of other organization members. That is, the replication of a routine involves the transfer of the capacity to develop a set of rudimentary habits so they become a set of established dispositions that reliably trigger each other. The result is an observable recurrent pattern of interaction among people.[15] Notably, a routine is a reciprocally-triggered disposition rather than an observable recurrent pattern of behaviour.

Generally, the copying of complex replicators, such as routines, involves the transfer of a multitude of information because many elements and their constituent coordinating mechanisms must be copied. With complex replicators the efficient transfer of information favours a truncated highly symbolic format (Szathmáry and Maynard Smith, 1997). Therefore, the copying of routines and other complex replicators becomes more incomplete, and the role of development becomes more significant as a process that produces interacting entities. The rudimentary structures of complex replicators are transferred through incomplete copying; the capacity to interact and replicate develops through processes that can be emergent as well as deliberate.[16]

Families and firms are organizations in which routines emerge, partly as a result of deliberate design. Such routines spread across time and space and in some instances they qualify as replicators. However, because routines are complex replicators, organizational routines are usually transferred through incomplete copying. In addition to overlap among key personnel, a template that can be used as a reference point in the development of a copy has been reported as critical in routine replication. Such support in the development of routines lies at the core of the 'McDonalds approach' where a successful business model is replicated in a large number of similar outlets that deliver a product or perform a service (Winter and Szulanski, 2001). More generally, as emphasized in the literature on entrepreneurship and knowledge transfer (Agarwal et al., 2004; Aldrich, 1999; Helfat and Lieberman, 2002), new firms in a number of cases, such as spin-offs, spin-outs, joint ventures and new subsidiaries, replicate a significant part of the routines of established firms.

According to the empirical evidence, routines function as replicators in many cases. When the interaction of social organizations leads to differential replication of routines, it is a generative selection process. We have thus arrived at a characterization of an important role of organizational routines in evolutionary theory. They are replicators in generative selection processes.[17]

Adapting the specification from Hull et al. (2001), *generative selection processes involving features of higher-order entities such as families and firms can be defined as repeated cycles of replication, variation and environmental interaction so structured that the environmental interaction causes the replication of routines to be differential.*[18] When social organizations interact, their features have consequences, which lead to changes in their routines, which in turn alter their features. Similarly, generative selection processes involving social features of human individuals are defined as repeated cycles of replication, variation and environmental interaction so structured that the environmental interaction causes the replication of *habits* to be differential.

In summary, the role of replication and interaction concern the mechanisms producing generative selection. Human individuals are interactors and the way they interact causes differential replication of their habits. Families, firms and other social organizations are higher-level interactors, where interactions cause differential replication of their routines. Routines are more complex replicators composed of a bundle of individual habits. Therefore, the developmental phase is much more critical for the replication of organizational routines than it is when habits are copied.

4   Routines in prominent theories of organizational evolution

Prominent organizational variants of evolutionary theory include the learning theory of March and co-authors (Levinthal and March, 1981; March, 1988; March et al., 2000), Nelson and Winter's (1982) evolutionary theory of economic change, and population ecology (Hannan and Freeman, 1989).[19] These literatures share an emphasis on habitual and routinized behaviour even though they address distinct issues at different levels of analysis.

March and co-authors portray intraorganizational learning processes as routine-based behaviour that adapts to experience. The process is driven by the relation between targets and performance. Higher organizational performance relative to a target leads to less behavioural variation, and vice versa. Thus, routines can be viewed as an endogenous outcome of enduring success. Various work on organizational routines is based on a similar proposition that routines emerge as a result of problem-solving activities.[20] Notably, the learning theory of March and co-authors can be viewed as an instance of selection processes because it involves a population of organizations (or decision makers) with concurrent variation on important attributes, and with replacement of those who do not meet a performance criterion (e.g. March, 1988).

The learning theory of March and co-authors also lies at the heart of Nelson and Winter's (1982) evolutionary theory of economic change.[21] In the face of adverse environmental conditions, firms adapt their existing routines or, if the conditions are severe enough, they search for new routines to replace their existing routines. Successful firms will tend to be more routinized; failing firms less routinized. The generation of new variation in behaviour is caused by failure-induced problem-solving activities (problemistic search). Routines are retainers of the firm's behavioural procedures, the way it devises organizational solutions as a basis for production. When the current solutions do not appear to suit its purpose any longer, the firm engages in risky search for new ways of doing things. Thus, negative feedback induces a process where existing routines are adapted or even replaced. In the latter case, the change in the population of routines held by a firm can be viewed as a selection process. The firm's interaction with its environment results in negative feedback causing differential elimination of the existing routines (subset selection) as well as differential adoption of new routines (diffusion). In consequence, the firm's population of routines can change, as a result either of adaptation or of selection.

At a level above the individual firm, there is market selection. Failing firms tend to contract; their routines become unstable and lose weight relative to other routines present in the relevant population of firms (e.g. industry). The flip side of this process is that successful firms expand; their routines become stable and gain in weight relative to other routines. Drawing on behavioural learning theory associated with Herbert Simon, James March, Richard Cyert and others, Nelson and Winter (1982) assume that positive feedback leads to increased routinization. In addition, the growth of a successful firm implies that its existing routines are somehow self-expanded. Here we have, then, a possible case of generative selection with environmental interaction causing differential replication of a firm's existing routines (a process that gains in force when the firm is successful). Should the failing firms be able to copy the routines of a successful firm, generative selection may also include this case.

Population ecology, developed by Hannan and Freeman (1989) and co-workers, focuses on the foundings and failures of organizations, while assuming that their behavioural repertoires are (relatively) inert. Inertia in behavioural repertoires, it is argued, is caused by its effects. Observations from a large number of empirical studies appear to support the claim that change is usually detrimental to organizational survival. It is therefore assumed that selection processes increase inertia because procedures promoting change are dangerous and will tend to be eliminated. Even though the empirical observation that organizational change tends to be hazardous is also consistent with behavioural learning theory, population ecology draws its own conclusion. Population ecology views routines as gene-like containers of a frozen representation of the imprint an organization received at the time it was founded. In consequence, population ecology views organizational change as a result of differential elimination of organizations (subset selection) combined with the appearance of organizations with new features (diffusion). Notably, the changing environmental conditions that give rise to new organizational features tend to be left unexplained. However, recent work reported in Aldrich (1999) and elsewhere have begun to unravel the causes underlying the appearance of new (populations of) organizations. For example, Aldrich (1999, ch. 9) has an extensive discussion of an evolutionary view on where new populations come from, how they grow (or not), and how such growth is conditioned on wider sociopolitical conditions. Such work indicates that generative selection, involving a causal relation between interaction and replication, may be a critical explanatory principle, a view that is broadly supported in recent work in organization studies (Aldrich and Kenworthy, 1999; Galunic and Weeks, 2002; Warglien, 2002).

This broad survey of organizational routines in prominent theories of organizational evolution indicates common ground in viewing routines as persistent containers of behavioural repertoires that differentially gain in frequency (multiply) in response to environmental feedback. There are marked differences in the way environmental feedback is thought to bring about organizational changes. Environmental feedback can be viewed as a selection force causing differential elimination of organizations that hold inert routines, or it can be viewed as a force adjusting the variation among behavioural repertoires, which in turn forms the basis of internal adaptation and selection processes that change organizational routines. Population ecology favours the view that routines are inert, gene-like entities, while evolutionary economics in the spirit of Nelson and Winter and behavioural learning theory of March and co-authors view routines as subject to both adaptation and selection processes.

5 Conclusion

This chapter has considered three features of habits and routines accounting for their central role in evolutionary theories of cultural and economic change. Habits and routines are persistent, they multiply, and they contain ready-made solutions to common, recurrent problems. That is, habits and routines are stable containers of information that can be transferred in selection processes.

Even though the particular content of evolutionary theories of cultural and economic change is very different, there is a shared overlap. All of these theories include three Darwinian core principles: variation, selection and information transfer, which appear to be common to selection processes both in the social and the biological domain (Aldrich, 1999; Hodgson and Knudsen, 2005a; Winter, 1987).

Variation and information transfer are concepts that readily capture cultural and economic phenomena. However, a critical issue is to capture selection processes adequately (Axelrod and Cohen, 1999; Knudsen, 2004; Winter, 1971). Selection requires a stable component. Whether evolutionary theories are useful in explaining cultural and economic change, therefore, depends on the existence of a stable component. Organizational routines are fundamental sources of persistence in various organizational features, for which reason they possess the required stability. Therefore, selection can operate on routines.

Selection processes lie at the core of cultural and economic change. Through selection, a population of business organizations can gradually adapt in response to an environmental factor. Three forms of selection commonly occur at the social level: subset selection, diffusion and generative selection. Subset selection is a process in which differential elimination of entities is caused by their environmental interaction. A common instance of subset selection at the social level is the elimination of firms through bankruptcy. Diffusion is a process in which there is differential adoption of new entities. For example, diffusion occurs when bankrupt firms exit an industry and are replaced with new firms whose properties are partly generated from imitation of existing firms.

An important difference sets generative selection apart from both subset selection and diffusion. Only generative selection can accommodate an explanation of how new variation is created. Since some cultural and economic selection processes have remarkable endurance, the most likely explanation is that they are instances of generative selection involving a coupled process of interaction and replication. Such a process can, in principle, generate the variation necessary to continue indefinitely. Therefore, generative selection involving replicating habits and routines was considered in more detail. Generative selection involving habits and routines was defined in the following way: the environmental interaction of individual human beings gives rise to differential replication of *habits*; similarly, the environmental interaction of families, firms and other organizations gives rise to differential replication of *routines*.

A broad survey of organizational routines in prominent theories of organizational evolution indicates common ground in viewing routines as persistent containers of behavioural repertoires that differentially gain in frequency (multiply) in response to environmental feedback. This review included the learning theory of March and co-authors, Nelson and Winter's evolutionary theory of economic change, and population ecology.

There are marked differences in these theories regarding the way environmental feedback is thought to bring about organizational changes. Environmental feedback can be viewed as a selection force causing differential elimination of organizations that hold inert routines, or it can be viewed as a force adjusting the variation among behavioural repertoires, which in turn forms the basis of internal adaptation and selection processes changing organizational routines. Population ecology favours the view that routines are inert, gene-like entities, while evolutionary economics in the spirit of Nelson and Winter and behavioural learning theory of March and co-authors views routines as subject to both adaptation and selection, including the possibility of generative selection.

As should be clear, however, there is no straightforward analogy between the details of biological genes and the details of habits and routines. Not only do organizations to some extent choose and revise their routines, the human storage of habits also seems to be quite un-gene-like and, as a result of this, the details of persistence, expression-in-context, and transfer for habits and routines are very different from biological evolution.

Even though the general model of evolution has only one set of core principles (variation, selection and information transfer), the details are obviously very different in the case of economic and biological evolution. At the present time, little is known about the finer details of economic evolution. Open questions include the following two: what is the nature of the possibly coupled selection processes that take place within and between organizations? In what way are habits and routines transferred (replicated), and what are the factors determining the reliability of the transfer process?

The present chapter has focused on the central role of habits and routines in evolutionary theories of cultural and economic change. There has been considerable progress in research on this issue and there is considerable promise in efforts to uncover the details of cultural and economic selection processes.

Notes

1. The author thanks Howard E. Aldrich, Marion Blute, Michael R. Cohen, Nicolai J. Foss, Geoffrey M. Hodgson, David L. Hull, Daniel A. Levinthal, James G. March, Richard R. Nelson, Stephen Rosenbaum, Sidney G. Winter, Ulrich Witt and Wendy Wood for comments and discussions that have influenced this chapter in many kinds of ways. Comments from the editor, Markus C. Becker, and an anonymous reviewer are appreciated. Responsibility for any error is mine.
2. Habits have been studied in medical and psychological research during the last 100 years or more. It continues to be a topic of great interest to medical and psychological research. The empirical evidence on habits in the medical literature reported in the present chapter unless, explicitly referenced, is drawn from a scan of the MEDLINE database (medical research), the PsycINFO database (psychological research) and the CINAHL-database (research of allied health professionals). This evidence is clearly relevant also to research on habits and routines in the social sciences.
3. As further explained below, habits are usually suboptimal and possibly dysfunctional.
4. This definition has been developed in Hodgson (2003), and in Hodgson and Knudsen (2004a, 2004b).
5. This line of thought leads to a process definition of habits in terms of *if-then rules* (Knudsen, 2004): if circumstance C, then energize behaviour (thought) B, which is a subset S_j out of all possible behaviours (thoughts) S in that situation. The if-then rule is a function f that defines the actual content of S_j through assignment of elements from the global set S of all possible behaviours (thoughts). The term disposition, as used here, denotes the if-then rule f assigning the actual content of S_j from the global set S.
6. This translates into the variance of behaviour as a possible statistical measure of the strength of habits and routines.
7. The definition of habits as a disposition obviously gives rise to measurement problems surrounding disposition concepts in general (Malzkorn, 2001). We can observe behaviour, but we cannot observe the habit (routine) itself. More generally, the status of disposition concepts has been the source of dispute from the 1920s and up to the present

day in the philosophy of science literature (Malzkorn, 2001). The minimal position taken here is that dispositions are causally efficacious, a viewpoint that remains respectable (Malzkorn, 2001). For a discussion of measurement of habits in psychology, see, e.g., Verplanken et al. (1997) and Wood and Neal (2007).

8. Even though the distinction between habits and routines is somewhat fuzzy, it is found useful in a number of recent works. However, not all enforce it (e.g. Postrel and Rumelt, 1996; Wood and Neal, 2007).

9. Foss (2003) recently observed that an individual-'less' mode of theorizing, promoted in works on routines, partly explains an absence of micro-foundations of organizational routines. The stipulation that routines are driven solely by individual habituations, and thus originate in causes that can be traced to individual habits, goes a long way to meet this shortcoming.

10. This evidence includes inferential rules (Nisbett et al., 1987), which fall under the rubric of habits and routines as defined here. For a review of the empirical literature on routines, see Becker (2004).

11. Hodgson (1993) provides a broad account of the history of evolutionary thought in economics and Winter (2005) provides a comprehensive survey of current evolutionary theories for economics and management. For a comprehensive introduction to evolutionary theories of organizational change, see Aldrich (1999).

12. See Hodgson and Knudsen (2004d, 2005a) for a counter argument to common objections to the use of evolutionary theory in the social sciences, such as the role of self-organization and human intentionality.

13. The technical definition of selection is explored at greater length elsewhere (Price, 1995; Knudsen, 2004).

14. See Hodgson and Knudsen (2004b) for a discussion.

15. Routines have previously been defined as observable human action in terms of recurrent interaction patterns (Becker, 2004; Cohen et al., 1996). However, this definition is best viewed as an attempt to define a useful empirical measure. Empirical measures are imperfect proxies of theoretical constructs.

16. The concept of a reproducer (not to be confused with the reproducer–innovator distinction) has been suggested as a description of higher-order entities that multiply through processes where copying is very incomplete, and where most of the capacity to interact emerges in developmental processes (Griesemer, 1999; Szathmáry and Maynard Smith, 1997). However, there is no need to introduce a new concept to capture the role of development. Development can be made explicit by considering how the information transferred in replication, in conjunction with environmental influences, shapes the features of interactors. A critical issue is a mechanism, possibly facilitated by material overlap, minimizing error in the transfer of information.

17. The following section suggests a minimal characterization of the role of organizational routines in theories of organizational evolution, according to which they are stable properties of firms that subset selection and diffusion can work upon.

18. Multilevel selection involving a nested hierarchy of interactors and replicators can be conceptualized on the basis of this definition (Hodgson and Knudsen, 2004b). However, we must keep in mind that interaction at one level must cause differential replication at that level, i.e., the replication of routines is engendered by interaction at the level of social organizations.

19. The present treatment of routines in prominent theories of organizational evolution cannot possibly do justice to the very large number of theoretical and empirical studies that speak to this topic. For a more detailed exposition, see Aldrich (1999), Baum and McKelvey (1999), Baum and Singh (1994), Winter (2005) as well as Amburgey and Singh (2002), Baum and Amburgey (2002), Galunic and Weeks (2002), Greve (2002) and Warglien (2002) and other articles included in *The Blackwell Companion to Organizations*.

20. See Greve (2003) and Winter (2005) for a more detailed exposition.

21. See Winter (2005) for an illuminating account of the relation between Nelson and Winter's (1982) evolutionary theory and the Carnegie School including Herbert Simon, James March, Richard Cyert and others.

References

Aarts, Henk and Ap Dijksterhuis (2000), 'Habits as knowledge structures: automaticity in goal-directed Behavior', *Journal of Personality and Social Psychology*, **78**, 53–63.

Aarts, Henk, Ap Dijksterhuis and Cees Midden (1999), 'To plan or not to plan? Goal achievement or interrupting the performance of mundane behaviors', *European Journal of Social Psychology*, **29**, 971–9.

Agarwal, Rajshee, Raj Echambadi, April M. Franco and M.B. Sarkar (2004), 'Knowledge transfer through inheritance: spin-out generation, development and survival', *Academy of Management Journal*, **47**(4), 501–22.

Aldrich, Howard E. (1999), *Organizations Evolving*, London: Sage Publications.

Aldrich, H.E. and A.L. Kenworthy (1999), 'The accidental entrepreneur: Campbellian antinomies and organizational foundings', in Joel A.C. Baum and B. McKelvey (eds), *Variations in Organization Science. In Honor of Donald T. Campbell*, Thousand Oaks, CA: Sage, pp. 19–34.

Amburgey, T.L. and J. Singh (2002), 'Organizational evolution' in Joel A.C. Baum (ed.), *The Blackwell Companion to Organizations*, Oxford and Malden, MA: Blackwell, pp. 327–43.

Argote, L., S.L. Beckman and D. Epple (1990), 'The persistence and transfer of learning in industrial settings', *Management Science*, **36**, 140–54.

Arnould, Eric J. (1989), 'Toward a broadened theory of preference formation and the diffusion of innovations: cases from Zinder Province, Niger Republic', *Journal of Consumer Research*, **16**(2), 239–67.

Attewell, Paul (1992), 'Technology diffusion and organizational learning: the case of business computing', *Organization Science*, **3**(1), 1–19.

Aunger, Robert (2002), *The Electric Meme: A New Theory of how we Think*, New York: Free Press.

Axelrod, Robert and Michael Cohen (1999), *Harnessing Complexity: Organizational Implications of a Scientific Frontier*, New York: Free Press.

Baum, J.A.C. and T.L. Amburgey (2002), 'Organizational ecology', in Joel A.C. Baum (ed.), *The Blackwell Companion to Organizations*, Oxford and Malden, MA: Blackwell, pp. 304–26.

Baum, J.A.C. and B. McKelvey (eds) (1999), *Variations in Organization Science. In Honor of Donald T. Campbell*, Thousand Oaks, CA: Sage.

Baum, J.A.C. and J. Singh (eds) (1994), *Evolutionary Dynamics of Organizations*, New York and Oxford: Oxford University Press.

Becker, Markus C. (2004), 'Organizational routines. A review of the literature', *Industrial and Corporate Change*, **13**, 643–78.

Becker, Markus C. and Thorbjørn Knudsen (2004), 'The role of routines in reducing pervasive uncertainty', *Journal of Business Research*, **58**, 746–57.

Benner, Mary J. and Michael Tushman (2002), 'Process management and technological innovation: a longitudinal study of the photography and paint industries', *Administrative Science Quarterly*, **47**, 676–706.

Bergstrom, T.C. (2002), 'Evolution of social behavior: individual and group selection', *The Journal of Economic Perspectives*, **16**(2), 67–88.

Bowles, Samuel (2004), *Microeconomics: Behavior, Institutions, and Evolution*, Princeton, NJ: Princeton University Press.

Boyd, Robert and Peter J. Richerson (1985), *Culture and the Evolutionary Process*, Chicago, IL: University of Chicago Press.

Cohen, Michael D. and Paul Bacdayan (1994), 'Organizational routines are stored as procedural memory: evidence from a laboratory study', *Organization Science*, **5**(4), 554–68.

Cohen, Michael D., Barry R. Burkhart, Benjamin Coriat, Giovanni Dosi, Massimo Egidi, Luigi Marengo, Massimo Warglien and Sidney G. Winter (1996), 'Routines and other recurring action patterns of organizations: contemporary research issues', *Industrial and Corporate Change*, **5**(3), 653–98.

Cohen, Wesley M. and Daniel A. Levinthal (1990), 'Absorptive capacity: a new perspective on learning and innovation', *Administrative Science Quarterly*, **35**(1), 128–52.

Cyert, Richard M. and James G. March (1963), *A Behavioral Theory of the Firm*, Cambridge, MA: Blackwell Publishers.

Dawkins, Richard (1976), *The Selfish Gene*, Oxford, UK: Oxford University Press.

de Jong, Gerdien (1994), 'The fitness of fitness concepts and the description of natural selection', *The Quarterly Review of Biology*, **69**(1), 3–29.

Dosi, Giovanni, Richard R. Nelson and Sidney G. Winter (2000), 'Introduction: the nature and dynamics of organizational capabilities', in Giovanni Dosi, Richard R. Nelson and Sidney G. Winter (eds), *The Nature and Dynamics of Organizational Capabilities*, Oxford, UK: Oxford University Press, pp. 1–22.

Durham, William H. (1991), *Coevolution. Genes, Culture and Human Diversity*, Stanford, CA: Stanford University Press.

Feldman, Martha S. and Brian T. Pentland (2003), 'Reconceptualizing organizational routines as a source of flexibility and change', *Administrative Science Quarterly*, **48**, 94–118.

Finkelstein, Sydney and Jerayr Haleblian (2002), 'Understanding acquisition performance: the role of transfer effects', *Organization Science*, **13**(1), 36–47.

Fischer, David H. (1989), *Albion's Seed. Four Brittan Folkways in America*, New York and Oxford: Oxford University Press.

Foss, Nicolai J. (2003), 'Bounded rationality and tacit knowledge in the organizational capabilities approach: an evaluation and a stocktaking', *Industrial and Corporate Change*, **12**(2), 185–201.

Frank, Steven A. (1998), *Foundations of Social Evolution*, Princeton, NJ: Princeton University Press.

Galunic, D.R. and J.R. Weeks (2002), 'Intraorganizational ecology', in Joel A.C. Baum (ed.), *The Blackwell Companion to Organizations*, Oxford and Malden, MA: Blackwell, pp. 75–97.

Godfrey-Smith, Peter (2000), 'The replicator in retrospect', *Biology and Philosophy*, **15**, 403–23.

Greve, Henrich R. (2002), 'Interorganizational evolution', in Joel A.C. Baum (ed.), *The Blackwell Companion to Organizations*, Oxford and Malden, MA: Blackwell, pp. 557–78.

Greve, Henrich R. (2003), *Organizational Learning from Performance Feedback*, Cambridge, UK: Cambridge University Press.

Griesemer, James R. (1999), 'Materials for the study of evolutionary transition', *Biology and Philosophy*, **14**, 127–42.

Grunert, Klaus G. (1996), 'Automatic and strategic processes in advertising effects', *Journal of Marketing*, **60**, October, 88–101.

Hannan, Michael T. and John Freeman (1989), *Organizational Ecology*, Cambridge, MA: Harvard University Press.

Hawkins, Scott A. and Stephen J. Hoch (1992), 'Low-Involvement learning: memory without evaluation', *The Journal of Consumer Research*, **19**(2), 212–25.

Hayek, Friedrich A. (1988), *The Fatal Conceit: The Errors of Socialism. The Collected Works of Friedrich August Hayek, Vol. I*, ed. William W. Bartley, London: Routledge.

Helfat, Connie E. and M.B. Lieberman (2002), 'The birth of capabilities: market entry and the importance of pre-history', *Industrial and Corporate Change*, **11**, 725–60.

Hodgson, Geoffrey M. (1993), *Economics and Evolution. Bringing Life Back Into Economics*, Cambridge, UK: Polity Press.

Hodgson, Geoffrey M. (2003), 'The mystery of the routine: the Darwinian destiny of *An Evolutionary Theory of Economic Change*', *Revue Économique*, **54**(2), March, pp. 355–84.

Hodgson, Geoffrey M. (2004), *The Evolution of Institutional Economics: Agency, Structure and Darwinism in American Institutionalism*, London and New York: Routledge.

Hodgson, Geoffrey M. and Thorbjørn Knudsen (2004a), 'The complex evolution of a simple traffic convention: the functions and implications of habit', *Journal of Economic Behavior & Organization*, **54**, 19–47.

Hodgson, Geoffrey M. and Thorbjørn Knudsen (2004b), 'The firm as an Interactor: firms as vehicles for habits and routines', *Journal of Evolutionary Economics*, **14**(3), 281–307.

Hodgson, Geoffrey M. and Thorbjørn Knudsen (2004c), 'Habit Replication', mimeo, The University of Hertfordshire.

Hodgson, Geoffrey M. and Thorbjørn Knudsen (2004d), 'The Limits of Lamarckism Revisited: On the Importance of the Distinction Between Genotype and Phenotype, and

Other Matters Relating to Socio-Economic Evolution', mimeo, The University of Hertfordshire.

Hodgson, Geoffrey M. and Thorbjørn Knudsen (2005a), 'Why we need a generalized Darwinism: and why generalized Darwinism is not enough', *Journal of Economic Behavior & Organization* (forthcoming).

Hodgson, Geoffrey M. and Thorbjørn Knudsen (2005b), *The Nature and Units of Social Selection*, Working Paper, Jena, Max Planck Institute for Research into Economic Systems.

Hofbauer, Josef and Karl Sigmund (1998), *Evolutionary Games and Population Dynamics*, Cambridge, UK: Cambridge University Press.

Hull, David L. (1990), *Science as a Process*, Chicago, IL: University of Chicago Press.

Hull, David L., Rodney E. Langman and Sigrid S. Glenn (2001), 'A general account of selection: biology, immunology and behavior', *Behavioral and Brain Sciences*, **24**(3), 511–28.

Knudsen, Thorbjørn (2001), 'Nesting Lamarckism within Darwinian explanations: necessity in economics and possibility in biology?', in J. Laurent and J. Nightingale (eds), *Darwinism and Evolutionary Economics*, Cheltenham, UK and Northampton MA, USA: Edward Elgar, pp. 121–59.

Knudsen, Thorbjørn (2002a), 'Economic selection theory', *Journal of Evolutionary Economics*, **12**, 443–70.

Knudsen, Thorbjørn (2002b), 'The significance of tacit knowledge in the evolution of human language', *Selection*, **3**(1), 93–112.

Knudsen, Thorbjørn (2004), 'General selection theory and economic evolution: the price equation and the replicator/interactor distinction', *Journal of Economic Methodology*, **11**(2), June, 147–73.

Levinthal, Daniel A. (1997), 'Adaptation on rugged landscapes', *Management Science*, **43**(7), 934–50.

Levinthal, Daniel A. and James G. March (1981), 'A model of adaptive organizational search', *Journal of Economic Behavior and Organization*, **2**, 307–33.

Macready, Norra (1999), 'Early instruction for healthy living lasts longer than expected', *Lancet*, **354**(9175), 311.

Malzkorn, Wolfgang (2001), 'Defining disposition concepts: a brief history of the problem', *Studies in History and Philosophy of Science*, **32**(2), 335–53.

March, James G. (1988), 'Variable risk preferences and adaptive aspirations', *Journal of Economic Behavior and Organization*, **9**, 5–24.

March, James G. and Herbert A. Simon (1958), *Organizations*, New York: John Wiley.

March, James G., Martin Schulz and Xuegang Zhou (2000), *The Dynamics of Rules. Change in Written Organizational Codes*, Stanford, CA: Stanford University Press.

Mead, Margaret (1964), *Continuities in Cultural Evolution*, New Haven, CT and London: Yale University Press.

Metcalfe, J. Stanley (1998), *Evolutionary Economics and Creative Destruction. The Graz Schumpeter Lectures*, London: Routledge.

Miner, A.S. and S.V. Raghavan (1999), 'Interorganizational imitation. A hidden engine of selection', in Joel A.C. Baum and B. McKelvey (eds), *Variations in Organization Science. In Honor of Donald T. Campbell*, Thousand Oaks, CA: Sage, pp. 35–62.

Mokyr, Joel (1990), 'Punctuated equilibria and technological progress' (in The Economic History of Technology), *The American Economic Review*, **80**(2), 350–54.

Nelson, Richard R. and Sidney G. Winter (1982), *An Evolutionary Theory of Economic Change*, Cambridge, MA: Harvard University Press.

Nelson, Richard R., Alexander Peterhansl and Bhaven Sampat (2004), 'Why and how innovations get adopted: a tale of four models', *Industrial and Corporate Change*, **13**, 679–99.

Nisbett, Richard E., Geoffrey T. Fong, Darrin R. Lehman and Patricia W. Cheng (1987), 'Teaching reasoning', *Science*, **238**(4827), 625–31.

Pentland, Brian T. (2003), 'Conceptualizing and measuring variety in organizational work processes', *Management Science*, **49**(7), 857–70.

Pentland, Brian T. and Henry H. Rueter (1994), 'Organizational routines as grammars of action', *Administrative Science Quarterly*, **39**, 484–510.

Perlow, Leslie A. (1999), 'The time famine: toward a sociology of work time', *Administrative Science Quarterly*, **44**, 57–81.

Postrel, Steven and Richard P. Rumelt (1996), 'Incentives, routines and self-command', in Giovanni Dosi and Franco Malerba (eds), *Organization and Strategy in the Evolution of the Enterprise*, Basingstoke and London: Macmillan Press Ltd, pp. 72–102.

Price, George R. (1995), 'The nature of selection', *Journal of Theoretical Biology*, **175**(3), 389–96.

Richards, Richard J. (1987), *Darwin and the Emergence of Evolutionary Theories of Mind and Behavior*, Chicago, IL: University of Chicago Press.

Rogers, Everett M. (1983), *Diffusion of Innovations*, New York: The Free Press.

Romanelli, E. (1999), 'Blind (but not unconditioned) variation: problems of copying in sociocultural evolution', in Joel A.C. Baum and B. McKelvey (eds), *Variations in Organization Science. In Honor of Donald T. Campbell*, Thousand Oaks, CA: Sage, pp. 79–92.

Rosenberg, A. (1994), 'Does evolutionary theory give comfort or inspiration to economics?', in P. Mirowski (ed.), *Natural Images in Economic Thought, Historical Perspectives on Modern Economics*, Cambridge: Cambridge University Press, pp. 384–407.

Samuelson, Larry (1997), *Evolutionary Games and Equilibrium Selection*, Cambridge, MA: The MIT Press.

Simon, Herbert A. (1955), 'A behavioral model of rational choice', *Quarterly Journal of Economics*, **69**, 99–118.

Sperber, Dan (2000), 'An objection to the memetic approach to culture', in Robert Aunger (ed.), *Darwinizing Culture: The Status of Memetics as a Science*, Oxford and New York: Oxford University Press, pp. 162–73.

Sutton, Richard S. and Andrew G. Barto (2000), *Reinforcement Learning*, Cambridge, MA.: The MIT Press.

Szathmáry, Eörs and John Maynard Smith (1997), 'From replicators to reproducers: the first major transitions leading to life', *Journal of Theoretical Biology*, **187**(4), 555–71.

Van de Ven, Andrew H. and Marshall Scott Poole (1995), 'Explaining development and change in organizations', *Academy of Management Review*, **20**(3), 510–40.

Verplanken, Bas, Henk Aarts and Ad Van Knippenberg (1997), 'Habit, information acquisition, and the process of making travel mode choices', *European Journal of Social Psychology*, **27**, 539–60.

Vincenti, Walter G. (1994), 'The retractable airplane landing gear and the Northrop "Anomaly": variation-selection and the shaping of technology', *Technology and Culture*, **35**(1), 1–34.

Vromen, Jack J. (1995), *Economic Evolution. An Enquiry into the Foundations of New Institutional Economics*, London and New York: Routledge.

Warglien, M. (2002), 'Intraorganizational evolution', in Joel A.C. Baum (ed.), *The Blackwell Companion to Organizations*, Oxford and Malden, MA: Blackwell, pp. 327–43.

Winter, Sidney G. (1971), 'Satisficing, selection and the innovating remnant', *Quarterly Journal of Economics*, **85**(2), May, 237–61.

Winter, Sidney G. (1987), 'Natural selection and evolution', in J. Eatwell, M. Milgate and P. Newman (eds) (1987), *The New Palgrave Dictionary of Economics*, vol. 3, London: Macmillan, pp. 614–17.

Winter, Sidney G. (2003), 'Understanding dynamic capabilities', *Strategic Management Journal*, **24**, 991–5.

Winter, Sidney G. (2005), 'Developing evolutionary theory for economics and management', in M. Hitt and K.G. Smith (eds), *The Oxford Handbook of Management Theory*, Oxford: Oxford University Press, (Forthcoming).

Winter, Sidney G. and Gabriel Szulanski (2001), 'Replication as strategy', *Organization Science*, **12**(6), 730–43.

Witt, Ulrich (2003), *The Evolving Economy: Essays on the Evolutionary Approach to Economics*, Cheltenham UK and Northampton, MA, USA: Edward Elgar.

Witt, Ulrich (2004), 'On the proper interpretation of "evolution" in economics and its implications for production theory', *Journal of Economic Methodology*, **11**(2), 125–46.

Wood, W. and D.T. Neal (2007), 'A new look at habits and the interface between habits and goals', *Psychological Review*, **114**(4), 843–63.

Yin, Henry H., Barbara J. Knowlton and Bernard W. Balleine (2004), 'Lesions of dorslateral striatum preserve outcome expectancy but disrupt habit formation in instrumental learning', *European Journal of Neuroscience*, **19**, 181–9.

Zollo, Maurizio and Sidney G. Winter (2002), 'Deliberate learning and the evolution of dynamic capabilities', *Organization Science*, **13**(3), 339–51.

8 Organizational routines and organizational learning

Anne S. Miner, Michael P. Ciuchta and Yan Gong

This chapter tackles the relationship between organizational routines and organizational learning. Specifically, we propose that (1) routines serve as organizational memory, (2) organizations adapt and learn through changes in the mix of stable routines that they enact, (3) organizations adapt and learn through the transformation of routines themselves, and (4) organizations deploy routines specifically aimed at generating learning. In a subsection on each of these ideas, we describe ways that routines inform organizational learning and offer illustrative evidence from empirical research. We flag selected issues that seem especially promising for further research.

The topics of routines and organizational learning inspire both vivid and fascinating theorizing in the domain of organizational studies. They also both present tough challenges for doing systematic empirical research. In this chapter, we put special emphasis on ideas with empirical grounding. As a result, we allocate a substantial portion of the chapter to processes that generate systematic change in the nature and mix of routines enacted in organizations and extinguish both internal/external and deliberate/emergent sub-processes. At the same time, we believe that the organizational learning literature has reached an especially promising period for testing more powerful theory that links learning and routines. Overall, then, the sub-sections highlight the importance of emerging work on the interaction of multiple learning processes and sources, the importance of imaginative processes that generate new-to-the-world routines and routines for learning itself.

Definitions   We adopt an inclusive definition of organizational learning: it occurs when experience systematically alters an agent's behaviour and/or its knowledge (Argote, 1999; Miner and Anderson, 1999). Learning, then, is not random change. Rather, it involves patterned change over time. The specific learning pattern must relate to prior experience. Studying learning in the broadest sense forces our attention to prior experience rather than to expectations as a major driver of action. It offers an alternative framework to the emphasis on calculated expectations of future outcomes as the most vital issue in organizational action. We focus on learning as a *process*, although we also discuss learning outcomes. Organizations can learn from their own experience, or through vicarious learning, in which organizations observe the experience of others (Haunschild and Miner, 1997). Individuals, groups, organizations, and whole organizational populations or industries can learn (Levitt and March, 1988; Miner and Anderson, 1999). There are many learning sub-processes such as search, discovery, trial-and-error learning, knowledge creation or forgetting – and many ways to bundle them together. Our approach embraces both *behavioural* learning in which the organization shifts activities or structures based on prior experience (perhaps following automatic rules) and *cognitive* learning in which the organization revises shared mental maps or beliefs (Argote, 1999; Argyris and Schon, 1978; Lant and Mezias, 1990; Levinthal and March, 1993; Miner and Mezias, 1996).

We focus on *organization*-level routines as a crucial element in organizational learning, as distinct from individual level habits. We define an organizational routine as a *coordinated, repetitive set of organization activities or sustained shared cognitive bundle.* This definition extends Miner's (1991) definition by accommodating both the behavioural and the cognitive regularities of organizational routines (e.g., Feldman, 2000; Hodgson and Knudsen, 2004). Routines can be present in the form of rules, reflected in the structure of 'if-then' statements within organizations (Becker, 2004). Organizations deploy many such 'if-then' rules, which are frequently codified as standard operating procedures (Cyert and March, 1992[1963]).

Argote (1999) provides a simple example of an organizational routine in use that involves applying two-tone paint to vehicles in an automobile manufacturing plant. The plant first covers part of the vehicle with a protective plastic sheet ('masking') while painting the uncovered part. Next, the plant reverses the process, placing a plastic sheet over the newly painted part while the remaining sections are painted another colour. These steps embody a set of repetitive coordinated activities. They may also, but do not necessarily, involve shared cognition about why this is done. Routines also represent collective stored behavioural capacities or potential bundles of action (Hodgson and Knudsen, 2004). For example, when office workers go home on Friday evening, the organizational routines do not disappear over the weekend; they are triggered the following Monday by the appropriate stimuli (Hodgson and Knudsen, 2004: 290).

Routines involve two interrelated dimensions of representation and enactment. Feldman and Pentland (2003: 94) label the representation of a routine as its *ostensive* aspect. They label its actual enactment as its *performative* aspect. In the previous vehicle painting example, the general idea or even norm, written or unwritten, of applying two-tone paint to a vehicle represents its ostensive dimension. The performative part corresponds to what the workers actually do and how they interact on the shop floor. As this brief review suggests, the routine construct is multifaceted. In this chapter we demonstrate how the framework we describe links organizational routines to organizational learning.

The chapter explores this link, starting from the simplest relationship between learning and routines, and then moves to more complex or dynamic theories. Section 1 reviews the basic idea that routines serve as one form of organizational memory. Section 2 then describes organization-level learning that occurs when the mix of relatively stable routines within a given organization change over time. We propose that the creation and selective retention of routines represents a form of learning, no matter what mechanisms are involved. We describe how both internal and external processes can drive variation, selection and retention of routines. Each of these processes may arise through deliberate choice at higher levels or through emergent processes. Section 2 explores and provides illustrative evidence for these distinct processes. Section 3 relaxes the assumption that routines themselves remain internally consistent, and describes how organizational learning can occur through the morphing of the routines themselves. Figures 8.1 to 8.3 illustrate the basic frameworks for these sections. Section 4 then discusses routines that enable learning itself, a topic that raises issues of learning capabilities and routines. We propose there that some learning capabilities involve routines, but some do not.

1 Routines serve as organizational memory

Organizational learning researchers have long argued that routines play a key role in organizational learning because they serve as one form of organizational memory (Levitt and March, 1988). Scholars in many fields have observed that organizations sometimes engage in varied behaviour, but at some point cut back in the range of activities into more narrow and consistent activities – i.e. develop routines – as a result of their ongoing experience. Berger and Luckmann (1966) call this process one of institutionalization. Walsh and Ungson (1991) see standard operating procedures, a special type of routine, as a 'storage bin' within the organization's memory system. Routines serve as memory, not just in terms of encoding prior experience, but also represent codes for action (Rura-Polley and Miner, 2002). Figure 8.1 presents a stylized image of this basic process.

As we discuss in more detail in Section 2, organizations sometimes deliberately choose to create a new routine so that some activities will now occur repetitively or some cognitive maps become more widespread. An organization may write a new policy or rule to capture previously uncoordinated activities, for example (Schulz, 1992). Organizations may also deliberately encode their experience in informal ways, through creating unwritten

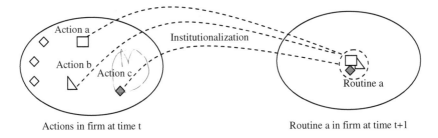

Figure 8.1   Routines as organizational memory

traditions, or rules-of-thumb or informal standard operating procedures (Darr et al., 1995).

Experience may also become encoded in an organization through less deliberate processes. Drawing on a series of card-playing experiments, Cohen and Bacdayan (1994) found that stable patterns of actions emerged among pairs of players. Coordinated repetitive blocks of moves appeared over time. In further corroboration of the routinized as opposed to calculated nature of the basis for action, pairs executed their existing routines in such an automatic way that they frequently overlooked obvious superior alternative actions. The authors argue that these routines tend to embody *procedural* knowledge (knowing how to do things) as opposed to *declarative* knowledge (knowing why to do things).

Hutchins (1991) presents important qualitative evidence that organizational routines can embody a procedural knowledge accumulation process without deliberate knowledge. He shows with careful analysis of ship records that the crew developed a collective navigation routine to deal with a broken steering system. Crucially, the participating individuals could not explain or describe the higher-level routine they were implementing.

Challenges and future research
There is ample evidence that routine development can represent a useful form of learning (Winter and Szulanski, 2001); memory encoded in routines can guide current action in very useful ways. The literature on Total Quality Management ('TQM') provides many examples of how the deliberate act of encoding or routinizing some practices can provide value, especially in efficiency, for organizations (Winter and Szulanski, 2001). The evidence for specific improvements remains solid, even if the causal link between TQM and global outcomes has been questioned (Hackman and Wageman, 1995). Previous classical learning curve research results are also consistent with the idea that experience can lead to routines that then

increase efficiency (Yelle, 1979), although this work does not typically examine individual routines.

Memory encoded in routines can also prove problematic for organizations. First, the organization can encode something that is simply false (Levinthal and March, 1993; Levitt and March, 1988). Second, an organization can enact obsolete routines that no longer have value in a new context. For example, Morison (1966) recounts the puzzlement of a time-and-motion expert who was called in to improve the firing efficiency of British artillery in World War II. Perplexed by a particular delay the soldiers took during preparation to fire, the expert went to an old colonel for advice. After giving it some thought, the old colonel explained that the soldiers were pausing to 'hold the horses', even though horses were no longer part of the artillery. They were enacting a routine based on experience from a different era. If a routine stores memory that is still applicable, automatic enactment increases its value, reducing time spent on considering what to do. To the degree the stored memory is no longer applicable, automatic enactment can become a dangerous threat to currently useful action. Finally some aspects of the memory encoded in a given routine may still apply while others do not, presenting a major challenge to using them as reliable forms of memory.

Routines represent only one form of organizational memory. Organizational knowledge can also be stored in technologies, physical objects, individuals, and culture (Argote, 1999; Starbuck, 1992; Walsh and Ungson, 1991). Contemporary efforts to execute 'knowledge management' demonstrate that the appropriate and timely use of stored knowledge is difficult to achieve (Haas and Hansen, 2005; Orlikowski, 2002). Memory stored in routines also presents challenges to appropriate deployment. A routine's existence does not assure its enactment. Even among routines in use, Rura-Polley and Miner (2002) found that some routines are incorporated in the daily operations of an organization more than others. In established organizations, top management typically works in a landscape of action and assumptions populated by routines.

Assuming that these routines embody the organization's memory, current leaders can affect current outcomes by diagnosing which routines to activate and how to deploy them usefully, even though these actions do not sound heroic. Even though learning research has long embraced the notion that routines represent a form of memory, then, research on competencies in accessing and using organizational memory stored in routines still represents a vital area for research.

2   Organizations learn through change in the mix of stable routines

The behavioural theory of the firm (Cyert and March, 1992[1963]) envisions organizations as enacting standard operating procedures, which represent one type of routine. In this model, organizations continue to implement these routines until a gap appears between organizational aspirations and organizational outcomes. When that happens, the organization searches for new possible behaviours. It then develops new routines. This model has persisted for more than 40 years and informs the important line of work developed by Greve in this volume.

In this section, however, we do not assume that performance gaps repre-×
sent the major engine of change in action. This perspective offers a broader menu of organizational learning processes involving routines. We presume that an organization begins with one mix of routines, which are then changed, based on experience. We break the total learning cycle into processes that (1) *create variation* in the routines available to the organization, (2) *select among these routines* for which ones to enact in the future, and (3) *retain* the new mix of routines. In this overall system, the routines themselves are stable in nature. As the three variation–selection–retention (V-S-R)) phases unfold an organizational learning cycle occurs. Although we use the familiar V-S-R framework from evolutionary discourse, the processes we describe embrace some activities for which it is hard to find analogies in evolutionary processes in the biological world. Figure 8.2 offers a schematic view of the overall process.

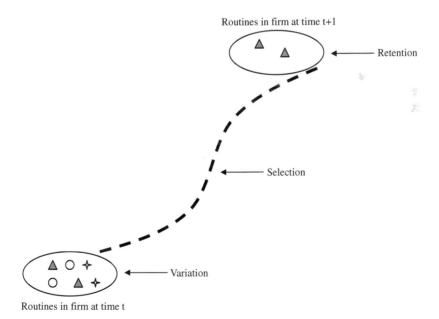

Figure 8.2   Organizational adaptation based on V-S-R routines

Crucially, each step may arise through many other sources beyond those emphasized in the work of Cyert and March 1992[1963]. Variation can occur through many sources other than deliberate search based on performance gaps or slack search. Selection occurs because of many other processes than outcome comparisons triggered by such gaps. Retention may be achieved through a variety of different factors in addition to the value of standard operating procedures due to bounded rationality.

In the descriptions below, we review theory and evidence concerning each of the three sub-processes of variation, selection and retention. While easily imagined in a general way, this vision of selective replacement offers a surprisingly rich palette of organizational learning based on routines. Each of the three processes may unfold through deliberate top-level organization-level choices. Each can also occur because of emergent and political actions, providing a form of unintended learning (Miner, 1990). Further, either internal or external sources can drive the V-S-R processes. Tables 8.1a and 8.1b summarize selected prior work that explores these different steps.

Prior work on changes in the mixes of routines in an organization has sometimes caused confusion about whether V-S-R sequences of routines automatically represent organizational evolution or organizational learning, or both. In our framework, any systematic change in the mix of routines tied to prior experience represents a form of organizational learning. Evolutionary approaches largely focus on random sources of variation or recombinations of existing routines, and/or on fitness or competition as drivers of selection (Aldrich, 2001; Baum and Singh, 1994; Schulz, 1992). Analogies with biological evolution do not easily match up with imaginative and deliberate creation of new-to-the-world routines. The representational or ostensive aspect of routines present special challenges in applying analogies from the biological world, as do processes involving interpretation and identity. The discourse of learning offers a wider array of appropriate theoretical processes and elements for social systems than can traditional evolutionary models. From this viewpoint, standard evolutionary models of change represent a special type of learning.

Variation in organizational routines
Column 1 of Table 8.1a provides examples of work that focuses on the pre-planned creation of new routines by organizations.

Pre-planned variation from internal sources   In their study of the cochlear implant industry, Van de Ven and Garud (1994) explored the origins of this new-to-the-world technology that brings hearing to profoundly deaf people. Using a combination of field observations, interview, and archival

Table 8.1a Variation–selection–retention of routines (pre-planned)

Mode	Variation	Selection	Retention
Internal – *Pre-planned*	Ingram and Roberts (2000) Routine – new product development Process – prior experience	Miner (1990, 1991) Routine – jobs Process – outcome-based selection	Miner (1990, 1991) Routine – jobs Process – outcome-based retention
	Thurston (1983) Routine – routines in new firms Process – planning for new routines	Van de Ven and Garud (1994) Routine – hearing product development Process – outcome-based selection	Schulz (1992) Routine – organizational rules Process – learning and depleting of organizational knowledge
	Powell et al. (1996) Routine – setting up alliance Process – prior alliance experience	Henderson and Stern (2004) Routine – new products Process – financial or reprocess constraints	Greve (1996) Routine – radio station format Process – performance feedback
	Darr et al. (1995) Routine – making pizza Process – internal R&D	Greve (1996) Routine – radio station format Process – performance feedback	
	Murray and Tripsas (2004) Routine – technical development Process – purposeful experimentation	Other related processes: Real options Multi-gate model	
	Van de Ven and Garud (1994) Routine – hearing product development Process – trial-and-error learning		

159

Table 8.1a (continued)

Mode	Variation	Selection	Retention
	Other related processes: Recombination		Sine et al. (2005) Routine – production technology Process – legitimacy
External – Pre-planned	Haunschild and Miner (1997) Routine – investment bank selection Process – vicarious learning	Henderson and Stern (2004) Routine – new products Process – market competition	
	Miner and Haunschild (1995) Routine – setting up association Process – population level learning	Other related processes: Selection of internal routines due to technology progress Selection of internal routines due to regulatory changes	
	Haunschild and Ni Sullivan (2002) Routine – airline accident Process – complexity of rules expands the definition of accidents		
	Sine et al. (2005) Routine – production technology Process – regulatory incentives for increasing variation and innovation		
	Other related processes: Extreme-value based competition Innovation based competition		

160

Table 8.1b *Variation–selection–retention of routines (emergent)*

Mode	Variation	Selection	Retention
Internal – Emergent	Hannan and Freeman (1984) Routine – general Process – blind variation	Burgelman (1994) Routine – new product development Process – internal resource allocation rule	Cohen and Bacdayan (1994) Routine – card playing Process – procedural memory
	Miner (1990, 1991) Routine – creation of new jobs Process – unplanned variation	Narduzzo et al. (2000) Routine – maintenance and installation of telecom equipment Process – situated interpretation based on local context	Reagans et al. (2005) Routine – joint replacement procedure Process – transactive memory
	Burgelman (1994)	Cohen and Bacdayan (1994)	
	Routine – new product development Process – middle-level manager initiatives	Routine – card playing Process – procedural memory	
	Feldman and Pentland (2003) Routine – hiring Process – 'performative' or execution	Tripsas and Gavetti (2000) Routine – new product development Process – managerial cognitive inertia	
	Miner et al. (2001a) Routine – new product development Process – improvisation	Rura-Polley and Miner (2002) Routine – job Process – logic of appropriateness	
	Gong et al. (2005) Routine – a variety of routines Process – generative bricolage		

Table 8.1b (continued)

Mode	Variation	Selection	Retention
	Narduzzo et al. (2000) Routine – maintenance and installation of telecom equipments Process – local reprocessing of global routines		
	Hutchins (1991) Routine – navigation of warship Process – improvisation		
	Cohen and Bacdayan (1994) Routine – card playing Process – experimentation or practice		
External – Emergent	Beckman and Haunschild (2002) Routine – acquisition premium Process – heterogeneous experience of network	Hargadon and Douglas (2001) Routine – electricity generation system Process – technology trajectory lock-in	Hargadon and Douglas (2001) Routine – electricity generation system Process – technology trajectory lock-in
	Haunschild and Ni Sullivan (2002) Routine – airline accident Process – technological complexity	Anderson and Tushman (1990) Routine – dominant design Process – multi-dimensional selection	Anderson (1999) Routine – cement production procedure Process – population-level learning

Ingram and Baum (1997)
Routine – hotel operations
Process – congenital learning

Phillips (2002)
Routine – law firm operations
Process – genealogical relationship

Gong et al. (2005)
Routine – a variety of routines
Process – automatic bricolage

March (1991)
Routine – organizational 'code'
Process – individual newcomers

Miner et al. (2001b)
Routine – technology commercialization
Process – social movement

Argote (1999)
Routine – liberty ship building
Process – forgetting

data, they found that novelty emerged not simply from blind processes. Rather, the authors portray organizational activity that includes the imaginative design of novel technological routines, and conscious experimentation with processes as well as technological features.

Purposeful experimentation can also provide a source of internal variation. Murray and Tripsas (2004) demonstrated how a particular entrepreneurial firm used technical, market/technical, and business model experiments to generate variation in the creation of new routines. For instance, the organization conducted internal research projects on two separate potential applications to determine whether one or both were viable applications for the organization's technology. Miner et al. (2001a) observed deliberate technical and market experimentation during product development. Other settings demonstrating pre-planned internal variation of routines include the design of a more efficient means of distributing pepperoni on a pizza (Darr et al., 1995), the impact of a biotechnology firm's position in a network on R&D collaborations (Powell et al., 2005), and the contingent nature of business planning in smaller organizations (Thurston, 1983).

The existence of deliberate, imaginative and creative activities that can be later encoded into routines represents a crucial element of a learning approach to V-S-R processes that contrasts to some evolutionary discourses. Conscious creative imagination represents a distinct causal mechanism above and beyond simple recombination of pre-existing elements, and a challenging but crucial domain for further work.

Pre-planned variation from external sources   On some occasions preplanned variations emanate from outside the system. First, external actors create new routines that organizations then deliberately import from outside their own borders. For example, Edmondson et al. (2001) show the introduction of a new routine, minimally invasive cardiac surgery (MICS), across 16 hospitals. Because MICS was developed and manufactured by a medical device company actively seeking to encourage adoption, this case illustrates external variation then followed by internal adoption. The enormous literature that documents the diffusion of innovations often emphasizes new physical technologies (Rogers, 1995). However, some studies examine the creation and promotion of new organizational routines. This may occur when consultants, business schools and thought leaders promote new practices, which are then imported by a focal organization (Burns and Wholey, 1993; Strang and Tuma, 1993; Westphal et al., 1997).

Second, pre-planned external variation often occurs when legislators or governments pass laws to force or entice organizations to import new routines (Miner and Haunschild, 1995; Tolbert and Zucker, 1983). For example, certain regulations contributed to the heterogeneity of organizational forms and technologies that were adopted in the new independent power sector (Sine et al., 2005).

Emergent variation from internal sources   Column 1 of Table 8.1b provides examples of work that focuses on emergent processes of routine creation. The field of organization theory has started to explore emergent processes of routines in a wide variety of research settings. In contrast to models that emphasize a 'blind variation' process, this work includes processes that can embrace mindful or creative processes but do not represent future-oriented instrumental action.

In research on emergent routines, Miner (1990; 1991) argues that jobs in a formalized bureaucracy represent organizational routines. Miner (1991) reported that many jobs were planned in advance on the organization's collective behalf. However, she also provides compelling evidence that a non-trivial number of new jobs were created through ongoing organizational activity, with some formal jobs created after the job-holder had already been performing its duties. In some cases there was no prior planning by the job-holder or his/her supervisor at all. In others the job-holder may have deliberately pursued a vision of a possible job, and through action convinced others of the value of its activities. In either case, the new job was not planned by top management or the organization as a whole. At the same time, newly created jobs were not simply a random recombination of activities already in existence.

In a research setting of new product development, Burgelman (1994) describes similar bottom-up processes in relation to organizational strategies, some of which can be regarded as a higher level of routine. Local actors started enacting new routines that were not planned in advance or even induced by higher management through setting specific priorities. As was the case with emergent jobs, the local strategy may have emerged from interactions of lower-level units with technical or market realities, or may have been deliberate from an individual employee's point of view, but they represented unplanned variation at the organizational level of analysis. A localized routine creation process is also documented in Narduzzo et al. (2000). Observing the behaviour of sub-units on maintaining and installing telecommunications equipment, they found that the local units followed the standard installation routines set by the headquarters but with a changed order of execution, which unintentionally created new routines for equipment installation.

Bricolage and improvisation can also lead to the emergent routines within organizations. Miner and colleagues (2001a) describe how organizations sometimes improvise new processes while executing product development projects, and routinize some of them, based on positive outcomes. Relatedly, Hutchins (1991) describes the creation of a collective manual navigation routine as a result of improvisation, without deliberate pre-planning or even general awareness from the individual crew members on the creation of such collective routine. Gong and colleagues (2005) document that new firms sometimes unwittingly extend and apply an existing routine to a novel managerial challenge. In doing so, they sometimes create new sets of standard procedures in the areas where they previously did not have any routines. Gong et al. (2005) define this process as 'generative bricolage' because the organization used old routines for a new purpose (Baker and Nelson, 2005; Baker et al., 2003). Emergent routines derived from improvisation or bricolage provide further examples of internally generated routines not planned in advance by management or the organization as a whole.

Emergent variation from external sources Phillips (2002; 2005) has described transfers of routines across generations of law firms in Silicon Valley. He identifies the mobility of employees of law firms, particularly higher-level partners, as a major driver for the diffusion and variation of routines across boundaries of law firms. Similarly, Gong et al. (2005) describe how firm founders unwittingly import organizational routines from their prior organizations in the early years of a firm's existence. The somewhat automatic routine transfer across generations of firms has also been examined in Klepper and Sleeper (2005) and Usselman (1993).

Social networks also represent an important source of unintended routine variation drawn from external sources. Knowledge about specific managerial practices can move through social networks into a focal firm's menu of routines, sometimes without deliberate managerial or formal organizational choice (Miner and Raghavan, 1999). Beckman and Haunschild (2002) found that firms paid lower acquisition premiums if their network partners had more diverse acquisition premium experience. Beckman and Haunschild (2002) offer several ideas about why this may occur, including the notion that the focal firm may acquire a mixture of practices and novel mental models through interaction with others, not all of which arise through deliberate vicarious learning.

Selection of organizational routines
Selection of some but not other routines that appear in the variation process represents a powerful learning step through which experience drives organization-level change. Column 2 of Table 8.1a provides examples of work that focuses on the pre-planned selection of organizational routines.

Pre-planned selection through internal processes   Traditional learning research offers a basic cycle of learning with three steps: organizations act, then observe outcomes, and next selectively repeat actions that appear to produce good outcomes (March and Olsen, 1976). This classic framework highlights one basic selection rule that organizations may deliberately follow: repeat routines that generate useful outcomes and abandon routines with harmful or useless outcomes (Levitt and March, 1988).

Lant et al.'s (1992) analysis of firms operating in the furniture and computer software industries suggested that poor past performance leads to the designed replacement of routines on strategic reorientation. In the cochlear implant context, Van de Ven and Garud (1994) found that internal rule making played a key role in selection of internal technical routines in the process of new product developments. Similarly, Miner et al. (2001a) reported that during the new product development process organizations sometimes deliberately observed new mixes of routines and retained routines that appeared to have value. Studies of the implementation of total quality programmes similarly describe selective retention based on the apparent outcomes of implementing routines (Westphal et al., 1997).

Greve (see Chapter 9 of this volume) reviews evidence about the impact of performance gaps on the selective retention of routines. This represents a special case of outcome-based selection of routines. Schematically, a performance gap triggers attention to the outcomes of routines, and prompts search for new ones and replacement of apparently weaker practices. In one important early study, for example, Greve (1996) explored the effect of performance gaps on choice of format among radio stations. He found that deliberate routine replacement (i.e., broadcasting format of production) declined when a station's performance exceeded aspiration levels, and increased when performance fell short of aspiration levels, thus broadly supporting a performance gap feedback model. Further studies by Greve (2003) show more detailed nuances of performance gap selection processes.

Pre-planned selection through external processes   Deliberate external processes like market interactions can play a decisive role in which routines remain influential in a focal organization. However, emerging work presents a more intricate selection mechanism than simple market selection of internal practices. In his study of computer workstation manufacturers, Sorenson (2000) observes that organizations that select internally through the culling of products might deprive themselves of useful information the market can provide.

Henderson and Stern (2004) studied the interaction between internal and external selection processes within a population of firms in the US personal computer industry. Internal selection occurred when a firm removed a viable product. Partial external selection was said to occur when an unviable product was removed. Full external selection was said to occur when the entire focal firm died. Their results indicated that internal selection events had a positive and cumulative effect on new product development. At the same time, new product development had a negative effect on organizational failure (full external selection). Thus, organizations that killed off viable products tended to have more new product introductions which in turn increased their chance of survival. These papers present important models of the role of instrumental or deliberate external selection processes and its interaction with deliberate internal selection. Column 2 of Table 8.1b provides examples of work that focuses on the emergent selection processes.

Emergent selection through internal processes   Burgelman (1994) provides a novel look at how internal resource allocation rules can drive selection of important routines, in this case both the manufacturing and resulting strategic action of a major firm. Despite upper management's commitment to the DRAM business within a major semi-conductor firm, lower-level rules about the allocation of manufacturing space and time led the firm to produce more and more microprocessors. Over time, these processes led to the domination of the microprocessors in the firm's actual commercial activity, even as top management debated whether or not to make the shift to intentionally focusing on microprocessors. In this case, an internal allocation rule (one higher-level process routine) led to a change in the mix of production routines, which led to product-market outcomes that in turn changed the competitive situation of the firm itself. The unintended internal selection process, according to this view, accidentally generated a mix in routines that had adaptive value (Burgelman, 1994: 53).

Miner (1991) provides systematic data on the actual selection rates for routines in the form of formalized jobs. She studied the survival rate of the jobs, not the persistence of individual employees. In discussing underlying processes driving her results, she suggests that the survival of jobs (selection of a given routine) may spring from competition between departments, imitative processes across departments, social and emotional interaction, and influence efforts by job holders, above and beyond any impact of the job (routine) itself (Miner, 1990, 1991).

Another less obvious selection force comes from the fact that some routines appear to drive action more than others (Rogers, 1995: 399). Some routines are deeply entrenched in the normal workings of their organizations, as when naval blockade procedures, developed in the age of pirates, guided actions in the 1964 Missile Crisis (Allison, 1971). Rura-Polley and

Miner (2002) found that jobs (routines) rated as making the highest contributions to the department's mission were most likely to be reported as part of the regular workings of the department. This is consistent with a selection process of most actively implementing useful routines and may well reflect deliberate managerial action. However, Rura-Polley and Miner found, when the apparent value of jobs was intermediate, social factors influenced which jobs apparently played a key role in departmental activity. In these cases, it seems more likely that the selection process involved social interactions outside of management control and/or formal organizational processes.

March and Olsen (1998) distinguish the logic of consequences – when actions are driven by expectations of their consequences – from the logic of appropriateness, which includes enacting behaviour consistent with an identity. Qualitative evidence suggests that some routines are culled, not because of their observed outcomes, but because they are perceived as inappropriate given the identity of the organization (Porac et al., 1989).

Emergent selection through external processes   Emergent external selection forces can also play a key role in unintended selection processes. Case studies of technology lock-in often describe how external factors shape an organization's technical routines in enduring ways not linked to deliberate actions by outside or internal actors. In one example, Hargadon and Douglas (2001) describe how the technically inferior AC system surpassed the DC system in part through accidental external events. Historians have argued that external factors such as the impact of personal skill in a typing competition or rainfall level during contests between steam and gas-fuelled cars decisively led to the culling of technical routines in participating organizations (Rosenberg, 1996; Tushman and Murmann, 1998). In a less celebrated process, the 'forgetting' of technology can also unintentionally select routines along the development of technology. Argote (1999), for example, showed that some routines of liberty warship building were selected out owing to the forgetting by the industry as a whole.

Social movements act as an emergent external selection process for nontechnical organizational routines as well. Miner et al. (2001b) argued that world-wide activities to commercialize university technologies through the creation of start-ups (as opposed to licensing) represented a broad social movement. She provides indirect evidence that some universities ended up enacting routines unlikely to work in their local context. Miner argues that in some cases accidental organizational interactions with advocates and developing ideologies led to selection of these activities for implementation.

Retention of organizational routines
Retention of the new routines completes the V-S-R organization-level learning process. Column 3 of Table 8.1a provides examples of work that focuses on the deliberate retention of organizational routines.

Pre-planned internal retention processes   Systems can store memory in routines but memory does not automatically persist. Rather, system memory is subject to depreciation (Darr et al., 1995). Further, a routine does not flow equally in all directions. As Darr et al. (1995) found in their study of pizza franchises, routines transferred more readily across franchises sharing an owner than across franchises with different owners. Even when the organization repeatedly enacts a routine, then, varied retention mechanisms affect its ongoing implementation.

Schulz and Jobe (2001) present an intriguing study that examines the effects on performance of two different types of routine retention mechanisms – codification strategies and tacitness strategies. In their study of Danish subsidiaries of US multinationals, the authors found that technical routines are best codified in numbers and codes, marketing and sales routines are best codified in text and language-based forms, and strategic routines are best encoded in objects and people. Miner (1991) argues that formalized job systems represent a retention system, whereby written job classifications and individual job descriptions codify existing sub-routines with the job's performance, form expectations about what those jobs entail and create structure through which elements are reinforced, as when supervisors or employees use them to justify action or resolve disagreements (Miner, 1990).

Pre-planned external retention processes   Important retention support for routines sometimes occurs outside the organization. For example, in a new industry sector seeking legitimacy, external media may serve as a source of retention. The media disseminate information about a sector and endorse certain routines within the sector, helping retain their credibility and influence on action (Sine et al., 2005). External retention from the viewpoint of a focal organization can also be seen as part of an expanded view of the system in which this routine has become standard. For example, buyer–supplier relationships can retain routines of practice which are unique to those relationships (Dyer and Hatch, 2006). In their study of Toyota suppliers, Dyer and Hatch (2006) found that, when Toyota representatives engaged in more knowledge sharing with the suppliers, productivity at the suppliers improved, but that these improved practices frequently did not migrate to other cells within the suppliers' plants. Knowledge brokers, who can be organizations such as design firms or specific sub-groups within a given organization, are yet another conduit for the retention of routines. These knowledge brokers rely on their previous experiences to recognize non-obvious connections between past problems and solutions and current projects (Hargadon, 2002: 67). As such, knowledge brokers fulfil a critical retention role by linking technological know-how across a domain of organizations or across multiple domains within an organization. Column 3 of Table 8.1b provides examples of work on the non-deliberate retention of organizational routines.

Emergent internal retention processes   Organizational routines can be retained in the form of procedural memory, with individual actors involved sometimes unaware of the existence of such routines (Cohen and Bacdayan, 1994). In the group setting, scholars have identified transactive memory – knowing who is good at what in the group and how the group works together – as an important emergent internal retention mechanism for group-level routines (Ren et al., 2006). Reagans et al. (2005) investigated different determinants for the speed of executing a particular medical routine in hospitals. They found that the level of transactive memory in the group was positively associated with the procedure's outcome.

Forces that affect the ongoing replication of routines also include emotions, although this has received less attention in work to date. In a novel study of symphony orchestras' decisions to 'let go' a particular performer, Maitlis and Ozcelik (2004) found that emotions like fear and anger could be triggered by the carrying out of particular actions. The spread of these emotions into shared organizational awareness and action can affect how the routine is perceived and ultimately enacted over time within an organization.

Emergent external retention   The retention of routines sometimes results from external forces that are unrelated to deliberate efforts of external groups to encourage replication of a given routine. Anderson (1999) describes how the cement industry shifted from a dry process to a wet process and back to a dry process again. Individual firms engaged in repeated vicarious learning by adjusting their production routines, based on observing the use of wet or dry practices by others. Anderson argues, however, that certain cement attributes, which tended to favour cement produced by the wet process, emerged as the collective definition of 'good' cement. This led to the emergence of the wet process, though it did not completely displace the dry process. Years later, after subsequent innovations and continuing industry interactions, the dry process re-emerged as the favoured routine across the industry. Accidental external patterns and interactions, then, played a role in the ongoing retention of the dry process in this industry. If a routine acquires legitimacy over time, although it has no deliberate advocates, this may also serve as an external factor promoting retention of this routine in a focal organization (King et al., 2005; Sine et al., 2005; Tolbert and Zucker, 1983).

Challenges and future research

We began with the simple idea that an organization can adapt and learn through systematic changes in the nature and mix of relatively stable routines it enacts or embodies. Tracing credible reports on organizational activity, we then described variation, selection and retention processes supported by scholarly research. Does this body of prior work simply create an unintelligible stew of potential sub-processes that have little value for understanding either routines or organizations, or does it offer a platform for important new work?

After considering emerging work and cumulative evidence, we conclude that it represents a critical frontier for new work. We propose that research on organizational learning through changes in mixes of routines has reached a new level of important emerging inquiry. Accumulated work offers a simple but credible set of insights about routines and learning. This vision has already provided important insights into learning, and we see several areas where it has great promise.

Promising frontiers   Three frontiers stand out as especially promising regarding learning through variation, selection and retention of routines. First, the rich field descriptions available of different V-S-R mechanisms highlight the importance of a new generation of work that more explicitly contrasts the adaptive consequences of different forms of each mechanism. Studies that contrast internal and external selection mechanisms (Henderson and Stern, 2004; Sorenson, 2000) offer important exemplars of this approach. We know that some organizational systems such as governments or research and development firms deliberately set up political processes to act as the selection mechanisms for creating new routines (Miner and Raghavan, 1999). Under what circumstances will adversarial or bargaining selection processes produce helpful outcomes for the adaptation of the system as a whole? (See Chapter 3 of this volume regarding political processes and routines.) Does the encoding of prior experience in procedural knowledge (in the form of action routines) make it harder to learn from organizational failure than encoding insights from experience into declarative knowledge such as principles (Gong et al., 2005)?

Formal modellers of adaptive learning systems have generated many creative simulations and agent-based models that provide systematic reasoning about these and more complex models of changes in routines. Well crafted,

tightly argued and systematic empirical research is needed to test implications of major predictions and examine simple heuristics in working
organizations.

Second, although theorists have long envisioned routines as nested in
hierarchical structures of other routines (Baum and Singh, 1994), the time
is ripe for empirical research on interactions between levels of routines.
Top simulation work on learning has long embraced fascinating issues
concerning learning and routines on more than one level (Lounamma and
March, 1987; March, 1991; Siggelkow and Rivkin, 2006). Unfortunately,
we lack well-grounded field research to test the actual impact of potential
interactions. For example, lower and higher-level processes of variation,
selection or retention of routines can complement each other, or substitute
for each other or even have no impact on each other (March, 1991).
Schwab et al. (2004) found that organizational and industry-level experience implementing farm team system routines in professional baseball
enhanced each other's positive impact on team performance, but other
work on knowledge and routines sometimes suggests substitution effects
(Beckman and Haunschild, 2002), highlighting the importance of additional work.

In one important variant of work on interactions between levels, Miner,
et al. (2003) argue that interaction of the implementation of routines at
different levels not only will affect adaptation of individual organizations,
but can increase variation in the mix of routines in a whole population of
organizations. This in turn determines whether a whole industry or region
can learn through selective retention of routines at that level of analysis
(Miner and Anderson, 1999). Finally, general models of V-S-R within evolutionary theory highlight that multi-level processes raise questions of the
viability of group selection mechanisms (Campbell, 1994; Hodgson and
Knudsen, 2004). Multi-level work on interactions of V-S-R processes on
mixes of routines offers a potential window for probing that important
issue.

The question of origins of variation in routines offers a third, and an
exceptionally promising, domain for renewed empirical work. The assumption that novel routines appear from random recombinations of prior routines has offered a helpful modelling assumption, and is the subject of
considerable debate by innovation researchers (Fagerberg, 2005). We conclude from close field observation and published research that the time has
come to embrace a more complete view of the creation of routines.
Organizations sometimes deliberately plan new routines using imagination
and insight, designing routines that at least in some cases do not represent
recombinations of prior routines (Baker et al., 2003; Dougherty, 1992).
Improvisation can also sometimes play a role generating the variation in

routines and, while often combining prior routines, sometimes reflects new-to-the-world patterns of action (Miner et al., 2001a). Further work can explore whether treating mindful de novo creation as a negligible factor in routine-based learning models creates biased predictions, and explore how to incorporate them into models of changes in the mix of routines.

Implications of prior research   Learning through changes in the mix of routines generated by V-S-R processes may seem so familiar as to be theoretically uninspired, but it remains a fertile model of adaptive change in the behaviour and cognition of organizations. Some simple but meaningful conclusions emerge from the combined body of empirical work from which we have drawn illustrations above. First, organizations can and do engage in the deliberate variation, selection and retention processes with an eye to adapting, and in some instances these learning efforts clearly provide value. The total quality management and process re-engineering movements in the 1980s and 1990s (Deming, 1986; Ishikawa, 1985; Juran, 1988) included systematic efforts to seek variation in routines and deliberately change mixes of routines. These normative schools have influenced manufacturing and production functions in organizations, and even had enduring influence on some large public organizations (Sodhi and Sodhi, 2005). Although the language of these movements, as expected, has changed, the actual organizational practices of reviewing and replacing routines remain important in contemporary industry and are valued by many organizations (Westphal et al., 1997). One way to conceptualize contemporary activities in the TQM and process engineering movements is that key micro-practices designed to select routines and increase reliability have become embedded in the taken-for-granted practices of many organizations, so no longer required explicit ideology.

Second, non-deliberate sub-processes of changing mixes of routines also sometimes have adaptive value, as shown in a substantial body of prior work (Baker et al., 2003; Burgelman, 1994; Eisenhardt and Tabrizi, 1996; Miner, 1990; Miner et al., 2001a). The cumulative work in this domain continues to support the idea that adaptation can occur through hybrid organizational systems in which deliberate and other emergent processes occur. Contemporary research often emphasizes that some organizations deliberately combine directed efforts to generate variation with openness to unintended variation sources (Gavetti, 2005; Levinthal and Rerup, 2006).

Third, even though deliberate and emergent V-S-R processes involving internal and external sources *can* generate adaptive learning, achieving useful learning through changing mixes of routines presents considerable challenges – a familiar but still important insight. Research clearly shows many conditions in which both mindful and emergent V-S-R processes generate inefficient or harmful outcomes. In their study of trading room activity, Madsen et al. (1999) found results that highlight how selection, and the convergence to successful routines, can drive out exploration (Levinthal and March, 1993), a familiar danger in the learning literature. Benner and Tushman (2002) found similar results in their study of ISO 9000 adoption effects on patenting activity. In the contemporary learning discourse, executing routines permits the organization to exploit its knowledge, while generating variation in routines can represent exploration that offers long-term value but creates harmful short-term disruption (March, 1991).

Findings to date are also consistent with the standard notion that adaptation through change in the mixes of routines requires rates (and content) of variation and selection relevant to changes in an exogenous environment, including competitive dynamics (Baum and Singh, 1994). In a stable, clear environment, variation can be represented rather well in thought experiments in the planning process and in traditional managerial control mechanisms (Gavetti and Levinthal, 2000). Even if causal processes are not known, effective trial-and-error learning can occur. Visibly effective procedures, machines, policies or people can be selected and sustained for long periods, even if the reason they are effective is unknown. The crucial task is to maintain high consistency in organizational action (retention) (Deming, 1986; Levinthal, 1997). In a stable environment retention should be strong relative to variation. Dynamic environments challenge the system to find balances between retention and variability that sustain the value of prior learning while avoiding obsolescence (Benner and Tushman, 2003).

3 Organizations learn through the transformation of routines

In this section we relax the assumption that routines themselves remain stable and explore related organizational learning processes related to their transformation. Figure 8.3 illustrates the process of routine transformation.

Although it seems counterintuitive, a routine can undergo transformation and still remain the same routine, for two reasons. First, routines often have both a representational, or ostensive dimension and an expressive or performative dimension (Feldman and Pentland, 2003). Second, researchers in many fields acknowledge that using the general word 'routines' provides shorthand for what are more accurately seen as nested systems of sub-routines, routines and meta-routines embedded in organizational action (Nelson and Winter, 1982; Winter, 2003). These factors imply that parts of a routine or levels of a routine may change even as the higher level routine retains consistency of action or identity.

Feldman and Pentland (2003) make the important argument that routines not only can, but often do, change through the very process of their enactment. In some cases, the exemplars primarily describe small steps of

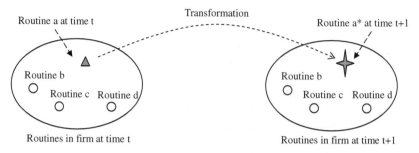

Figure 8.3   Organizational learning through transformation of routines

trial-and-error learning about specific sub-routines. For example, one case demonstrated how a university coordinated student move-in each fall. Initially, each residence hall handled the move-in in its own way, resulting in numerous traffic jams on surrounding streets. But then the routine changed. It was taken over by a central administrator who coordinated with police to improve traffic flow (Feldman, 2000). In this case, as in others, it is not really clear that the process differs from a multi-level process of changing the mix of routines – especially at lower levels. That is, a higher-level routine may stay in place, but lower-level micro-routines that enact it may be changing. We propose that distinguishing this situation from change at the original higher level offers an important area for further work.

Feldman and Pentland (2003) make a deeper claim as well, however. They argue that interactions during the implementation process can produce changes in shared understanding of what it means to do a particular routine. The ostensive or representation of the routine may change. This in turn may not only change the routine's ostensive nature or its representation, but represent another form of organizational learning. The experience implementing the routine does not lead to a new routine at the same level, but transforms the shared understanding of the purpose of the higher-level routine, or its meaning in ongoing organizational life, in addition to any refinements of implementation. This clearly represents organizational learning through a change in shared cognition, since the implementation experience drives the transformation.

Related findings
Much of the research that adopts this framework in studying routines tends to be case-oriented and has adopted various unique research settings. For example, Narduzzo et al. (2000) found that, within certain equipment installation or repair routines, the performative aspect of the routine (i.e., what the technicians actually *did*) showed considerable variation in actions.

The technicians rarely repeated the same exact behaviour and were able to adapt to different situations with different behaviours. In some cases, the technicians did not appear to draw on a fixed repertoire of behaviour, but carried out actions related to their interpretation of the situation itself. Using our definitions, the activity nonetheless remained a 'routine' because the ostensive routine of going to install something or make it work remained intact, as did higher-level routines about how and when the technician appeared, or did the work.

Lazaric and Denis (2005) also recognize the distinction between performative and ostensive aspects of routines in their study of a meat-processing company. They see one purpose of ISO standards as reducing the gap between these two components of routines. In their study, the introduction of this new norm created its own tension by highlighting discrepancies between what managers thought operators were doing and what the operators were actually doing. Through the process of reconciling these discrepancies, new declarative memory emerged, along with the creation of new routines embodying procedural memory. According to the authors, new information flows in the documentation system created new declarative memory. In addition, ISO implementation led to change in recurrent interaction patterns which resulted in increased procedural memory.

Reynaud (2005) examined the impact of the introduction of a new form of incentive compensation (a new 'rule') on existing routines in a maintenance workshop of the Paris Métro. Reynaud portrays the role of routines as managing the incompleteness of rules. Routines emerge as one of the ways of following rules, including new ones. However, Reynaud points out that, in the context he studied, the rule followers were able to change the rules or to pick different ones to follow, when faced with radically new problems. The introduction of new rules did not lead to replacing old routines with new ones, but allowed new interpretations of old rules and routines. Organizational learning occurred here when the organization developed new interpretations of old rules through its own experience. Howard-Grenville (2005) provides yet another case analysis which adopts the perspective that routines can serve as sources of both stability and change within organizations. In her analysis of how a particular roadmapping routine takes place within a high-tech manufacturing organization, Howard-Grenville also explicitly looks at the role of power and position of those who engage routines. The roadmapping routine involved a series of actions in support of addressing anticipated future needs. In one case, Howard-Grenville demonstrated how a senior executive reframed a particular problem to reflect his formal authority to set strategic direction. Thus, this executive was able to influence what the organization perceived as a critical need, a crucial element of the roadmapping routine.

Challenges and future research

Since continuity or consistency represents a core aspect of the definition of routines, theories that embrace change in routines will benefit from explicit boundary conditions around when and what types of routines change and which lead to stability (Obstfeld, 2006). Howard-Grenville's (2005) is an important step in this direction, but more systematic empirical work can fruitfully be directed in this effort.

The identification of ostensive and performative dimensions of routines clearly offers an important platform for work on more cognitive dimensions of routine-based organizational learning. For example, it gives rise to the question of when or how organizations can shift between being mindful and less mindful (Levinthal and Rerup, 2006). One suggestion is that interruptions might cause organizations to switch between action modes (Zellmer-Bruhn, 2003). This perspective also suggests greater emphasis on the formation and persistence of group or other collective mental models (Lim and Klein, 2006; Porac et al., 1989). It opens a door between theories that emphasize interpretation or identity with the idea of changes of routines as engines of learning. For example, a routine may remain stable in its performative aspect, but have a different ostensive meaning in this framework. This can permit learning through hypocrisy, where an organization represents its routines one way and acts another way, but over time comes to change both. These types of more nuanced processes can be represented more precisely in a world where parts of a routine can change while other parts do not.

4   Routines for learning

When we describe learning as change in the mix of routines in an organization and/or changes in shared cognition, the routines in question can involve hiring, production, planning, communication, financial exchange and any other organization-level activity. Some routines, however, can themselves embody a learning process. That is, the routine may involve a learning process such as search, discovery, or encoding experience into memory. *The Behavioral Theory of the Firm*, for example, proposed that search activities can be routinized, possibly with different types of search routines (Cyert and March, 1992[1963]). Learning routines constitute a special subset of all routines. By definition they play a role in generating systematic change in the organization's behaviour or knowledge.

Specific learning routines

Examples of learning routines include organizational *search* and *experimentation* (Gavetti and Levinthal, 2000) . If the organization has standard ways of creating interpretations of experience, or even of taking diffuse experience and encoding it in new routines, these too would represent learning routines. In a variation-selection-retention framework, search and experimentation routines produce organization-level variation.

Greve's chapter in this volume offers important insight into organizational search processes, including organizational search routines. Prior work has distinguished problemistic search focused on a specific obstacle from slack research which arises in the presence of extra resources (Cyert and March, 1992[1963]). Observers have also argued that organizational meta-routines can structure formal research processes (Nelson and Winter, 1982; Winter, 2003). A laboratory may sustain conventions for the way research problems are addressed, for picking which research projects to address first or strategies for examining possible answers to questions. Although social science research over many decades in many fields has provided important evidence about research and development expenditures and outcomes, it has not generally directly observed specific meta-level R&D routines. Eisenhardt and Trabrizi (1996) make an important contribution by proposing higher-level R&D processes.

Miner et al. (2001a) describe new product development routines in a study on improvisation in that context. The organizations had routines for preparing market or technical feasibility analyses, conducting prototyping experiments, assessing customer preferences, or designing for manufacturing. The total quality movement deliberately sought to formalize steps in the new product development and included audits of whether required routines were carried out (Wruck and Jensen, 1994). Miner et al. (2001a) highlight that there is no logical inconsistency in having routines that promote discovery or even creation of new-to-the-world actions or concepts.

Theorists who emphasize political and interpretive processes related to routines provide the crucial insight about how routines may involve learning processes, but not actually produce valid knowledge about the world or useful action (see McKeowen in this volume). Feldman and March (1981) describe how an organization may deploy a learning routine – e.g. routines for collecting data – but collect the data after the related decision is already made, for example. In our framework, routines describe processes that can produce systematic change based on experience. These changes may or may not have value or involve valid knowledge about the world (Levinthal and March, 1993).

Learning routines as capabilities
If organizations have effective routines for conducting research and development, problem finding or creating new knowledge, these can be seen as learning capabilities as well as learning routines (Teece et al., 1997; Winter, 2003). The webs of definitions created by this line of thinking carry high

risks of conceptual confusion. Nonetheless we agree with those who propose that learning capabilities and learning routines represent an important research frontier.

The bulk of work to date has suggested or assumed that organizations build learning capabilities (like other capabilities) from existing routines or enhance capabilities through replacement of obsolete routines (Leonard-Barton, 1992; Nelson and Winter, 1982; Teece et al., 1997). Organization theorists describe steps through which organizational routines precede and serve as the building blocks for organizational capabilities (Eisenhardt and Martin, 2000; Helfat and Peteraf, 2003; Zollo and Winter, 2002), often under the rubric of dynamic capabilities.

However, although organizational capabilities often comprise routines, routines are neither the only nor essential elements of capabilities (Gong et al., 2005). Organizations can develop learning capabilities that do not necessarily involve routines, in spite of the counterintuitive flavour of this idea. In one concrete example, behaviours other than routines – for example improvisation – can play a role in a new firm developing a new capability, which is a learning process (Baker et al., 2003; Levinthal and Rerup, 2006). Sometimes organizations respond to challenges and opportunities by improvising repeatedly. Improvisation involves combining real-time information and prior expertise, often (but not always) recombining prior routines in novel ways for new purposes (Baker et al., 2003). Improvisation also involves repeated de novo imaginative actions and energy from the organization.

Gong et al. (2005) report a case in which an organization repeatedly improvises in product development contexts, engaging in a form of organizational discovery. They repeatedly improvised new software products on the fly, improvising in new ways each time. Only after a long time, after observing the outcomes of their repeated improvisations did they invest resources and time to develop routines related to discovering new software products to match local context (Gong et al., 2005). This backfilling process can be seen as a separate step in a higher-level trial-and-error learning process. The firm's original repeated improvisational activity represented an ongoing learning capability but not a learning routine. Their later routines in software development represent a learning capability and a set of learning routines.

These findings highlight the role of imagination and creativity in the development of routines and capabilities, going beyond mechanical visions of capabilities as simple assemblies of prior routines gradually accrued from prior experience. These processes may be especially visible in new organizations (Gong et al., 2005) but may well be universal. For us, they underscore once more the importance of ongoing investigation of the origins of routines and micro-processes that intertwine to link routines and organizational learning.

Conclusions

This chapter offers a theoretical and empirical overview of several distinct roles that routines play in organizational learning. We first tackled how routines serve as organizational memory, a well-accepted idea. Future research can further extend this line of work for a more nuanced treatment of this role. It could usefully tackle issues such as how faulty memories are created, how organizational forgetting leads to certain outcomes, and how memory can be used to trigger and deploy routines in novel situations.

Built on the notion that stable routines serve as important vehicles of organizational adaptation, our work differentiates between pre-planned and emergent variation-selection-retention processes, which can occur both within and outside a learning system. Both deliberate and emergent sub-processes of changing mixes of routines can generate adaptive value under certain boundary conditions. Adaptation can also occur through hybrid organizational systems in which deliberate and other emergent processes interact. We explore research frontiers of organizational learning via changes in the mix of routines, and suggest that further research can usefully be directed toward the interactions across levels of routines, as well as the inherent tensions between deliberate and emergent V-S-R processes.

We also describe work in which routines themselves change, with an emphasis on related work on ostensive and performative dimensions of routines. Contemporary work has embraced increasingly nuanced models of the interplay between stability and change, between mindfulness and habit and outcome-based versus other forms of learning. Built on this emerging line of work, we highlight work that proposes that interruptions can cause organizations to switch between learning modes, and both interpretation and identity play important roles for routines as engines of learning. We suggest two additional areas for future study. Researchers can fruitfully direct more attention towards the emergence of routines in nascent organizations, not just for the empirical advantage such settings provide, but for the opportunity to develop a richer understanding of the creation of new routines.

Finally, although the notion of search routines lies at the heart of many decades of learning research, additional learning routines deserve attention, as does their link to capability development and deployment.

Overall, then, our overview of prior work implies that routines play a vital role in organizational learning in four key ways: through the creation of organizational memory; through changes in the mix of stable routines; through transformation of the routines themselves; and through the deployment of routines designed to generate learning, such as search or encoding experience. In each area, prior work offers important insights, and new work can take current understanding to a new level of impact.

References

Aldrich, H. (2001), *Organizations Evolving*, London: Sage Publications.

Allison, G.T. (1971), *Essence of Decision: Explaining the Cuban Missile Crisis*, Boston, MA: Little, Brown.

Anderson, P. (1999), 'Collective interpretation and collective action in population-level learning: technology choice in the American cement industry', *Advances in Strategic Management*, **16**, 277–307.

Anderson, P. and M.L. Tushman (1990), 'Technological discontinuities and dominant designs: a cyclical model of technological change', *Administrative Science Quarterly*, **35**, 604–33.

Argote, L. (1999), *Organizational Learning: creating, retaining and transferring knowledge*, Boston, MA: Kluwer Academic Publishers.

Argyris, C. and D.A. Schon (1978), *Organizational Learning*, Reading, MA: Addison-Wesley.

Baker, T. and R.E. Nelson (2005), 'Creating something from nothing: resource construction through entrepreneurial bricolage', *Administrative Science Quarterly*, **50**, 329–66.

Baker, T., A.S. Miner and D.T. Eesley (2003), 'Improvising firms: bricolage, account giving and improvisational competencies in the founding process', *Research Policy*, **32**(2), 255–76.

Baum, J.A.C. and J.V. Singh (1994), 'Organizational hierarchies and evolutionary processes: some reflections on a theory of organizational evolution', in J.V. Singh (ed.), *Evolutionary Dynamics of Organizations*, New York: Oxford University Press.

Becker, M.C. (2004), 'Organizational routines: a review of the literature', *Industrial and Corporate Change*, **13**(4), 643–77.

Beckman, C.M. and P.R. Haunschild (2002), 'Network learning: the effects of partners' heterogeneity of experience on corporate acquisitions', *Administrative Science Quarterly*, **47**(1), 92–124.

Benner, M.J. and M.L. Tushman (2002), 'Process management and technological innovation: a longitudinal study of the photography and paint industries', *Administrative Science Quarterly*, **47**(4), 676–706.

Benner, M.J. and M.L. Tushman (2003), 'Exploitation, exploration, and process management: the productivity dilemma revisited', *Academy of Management Review*, **28**(2), 238–56.

Berger, P. and T. Luckmann (1966), *The Social Construction of Reality; a Treatise in the Sociology of Knowledge*, Garden City, NJ: Doubleday.

Burgelman, R.A. (1994), 'Fading memories: a process theory of strategic business exit in dynamic environments', *Administrative Science Quarterly*, **39**, 24–56.

Burns, L.R. and D.R. Wholey (1993), 'Adoption and abandonment of matrix management programs – effects of organizational characteristics and interorganizational networks', *Academy of Management Journal*, **36**(1), 106–38.

Campbell, D.T. (1994), 'How individual and face-to-face-group selection undermine firm selection in organizational evolution', in J.A.C. Baum and J.V. Singh (eds), *Evolutionary Dynamics of Organizations*, New York: Oxford University Press.

Cohen, M.D. and P. Bacdayan (1994), 'Organizational routines are stored as procedural memory: evidence from a laboratory study', *Organization Science*, **5**, 554–68.

Cyert, R.M. and J.G. March (1963), *A Behavioral Theory of the Firm*, Englewood Cliffs, NJ: Prentice-Hall.

Darr, E.D., L. Argote and D. Epple (1995), 'The acquisition, transfer, and depreciation of knowledge in service organizations: productivity in franchises', *Management Science*, **41**(11), 1750–62.

Deming, W.E. (1986), *Out of the Crisis*, Cambridge, MA: MIT, Center for Advanced Engineering Study.

Dougherty, D. (1992), 'Interpretive barriers to successful product innovation in large firms', *Organization Science*, **3**, 179–202.

Dyer, J.H. and N.W. Hatch (2006), 'Relation-specific capabilities and barriers to knowledge transfers: creating advantage through network relationships', *Strategic Management Journal*, **27**(8), 701–19.

Edmondson, A.C., R.M. Bohmer and G.P. Pisano (2001), 'Disrupted routines: team learning and new technology implementation in hospitals', *Administrative Science Quarterly*, **46**(4), 685–716.

Eisenhardt, K.M. and J.A. Martin (2000), 'Dynamic capabilities: what are they?', *Strategic Management Journal*, **21**(10–11), 1105–21.

Eisenhardt, K.M. and B.N. Tabrizi (1996), 'Accelerating adaptive processes: product innovation in the global computing industry', *Administrative Science Quarterly*, **40**, 84–110.

Fagerberg, J. (2005), 'Innovation: a guide to the literature', in J. Fagerberg, D.C. Mowery and R.R. Nelson (eds), *The Oxford Handbook of Innovation*, Oxford: Oxford University Press.

Feldman, M.S. (2000), 'Organizational routines as a source of continuous change', *Organization Science*, **11**(6), 611–29.

Feldman, M.S. and J.G. March (1981), 'Information in organizations as signal and symbol', *Administrative Science Quarterly*, **26**(2), 171–86.

Feldman, M.S. and B.T. Pentland (2003), 'Reconceptualizing organizational routines as a source of flexibility and change', *Administrative Science Quarterly*, **48**(1), 94–118.

Gavetti, G. (2005), 'Cognition and hierarchy: rethinking the microfoundations of capabilities development', *Organization Science*, **16**(6), 599–617.

Gavetti, G. and D. Levinthal (2000), 'Looking forward and looking backward: cognitive and experiential search', *Administrative Science Quarterly*, **45**(1), 113–37.

Gong, Y., T. Baker and A.S. Miner (2005), 'Dynamics of routines and capabilities in new firms', *Working Paper*.

Greve, H.R. (1996), 'Patterns of competition: the diffusion of a market position in radio broadcasting', *Administrative Science Quarterly*, **41**(1), 29–60.

Greve, H.R. (2003), *Organizational Learning from Performance Feedback: A Behavioral Perspective on Innovation and Change*, Cambridge: Cambridge University Press.

Haas, M.R. and M.T. Hansen (2005), 'When using knowledge can hurt performance: the value of organizational capabilities in a management consulting company', *Strategic Management Journal*, **26**(1), 1–24.

Hackman, J.R. and R. Wageman (1995), 'Total quality management – empirical, conceptual, and practical issues, *Administrative Science Quarterly*, **40**(2), 309–42.

Hannan, M.T. and J. Freeman (1984), 'Structural inertia and organizational change', *American Sociological Review*, **49**(2), 149–64.

Hargadon, A.B. (2002), 'Brokering knowledge: linking learning and innovation', *Research in Organizational Behavior*, **24**, 41–85.

Hargadon, A.B. and Y. Douglas (2001), 'When innovations meet institutions: Edison and the design of the electric light', *Administrative Science Quarterly*, **46**(3), 476–501.

Haunschild, P.R. and A.S. Miner (1997), 'Modes of interorganizational imitation: the effects of outcome salience and uncertainty', *Administrative Science Quarterly*, **42**, 472–500.

Haunschild, P.R. and B. Ni Sullivan (2002), 'Learning from complexity: effects of prior accidents and incidents on airlines learning', *Administrative Science Quarterly*, **47**(4), 609–43.

Helfat, C.E. and M.A. Peteraf (2003), 'The dynamic resource-based view: capability lifecycles', *Strategic Management Journal*, **24**(10), 997–1010.

Henderson, A.D. and I. Stern (2004), 'Selection-based learning: the coevolution of internal and external selection in high-velocity environments', *Administrative Science Quarterly*, **49**(1), 39–75.

Hodgson, G.M. and T. Knudsen (2004), 'The firm as an interactor: firms as vehicles for habits and routines', *Journal of Evolutionary Economics*, **14**(3), 281–307.

Howard-Grenville, J. (2005), 'The persistence of flexible organizational routines: the role of agency and organizational context', *Organization Science*, **16**, 618–36.

Hutchins, E. (1991), 'Organizing work by adaptation', *Organization Science*, **2**(1), 14–39.

Ingram, P. and J. Baum (1997), 'Chain affiliation and the failure of Manhattan hotels, 1898–1980', *Administrative Science Quarterly*, **42**, 68–102.

Ingram, P. and P. Roberts (2000), 'Friendships among competitors in the Sydney Hotel industry', *American Journal of Sociology*, **106**, 387–423.

Ishikawa, K. (1985), *What is Total Quality Control? The Japanese Way* (D.J. Lu, Trans.), Englewood Cliffs, N.J.: Prentice-Hall.

Juran, J.M. (1988), *Juran on Planning for Quality*, New York: The Free Press.

King, A.A., M.J. Lenox and A. Terlaak (2005), 'The strategic use of decentralized institutions: exploring certification with the ISO 14001 management standard', *Academy of Management Journal*, **48**(6), 1091–1106.

Klepper, S. and S. Sleeper (2005), 'Entry by spinoffs', *Management Science*, **51**(8), 1291–1306.

Lant, T.K. and S.J. Mezias (1990), 'Managing discontinuous change: a simulation study of organizational learning and entrepreneurship', *Strategic Management Journal*, **11**, 147–79.

Lant, T.K., F.J. Milliken and B. Batra (1992), 'The role of managerial learning and interpretation in strategic persistence and reorientation – an empirical exploration, *Strategic Management Journal*, **13**(8), 585–608.

Lazaric, N. and B. Denis (2005), 'Routinization and memorization of tasks in a workshop: the case of the introduction of ISO norms', *Industrial and Corporate Change*, **14**(5), 873–96.

Leonard-Barton, D. (1992), 'Core capabilities and core rigidities – a paradox in managing new product development', *Strategic Management Journal*, **13**, 111–25.

Levinthal, D.A. (1997), 'Adaptation on rugged landscapes', *Management Science*, **43**(7), 934–50.

Levinthal, D.A. and J.G. March (1993), 'The myopia of learning', *Strategic Management Journal*, **14**, 95–112.

Levinthal, D.A. and C. Rerup (2006), 'Crossing an apparent chasm: bridging mindful and less-mindful perspectives on organizational learning', *Organization Science*, **17**(4), 502–13.

Levitt, B. and J.G. March (1988), 'Organizational Learning', *Annual Review of Sociology*, **14**, 319–40.

Lim, B.-C. and K.J. Klein (2006), 'Team mental models and team performance: a field study of the effects of team mental model similarity and accuracy', *Journal of Organizational Behavior*, **27**, 403–18.

Lounamaa, P. and J.G. March (1987), 'Adaptive coordination of a learning team', *Management Science*, **33**(1), 107–23.

Madsen, T.L., E. Mosakowski and S. Zaheer (1999), 'Static and dynamic variation and firm outcomes', in J.A.C. Baum and B. McKelvey (eds), *Variations in Organization Science*, Thousand Oaks, CA: SAGE Publications.

Maitlis, S. and H. Ozcelik (2004), 'Toxic decision processes: a study of emotion and organizational decision making', *Organization Science*, **15**(4), 375–93.

March, J.G. (1991), 'Exploration and exploitation in organizational learning', *Organization Science*, **2**, 71–87.

March, J.G. and J.P. Olsen (1976), *Ambiguity and Choice in Organizations*, Bergen: Universitetsforlagt.

March, J.G. and J.P. Olsen (1998), 'The institutional dynamics of international political orders', *International Organization*, **52**(4), 943–69.

Miner, A.S. (1990), 'Structural evolution through idiosyncratic jobs: the potential for unplanned learning', *Organization Science*, **1**(2), 195–210.

Miner, A.S. (1991), 'Organizational evolution and the social ecology of jobs', *American Sociological Review*, **56**(6), 772–85.

Miner, A.S. and P. Anderson (1999), 'Industry and population-level learning: organizational, interorganizational and collective learning processes', in J.A.C. Baum (ed.), *Advances in Strategic Management: Population-Level Learning and Industry Change*, Vol. 16, 1–30, Stamford, CT: JAI Press.

Miner, A.S., P. Bassoff and C. Moorman (2001a), 'Organizational improvisation and learning: a field study', *Administrative Science Quarterly*, **46**, 304–37.

Miner, A.S., D.T. Eesley, M. DeVaughn and T. Rura-Polley (2001b), 'The magic beanstalk vision: commercializing university inventions and research', in C.B. Schoonhoven and E. Romanelli (eds), *The Entrepreneurship Dynamic*, Stanford, CA: Stanford University Press.

Miner, A.S. and P.R. Haunschild (1995), 'Population level learning', in L.L. Cummings (ed.), *Research in Organizational Behavior*, Greenwich: JAI Press.

Miner, A.S. and S.J. Mezias (1996), 'Ugly duckling no more: pasts and futures of organizational learning research', *Organization Science*, **7**(1), 88–99.

Miner, A.S. and S.V. Raghavan (1999), 'Interorganizational imitation', in J.A.C. Baum and B. McKelvey (eds), *Variations in Organization Science*, Thousand Oaks, CA: Sage.

Miner, A.S., P.R. Haunschild and A. Schwab (2003), 'Experience and convergence: curiosities and speculation', *Industrial and Corporate Change*, **12**(4), 789–813.

Moorman, C. and A.S. Miner (1998), 'Organizational improvisation and organizational memory', *Academy of Management Review*, **23**(4), 698–723.

Morison, E.E. (1966), *Men, Machines, and Modern Times*, Cambridge, MA: The MIT Press.

Murray, F. and M. Tripsas (2004), 'The exploratory processes of entrepreneurial firms: the role of purposeful experimentation', *Business Strategy over the Industry Life Cycle*, **21**, 45–75.

Narduzzo, A., E. Rocco and M. Warglien (2000), 'Talking about routines in the field', in G. Dosi, R.R. Nelson and S.G. Winter (eds), *The Dynamics of Organizational Capabilities*, New York: Oxford University Press, pp. 27–50.

Nelson, R.R. and S.G. Winter (1982), *An Evolutionary Theory of Economic Change*, Cambridge, MA: The Belknap Press.

Obstfeld, D. (2006), 'Engineering knowledge: innovation and knowledge work as collective action', *Working Paper*.

Orlikowski, W.J. (2002), 'Knowing in practice: enacting a collective capability in distributed organizing', *Organization Science*, **13**(3), 249–73.

Phillips, D.J. (2002), 'A genealogical approach to organizational life or chances: the parent–progeny transfer among Silicon Valley law firms, 1946–1996', *Administrative Science Quarterly*, **47**(3), 474–506.

Phillips, D.J. (2005), 'Organizational genealogies and the persistence of gender inequality: the case of Silicon Valley law firms', *Administrative Science Quarterly*, **50**(3), 440–72.

Porac, J.F., H. Thomas and C. Badden-Fuller (1989), 'Competitive groups as cognitive communities: the case of Scottish knitwear manufacturers', *Journal of Management Studies*, **26**(4), 397–416.

Powell, W.W., K.W. Koput and L. Smith-Doerr (1996), 'Interorganizational collaboration and the locus of innovation: networks of learning in biotechnology', *Administrative Science Quarterly*, **41**, 116–45.

Powell, W.W., D.R. White, K.W. Koput and J. Owen-Smith (2005), 'Network dynamics and field evolution: the growth of interorganizational collaboration in the life sciences', *American Journal of Sociology*, **110**(4), 1132–1205.

Reagans, R., L. Argote and D. Brooks (2005), 'Individual experience and experience working together: predicting learning rates from knowing who knows what and knowing how to work together', *Management Science*, **51**, 869–81.

Ren, Y., K.M. Carley and L. Argote (2006), 'The contingent effects of transactive memory: when is it more beneficial to know what others know?', *Management Science*, **52**, 671–892.

Reynaud, B. (2005), 'The void at the heart of rules: routines in the context of rule-following. The case of the Paris Metro Workshop', *Industrial and Corporate Change*, **14**(5), 847–71.

Rogers, E.M. (1995), *Diffusion of Innovations*, New York: Free Press.

Rosenberg, N. (1996), 'Uncertainty and technological change', in R. Landau, T. Taylor and G. Wright (eds), *The Mosaic of Economic Growth*, Stanford, CA: Stanford University Press.

Rura-Polley, T. and A.S. Miner (2002), 'The relative standing of routines: some jobs are more equal than others', in J.G. March (ed.), *The Economics of Choice, Change and Organization*, Cheltenham, UK and Northampton, MA: Edward Elgar.

Schulz, M. (1992), 'A depletion of assets model of organizational learning', *Journal of Mathematical Sociology*, **17**, 145–73.

Schulz, M. and L.A. Jobe (2001), 'Codification and tacitness as knowledge management strategies: an empirical exploration', *Journal of High Technology*, **12**, 139–65.

Schwab, A., A.S. Miner and C.A. Olson (2004), 'Ecologies of exploitation learning: the impact of implementation experience on organization-level and industry-level outcomes', *Working Paper*.

Siggelkow, N. and J.W. Rivkin (2006), 'When exploration backfires: unintended consequences of multilevel organizational search', *Academy of Management Journal*, **49**, 779–95.

Sine, W.D., H.A. Haveman and P.S. Tolbert (2005), 'Risky Business? Entrepreneurship in the new independent power sector', *Administrative Science Quarterly*, **50**, 200–232.

Sodhi, M.S. and N.S. Sodhi (2005), 'Six sigma pricing', *Harvard Business Review*, **83**(5), 135–42.

Sorenson, O. (2000), 'Letting the market work for you: an evolutionary perspective on product strategy', *Strategic Management Journal*, **21**, 577–92.

Starbuck, W.H. (1992), 'Learning by knowledge-intensive firms', *Journal of Management Studies*, **29**(6), 713–40.

Strang, D. and N.B. Tuma (1993), 'Spatial and temporal heterogeneity in diffusion', *American Journal of Sociology*, **99**, 614–39.

Taylor, A. and H.R. Greve (2006), 'Superman or the fantastic four? Knowledge combination and experience in innovative teams', *Academy of Management Journal*, **49**, 723–40.

Teece, D.J., G. Pisano and A. Shuen (1997), 'Dynamic capabilities and strategic management', *Strategic Management Journal*, **18**(7), 509–33.

Thurston, P.H. (1983), 'Should smaller companies make formal plans?', *Harvard Business Review*, **61**(5), 162–70.

Tolbert, P.S. and L.G. Zucker (1983), 'Institutional sources of change in the formal structure of organizations: the diffusion of civil service reform', *Administrative Science Quarterly*, **28**, 22–39.

Tripsas, M. and G. Gavetti (2000), 'Capabilities, cognition, and inertia: evidence from digital imaging', *Strategic Management Journal*, **21**, 1147–62.

Tushman, M.L. and J.P. Murmann (1998), 'Dominant designs, technology cycles, and organizational outcomes', in B.M. Staw and L.L. Cummings (eds), *Research in Organizational Behavior*, **20**, 231–66.

Usselman, S.W. (1993), 'IBM and its imitators: organizational capabilities and the emergence of the international computer industry', *Business and Economic History*, **22**(2), 1–35.

Van de Ven, A.H. and R. Garud (1994), 'The coevolution of technical and institutional events in the development of an innovation', in J.V. Singh (ed.), *Evolutionary Dynamics or Organizations*, New York: Oxford University Press.

Walsh, J.P. and G.R. Ungson (1991), 'Organizational memory', *Academy of Management Review*, **16**(1), 57–91.

Westphal, J.D., R. Gulati and S.M. Shortell (1997), 'Customization or conformity? An institutional and network perspective on the content and consequences of TQM adoption', *Administrative Science Quarterly*, **42**(2), 366–94.

Winter, S.G. (2003), 'Understanding dynamic capabilities', *Strategic Management Journal*, **24**(10), 991–5.

Winter, S.G. and G. Szulanski (2001), 'Replication as strategy', *Organization Science*, **12**(6), 730–43.

Wruck, K.H. and M.C. Jensen (1994), 'Science, specific knowledge, and total quality management', *Journal of Accounting & Economics*, **18**(3), 247–87.

Yelle, L.E. (1979), 'The learning curve: historical review and comprehensive survey', *Decision Sciences*, **10**, 302–28.

Zellmer-Bruhn, M.E. (2003), 'Interruptive events and team knowledge acquisition', *Management Science*, **49**(4), 514–28.

Zollo, M. and S.G. Winter (2002), 'Deliberate learning and the evolution of dynamic capabilities', *Organization Science*, **13**(3), 339–51.

9 Organizational routines and performance feedback
Henrich R. Greve

Introduction

Organizational routines and similar concepts have been prominent in organizational theory since March and Simon (1958) discussed performance programmes. The focus on routines increased after work defining organizational routines as 'regular and predictable behavioral patterns of firms' and showing their importance for organizational evolution (Nelson and Winter, 1982: 14). Later work has expanded this definition to clarify that routines are constructs at the group level of analysis rather than the individual one (Dosi et al., 2004). A focus on routines in organizational behaviour implies attention to behavioural stability in organizations rather than to change, yet it also implies an interest in how routines are changed. If organizations are taken to be primarily bundles of routines, and organizational distinctiveness mainly comes from differences in their routine bundles, then a central question in organizational theory and strategy is how routines are changed. What each organization does is a function of all past routine changes, and how long it persists in doing it is determined by the processes that generate change in routines.

Change of routines is a central research question in the theory of organizational routines, and is also a question that links theory of organizational routines to theory of organizational learning. Because change of routines encodes interpretations of organizational experience into future behaviours, it is an important component of organizational learning processes (Levitt and March, 1988). Since its inception, learning theory has been used to explain how organizational change occurs, and it contains specific mechanisms that cause change in organizational routines (Cyert and March, 1963). The two processes first specified were problemistic search, which is search in response to a problem, and slack search, which is search as a result of having slack resources. Later work has added institutionalized search, which is search conducted in organizational units established to search (such as research and development) as the final intraorganizational process causing routine change. Inter-organizational search processes have also been proposed, however, as learning from the experiences of others through mechanisms such as imitation also changes organizational routines (Levitt and March, 1988). These can be viewed as independent processes, each of which has the potential for modifying organizational routines.

Performance feedback theory is founded on the theory of problemistic search, but some treatments add theory of decision maker risk preferences (Kahneman and Tversky, 1979), self-efficacy (Locke et al., 1984) and organizational inertia (Hannan and Freeman, 1984). Performance feedback theory exists as a micro-level research tradition investigating the behaviours of individuals and small groups, a meso-level research tradition investigating the behaviours of organizational units, and as a macro-level research tradition investigating the behaviour of whole organizations. These research traditions often investigate other outcomes than routines, such as task performance or organizational change events, but each also has findings on organizational routines. This chapter concentrates on performance feedback theory, as other parts of learning theory are treated separately in this volume (Miner et al., 2008). It emphasizes work within performance feedback theory that is most relevant to routines, as work on other dependent variables is less relevant to this volume and is reviewed elsewhere (Greve, 2003c; Locke and Latham, 1990).

Performance feedback theory

Figure 9.1 shows the main causal paths of performance feedback theory. It is based on the behavioural theory of the firm (Cyert and March, 1963: 114–27), but item 4 below has been added, based on prospect theory and related work on risk taking (Kahneman and Tversky, 1979; Lopes, 1987; March, 1994: 35–49; Shapira, 1994). The following process guides the rate of routine change in organizations (Greve, 2003b;2003c).

1. A decision maker compares organizational, subunit, or individual performance with an aspiration level that specifies the level of performance that the decision maker would view as satisfactory. The aspiration level helps a boundedly rational decision maker interpret performance by dividing it into a success range above the aspiration level and a failure range below the aspiration level (March and Simon, 1958). It is determined by the past performance, by the performance of a peer group, or by a formal goal-setting system.
2. Performance below the aspiration level creates a problem and causes search for solutions. This problemistic search is driven by heuristic rules such as searching for solutions that are proximate to the symptom and the current set of organizational routines (Cyert and March, 1963).

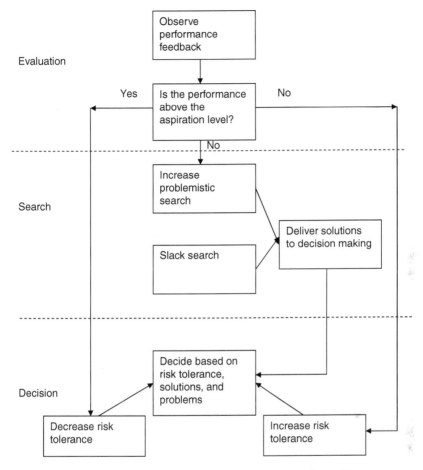

Source: Organizational Learning from Performance Feedback: A Behavioral Perspective on Innovation and Change (Henrich R. Greve, 2003c, Cambridge, UK: Cambridge University Press, p. 60). Reprinted by permission.

Figure 9.1 Performance feedback and decision making

3. Search also occurs when slack resources are available, such as extra
    time and funds that can be channelled into activities that the decision
    maker finds rewarding.
4. Solutions generated by problemistic and slack search are evaluated for
    their risk and fit to broader organizational goals. Risk evaluation is
    done by comparing the potential loss of making the change with the
    decision maker's risk tolerance (Shapira, 1994), which is influenced by
    performance. Performance below the aspiration level increases the risk

tolerance,[1] and performance above the aspiration level decreases the risk tolerance (Kahneman and Tversky, 1979).

5. Decisions are made based on the available problems and solutions and the decision maker risk tolerance.

This basic form of the theory has performance and slack as its causal drivers and routine change as the final outcome to predict, but additional causal paths can be added, and other outcomes (such as aspiration levels or search) can be studied.

Selection of goal variables is an important step prior to the causal process described by performance feedback theory, as the theory predicts attention to goals that are monitored before other goals (Cyert and March, 1963). In the behavioural theory of the firm, selection of organizational goals was seen as an outcome of intraorganizational negotiation processes resulting in a dominant coalition (ibid.). Later work has emphasized goals emanating from external actors with an interest in the organization's work and ability to enforce their preferences on it, as in institutional theory (DiMaggio and Powell, 1983; Meyer and Rowan, 1977) and resource dependence theory (Pfeffer and Salancik, 1978).

Goals at lower levels of the organization are thought to cascade down from higher level goals, with the means at each higher level becoming goals for the level below (March and Simon, 1958). Performance feedback research often looks at goals imposed from higher levels of management, though without assuming that they form a consistent goal hierarchy. Even so, it shows some negotiation or slippage in goals, as workers may choose not to take the goal variables or goal levels as given, and instead substitute their own. Such goal negotiation has been known for some time for both group goals and individual goals (Locke and Latham, 1990; Roethlisberger and Dixon, 1939).

Aspiration levels are central in performance feedback theory, as comparison of performance and aspirations is the engine driving behaviours in this model. It follows that knowledge of how aspiration levels are made is crucial for understanding performance feedback processes. The initial model of the aspiration level specified that it was made as a weighted average of past aspirations, current performance and the performance of a reference group of peers (Cyert and March, 1963), as in the following formula:

$$L_t = (1 - \beta_h - \beta_s)L_{t-1} + \beta_h P_{t-1} + \beta_s L_{st}.$$

Here, L_t is the aspiration level in time t and L_{st} is the social (peer group) aspiration levels. The formula makes the new aspiration a weighted sum of the past aspiration level, most recent performance, and social aspiration level, where the coefficients β_h and β_s determine the relative weight of the most recent own performance and the performance of others. The weights are assumed to sum to one, which is why the past aspiration level has a coefficient equal to $(1-\beta_h-\beta_s)$.

This formulation has been tested in both experimental and field studies with supportive results (Lant, 1992; Mezias et al., 2002). The findings also suggest potential modifications of the basic formulation of the aspiration level updating, however, as one study found an upward striving bias in the aspiration level through estimates of the weights that summed to more than one (Lant, 1992). Another study found that managers appeared to seek to even out performance differences among different units of the same organization (Mezias et al., 2002). Also, theory proposing that social similarity judgments influence how the performance of others influences aspiration levels has been proposed but not tested (Greve, 2003c). Thus, more work on aspiration levels can be expected.

Individual habits and group routines

Performance feedback as a cause of individual behavioural change has been extensively investigated in the goal setting literature (Locke and Latham, 1990). The basic proposition is that individuals who are given information on their performance and a goal will monitor their performance relative to the goal, and will change their behaviours if the performance is below the goal. Such goal seeking behaviour can be strengthened by attaching rewards to goal fulfillment, but appears not to be driven by rewards alone (Hogarth et al., 1991). Goal-seeking behaviour occurs because individuals may derive intangible rewards such as pride or social esteem from goal fulfillment, or they may simply use the goals as guides to what performance is possible. Goal seeking is distinctively effective in improving performance, as individuals who are given specific, challenging goals and performance feedback improve at a greater rate than individuals given feedback but not goals or feedback and unspecific goals such as 'do your best' (Locke and Latham, 1990).

Goal-setting research has investigated effects of goals on change in both individual and small-group behaviours, and has found similar effects on both outcomes. Researchers on organizational routines find it useful to distinguish routines as multi-person regularized behaviours from individual regularized behaviours, and denote the latter as habits, (Hodgson, 2008, this volume). In the following, the term 'routine' will be used for theory and findings that apply to multi-person behaviours, and the term 'habit' will be used for single-person behaviours. Routine will also be used when both single and multi-person behaviours are covered.

Much work on goal seeking has studied routine change indirectly through its effect on individual or group performance, and has a long record of showing strong effect in a variety of experimental and field settings (Kluger and DeNisi, 1996; Locke and Latham, 1990). While this work is useful in order to indicate that performance feedback is causing the actor to do 'something', it does not directly investigate how habits and routines are changed. The distinction is important because performance feedback appears to have strong effects on goals that can be reached by simple increase of effort, and has weaker effects on complex tasks (Wood et al., 1987). Thus, some of the effect on performance may be due to a simple strategy of performing the same behaviours faster, suggesting that more detailed investigation is needed to conclude that routine change has occurred.

Some investigations have, however, offered evidence of routine change. First, some behavioural simulations use complex decision-making tasks designed so that exertion (except mental) has no effect and speed is not rewarded, leaving quality of information collection and decision making as the variables explaining performance differences. In such work, it has been shown that individuals use performance feedback to obtain higher performance in complex tasks because they concentrate better and use more sophisticated problem-solving strategies when they are seeking to fulfil a goal (Bandura and Jourden, 1991; Chesney and Locke, 1991).

The studies also offer additional evidence on how decision-making routines are improved. For example, one study showed that individuals who received feedback indicating that they were progressively improving relative to their peers employed a systematic strategy of making small adjustments to their past decisions, whereas individuals who thought they were doing progressively worse appeared to flounder, making many simultaneous changes (Bandura and Jourden, 1991). The former strategy is more effective in complex decision making, and indeed led to higher performance.

Other studies have shown that individuals who were given a goal of learning a decision-making task collected more information, allowing them to reach higher performance than individuals who were given a goal to reach a certain level of performance or simply being told to do their best (Seijts, Latham, Tasa and Latham, 2004; Wood and Bandura, 1989). Thus, better information collection or better experimentation strategies are two approaches to effective learning of new habits, and both are stimulated by setting goals and providing performance feedback. The finding is interesting because it shows that telling subjects to become familiar with a decision-making task actually results in higher performance than telling them to perform well on the task. Presumably, this effect will vary, depending on the complexity of the task.

A problem with experimental studies is that they tend to use tasks that the subjects are not familiar with, and thus show the subjects establishing new habits and routines rather than modifying existing ones. The same processes appear to operate when modifying existing routines, however, as seen in field studies where workers seek to improve the performance on tasks that they have experience with, and thus presumably have routines in place already. In such settings, individuals have spontaneously started information-collection and coordination behaviours when they were given goals and performance feedback (Campbell and Gingrich, 1986; Latham and Saari, 1979). Workers who are not managers, such as the truck drivers studied in one experiment (Latham and Saari, 1979), established routines that included managerial tasks such as information exchange and scheduling. Similar findings have been produced in other field studies (e.g., Campbell and Gingrich, 1986; McCuddy and Griggs, 1984).

Except in simple settings such as salespersons working as individuals, field studies tend to encounter the usual organizational reality of routines involving multiple individuals executing a routine together. The shift from a single-person habit to multiple persons executing a routine has theoretical significance, as will be discussed in the next section.

Intraorganizational routines

Internal routines involving multiple organizational members are thought to be the most interesting part of research on organizational routines, as such routines are 'truly organizational', as opposed to the habits of an individual. This property of multi-person routines raises a range of interesting questions. For example, they may persist even though one or more of the persons executing them leave the organization, but the degree to which they persist (and what the organization can do to make them persist) has seen little field evidence. Experimental work has shown high persistence because of training of newcomers by senior workers (Zucker, 1977). It is already well known that organizations with substantial turnover of personnel and a need for consistency in behaviours, such as fast-food franchises, rely heavily on documenting routines and embedding routines in the production machinery (Bradach, 1997). Organizations with less turnover use selection and socialization for the same purpose (Chatman, 1991). Hiring has also been shown to alter organizational routines (Miner, 1990), however, so it is clearly a behaviour that involves the potential for change unless countered by some stabilizing mechanism.

It is less clear how a multi-person routine is changed than a single-person habit, as the allocation of formal and actual authority to change and the use of change strategies such as deliberately decided variation or simple mutual adjustment may vary across organizations. Even in simple experimental settings with as few as two persons executing a routine, it has been shown that multi-person routines are rather rigid (Cohen and Bacdayan, 1994). Whereas an individual can be very flexible in selecting one out of multiple habits or modifying habits as needed, persons working together engage in interlocking behaviours (Weick, 1979) that may cause them to make fewer changes in order to be predictable to the other person. Thus, there are good reasons to concentrate the empirical effort on empirical research on multi-person intraorganizational routines. Such research involves difficulties in gaining access and in getting data with sufficient experimental control or natural variation for causal attribution, however, and indeed there is less work done here than on individual behaviours.

Work on the learning of new routines in surgical teams has shown considerable variation in the degree of successful implementation (Edmondson et al., 2001), in part as a result of different degrees and types of preparations for the change. Interestingly, the ability of team members to speak up when discovering problems during the execution of a routine proved to be an important variable explaining the speed of learning new routines (Edmondson, 2003). The observation is important because status differences in organizational teams causing subordinates not to speak up have been implicated in the literature on mistakes and accidents in the execution of routines (Gersick and Hackman, 1990; Lanir, 1989). Also, performance feedback obtained and communicated during the execution of a routine may have a more rapid effect on learning than performance feedback based on the final outcome after the routine has been completed (Edmondson, 2004).

Organizations have been observed to meet unexpected challenges by reconstructing new routines from the ground up (Hutchins 1991) or by improvising nonroutine actions (Miner et al., 2001). Such behaviour is clearly different from the usual incremental and conservative updates of routines, and seems to require strong signals that continuation of the routine would lead to disastrous outcomes, that the context for executing the known routine is clearly inappropriate, or that necessary conditions for executing the known routine are absent (Gersick and Hackman, 1990; Hutchins, 1991; Miner et al., 2001). Misapplication of known routines occurs frequently enough for it to be an open question just how strong such signals need to be (or how receptive the organization needs to be) in order for the routine to be interrupted (Gersick and Hackman, 1990).

An important feature of formal organizations is the ability to have multiple managerial layers with responsibility for fulfilling the goals of their subunit. The design of such goal hierarchies was one of the first issues raised in organizational theory (March and Simon, 1958), and the issue remains important given later evidence of the effectiveness of goals in influencing behaviours, including in ways not intended by the designers of the goal system (Kerr, 1975). From the individual-level performance feedback literature we know that performance feedback drives not only effective habit execution, but also development of new habits. We may expect similar effects on the routines executed by groups. A natural implication is that removal of managerial layers and goal systems will cause less maintenance of existing routines and development of new routines. One study tested this proposition on organizations that left a franchise system, finding evidence that this caused less reliable execution of existing routines, less creation of new routines, and lower overall performance (Knott and McKelvey, 1999).

Work on the effects of different types of performance feedback has also shown how organizational design of a goal system affects routine execution and change. A study of control systems in research and development distinguished between performance feedback systems focused on unit inputs, unit outputs or unit processes, and found that these had surprisingly similar effects on the development of incremental and radical innovations (Cardinal, 2001). Input and output controls enhanced both kinds of innovations, while process controls enhanced only radical innovations. The findings seem to support the idea that performance feedback generates both efficient execution of routines, as in the development of incremental innovations, and introduction of new routines or non-routine behaviour, as in the development of radical innovations.

Organizational routines
Each activity performed by an organization constitutes a macro level routine that contains micro-level routines for executing the activity. For example, the product market niches covered by an organization is a set of macro-level routines and, within each of these niches, numerous routines for producing and delivering the product are found. Change in macro-level routines create large-scale changes in the constituent routines, with new routines established when a new activity is started, existing routines removed when an activity is terminated, and existing routines modified when an activity is modified. Just as the environment forms the context for organizational changes in these macro routines, the macro routines form the context for changes in micro routines. Routine changes can be seen to cascade from the environment through macro routines to micro routines and, in the final instance, to behavioural change by individuals.

Performance feedback theory has been applied to change in macro routines as well, showing the expected decline in the rate of change when the performance is high relative to the aspiration level. Work on curriculum change in universities found that times of financial adversity caused more change in departments with relatively low research reputations, suggesting that the rate of change is function of performance feedback on both financial and reputational variables (Manns and March, 1978). Later work has found the adoption of entire programmes to be guided by performance feedback along with other mechanisms such as mimetic pressures, and despite pressures against adopting by alumni and other groups seeking to preserve the existing set of programmes (Kraatz, 1998; Zajac and Kraatz, 1993).

In one study, a compound measure using a range of different strategic changes was used to show that firms with low performance relative to the aspiration level changed more than firms with high performance (Lant et al., 1992). Another study examining a variety of change behaviours gave a similar finding, and also showed that the changes were preceded by a period of search (Grinyer and McKiernan, 1990). Findings of greater rates of market niche change and other changes in macro routines have been reproduced in a variety of industries (Audia et al., 2000; Boeker, 1997; Burgelman, 1994; Miller and Chen, 1994; Mitsuhashi and Greve, 2004).

These studies have also revealed additional details on how the change process functions. Performance has a greater effect on the change of lower-level tactical actions than on actions that determine the strategy of the firm, though it affected both kinds of actions (Miller and Chen, 1994). Low performance interacted with management characteristics such that the combination of low performance and management characteristics had a stronger effect than the main effects these would suggest (Boeker, 1997; Mitsuhashi and Greve, 2004). Low performance from one set of routines has a particularly high effect on change in macro routines if there is also high performance from an alternative set of routines so that managers can see an alternative strategy (Burgelman, 1994). Long-lasting high performance can make managers too confident in the organizational strategy to implement changes following a major change in the organizational environment (Audia et al., 2000).

Recent work on macro routines has modified performance feedback theory to take into account concerns of risk taking (Bromiley, 1991) and organizational inertia (Greve, 1998) that become salient at the level of the macro routine. The baseline prediction of a linear decline in the rate of change when performance relative to the aspiration level has been modified is shown in Figure 9.2. Here, the straight line (centre) shows a decline in the probability of change as performance increases relative to the aspiration level, as predicted by problemistic search. Change in macro-level routines involves risk, however, which means that prospect theory can be used to

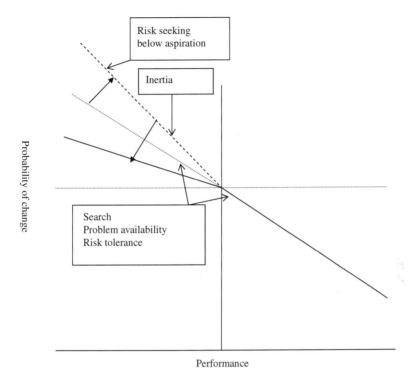

Source: *Organizational Learning from Performance Feedback: A Behavioral Perspective on Innovation and Change* (Henrich R. Greve, 2003c, Cambridge, UK: Cambridge University Press, p. 63). Reprinted by permission.

Figure 9.2   Predicted effect of performance feedback

predict a shift towards more risky behaviours and, accordingly, an even greater increase in the likelihood of change as performance falls below the aspiration level (Bromiley, 1991; Fiegenbaum and Thomas, 1986; Kahneman and Tversky, 1979). Countering this effect, however, is organizational inertia caused by internal and external resistance to radical change (Hannan and Freeman, 1977). The inertia effect is triggered by the attempts to change the organization that occur when the performance falls below the aspiration level, and reduces the effect of performance feedback to the solid line at the bottom (Greve, 1998). High performance reduces the rate of change more effectively than low performance increases the rate of change.

The relation from performance feedback to macro-routine change was first tested on changes in product-market niches (Greve, 1998), showing the predicted effect of a declining rate of change as performance increased and a greater rate of decline above the aspiration level. Moreover, the estimated curve was nearly linear for a low-risk type of change, but highly bent (the left-hand side was nearly level) for the adoption of an innovative product-market niche, suggesting that inertia is actually strengthened when unusual or risky alternatives are considered. Later work on the launch of innovative products has supported these findings, showing a strong decline in the rate above the aspiration level but a nearly level curve (no effect) below the aspiration level (Greve, 2003a).

Integrated model

The multi-level nature of performance feedback effects on routines should be clear from the preceding review. Performance feedback operates on the organization, on work groups in the organization, and on individuals, though the goals and consequences differ in each case. Table 9.1 depicts the processes discussed here. At the organizational level, performance feedback causes entire activity sets to be added, modified or replaced. The goals are typically negotiated or imposed on the organization by external actors, and tend to be profitability or stock price goals for private sector firms. At the work group level, performance feedback causes modification of production routines when goals emphasized in the internal goal-setting system are not met. At the individual level, persons who are not constrained by the stabilization of routines at the work group level may use performance feedback to modify their own habits, and the goals will either be set by the organization or created by the individual.

The performance feedback at multiple levels constitutes a system, but the system is not likely to be consistent in the sense imagined in early work on organizations as hierarchical, self-regulating systems (March, 1981). Rather, organizations are drawn to pursue goals that happen to be salient

Table 9.1   Cross-level performance feedback

Level	Goal source	Actions
Organization	Environment and dominant coalition	Select and modify macro routines Update own aspiration levels Design goal systems for lower levels Influence lower-level aspiration levels
Work group	Organization and group	Select and modify work group routines Update own aspiration levels
Individual	Organization, group and individual	Select and modify individual routines Update own aspiration levels Modify individual actions used in work group routines

at the moment through processes of allocation of attention that still have seen little investigation (Ocasio, 1997). Work on rule changes indicates that an interplay of environmental signals and internal organizational dynamics turns attention to specific areas of organizational activities (March et al., 2000), and presumably also makes goals on those areas of activities salient.

The multi-level nature of organizational goals and performance feedback processes suggest that the levels may influence each other, and thus that research done at one level of analysis may need to take into account influence from adjacent levels. As Table 9.1 shows, some of the interactions are indirect: if the model is correct, the organization level sets the goal variables for lower levels (and influences the aspiration levels), but does not directly influence lower-level routine modification. Nor are the influences from lower levels to the organizational level strong. On the other hand, the individual and work group levels are tightly intertwined and may need to be considered jointly.

Unanswered questions
There are unanswered questions on performance feedback effects on routine change at all levels of analysis and on cross-level effects. At the individual level, much of the work has taken the natural first step of investigating the effect of goals assigned to an individual on decisions controlled by that individual. Such work has been performed both in experimental and in field settings. It has resulted in important progress, but has ignored important features of routines. First, often the individual behaviour is part of a multi-person routine, so the individual control over own behaviours is modified by the individual's wish to effectively interlock behaviours with the others performing the routine. As a result, the person and the decision are not tightly associated. Second, the goal is often assigned at a higher level than the specific routines, as when a work unit has a production goal, but the production involves multiple steps (each with one or more routines) and the steps may involve selection between routines depending on the context. As a result, the goal and the routine are not tightly associated. In such cases, it is often not clear whether the individual will feel responsible for making any specific change, and that the change will be a modification of a routine. Hence, showing change in individual contributions to multi-person routines in a field setting is an important challenge for micro research.

Parallel with this challenge is one of expanding work on how multi-person routines change as a whole. This is the smallest part of performance research so far, and possibly the one with the highest potential for future work. The dissociation of goals and routines will most likely turn out to modify the predictions and findings here as well. Still, there is strong hope that performance feedback effects on routine change will be easy to find, as the problem of dissociation is similar to one that has been successfully resolved at the macro level: it is not clear which strategic action managers should take when organizational goals are not met, but it nonetheless turns out that effects on multiple types of actions can be shown. The reason is probably that managers pick from a wide range of potential actions with no particular bias for certain types of actions. As long as the work group members do not have a specific reason for avoiding change to a given routine, such as commitment (Staw, 1981) or power relations (Barley, 1986), it is more likely to change when the performance declines.

Macro research on performance feedback has so far focused on strategic changes that alter the domain of activity for the organization, and thus selects among macro routines. In Table 9.1, an important action controlled by the top management is the design of goal systems for the organization as a whole. There is abundant anecdotal evidence that managers do over- haul goal systems as a result of performance feedback, but systematic investigation of this action seems to be missing. It is an important missing link in work on performance feedback effects on routines, as modification of goals and aspiration levels can have effects that reverberate across the organization. If these changes are accepted at the work group and individ- ual level, the result is reassessment of the performance relative to the aspir- ation level and possibly changes in which parts of the organization will engage in problemistic search. The central insight in performance feedback research is that problems drive change more effectively than opportunities do, so change in the definition of a problem is consequential.

There are many challenges for cross-level research. Perhaps the most significant is the linking of research on individual change in the contribu- tion to a multi-person routine and change in the multi-person routine as a whole. Also, there is important work to do on the mutual influence of aspir- ation levels assigned from higher levels (Erez and Kanfer, 1983; Latham and Saari, 1982), social aspiration levels in the work group (Jones, 1990) and individual aspiration levels (Lant, 1992). Again, knowing how the definition of a problem is made is fundamental to investigation of how problems are solved.

Discussion and conclusions

The micro, meso, and macro research traditions that constitute organiza- tional research on performance feedback effects on routines have made impressive progress. Still, comparison of the findings suggests that there are unexploited opportunities for cross-fertilization, and there are also areas of research within each tradition that call for more work. More knowledge on performance feedback effects seems important because the effects are very strong and consistent across levels of analysis, suggesting that performance feedback is a major mechanism contributing to changes in organizational routines. Thus, of the two interests of research on routines – that of routines stabilizing organizational behaviour and that of routines changing – performance feedback research has a clear contribution to make on the second.

An important feature of performance feedback research is that much of the work done is not explicitly on routines. The bulk of work at the micro level is on performance, the bulk of work at the macro level is on strategic changes and risk taking, and the meso level research, which is mostly about routines, is not yet a large tradition. The theory seems to generalize across a wide range of outcomes including routines, however, so performance feedback is a theory that links research on routines to research on other organizational outcomes. In principle, future investigations might show that there is nothing special about routines: they are changed according to the same mechanisms as other organizational decisions change. In practice, we can anticipate that further work on routines will show that the interlocking of behaviours and lack of a distinct decision maker and decision-making opportunity causes change in routines to be different from other organizational decisions.

Routines have been central to organizational theory from the start, and learning theory has been central to investigations of routines from the start (Cyert and March, 1963; March and Simon, 1958). Learning theory makes progress on a wide range of learning mechanisms including performance feedback, and both theoretical developments and empirical findings have increased recently. This progress has led to additional knowledge bringing researchers into contact with additional unexplored questions, as when an inflated balloon gains a larger surface, giving a long agenda for future research. A recent increase in the pace of work on performance feedback suggests that it will not be long until the new questions have answers.

Note

1. Risk tolerance can range from strong risk aversion (risks are taken only in exchange for large gains in expected value) through risk neutrality to strong risk seeking (risky alternatives are chosen over safe ones with much higher expected value).

References

Audia, Pino G., Edwin A. Locke and Ken G. Smith (2000), 'The paradox of success: an archival and a laboratory study of strategic persistence following a radical environmental change', *Academy of Management Journal*, **43**(5), 837–53.

Bandura, Albert and Forest J. Jourden (1991), 'Self-regulatory mechanisms governing the impact of social comparison on complex decision making', *Journal of Personality and Social Psychology*, **60**(6), 941–51.

Barley, Stephen R. (1986), 'Technology as an occasion for restructuring: evidence from obser-
vations of CT scanners and social order of radiology departments', *Administrative Science
Quarterly*, **31**(March), 24–60.
Boeker, Warren (1997), 'Strategic change: the influence of managerial characteristics and
organizational growth', *Academy of Management Journal*, **40**(1), 152–70.
Bradach, Jeffrey L. (1997), 'Using the plural form in the management of restaurant chains',
Administrative Science Quarterly, **42**(June), 276–303.
Bromiley, Philip (1991), 'Testing a causal model of corporate risk taking and performance',
Academy of Management Journal, **34**(1), 37–59.
Burgelman, Robert A. (1994), 'Fading memories: a process theory of strategic business exit in
dynamic environments', *Administrative Science Quarterly*, **39**(1), 24–56.
Campbell, Donald J. and Karl F. Gingrich (1986), 'The interactive effects of task complexity
and participation on task performance: a field experiment', *Organizational Behavior and
Human Decision Processes*, **38**, 162–80.
Cardinal, Laura B. (2001), 'Technological innovation in the pharmaceutical industry: the use
of organizational control in managing research and development', *Organization Science*,
12(1), 19–36.
Chatman, Jennifer A. (1991), 'Matching people and organizations: selection and socialization
in public accounting firms', *Administrative Science Quarterly*, **36**(September), 459–84.
Chesney, Amelia A. and Edwin A. Locke (1991), 'Relationships among goal difficulty, busi-
ness strategies, and performance on a complex management simulation task', *Academy of
Management Journal*, **34**(2), 400–424.
Cohen, Michael D. and Paul Bacdayan (1994), 'Organizational routines are stored as proce-
dural memory: evidence from a laboratory study', *Organization Science*, **5**(4) (November),
554–68.
Cyert, Richard M. and James G. March (1963), *A Behavioral Theory of the Firm*, Englewood
Cliffs, NJ: Prentice-Hall.
DiMaggio, Paul J. and Walter W. Powell (1983), 'The iron cage revisited: institutional iso-
morphism and collective rationality in organizational fields', *American Sociological Review*,
48, 147–60.
Dosi, Giovanni, Richard R. Nelson and Sidney G. Winter (2004), 'Introduction: the nature
and dynamics of organizational capabilities', in G. Dosi, R.R. Nelson and S.G. Winters
(eds), *The Nature and Dynamics of Organizational Capabilities*, Oxford: Oxford University
Press, pp. 1–24.
Edmondson, Amy C. (2003), 'Speaking up in the operating room: how team leaders promote
learning in interdisciplinary action teams', *Journal of Management Studies*, **40**(6), 1419–52.
Edmondson, Amy (2004), 'Learning from mistakes is easier said than done', *Journal of
Applied Behavioral Science*, **40**(1).
Edmondson, Amy C., Richard M. Bohmer and Gary P. Pisano (2001), 'Disrupted routines:
team learning and new technology implementation in hospitals', *Administrative Science
Quarterly*, **46**(December), 685–716.
Erez, Miriam and Frederick H. Kanfer (1983), 'The role of goal acceptance in goal setting and
task performance', *Academy of Management Review*, **8**(3), 454–63.
Fiegenbaum, Avi and Howard Thomas (1986), 'Dynamic and risk measurement perspectives
on Bowman's risk-return paradox for strategic management: an empirical study', *Strategic
Management Journal*, **7**, 395–407.
Gersick, Connie J.G. and J. Richard Hackman (1990), 'Habitual routines in task-performing
groups', *Organizational Behavior and Human Decision Processes*, **47**(1), 65–97.
Greve, Henrich R. (1998), 'Performance, aspirations, and risky organizational change',
Administrative Science Quarterly, **44**(March), 58–86.
Greve, Henrich R. (2003a), 'A behavioral theory of R&D expenditures and innovation: evi-
dence from shipbuilding', *Academy of Management Journal*, **46**(6), 685–702.
Greve, Henrich R. (2003b), 'Investment and the behavioral theory of the firm: evidence from
shipbuilding', *Industrial and Corporate Change*, **12**(5), 1051–76.
Greve, Henrich R. (2003c), *Organizational Learning From Performance Feedback: A Behavioral
Perspective on Innovation and Change*, Cambridge, UK: Cambridge University Press.

Grinyer, Peter and Peter McKiernan (1990), 'Generating major change in stagnating companies', *Strategic Management Journal*, **11**, 131–46.

Hannan, Michael T. and John Freeman (1977), 'The population ecology of organizations', *American Journal of Sociology*, **82**, 929–64.

Hannan, Michael T. and John Freeman (1984), 'Structural inertia and organizational change', *American Sociological Review*, **49**, 149–64.

Hodgson, Geoffrey M. (2008), 'The concept of a routine', in Markus C. Becker (ed.), *Handbook of Organizational Routines*, Cheltenham, UK and Northampton, MA, USA: Edward Elgar, pp. 15–28.

Hogarth, Robin M., Brian J. Gibbs, Craig R.M. McKenzie and Margaret A. Marquis (1991), 'Learning from feedback: exactingness and incentives', *Journal of Experimental Psychology: Learning, Memory, and Cognition*, **17**(4), 734–52.

Hutchins, Edwin (1991), 'Organizing work by adaptation', *Organization Science*, **2**(1), 14–39.

Jones, Stephen R.G. (1990), 'Worker interdependence and output', *American Sociological Review*, **55**(April), 176–90.

Kahneman, Daniel and Amos Tversky (1979), 'Prospect theory: an analysis of decision under risk', *Econometrica*, **47**(2), 263–91.

Kerr, Steven (1975), 'On the folly of rewarding A, while hoping for B', *Academy of Management Journal*, **18**, 769–83.

Kluger, Avraham N. and Angelo N. DeNisi (1996), 'The effect of feedback interventions on performance: a historical review, a meta-analysis, and a preliminary feedback intervention theory', *Psychological Bulletin*, **119**(2), 254–84.

Knott, Anne Marie and Bill McKelvey (1999), 'Nirvana efficiency: a comparative test of residual claims and routines', *Journal of Economic Behavior & Organization*, **38**(4), 365–83.

Kraatz, Matthew S. (1998), 'Learning by association? Interorganizational networks and adaptation to environmental change', *Academy of Management Journal*, **41**(6 December), 621–43.

Lanir, Zvi. (1989), 'The reasonable choice of disaster: the shooting down of the Libyan airliner on 21 February 1973', *The Journal of Strategic Studies*, **12**(4), 479–93.

Lant, Theresa K. (1992), 'Aspiration level adaptation: an empirical exploration', *Management Science*, **38**(5), 623–44.

Lant, Theresa K., Frances J. Milliken and Bipin Batra (1992), 'The role of managerial learning and interpretation in strategic persistence and reorientation: an empirical exploration', *Strategic Management Journal*, **13**, 585–608.

Latham, Gary P. and Lise M. Saari (1979), 'The effect of holding goal difficulty constant on assigned and participatively set goals', *Academy of Management Journal*, **22**, 163–8.

Latham, Gary P. and Lise M. Saari (1982), 'The importance of union acceptance for productivity improvement through goal setting', *Personnel Psychology*, **35**(4), 781–7.

Levitt, Barbara and James G. March (1988), 'Organizational learning', in W.R.Scott and J. Blake (eds), *Annual Review of Sociology*, Palo Alto, CA: Annual Reviews, pp. 319–40.

Locke, Edwin A. and Gary P. Latham (1990), *A Theory of Goal Setting and Task Performance*, Englewood Cliffs, NJ: Prentice-Hall.

Locke, Edwin A., Elizabeth Frederick, Cynthia Lee and Philip Bobko (1984), 'Effect of self-efficacy, goals, and task strategies on task performance', *Journal of Applied Psychology*, **69**(2), 241–51.

Lopes, Lola L. (1987), 'Between hope and fear: the psychology of risk', *Advances in Experimental Social Psychology*, **20**, 255–95.

Manns, Curtis L. and James G. March (1978), 'Financial adversity, internal competition, and curriculum change in a university', *Administrative Science Quarterly*, **23**, 541–52.

March, James G. (1981), 'Footnotes to organizational change', *Administrative Science Quarterly*, **26**, 563–77.

March, James G. (1994), *A Primer on Decision Making: How Decisions Happen*, New York: Free Press.

March, James G. and Herbert Simon (1958), *Organizations*, New York: Wiley.

March, James G., Martin Schulz and Xueguang Zhou (2000), *The Dynamics of Rules: Change in Written Organizational Codes*, Stanford, CA: Stanford University Press.

McCuddy, M.K. and M.H. Griggs (1984), 'Goal setting and feedback in the management of a professional department: a case study', *Journal of Organizational Behavior Management*, **6**, 53–64.

Meyer, John W. and Brian Rowan (1977), 'Institutionalized organizations: formal structure as myth and ceremony', *American Journal of Sociology*, **83**, 340–63.

Mezias, Stephen J., Ya Ru Chen and Patrice R. Murphy (2002), 'Aspiration-level adaptation in an American financial services organization: a field study', *Management Science*, **48**(10), 1285–1300.

Miller, Danny and Ming-Jer Chen (1994), 'Sources and consequences of competitive inertia: a study of the US airline industry', *Administrative Science Quarterly*, **39**(March), 1–23.

Miner, Anne S. (1990), 'Structural evolution through idiosyncratic jobs: the potential for unplanned learning', *Organization Science*, **1**, 195–250.

Miner, Anne S., Paula Bassoff and Christine Moorman (2001), 'Organizational improvisation and learning: a field study', *Administrative Science Quarterly*, **46**(June), 304–37.

Miner, Anne S, Michael P. Ciuchta and Yan Gong (2008), 'Organizational routines and organizational learning', in Markus C. Becker (ed.), *Handbook of Organizational Routines*, Cheltenham, UK and Northamption, MA, USA: Edward Elgar, pp. 152–86 .

Mitsuhashi, Hitoshi and Henrich R. Greve (2004), 'Powerful and free: intraorganizational power and the dynamics of corporate strategy', *Strategic Organization*, **2**(1), 107–32.

Nelson, Richard R. and Sidney G. Winter (1982), *An Evolutionary Theory of Economic Change*, Boston, MA: Belknap.

Ocasio, William (1997), 'Towards an attention-based theory of the firm', *Strategic Management Journal*, **18**(Summer), 187–206.

Pfeffer, Jeffrey and Gerald R. Salancik (1978), *The External Control of Organizations*, New York: Harper & Row.

Roethlisberger, F.J. and William J. Dixon (1939), *Management and the Worker*, Cambridge, MA: Harvard University Press.

Seijts, Gerard H., Gary P. Latham, Kevin Tasa and Brandon W. Latham (2004), 'Goal setting and goal orientation: an integration of two different yet related literatures', *Academy of Management Journal*, **47**(2), 227–39.

Shapira, Zur (1994), *Risk Taking*, New York: Russel Sage.

Staw, Barry M. (1981), 'The escalation of commitment to a course of action', *Academy of Management Review*, **6**(4), 577–87.

Weick, Karl E. (1979), *The Social Psychology of Organizing*, Reading, MA: Addison-Wesley.

Wood, Robert E. and Albert Bandura (1989), 'Impact of conceptions of ability on self-regulatory mechanisms and complex decision making', *Journal of Personality and Social Psychology*, **56**, 407–15.

Wood, Robert E., Anthony J. Mento and Edwin A. Locke (1987), 'Task complexity as a moderator of goal effects: a meta-analysis', *Journal of Applied Psychology*, **72**(3), 416–25.

Zajac, Edward J. and Matthew S. Kraatz (1993), 'A diametric forces model of strategic change: assessing the antecedents and consequences of restructuring in the higher education industry', *Strategic Management Journal*, **14**(Summer special issue), S83–S102.

Zucker, Lynne G. (1977), 'The role of institutionalization in cultural persistence', *American Sociological Review*, **42**, 726–43.

10 Routines and routinization: an exploration of some micro-cognitive foundations

Nathalie Lazaric

Introduction

The aim of this chapter is to explore the cognitive micro foundations of routines in order to understand the drivers and the triggers of the routinization process. The evolution of routines and their transformation at the individual and collective levels is questioned here with an explicit detour within the cognitive debate for having an accurate vision of concepts such as memorization or cognitive mechanisms. These notions are not neutral in explaining the evolution and stability of routines. I shall try to provide a more explicit overview, examining changes occurring inside organizational routines.

For this purpose, it seems important to explain how individual and collective memorization occurs, so as to grasp how knowledge can be converted into routines, that is to say, reach a level of stability and automaticity at a given time. Although memorization and routinization mechanisms imply a degree of permanence, our procedural and declarative knowledge, and our memorization processes, evolve so that individuals and organizations can project themselves into the future and innovate. The setting up of cognitive automatisms contributing to the creation of procedural knowledge has, in the field of cognitive science, been the object of intensive debates concerning the question of their complexity and of the deliberation process involved. An overview of this debate is necessary, as the latter has had several implications in the observation of organizational routines.

The cognitive dimension will be explored in order to have a clear picture of the memorization process which is a first step inside the routinization process. Some authors highlight the necessity of dreaming and forgetting (Bergson, 1896); others believe that emotions play a role in our memorization processes (Damasio, 1994). These dimensions are not only important at the individual level but also in an organizational context (Lazaric and Denis, 2005; Reynaud, 2005; Pentland and Feldman, 2005). Firms do not just need to preserve their knowledge; they must also forget some of it. Furthermore, political conflicts create tensions at the level of these memorization processes that can potentially lead to inertia in procedural knowledge.

In the first section of this chapter, I review the individual dimension of these memorization processes, using the latest studies in cognitive science that are based on Anderson's distinction between procedural knowledge and declarative knowledge (Anderson, 1976). The intentional and controlled nature of the creation of procedural knowledge will be discussed here. In the second section, I present some difficulties of memorization and routinization in organizations. Although memorization mechanisms in organizations are similar to the ones discussed above, the organizational context produces an additional complexity by creating a filtering mechanism that interferes with collective representations and individual memorization processes. In my conclusion, I observe these processes and discuss the difficult transition between procedural and declarative knowledge.

I   The various forms of individual and organizational memorization and
their impact on routinization processes

Cohen and Bacdayan (1994) define routines as procedural knowledge. In order to introduce this issue, the content of this knowledge and its opposite form has to be debated. Anderson was one of the first authors to have made a distinction between declarative and procedural memory and to have popularized these notions. In this section, I shall talk about Anderson's distinction between procedural knowledge and declarative knowledge, and will show that 'proceduralization' processes are in no way automatic and that individuals can consciously choose the degree of stability within their knowledge. Studies in cognitive science have discussed the notion of cognitive automatisms (Shiffrin and Schneider, 1977) and have pointed to their temporal and contextual nature (Cohen, 1991; Cohen and Bacdayan, 1994). Emotions are also a determining factor in our memorization processes and it is therefore important to observe them closely if one is to grasp the difficulties of individual memorization and routinization processes. They impact on the quality of the memorization process and on the setting up of potential cognitive automatisms.

1   The distinction between procedural knowledge and declarative knowledge

Many authors regard the distinction between procedural knowledge and declarative knowledge as fundamental to understanding the development of routines. I have used the research done by Cohen (1991) who, based on Anderson's works, distinguishes two forms of memorization: the memorization of procedural knowledge and that of declarative knowledge.

Taking into account the studies on artificial intelligence (Winograd, 1975) and a criticism of behaviourist analyses, which focused on the external

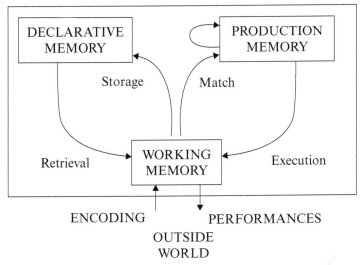

Source: Anderson (1976)

Figure 10.1 *The declarative memory between production memory and working memory*

manifestation of behaviour and not its content, Anderson, following Simon's footsteps, observed the course of mental processes in order to understand their driving forces. Using Simon's distinction between short-term memory and long-term memory, Anderson introduced a key notion: that of declarative memory, which plays a key role between 'working memory' and 'production memory' (Anderson, 1976). Figure 10.1 summarizes his argument.

In 1976, Anderson developed the idea that one form of memory collected facts and that another stored and recorded them. This notion was refined and clarified in 1983, a time during which Anderson distanced himself from the Simonian approach, in order to concentrate on cognitive mechanisms per se.

Later on, Anderson's research used the criticisms of artificial intelligence to go beyond the metaphor of the mind as a simple computer and to explore new directions. Indeed, starting from Ryle's distinction between 'know that' and 'know how', Winograd underlines why the expert system can only encode two representations of knowledge: the knowledge encoded independently from the programme and the knowledge mobilized when the programme is being used. In this context, declarative knowledge does not depend on any pre-existing programme and therefore exists independently of its use, whereas procedural knowledge translates into in a specific behaviour. This makes it possible to separate operationally the knowledge that is easily accessible, communicable and usable because it is independent and varied, from the knowledge that is used to solve a problem.

Anderson distances himself from the artificial intelligence approach and bases his analysis on his 'Adaptive Control of Thought' (or ACT) theory, to understand the transition from the status of declarative intelligence to that of procedural intelligence.

Declarative memory concerns more specifically the recollection of facts, events and propositions (Anderson, 1983; Cohen, 1991). It is not linked to a specific use and can be used for several purposes. In particular, it can be 'reorganized' in order to find the solution to a problem. It therefore mobilizes facts and technical or scientific principles that are different from know-how. Procedural memory, on the other hand, concerns know-how, how things are done, the knowledge that is put to use. Part of this knowledge can be expressed through routines and rests on 'patterned sequences of learned behaviour involving multiple actors' (Cohen and Bacdayan, 1994: 557).

Anderson focuses more particularly on the creation of procedural knowledge. Indeed, he believes that declarative knowledge is converted into procedural knowledge thanks to processes through which declarative knowledge is interpreted and selected. Interpretation leaves a trace in the working memory and repetition converts this declarative knowledge into procedural knowledge thanks to a compilation mechanism. The creation of some 'production rules' and their successful repetition increases their efficiency and, thus, their probability of being selected again. Anderson explains that 'knowledge automatization' occurs once knowledge has been used repeatedly over time for a specific purpose, consequently increasing performance and speed. This observation refers to the research in cognitive psychology and to the several clinical studies that have shown that, in some pathology, the two forms of memory are dissociated. A patient suffering from amnesia, for example, might no longer memorize declarative knowledge but his memorization of procedural knowledge is not affected. The case of a patient who did not remember the daily visits of his doctor, but could still play chess with great precision (Cohen, 1991) is but one of many cases that have made it possible to distinguish several types of memorization in individuals (Cohen, 1984; Cohen and Eichenbaum, 1993).

These two forms of memory do not have implications at the level of individual memorization alone. Indeed, as I shall see later, they generate specific representations of knowledge, creating different forms of organizational memory. Furthermore, they can promote the creation of cognitive automatisms that play a role in the individual and collective routinization process. This is the reason why Anderson's distinction is based on two questions that have been fundamental to the study of routines: are there automatic procedures that make it possible to convert declarative knowledge into procedural knowledge? Are there cognitive automatisms that can govern the human spirit? These questions, which many in cognitive science have tried to answer, deserve to be examined here.

2   The implications of cognitive automatisms   The question of cognitive automatisms was first addressed from the perspective of individuals' attention and their limited capacities: limited capacities that make them more or less capable of adapting to a complex environment. Shiffrin, with Atkinson, started his work in 1968, focusing more particularly on memory control processes (Atkinson and Shiffrin, 1968). A few years later, he and Schneider started their research on cognitive automatisms (Shiffrin and Schneider, 1977), distinguishing two types of information processing. The controlled process is performed more slowly and requires great attention. The automatic process, on the contrary, does not require attention in order to be performed; in other words, it 'consumes' very few attention resources. Automatic processing is anchored in long-term memory and does not disrupt the working memory; controlled processing, on the other hand, is maintained in the working memory, which requires conscious effort and sustained attention (Camus, 1988: 64). Furthermore, as Camus underlines, automatization can be mobilized consciously.

> An automatic process can be prepared by a controlled process. That is to say that an individual can consciously decide to enact an automatic activity. Controlled processing can help improve automatic processing of information. Indeed, the information processed automatically is transient and labile and its storing in the working memory takes no longer than a few seconds. If automatic processing requires more time, controlled processing enables individuals to maintain active the information that is necessary for automatic processing. (Camus, 1988, p. 66)

Schneider and Shiffrin's research has influenced the research protocol in cognitive science. Their work is based on the fact that visual automatism is different from motor-sensory automatism. Schmidt reckons that, in the context of motor-skill development, automatism is comparable to a flexible and parametrizable pattern more than to a rigid process (Schmidt, 1975). In keeping with this line of research on visual capacities and their automatic encoding, Kahneman distinguishes several levels of automatism: a highly automatic type of information processing that does not require any particular attention, a partly automatic process which attention can influence, and finally information processing that is occasionally automatic and requires attention (Kahneman and Charzyk, 1983; Kahneman and

Treisman, 1984). This distinction has led cognitive science to put into perspective these forms of automatism:

> There is widespread consensus around the notion that, notwithstanding exceptions, a behaviour understood as an observable response to a given situation cannot be considered as totally automatic: Only some components of the processing underlying this behaviour can be considered totally automatic. (Perruchet, 1988: 9)

These studies concur with and complement the work of Anderson. They explain and put into perspective the automatization mechanisms implemented by individuals. In the so-called 'proceduralization' phase, domain knowledge is directly incorporated into procedures for the execution of skills, which makes it possible to mobilize working memory less, but can also lead to errors or misses if the compilation phase is too short. In other words, the transition from declarative knowledge to procedural knowledge remains a delicate operation because the potential automatism can lock some know-how into tight procedures. Human judgement is necessary to update certain procedures.

At the individual level, therefore, it is important to find the right 'dosage' of automatisms. Individuals can learn to create certain types of automatisms in order to save their energy, and to keep certain pieces of knowledge in the realm of judgement. Thus, it is evident here that routines that are based on procedural knowledge must be learned and unlearned. At the organizational level, this has significant implications as indeed the organizations that rely on routines might, in their daily mobilization, forget the context in which they were learned and their significance. This is the reason why in some organizational contexts and certain collective tasks, some groups may tend to rely on old procedural knowledge without questioning its adequacy. This can lead to organizational inertia, conservatism and even to spectacular catastrophes. The best known is that analysed by Gersick and Hackman (1990). These researchers have shown why certain groups of individuals tend to rely on old know-how without being able to call it into question when the situation requires such a change. This can lead to an individual and/or collective inability to recognize new information and to consciously encode it into procedural memory. In the case of the air disaster of 13 January 1982, the crew proved incapable of questioning the usual procedures and to recognize that they were faced with a new situation in which heavy snow falls and the presence of ice in the engines called for the activation of the engine anti-ice system. The members of the crew seemed 'locked' in traditional procedures and performed the usual tasks (check list) without modifying any. This accident has led researchers in social sciences to discuss the organizational problems that can arise within groups of individuals and the maintenance of certain automatic procedures that should have been eliminated. The failure of the aircraft crew to question their procedural knowledge could have been avoided if they had acted in a less routine-like fashion and had trusted their common sense. This shows the strength and weakness of procedural knowledge. Indeed, it is used to stabilize information but can also become a trap if its carriers do not call it into question on a regular basis. As highlighted by Perrow (1984), this type of incident often occurs in situations of extreme technological complexity, where individuals have difficulty focusing on new information. Furthermore, the transfer of procedural knowledge can be difficult within teams of operators with a high turnover of personnel; this might result in the knowledge not being transferred, which can be detrimental to safety.

This is one of the reasons why routines and routinization processes should be understood, not as processes that 'freeze' procedural knowledge once and for all, but as processes through which knowledge evolves. Indeed, the procedural and declarative knowledge held by individuals is not inert but memorized in a certain social and political context, which leads individuals to reconfigure it actively in order either to question or to modify it in the course of action according to their understanding of a situation. As Martha Feldman has highlighted in this regard:

> Routines are performed by people who think and feel and care. Their reactions are situated in institutional, organizational and personal contexts. Their actions are motivated by will and intention. They create resist, engage in conflict, and acquiesce to domination. All these forces influence the enactment of organizational routines and create a tremendous potential for change. (Feldman, 2000: 614)

This free will dimension, observed in cognitive science and other fields of research, has led authors to refine the description of memorization procedures traditionally provided by Anderson, and to extend and integrate them into various contingent processes such as individuals' emotions or free will. Indeed, these dimensions are essential to understanding memorization processes. This dimension of free will in memorization processes had been clearly underlined in Bergson's works. Recent research in cognitive science emphasizes the pioneering role played by this French author and describes the various forms of memorization: declarative and non-declarative memorization.

3 The forms of memorization according to Bergson and Squire
Bergson's works were pioneering in their conceptualization of memorization processes (Squire, 2004).[1] Indeed, for this French philosopher, there

are two forms of memorization: memorization in the form of representations, and memorization in action. Bergson distinguishes a memory that stores the facts of our daily life, such as images, from a memory that materializes into motor mechanisms through the recollection of stored facts.

> The first records, in the form of memory-images, all the events of our daily life as they occur in time; it leaves to each fact, to each gesture, its place and date. Regardless of utility or of practical application, it stores up the past by the mere necessity of its own nature. But every perception is prolonged into a nascent action; and while the images are taking their place and order in this memory, the movements which continue them modify the organism, and create in the body new dispositions towards action. (Bergson, 1896: 92)

Bergson takes the example of the lesson learnt by heart, and which, through repetition, results in a form of automatism. He likens this form of memory to habit-memory, opposing it to image-memory that does not rely on pure repetition and maintains an important degree of imagination:

> To call up the past in the form of an image, we must be able to withdraw ourselves from the action of the moment, we must have the power to value the useless, we must have the will to dream. (Bergson, 1896: 94)

Both forms of memory being closely interwoven, Bergson puts automatic memorization processes in perspective by highlighting the role played by individuals' free will and freedom in the process of memorization.

> We are right when we say that habit is formed by the repetition of an effort; but what would be the use of repeating it, if the result were always to reproduce the same thing? The true effect of repetition is to decompose, and then to recompose, and thus appeal to the intelligence of the body. In this sense, a movement is learnt when the body has been made to understand it. (Bergson, 1896: 137)

Furthermore, Bergson shows that, although our memory is tuned to our body, 'what is automatic in the evocation of remembrances' has been greatly exaggerated (Bergson, 1896: 117). And in this automatic memorisation tendency there are 'inner movements of repeating and recognizing that are like a prelude to voluntary attention. *They mark the limit between the voluntary and the automatic*' (ibid: 145, my emphasis).

With both forms of memorization, there is permanent tension between the memory turned towards the present action and the memory that tends to distance itself from action. Hence the selection between motor habits and their representations: 'The nascent generality of the idea consists, then, in a certain activity of the mind, in a movement between action and representation' (ibid: 324).

Bergson's ideas remain relevant today because they express, in a literary manner, what cognitive science formulated subsequently; i.e. the contextual and temporal nature of cognitive automatisms. Moreover, Bergson goes further in his description of the memorization process in that he emphasizes how the body accompanies the memorization process. The body is involved in this cognitive effort in that together the body and spirit provide direction and meaning to the memorization process. Squire's approach (2004) might initially be disconcerting because it seems to point to the existence of a multitude of memorization processes, but, in fact, it is more a decomposition of the procedural memory into different facets and learning zones that it describes. Indeed, following Bergson, we could subdivide memory into a declarative form (where we build representations) and a non-declarative form (zone of reflex and automatisms). This recent concept makes it possible to locate the areas in the body where different types of knowledge are created and stabilized. Emotions are part of this configuration and correspond to a specific area that stores long-term memories.

Squire (2004) uses and extends Bergson's distinction to the principle of declarative and non-declarative knowledge. Like James, he underlines that there are many forms of memorization. Some are more able to collect facts, whereas others are directly operational, while others still are related to more emotional forms of memorization located in other parts of the brain, particularly in the 'amygdala' area. Each specific form of memorization is associated with a physiological area. This does not constitute a break from Anderson's work, but a diversification of the non-declarative form of memorization, which helps to gain a better understanding of the various learning processes where emotions and reflexes are included as specific types of functioning located in a particular area. According to Squire (2004):

> Declarative memory allows remembered material to be compared and contrasted. It supports the encoding of memories in terms of relationships among multiple items and events. The stored representations are flexible and can guide performance under a wide range of test conditions. Declarative memory is representational. It provides a way to model the external world and a model of the world, it is either true or false. It is dispositional and expressed through performance rather than recollection. Non-declarative forms of memory occur as modifications within specialized performance systems. The memories are revealed through reactivation of the systems within the learning originally occurred. (Squire, 2004: 172–3)

This idea is accepted with increasing unanimity within the cognitive science community (Eichenbaum, 1997; Eichenbaum and Cohen, 2001; Milner et al., 1998; Schacter et al., 2000). This argument is partly based on James' pioneering works, which underlined the flexibility of habits and showed that the various forms of memorization are found in different parts of the brain and are interconnected (James, 1890, in Thompson, 1990).

Eichenbaum argues that there is no unique circuit through which non-declarative knowledge is converted into declarative knowledge during the execution or modification of a task; different circuits ('brain circuits') are at play and have distinct functions in the hippocampus. Declarative knowledge is essential here in that it makes it possible to avoid over-simplified behaviours characterized by some rigidity in a context of repetition. Declarative memory is characterized by 'representational flexibility' enabling it to adapt to new situations, contrary to the non-declarative forms of memorization that are thought to be more rigid (Eichenbaum, 1997, p. 554).

The question here is therefore to determine, in cognitive and social sciences, the degree of plasticity of both forms of memory. Indeed, although non-declarative memory involves an emotional zone that has an impact on motor sensory processes, it is highly probable that these forms of memorization are far from inert. This is precisely what Damasio suggests when he argues that emotions play an important role in our cognitive faculties.

Our memory does not merely consist of archiving or storing documents or images that enable us to observe the past. On the contrary, our memory rests on representations made of recollections that enable us to implement our potential representations and use them. This notion of images is not just Damasio's (1994). It is also found in Boulding's work (1956) for whom our knowledge base is built around our recollection of images that guide our future and present behaviour, a 'vision of the world' so to speak.[2] Representations serve to build the future, to create new knowledge and to stabilize the knowledge we use daily. They are made not only of images but also of emotions.

When an individual faces a difficult situation and needs to make a precise choice, or elaborate a strategy, the challenge is to be able to implement a solution that will not be the fruit of past learning only. The act of inventing then rests on analogies and action combined with intuition and reason. Damasio (1994) shows that, if a truly new situation emerges, intense emotions play a role in the resolution of this problem. Emotions then serve to project oneself into the future and to make decisions. Contrary to what one could think, they are not the enemy of the mind but accompany the latter; otherwise, there could be no true invention or creativity. This work is based on the somatic markers hypothesis which, based on clinical observations, has shed light on how the brain, when faced with a new situation, activates part of its resources in different ways. Indeed, the attention required to carry out a new task, or face a new problem, mobilizes a certain somatic state that activates the biological regulation of the dorso-lateral area.

The somatic marker mechanism stimulates those of the working memory and of the attention related to future scenarios. In short, we cannot form an appropriate theoretical representation of our own psychological state and that of others if we do not have a mechanism such as that of somatic markers. (Damasio, 1994: 278)

The concept of somatic markers is particularly interesting here. Indeed, using the latest studies in cognitive science, Damasio has shown that, every time a cognitive effort is made, there is a localized activation of our neurons. Neurologists have been able to visualize this cognitive effort that activates certain localized zones of our brains and bodies. This example shows that the creation of individual routines is in no way automatic, but implies intense attention and decision making.

Thus the implications of this research at the organizational level are now clear. The development of routines appears to require will and sustained effort so that new procedural memory can be created. The organizational dimension deserves careful observation because it is through this dimension that the individual and collective efforts are coordinated and that an appropriate incentive regime can be developed ('sense-making routines' according to Reynaud, 2005). On the whole, this shows the complexity and scope of our memorization processes. They are not limited to the activation of cognitive automatism or of simple and inert procedural knowledge; they rest on an evocation process through which we can invent new strategies, face uncertainty and project into the future. This debate is important to understanding the evolution and stability of routines because the processes of collective memorization implemented also change and evolve. This shows that memorization processes are dynamic as our cognitive and social representations evolve and the routines implemented express this potential change.

The aim of this first section was to position ourselves at the heart of the debates concerning memorization at the individual level. Indeed, individual and collective routines rest on pieces of procedural knowledge that are in no way cognitive automatisms. And routines, in the current sense of the term, are sometimes likened to those simple soulless acts. In this context, providing a review of this debate seemed necessary to be able to show the richness and the relative stability of our knowledge and memorization processes, which evolve with time. This debate concerns organizations as their organizational memory also evolves and activates part of their existing knowledge. Though the repetition of some of this knowledge may seem automatic, it is simply aimed at promoting a degree of efficiency, which is limited in time and in context. In the second section, we shall show how organizations, just as individuals, rest on various memorization processes, and why it is often difficult to learn and unlearn procedural knowledge in an organizational context.

II   Organizational routines: between creation, repetition and sense making
To illustrate the implications of this debate on organizational routines, I shall make use of existing studies on the content of organizational memory and on how firms determine the right balance between declarative knowledge and procedural knowledge. Within organizations, also, there is a will to find a balance between stability – or even inertia – evolution and change in the content and boundaries of organizational memory.

Furthermore, I shall show that this tension reveals, at the individual and organizational levels, a will to prevent routines from becoming rigid and to maintain a degree of creativity in the latter. Indeed, if, as Feldman (2000) summarizes, routines are 'effortful accomplishments' and 'emergent accomplishments', it is essential to understand the practical mechanisms through which routines are stabilized and can evolve. I shall illustrate these difficulties and mechanisms by comparing the theoretical propositions provided in the existing literature to the results of an empirical study that I have conducted.

1   The content of organisational memory and the content of routines

ORGANISATIONAL MEMORY AND THE DEBATES   This debate, which has brought us into the heart of cognitive science, has raised the fundamental methodological question of how analyses of individual knowledge could be transposed to the level of organizational knowledge. This debate is certainly not new, but it is necessary to describe it briefly. Indeed, several authors consider that organizations do not 'remember' in the literal sense of the term. Bartlett (1961), although he shared Bergson's point of view concerning the recomposition within individual learning processes, had his doubts concerning organizational memory. He favoured the term 'memory within the group' to the term 'memory of the group' (Paoli and Prencipe, 2003). Thus, it appears that the term 'organizational memory' should not be understood literally but at the metaphoric level (Divry and Lazaric, 1998).

The term 'routine', understood as organizational memory, was popularized by Nelson and Winter (1982) who insisted on organizations' ability to memorize individuals' skills and to encode them within the organization so as to be able to respond coherently to changes in their environment. Organizational memory necessitates a degree of organizational coherence in individual routines so that coordination, in the primary sense of the word, can exist. Depending on the type of organization, this discipline necessitates a more or less efficient conflict resolution system.[3]

THE MEMORY DISTRIBUTED AMONG A GROUP OF INDIVIDUALS   The hypothesis that routines are distributed, confirmed through a study of card games, helps to understand how routines form at the individual level, and how they are transferred within a group, without the players having consciously to elaborate a strategy of knowledge exchange and transfer (Cohen and Bacdayan, 1994). Indeed, in their experiment, the card players do not speak to each other and yet develop common strategies and rules of action that are transferred within their group. This notion of routines seen as distributed procedural knowledge is very useful to understanding that individual knowledge can be transferred and shared among a group of individuals or an organization. Let us note here, again, that there are strong similarities between researches conducted at the individual level and those carried out at the collective level. The concept of 'transactive memory' (Wegner, 1987; Wegner et al., 1991) is useful in explaining how individuals' memory lies within a social context. This experience was repeated in a laboratory in order to test how well these groups performed a task.

Liang et al. (1995) identify three factors of performance that form the 'transactive memory'. The first effect is the specialization of certain aspects and the differences between the groups according to whether or not their members were trained together; the second is coordination, i.e. the individuals who know each other will cooperate more naturally and in a more flexible way; the third is knowing and being able to trust other individuals' skills. Liang et al.'s study shows that the groups whose members were trained together perform better than the groups whose members were trained individually, hence the importance of interactions between individuals and the development of a 'transactive memory'. This analysis of organizational performance also helps us understand the memorization mechanisms, which are essential to the activation and mobilization of organizational routines.

THE CHARACTERISTICS OF ORGANIZATIONAL MEMORY AND THE DIFFICULTY OF STRIKING THE RIGHT BALANCE BETWEEN DECLARATIVE AND PROCEDURAL MEMORIES   The literature on organizational memory provides an explanation for organizations' memory not being the sum of individual knowledge, but part of the latter, which will be used and activated within organizational routines. Organizational memory is thus 'collective beliefs, behavioural routines, or physical artefacts that vary in their content, level, dispersion and accessibility' (Moorman and Miner, 1997).

On the basis of this definition, several authors have attempted to determine the impact of the content of organizational memory. Indeed, the centralized or decentralized nature of an organization, as well as the level of memorization (intense or low) has an impact on the firm's creativity – for example on its economic performance and creativity during the launch of new products. Thus, Moorman and Miner (1997) underline the difficulty of determining, in practice, the right dosage of procedural memory and of declarative memory. Too much procedural memory within organizations can hinder creativity because, then, firms find it difficult to absorb new knowledge. This balance is very sensitive to changes in the environment. If organizational memory is dispersed but contains a minimal level of procedural knowledge, firms can then innovate and create new products even in a turbulent environment. However, the dispersion of knowledge can have a negative impact on competitiveness in the case of a turbulent environment, and a positive impact on creativity and performance in the context of a relatively stable environment. The conclusions of the study show that a sufficient degree of procedural knowledge enables firms to absorb new knowledge, but that the nature of this knowledge (centralized or scattered) has a structuring impact in the ability to assimilate (Moorman and Miner, 1997).

A complementary study was conducted in some firms of the food-processing industry; it shows that a high degree of procedural knowledge has a positive impact on efficiency but a negative impact on creativity, and that it is necessary for both forms of memory to evolve together in order to stabilize the organization and promote its creativity. Indeed, food-processing firms tend to codify extensively their practice, which creates important amounts of procedural knowledge but reduces their innovation capacity.

> Companies have been formalizing next product development activities, following ISO certification programmes, project management models (. . .) promulgated by the industry. In pursuit of this effort they try to codify successful own or others' practices and experience into a set of rules or recipes (. . .) to speed up activities and build up skills. One implication of our findings for product development practitioners is that companies need to exercise moderation in these practices. (Kyriakopoulos and de Ruyter, 2004, 1491)

Indeed, the combination of large amounts of procedural knowledge with internal or external information flows does not allow for creativity; this is due to the fact that the high degree of existing procedural knowledge hinders the absorption and assimilation of new information (Kyriakopoulos and de Ruyter, 2004). This result is in keeping with other studies concerning ISO standards that underline why the implementation of ISO standards has a positive impact on attention and detail at the expense of innovation capacities.

INDIVIDUALS' RESISTANCE   The resistance met during the setting up of codification procedures also indicates the difficulty for enterprises of maintaining a balance between sustained innovation and organizational stability. Indeed, codifying procedural knowledge, as in the context of ISO standards, responds to a need to articulate and memorize existing knowledge by giving less room for creativity. Nevertheless, behind managerial methods, there often are gaps between what individuals and organizations claim they do and what they actually put into practice. This gap can be analysed as a form of resistance or as a certain amount of discretionary power or leeway enjoyed by the individuals.

These evolutions are also observed at political level in organizations that claim to have implemented a certain level of organizational practices, but whose theoretical claims are not corroborated by reality. The discrepancy between 'ostensive routines' and 'performative' ones which has been studied theoretically and empirically (Feldman and Pentland, 2003) shows organizations' difficulty in controlling the routines developed and their lack of power in the face of individuals' free will.

In the nuclear industry, this gap between existing routines and the routines that should be implemented has been well described by the concepts of 'official memory' and 'underground memory' (Girod-Seville, 1998). In this industrial sector, the level of prescriptive specificity is quite high, which sometimes causes individuals to deviate from the administrative rules and to invent and combine their own practices to solve problems. This leads to differences between the official level of memory such as the management team sees it and the reality of this organizational memory. The individuals' creativity and resistance generate knowledge and cognitive representations that differ from the level prescribed by the management team. The political and cognitive dimensions are therefore the two hidden sides of one process through which routines develop, but whose content oscillates between repetition and creativity depending on circumstances and on individuals' and organizations' dispositions.

This is the reason why some authors recommend that attention be focused, not only on the accumulation of knowledge, but also on the destruction of the latter.[4] Indeed, there comes a time when individuals and organizations are incapable of absorbing new information. In this regard, Bergson thought it essential for individuals to dream in order to create new representations and to withdraw from the knowledge developed and destined for imminent use. Other authors suggest the importance, at organizational level, of forgetting in order to be able to carry on learning. This 'organizational forgetting' must be managed consciously and carefully so that crucial technological and organizational know-how is not occulted (Holan and Philips, 2004).

2   An illustration of the difficulty of memorizing tasks   Through a case study that Denis and I conducted in the mid-1990s, I was able to observe this difficult memorization and routinization of tasks (Lazaric and Denis,

2001, 2005). The firm we surveyed (Defial) was a food-processing enterprise that supplied meat to wholesalers and collective caterers. This company was in the process of implementing the ISO 9002 quality standard and for this purpose had to reconfigure its knowledge base (for a detailed analysis and an explanation of our empirical observations, see Lazaric and Denis, 2005).

This resulted in a new memorization and routinization of tasks, but involved great difficulties both socially and cognitively. In order to implement the ISO 9002 standard, Defial needed to reconfigure its organizational memory. Before the implementation of this standard, the employees – technicians and employees – had important discretionary powers with regard to quality control in the workshop and during the different stages of meat cutting and processing. However, the health safety crisis that affected the beef market in Europe led to the implementation of strict selective measures that forced meat suppliers to comply with new quality control procedures, or else face eviction from the market. Thus, Defial had to implement the ISO standard rapidly, for fear of losing its regular clients.

The introduction of the ISO 9002 standard represented a break from the traditional routines existing in the firm. Indeed, change occurred at two levels with the implementation of the standard. Firstly, new technological tools were introduced: scales, automatic measurement and tuning devices as well as computers for the follow-up and compilation of all technical data. The goal was to ensure traceability of the meat, and this could only be achieved by using new control and measurement tools. Secondly, the data collecting tasks were redistributed and centralized with the introduction of a quality manual in which were centrally memorized all the data related to organizational practices, the follow-up between the various groups and the different stages of production. Although this process of change does not, a priori, seem complex, it proved extremely difficult to implement. The reasons for this difficulty deserve careful examination.

In fact, one of the reasons for this difficulty was certainly related to the high level of procedural knowledge. Defial was a traditional family enterprise well established in the region, and whose functioning and organization had remained almost unchanged since the mid-1950s. The technical tools used evolved progressively but organizational practices had changed very little. With regard to the labour force, for example, the firm recruited and then trained local people with low levels of qualifications. Practices were therefore transferred 'on-the-job' by employees and the average productivity rate depended on the level of cooperation between the employees and their ability to reduce intraorganizational conflicts. The management team spent very little time in the workshop and trusted their foremen. As a result, the knowledge was transferred empirically without the management team intervening to verify the content of the work. Quality control was the responsibility of the maintenance team who collected samples of meat to have them controlled externally. In this context, the volume of procedural knowledge evolved progressively and regularly.

The introduction of the ISO norm had a significant impact on both forms of knowledge memorization. Indeed, declarative memory was disrupted by a sudden inflow of new organizational and technical procedures. The workers had to familiarize themselves with the new technological tools and learn how they functioned. In parallel to this, a new system of information flow management was implemented to facilitate information processing within teams, select significant practices that could serve as references, write the main control procedures implemented and transfer them to the following stage of production, and finally compile descriptions of all stages of production and make them available to the quality manager who could, if need be, modify the way in which certain tasks were performed. The volume of technical and organizational information needing processing was vast, especially for employees who were not used to high-tech tools and were not accustomed to using computers to compile lists of technical problems and transfer them to other departments. Furthermore, the management team, who seemed to have been 'dozing' for several years, got very involved in this process and started to communicate on a regular basis with the new recruits of the quality department. Through these conversations they were informed about the progress made and the results obtained in terms of quality control; they were informed, for example, about the rate of salmonella (close to zero or not) or about the performance of the equipment (whether the breakdown rate was low enough to ensure that the flow of information needed by the internal laboratory and the quality department was not interrupted).

The new division of labour required the employees to remain vigilant at all times, and 'unlearn' some of their old procedural knowledge. This process was difficult and necessitated the institution of a policy of incentives and of active training so that employees would accept this change and attach meaning to their new work. Indeed, the work pace was speeded up dramatically and operators were required to absorb vast amounts of technical information, to familiarize themselves with the new equipment used in the different stages of production and to compile data bases relevant to the quality department and laboratory. For most employees the new process of memorization was difficult and the routinization of the process was extremely slow, firstly because of the employees' resistance to the changes that were taking place, and secondly because the new declarative knowledge that was to generate new procedural knowledge was not introduced and assimilated in one day. The cognitive automatisms were acquired more or less easily during the training phase and the employees inevitably experienced the 'information overload syndrome'. An operator summarizes this well:

> At the beginning I was constantly wondering who I should receive data from and who I should transfer it to. I was never sure what I should take note of and what I shouldn't. Now I no longer ask myself the question; I just take notes and my colleagues do the same. They found their own adjustment marks for selecting data (for example by using average weekly data instead of daily data). (An operator on the production line, in Lazaric and Denis, 2005)

The process was eventually stabilized thanks to the implementation of a training course that increased the employees' empirical knowledge and taught them how to manage the various flows of information and synchronize it adequately even though the technical objects are highly dispersed. Moreover, the volumes of information, which had previously seemed unmanageable, were progressively processed and distributed more efficiently between the different actors. Learning to compile data efficiently was essential to the creation of procedural knowledge and to the acquisition of new automatisms in the workshop. This is well illustrated by a remark made by a member of the management team:

> Employees played their role, but the compilation of documents caused a major upheaval. In an effort to increase awareness among employees, we, along with the quality manager, summoned each team in turn and explained the role of the new procedures, why they were implemented, and why it was important for employees to record their actions. Although initially the operators recorded how they operate the controls, they soon stopped focusing and forgot to write down what they were doing. We [the management] had to constantly be there in order to observe them. *Now the practice of taking notes is carried out more automatically. It is becoming an automatism.* (The management, Defial, in Lazaric and Denis, 2005)

The difficulty of memorising tasks observed in Defial also explains why the creation of new procedural knowledge was also difficult. Indeed, individuals are very sensitive to the content and meaning of their work and might not always accept a reconfiguration of their knowledge and the implementation of new representations of the latter. This resistance is actually relatively healthy and makes it possible to maintain the firm's internal coherence by preventing organizational practices from changing incessantly according to managerial modes. Furthermore, and this is a question that deserves examination, the individuals who resist change because they do not wish to shake their habits or work in an environment that demands great attention and energy, are not necessarily the least capable of changing their procedural knowledge. These individuals can derive great pleasure from learning foreign languages or from trying a new sport. Consequently, the evolution of procedural knowledge in an organizational context, and simultaneously in a context of private life, needs to be explored to better understand the sources and content of procedural knowledge. The recent studies have made important contributions, but more in-depth observations are necessary to understand how the organizational context affects individual procedural knowledge and its representations (for a longer discussion, see Becker et al., 2005).

Using Defial's example of task memorization, I have tried to show why the creation of new automatisms was a delicate exercise. Indeed, individuals demonstrate some resistance to unlearning. Furthermore, although the incentive system plays a fundamental role, it does not solve all the problems because some problems require individual and collective involvement. This sustained effort is the keystone of the setting up of new organizational routines and implies genuine individual and collective motivation. We can clearly see here that the debate on cognitive science is relevant to the study of routines and that it helps understand the difficulty, for organizations, of changing routines. Motivation is a conscious and deliberate act and a commitment of individuals to take part in a new learning process and, as Leibenstein (1987) noted, authority and hierarchy cannot take the place of this deliberate effort.

Conclusion
In order to understand what drives change in routines, I made an exploration inside the heart of cognitive mechanisms for observing the development and evolution of declarative and procedural knowledge. Some cognitive processes in human beings remain a mystery but cognitive science research is gradually shedding light on some of their aspects. Furthermore, new dimensions must be taken into account to understand the creation of procedural knowledge: individuals' emotions and free will. With regard to declarative knowledge, dreaming and forgetting are also dimensions essential to stabilizing and renewing our individual representations. From this point of view, Bergson's contribution is invaluable and in keeping with many recent studies carried out in cognitive science.

Within organizations, the memorization mechanisms are at once similar and diverse. Indeed, organizations use their own filters and mechanisms to generate organizational coordination. This memory feeds on individual knowledge but also has its own dimension as it does not merely consist of the sum of individual knowledge and must be able to survive when individuals leave. Memorization processes are distributed, i.e. they are affected by the interactions of individuals with other people. The routines rest on the organizational memory implemented and on the procedural knowledge and representations of this knowledge (individual and collective representations). The organizational context where memorization processes and the creation of routines emerge can, in some measure, influence the creation of organizational procedural knowledge. However, as Leibenstein (1987) pointed out, a management team has limited control over the content of the work and the way in which it is performed and for this reason a sufficient amount of trust is necessary. An organization can create incentive measures, but is also faced with strong resistance. The 'information overload syndrome' is a good illustration of this difficulty. It shows how emotions interfere with the creation of new knowledge and why cognitive mechanisms cannot alone explain this process, which creates different dynamics depending on the individual and/or organizational context in which it is introduced.

More generally, the cognitive science debate is a detour that has enabled us to get to the heart of processes of individual memorization. This detour is essential if one is to include, in the study of organizational routines, new dimensions such as resistance, motivation, emotions and dreams. These dimensions must be taken account of when observing individuals' acquisition of new procedural knowledge (their resistance or their possible acceptance) and when trying to determine how organizations interfere in this process by 'smoothing' this learning process.

Notes

1. According to Squire, two pioneers have had great influence in the field of cognitive science. William James (1890) with his work, *Principles of Psychology*, and Henri Bergson, who was a French philosopher (1859–1941). Henri Bergson wrote the first edition of *Matter and Memory* in 1896 and *Creative Evolution* in 1907; he was highly influenced by Spencer's work. There are many similarities between Bergson's work and his book *Matter and Memory* and William James' approach to habits. Bergson grants great importance to the notion of perception initially developed by William James. Just as James did, he thought that perception and emotion play a key role in our cognitive faculties. Bergson was awarded the Nobel Prize for literature in 1927. Throughout his works, he strongly argued that intuition was deeper than pure reason and was also influenced by Spencer's evolutionist ideas. However, in Creative Evolution, Bergson argues that creative urge, not the Darwinian concept of natural selection, is at the heart of selection. It is also said that Bergson (who married Marcel Proust's cousin in 1881) gave Marcel Proust the idea for his great novel, *Remembrance of things past* (1913–1927).
2. For a survey on the theories of knowledge, see Lazaric and Lorenz (2003).
3. Indeed, organizations with decentralized management are more likely than highly centralized organizations to solve problems of coordination and conflicts because they can manage more efficiently their members' knowledge diversity and creativity (Lazaric and Raybaut, 2005).
4. The 'information overload syndrome' identified in literature is a process in which there is a cognitive and political blockage resulting in a saturation of individuals' cognitive capacities when they are faced with what they perceive as too much information. The difficulty of absorbing new information, or 'information overload syndrome', is a well-known phenomenon in organizations (Eppler and Mengis, 2004). This syndrome appears to affect both individuals – regardless of whether they are managers or employees – and organizations, and can be summarized as the inability to assimilate existing information when the volume of information is perceived as too important and unassimilable. This difficulty to create both declarative and procedural knowledge is due to the stress perceived by individuals having to deal with large amounts of information when a technological or

organizational change occurs (Sparrow, 1999; Walsh, 1995; Eppler and Mengis, 2004). This syndrome should not be seen as just the physical or technical inability to assimilate information, but also as the difficulty to create and transform organizational procedural knowledge. Furthermore, this reveals an individual or organizational resistance to the evolution of these forms of knowledge.

References

Anderson, J.R. (1976), *Language Memory and Thought*, Hillsdale, NJ: Erlbaum.

Anderson, J.R. (1983), *The Architecture of Cognition*, Cambridge, MA: Havard University Press.

Atkinson, R.C. and R.M. Shiffrin (1968), 'Human memory: a proposed system and its control process', in K.W. Spence and J.T. Spence (eds), *The Psychology of Learning and Motivation*, vol. 2, New York: Academic Press.

Bartlett, J. (1961), *Remembering*, Cambridge: Cambridge University Press.

Becker, M., N. Lazaric, R.R. Nelson and S.G. Winter (2005), 'Toward an operationalization of the routines concept', *Industrial and Corporate Change*, **14**(5), 775–91.

Bergson, H. (1991) [1896], *Matter and Memory* (trans. N.M. Paul and W.S. Palmer), New York: Zone Books.

Boulding, K. (1956), *The Image*, Michigan, MI: University of Michigan Press.

Camus, J.F. (1988), 'Distinction between controlled and automatic processes' in Schneider and Shiffrin: original French title: La distinction entre les processus contrôlés et les processus automatiques chez Schneider et Shiffrin, in P. Perruchet (ed.), *Les automatismes cognitifs*, Liège, Brussels: Pierre Mardaga.

Cohen, M.D. (1991), 'Individual learning and organisational routine: emerging connections', *Organization Science*, **2**, 135–9.

Cohen, M.D. and P. Bacdayan (1994), 'Organisational routines are stored as procedural memory: evidence from a laboratory study', *Organization Science*, **5**(4), 554–68.

Cohen, N.J. (1984), 'Preserved learning capacity in amnesia: evidence for multiple memory systems', in L. Squire and N. Butters (eds), *Neuropsychology of Memory*, New York: Guilford Press, pp. 88–103.

Cohen, N.J. and H. Eichenbaum (1993), *Memory Amnesia and the Hippocampal System*, Cambridge, MA: MIT Press.

Damasio, A. (1994), *Descartes' Error Emotion Reason and the Human Brain*, New York: Grosset Putman Books.

Divry, C. and N. Lazaric (1998), 'Organisational memory: original French title, *Mémoire Organisationnelle*, *Revue Internationale de Systémique*, **12**(1), 3–13.

Eichenbaum, H. (1997), 'Declarative memory: insights from cognitive neurobiology', *Annual Review of Psychology*, **48**, 547–72.

Eichenbaum, H. and N.J. Cohen (2001), *From Conditioning to Conscious Recollection: Memory Systems of the Brain*, New York: Oxford University Press.

Eppler, M.J. and J. Mengis (2004), 'The concept of overload: a review of literature from organization science, accounting, marketing, MIS and related disciplines', *The Information Society*, **20**, 325–44.

Feldman, Martha (2000), 'Organizational routines as a source of continuous change', *Organization Science*, **11**(6), 611–29.

Feldman, M. and B.T. Pentland (2003), 'Reconceptualizing organizational routines as a source of flexibility and change', *Administrative Science Quarterly*, **48**(1), 94–118.

Gersick, J.G. and J.R. Hackman (1990), 'Habitual routines in task-performing groups', *Organisational Behavior and Human Decision Process*, **47**, 65–97.

Girod-Seville, M. (1998), 'Memorisation and nuclear process: original French title: Mémorisation et ingénierie nucléaire, *Revue Internationale de Systémique*, **12**(1), 119–36.

Holan, M. De P. and N. Philips (2004), 'Remembrance of things past? The dynamics of organizational forgetting', *Management Science*, **50**(11), Nov., 1603–13.

James, W. (1890), *The Principles of Psychology*, 2nd vol., Henry Holt; reissued by Dower, New York, 1950.

Kahneman, D.A. and D. Charzyk (1983), 'Test of the automaticity of reading: dilution of the stroop effects by color irrelevant stimuli', *Journal of Experimental Psychology: Human Perception and Performance*, **9**, 497–509.

Kahneman, D.A. and A. Treisman (1984), 'Changing views of attention and automaticity', in R. Parasuram (ed.), *Varieties of Attention*, London: Academic Press.

Kyriakopoulos, K. and K. de Ruyter (2004), 'Knowledge stocks and information flows in new product development', *Journal of Management Studies*, **41**(8), 1469–98.

Lazaric, N. and B. Denis (2001), 'How and why routines change: some lessons from the artic- ulation of knowledge with ISO 9002 implementation in the food industry', *Economies et Sociétés*, **6**, 585–611.

Lazaric, N. and B. Denis (2005), 'Routinisation and memorisation of tasks inside a workshop: an illustration through a case study', *Industrial and Corporate Change*, **14**(5), 873–96.

Lazaric N. and E. Lorenz (2003), *Knowledge, Learning and Routines*, Critical Studies in Economic Institutions, 2 vols, Cheltenham, UK and Northampton, MA, USA: Edward Elgar.

Lazaric, N. and A. Raybaut (2005), 'Knowledge, hierarchy and the selection of routines: an interpretative model with group interactions', *Journal of Evolutionary Economic*, **15**(4), 393–421.

Leibenstein, H. (1987), *Inside the Firm: the Inefficiencies of Hierarchy*, Cambridge, MA: Harvard University Press.

Liang, D.W., R. Moreland and L. Argote (1995), 'Group versus individual training and group performance: the mediating role of transactive memory', *Personality and Social Psychology Bulletin*, **21**(4), 384–93.

Milner, B., L.R. Squire and E.R. Kandel (1998), 'Cognitive Neuroscience and the study of memory', *Neuron*, **20**, 445–68.

Moorman, C. and A.S. Miner (1997), 'The impact of organizational memory on the new product performance and creativity', *Journal of Marketing Research*, **34**(1), 91–106.

Nelson, R. and S. Winter (1982), *An Evolutionary Theory of Economic Change*, Cambridge, MA: Belknap Press of Harvard University Press.

Paoli, M. and A. Prencipe (2003), 'Memory of the organisation and memories within the organisation', *Journal of Management and Governance*, **7**, 145–62.

Pentland, Brian T. and Martha S. Feldman (2005), 'Organizational routines as a unit of analy- sis', *Industrial and Corporate Change*, **14**(5), 793–815.

Perrow, C. (1984/1999), *Normal Accidents. Living with High-Risk Technologies*, revised edn 1999, Princeton, NJ: Princeton University Press.

Perruchet, P. (ed.) (1988), *Cognitive Automatisms*: original French title, *Les automatismes cog- nitifs*, Liege-Brussels: Pierre Mardaga.

Reynaud, B. (2005), 'The void at the heart of rules: routines in the context of rule following observations from a workshop of the Paris Metro', *Industrial and Corporate Change*, **14**(5), 847–71.

Schacter, D.L., A.D. Wagner and R.L. Buckner (2000), 'Memory systems of 1999', in E. Tulving and F.I. Fraik (eds), *Oxford Handbook of Memory*, New York: Oxford University Press, pp. 627–43.

Schmidt, R.A. (1975), 'A schema theory of discrete motor skill learning', *Psychological Review*, **82**, 225–60.

Shiffrin, R.C. and W. Schneider (1977), 'Controlled and automatic human information pro- cessing perceptual learning automatic attending and a general theory', *Psychological Review*, **84**, 127–90.

Sparrow, P.R. (1999), 'Strategy and cognition: understanding the role of management knowl- edge structures, organizational memory and information overload', *Creativity and Innovation Management*, **8**(2), 140–48.

Squire, L.R. (2004), 'Memory of the brain: a brief history and current perspective', *Neurobiology of Learning and Memory*, **82**, 171–7.

Thompson, R.F. (1990), 'The neurobiology of learning and memory: William James in retro- spect', *Psychological Science*, **1**(3), May, 172–3.

Walsh, J.P. (1995), 'Managerial and organizational cognition. Notes from a trip down memory lane, *Organization Science*, **6**(3), 280–315.

Wegner, D.M. (1987), 'Transactive memory: a contemporary analysis of the group mind', in B. Mullen and G.B. Goethols (eds), *Theories of Group Behaviour*, New York: Springer Verlag.

Wegner, D.M., R. Erber and P. Raymond (1991), 'Transactive memory in close relationships', *Journal of Personality and Social Psychology*, **61**(6) 923–9.

Winograd, T. (1975), 'Frame representation and the declarative–procedural controversy', in D.G. Bobrow and A.G. Collins (eds), *Representations and Understanding*, New York: Academic Press.

11 Staying on track: a voyage to the internal mechanisms of routine reproduction
Martin Schulz[1]

> All evil deeds, all crimes, all self-sacrificing actions, all heroic exploits, as well as all the actions of ordinary life, are controlled by the moon. (Gurdjieff, 1949)[2]

Routines are a dominant feature of human existence. We use routines when we walk, talk, read, answer the phone, or write an email. It is hard to think of any domain of activity that does not involve some kind of routine. Even innovation, improvisation and thinking involve routines.[3] Our engagement with routines is so vast, it is almost nauseating (Sartre, 1965). It seems we are essentially Gurdjieffian meat machines, sleepwalking through our lives with *eyes wide shut*.

Clearly, such an autopilot perspective on human existence can be a bit disturbing, but it also highlights the most curious feature of routines – their capability of staying on track. Routine execution tends to follow automatically the path of prior iterations of the routine. The experience is a common one. We commute along the same routes, we shop at the same groceries, and we use the same tools. Of course, we do introduce variation occasionally – out of capriciousness or need – but such variations are merely dramatic punctuations on otherwise unremarkable paths of repetitive events (Lyman, 1990). Our experience with routines is dominated by sameness. We adhere to the cow paths of prior routine iteration even if alternatives are clearly available: there are different routes to work, different grocery stores to shop at, and different tools that could do the same job. In that view, one wonders, what keeps routines on track?

The question is not fortuitous. It is intimately related to the status of routines as core concepts in theories of social and economic order (where routines increasingly play a central role). If routines were merely transient phenomena, lacking internal forces that maintain their shape and boundary, there would be no point in making them the cornerstone of theoretical models that aim to explain how social and economic order emerges and persists. If routines can arbitrarily morph into each other, it would be impossible to observe them because we would not know when a routine starts or stops; nor would we be able to tell if a given routine has 're-occurred'. If routines can be readily reduced to external forces such as power or rationality there would be little need for a separate theory based on routines – the reduced form would be sufficient. However, if routines stay on track by virtue of routine-based mechanisms, they assume a degree of independence from external forces that justifies their theoretical treatment as autonomous units with causal effects of their own, e.g., in the form of 'genes of organizations', as 'grammars of organizational action', as 'building blocks of organizations', or as 'pillars of organizational legitimacy'.

The question of what keeps routines on track is different from the question of how routines change. Although staying on track implies routine stability (i.e., absence of change), falling off track normally introduces variation without shifting the average pattern. Of course, routine change can happen when departures from the normal track are systematic and regular, but that requires an additional account of the events that lead to such departures. This chapter focuses instead on the question of routine stability; how action comes to be locked into narrow channels that we recognize as 'same'; how action within routines stays on the 'normal' track. It aims to contribute to theories of order, and the issue of routine change is discussed only tangentially.[4]

So far, systematic research on what keeps routines on track is lacking. This chapter will attempt to carry together several strands of thought that have addressed this question from various perspectives. I will focus mainly on sociological and psychological work, although at times I also borrow from neighbouring disciplines. I start out with a review of several influential notions of routines as they were introduced in the social sciences and then proceed to a focused exploration of the mechanisms that keep action within routines on track.

Notions of routines

Routines have been approached from a number of different angles: if the field of routines were a meal, it would be a flavourful stew made from pungent ingredients and exotic spices. Thanks to the field's diverse roots, the literature on routines is multifaceted, rich and sometimes bewildering. Notions of routines are diverse and often overlapping and appear under a variety of guises. Many ideas are scattered around, and their potential has not yet been established. Any sampling from this flavourful stew will leave out important ideas. My sampling is less driven by adequate representation than by striving for maximum variety.

Early work considered routines in the context of system stability and rationality. In Weber's work on the 'routinization of charisma' (Weber, 1976: 143, 661), the development of routines marked the transition of an organization (or, more generally, a system of domination) from an extraordinary ('ausseralltägliche') state to an ordinary ('alltägliche', everyday) state. Through such routinization (which is essentially a low form of rationalization) the system can achieve significant stabilization. Weber argued that organizations based on charismatic authority are inherently unstable because the reaffirmation of supernatural powers of leaders is precarious[5] and the legitimacy of successors of the original leader is easily challenged (the problem of succession: Weber, 1976: 144). Those charisma-based organizations (e.g., religious movements) can achieve permanence and stability by routinization of charisma – by development of a staff to manage disciples (via recruiting and training), to collect resources (via donations), and elaborate and enforce the rules of the movement (Weber, 1976: 661). From this perspective, 'routine' captures a shift from passion to discipline, moving the system to a higher level of legitimacy and thereby assuring more reliable domination. At the same time, routinization marks a progression towards rationalization (Kieser, 1987) since routines are relatively more rational than revelations, epiphanies, or other forms of otherworldly inspiration (although, if they merely form traditions, they are inferior to the rational order prevailing in rational–legal forms of organization).

A quite different image of routines arose after World War II, when interest in cognition and its limitations started to gain attention. Scholars of the Carnegie School portrayed routines as fixed responses to defined stimuli (March and Simon, 1958: 142). This conceptualization was intended to capture the difference between two types of problem-solving situations: those involving complex search and those that had been simplified by the development of automatic (but not necessarily simple) responses to specific stimuli. Routine behaviour was thereby defined by the absence of complex search, and degrees of routine behaviour could be distinguished, based on the amount of complex search involved. Clearly, satisficing behaviour would be routinizable, and maximizing behaviour less so.

Closely related to and a derivative of the Carnegie approach, organizational learning theories have made major contributions to the notion of routine. Early work focused on how organizations develop routines. In their *Behavioral Theory of the Firm*, Cyert and March highlighted the role of organizational learning (Cyert and March, 1963). Organizations developed routines, or 'standard operating procedures' through a learning cycle where the organization responded to external shocks by varying the likelihood of reusing specific routines. Routines that led to preferred outcomes were subsequently used more frequently, and those that led to substandard performance were abandoned or revised. Subsequently, organizational learning evolved to become a key paradigm of organizational theory. Levitt and March (1988) made routines the cornerstone of their approach to organizational learning, defining organizational learning as a process of encoding experiential lessons into routines. Their work stressed the nested and path-dependent nature of routine-based learning. Routines were seen as subject to competency traps that can lock learning processes into suboptimal positions. This routine-based notion of learning gave rise to several streams of empirical research, including work on the evolution of jobs (Miner, 1987, 1991), the dynamics of organizational rules (March et al., 2000; Schulz and Beck, 2002; Beck and Kieser, 2003), and research on the relationship between rules and routines (Reynaud, 2005; Grote et al., 2007).

From an institutional perspective, routines can be considered as micro-institutions. Berger and Luckmann (1966) explored how 'habitualization' contributed to the formation of institutions: 'All human activity is subject to habitualization. Any activity that is repeated frequently becomes cast into a pattern, which, *ipso facto*, is apprehended by its performer *as* that pattern' (53). Habitualized patterns would 'become embedded as routines in his [the actor's] general stock of knowledge, taken for granted by him and at hand for his projects into the future' (53). Berger and Luckmann stressed the cognitive efficiencies that arise from habitualization: 'Habitualization carries with it the important psychological gain that choices are narrowed. While in theory there may be a hundred ways to go about the project of building a canoe out of matchsticks, habitualization narrows these down to one' (53). Social institutions would then arise when different actors would reciprocally typify each other's patterns and recognize these patterns as external and objective facts (Berger and Luckmann, 1966: 56, 58).

A different image of routines, called 'scripts', emerged from research on social cognition and artificial intelligence (roots shared with the Carnegie School) to describe the action sequences that occur in mundane situations, such as ordering food in a restaurant. The view was that many ordinary situations are scripted into 'a predetermined, stereotyped sequence of actions that define a well-known situation' (Schank and Abelson, 1977: 41). For example, Jack goes to a restaurant, he orders a hamburger and a coke, the waitress brings his meal, he eats and asks for the check, the waitress gives him the bill, he pays and leaves. The imagery is theatrical – both the customer and the waitress follow the lines of a script. Parts of the script are essentially expectations, shared by the participants, about the events that are to occur and the order of their occurrence. Scripts thus consist of actions that have a temporal relationship to each other (read menu first, then order food, then receive food, and so on). It is important to recognize a critical difference between scripts and the routines of the Carnegie School. While scripts are knowledge structures, routines in the sense of the

Carnegie School are real-world structures that focus more on observable stimuli than on internal states of actors.

A notion of routines related to the Carnegie approach was presented in the *Evolutionary Theory of Economic Change* (Nelson and Winter, 1982). Like the Carnegie School, the *Evolutionary Theory* is deeply sceptical about classical ('orthodox') notions of rationality in economic theory. It presents an inspiring vision of routines as essential ingredients of organizations and as a core concept of a new approach that aims to supersede the ortho-dox, rational choice-focused economic model. The conception highlights the suppression of choice as a key aspect of routines. In this view, routines are automatically executed without conscious volition, comparable to the execution of computer programs. Participants have mostly tacit knowl-edge of the routine and select options automatically (Nelson and Winter, 1982: 73, 75). As a result, routines have 'deep channels in which behavior normally runs smoothly and effectively.' (84). Because routines are com-paratively stable patterns of behaviour, they can act as organizational *genes* that reproduce behaviour and thereby facilitate the duplication and scaling of operations (135). They can recreate action patterns on individual and organizational levels. In evolutionary theory, the term 'routine' refers to three related things: 'a repetitive pattern of activity in an entire organiza-tion, to an individual skill, or, as an adjective to the smooth uneventful effectiveness of such an organizational or individual performance' (Nelson and Winter, 1982: 97). Although routines are characterized as effective ways of getting things done, routines are not considered to be optimal: 'one cannot infer from the fact that an organization functions smoothly and suc-cessfully in a particular range of observed environments that it is a rational and 'intelligent' organism that will cope successfully with novel challenges' (Nelson and Winter, 1982: 126). Even if an organization optimizes its rou-tines, or even builds dynamic capabilities that keep lower-order routines matched to changing environmental conditions, there is no guarantee that these efforts yield better results than 'ad hoc problem solving' (Winter, 2003: 994).

During the late eighties and early nineties, a series of articles emerged that shared a sceptical tenor about the benefits of routines. Routinized behaviour was considered to be of the 'non-thinking variety' (Weiss and Ilgen, 1985: 57), typically lacking 'depth of situational analysis and the explicit consid-eration of alternatives behaviors'. Routinization would involve a reduction of awareness apparently caused by repeated experience: 'if the same envi-ronment is repeatedly experienced there is little new to think about'.[6] 'Repeated successful responses to similar situations' (59) reduce uncertainty and cognitive activity and as a result, individuals 'acquire confidence in the validity of their behavior patterns' (59), problem-relevant cues are overlooked, and organizations can become 'desensitized to environmental changes' (64). Routines may even persist when outcomes are suboptimal because 'these outcomes may still be sufficiently positive to prevent noticing the possibility for even more satisfying outcomes which might be attainable by changing behaviors' (62), a notion that subsequently was explored under the heading of 'competency traps' (Levitt and March, 1988).

The mindlessness of scripted action in organizations was highlighted by Ashforth and Fried (1988). They identified six conditions that contribute to mindless enactment and cuing, including the existence of event schema, easily categorizable cues, minimal behavioural effort, absence of subroutines that require problem solving, and absence of interruptions. Because these conditions prevail in many work situations (including political settings), much of everyday organizational behaviour occurs quite mindlessly (Ashforth and Fried, 1988: 311). The outcomes are a lack of vigilance as workers 'go automatic', and a loss of authenticity that interferes with the display of emotions required by roles such as the friendly flight attendant or the hostile bill collector (317). Mindlessness would also negatively affect decision making because it 'effectively blinkers perceptions of the task environment', because initial cues can prematurely trigger the execution of entire scripts ('premature closure'), and because it perpetuates inaccurate causal attribution based on superstitious learning (Ashforth and Fried, 1988: 317–19).

The automatic launching of routines in response to stimuli was analysed by Gersick and Hackman (1990). Their paper starts out with the harrowing story of Air Florida Flight 90 which crashed because the pilots (who were from Florida where de-icing is not necessary) habitually skipped the de-icing of their airplane even though they were taking off in January from Washington, DC. The Gersick and Hackman approach appears to extend stimulus–response theory to the group level (and is similar in that respect to March and Simon, 1958: 149). They observed that the group 'exhibits a functionally similar pattern of behavior in a given stimulus situation without explicitly selecting it over alternative ways of behaving' (Gersick and Hackman, 1990: 69). This may explain why all life guards rush into the water after seeing one lifeguard racing to the water. The automatic triggering of routines has advantages for groups such as speed and comfort for members, but can have disadvantages, such as miscoding of stimuli, groupthink and stagnation. Habitual routines settle in over time and they are automatically repeated the next time the appropriate stimulus appears. They are often kept in place owing to sentimental attachments to the routine, social entrainment, when activity patterns become very persistent because of long or intensive training, or through reticence, when members wait for others to break out of the routine (Gersick and Hackman, 1990).

Connections between individual-level skills and organizational routines were drawn in research that explored how routines are stored in 'procedural memory' (Cohen, 1991; Cohen and Bacdayan, 1994). The argument builds up from the assumptions that 'routines are stored in procedural memory' of individuals, that organizations 'concatenate' (see below) individual routines to form multi-actor, organizational routines, and that routines on both levels have noteworthy features related to *procedural memory*. Procedural memory 'stores the components of individual skilled actions' involved in a routine and can be distinguished from *declarative memory* which stores 'facts, propositions, and events' (Cohen and Bacdayan, 1994: 557). Cohen and Bacdayan's laboratory-based study suggests that procedural and declarative memory have different features: 'Procedural knowledge is less subject to decay, less explicitly accessible, and less easy to transfer to novel circumstances' (Cohen and Bacdayan, 1994: 557). The arguments here appear to reflect the increasing enthusiasm within the organizational science field in the early nineties regarding the notion of tacit knowledge (e.g., Zander and Kogut, 1995). The key idea here is that the tacit, procedural memory of routines makes them inert: 'routines often emerge through gradual multi-actor learning, and exhibit tangled histories that may frustrate both understanding and reform' (Cohen and Bacdayan, 1994: 556). Cohen and Bacdayan illuminate their argument with Morison's fabulous example of 'British artillery crews pausing for three seconds before firing because they "were holding the horses"' (556). Apparently, routines can produce reliability and speed, but can also 'become "contaminated" with extraneous, historically specific and arbitrary components' (Cohen and Bacdayan, 1994: 556). They are also hard to change, and can misfire, as illustrated in Allison's (1971) story of the 'civilian-clothed Soviet troops arriving secretly in Cuba who nonetheless formed into ranks on the dock and marched conspicuously away' (Cohen and Bacdayan, 1994: 555). In that story, the collectively tacit side of this organizational routine reproduced a pattern that was easily identified by US spy satellites.

Routines exist on two levels – on the cognitive level in the form of conceptions held by participants, and on the empirical level in the form of factual actions. A routine held in the mind of participants can have a variety of functionally similar (Gersick and Hackman, 1990) observable instantiations (or 'performances'). For example, a restaurant routine might include various types of courses (dessert or not) and different types of payment (cash or credit). Pentland and Rueter (1994), building on Salancik and Leblebici's work (1988), explored these two sides of routines with a novel approach that compared routines to languages. Languages have grammars that determine the formation of proper sentences. In a similar manner, grammars of routines would determine the range of proper performances of the routine. The analogy implies that an 'organizational routine is not a single pattern but, rather, a set of possible patterns – enabled and constrained by a variety of organizational, social, physical, and cognitive structures – from which organizational members enact particular performances' (491). The conceptualization of routines as grammars of action is indeed intriguing, harking back to notions of social accounts and vocabularies of motive (Mills, 1940; Scott and Lyman, 1968). Just as grammars constrain language, so they might constrain action within routines. The identification of the grammatical rules of organizational routines is not easy, however. Pentland and Rueter analysed 335 customer support calls at a software company, each coded as a sequence of 'moves' such as opening, transfer responsibility to user, work on the call, etc. They used half the sample of calls to identify a series of grammar rules that they then tested on the other half of the sample. The grammar (consisting of 13 rules) was able to parse ('rewrite') more than half of the action sequences in the second half of the sample, meaning that a significant part of the firm's support calls would follow patterns consistent with the grammar,[7] suggesting that performances of routines share an underlying grammatical structure. What is less clear in this approach is how grammars become relevant for action. The authors suggest that grammars reflect constraints arising from the limited lexicon of moves available to actors and 'logical dependence' among moves (e.g., calls must be opened before they can be closed). But direct effects of grammars on actions of actors are so far not part of the model. Grammatical rules 'need not be thought of in the usual sense of rules that organizational members follow or refer to while doing their work . . . phrase structure rules of the kind used here are simply devices for describing patterns observed in the coded data' (498). It seems that more research will be needed to explore how routine grammars relate to action, where the grammars come from, how they evolve, and how they get transmitted between participants. Clearly, grammars are a promising and inspiring area for future research.

Routines are executed by agents (usually humans), and if one considers agents to be part of the routine itself, then the internal life of routines becomes much more complex and dynamic. Routines then can be seen as a source of change (Feldman, 2000). For example, in the student residences explored by Feldman, the building directors felt they had an educational mission regarding students who often would not assume personal responsibility for the damage they had incurred to their rooms, even though their parents usually paid for all damages, which then led to a modification of the check-out routine that assured that the students would personally meet staff members before they moved out. Feldman and Pentland (2003) propose to see the internal dynamic of routines driven by two key 'aspects' of routines, the ostensive and performative aspects: 'The ostensive aspect is the ideal or schematic form of the routines. It is the abstract, generalized idea of the routine, or the routine in principle. The performative aspect of the routine consists of specific actions, by specific people, in specific places and times. It is the routine in practice' (Feldman and Pentland, 2003: 101). According to Feldman and Pentland, change of routine comes about because '[p]eople combine elements of past repertoires of a particular routine . . . with present situations, with a view to how this particular combination affects future understandings of what the routine is. This movement between performative and ostensive provides many opportunities for people to produce variations on a routine, to select these variations, and to retain them as what it means to do this particular routine' (112–13). In later work, Pentland and Feldman (2005) added 'artifacts' as a third component of routines, and argued that divergence between the three would lead to routine change. The conceptual apparatus in this line of work is complex but intriguing, and leaves quite a few questions for future research.

In sum, it appears there are many diverse notions of routines in this field. Routines are seen as kernels of rationality, fixed responses to stimuli, repositories of organizational knowledge, micro institutions, theatrical scripts, genes of organizations, a reduction of awareness, mindless behaviour, functionally similar patterns of behaviour, procedural memory, grammars of action, and sources of change (for a more extensive review, see Becker, 2004). As a result, researchers have struggled to develop a unified conception of routine (e.g., Cohen et al., 1996). Nevertheless, there is a fair amount of agreement that routines involve recurrent patterns of action, that the cognitive effort required for their execution decreases with repeated performance, and that routines operate on multiple levels.

Research on routines is still very much in flux, however, and it might be premature at this point to impose a rigid definition of routines. Instead, it might be more productive to focus the analysis on those social situations we normally refer to as 'routine'. This means using language as a guide, or perhaps common cultural understandings of what routines are. This also means taking into account how we recognize routines. It is an approach that considers routines as curious phenomena that manage to coagulate separate actions into distinctive and persistent patterns.[8]

Internal mechanisms of routine reproduction

Although routines have found considerable attention over the last twenty years, we understand surprisingly little of how action within routines comes to be guided by forces that arise from within the routines. Such routine-based forces are strong and prevalent. They reproduce the same behaviour in individuals, groups, and organizations, and they can do so in a remarkably reliable fashion, yet, the degree to which routines stay on track varies considerably. Sometimes a routine situation is an exact replication of the sequence of steps taken in the past; sometimes there is only a rough resemblance, e.g., because steps are added or skipped or executed in a different manner. What determines the degree to which routines stay on track? What keeps action locked within narrow channels?

To some degree, the question of how routines stay on track is an epistemological one. How do we recognize routines as such? Apparently, routines emerge clearer to us the more the actions within them stay on track. The more action within routines stays on track, the more we get the *sense of sameness* so typical of our experience with routines. The more action goes astray, the more we lose that sense of sameness. The systematic sources of that sense of sameness are not too well understood (although its curiosity is recognized: e.g., Birnholtz et al., 2007). A key mechanism could likely be the inherent capability of intelligent agents to recognize repetition (e.g., Gupta and Cohen, 2002; Shanks and Perruchet, 2002). Our capacity to recognize things when they reappear is at the core of our experience of sameness and, more generally, is at the heart of all notions of identity.[9] We recognize routines because they repeat. Because they repeat, we recognize routines as separate entities that exist independently of us as exterior and objective phenomena (Berger and Luckmann, 1967; Zucker, 1977). Not only do routines repeat, the steps within routines repeat as well. We recognize the steps when we re-encounter them during another pass through the same routine (perhaps even backwards when we walk home from a trip to the post office). We recognize them as being part of the routine, and we expect to re-encounter them, and recognize them as the ones we took last time we passed through the routine. So, the capability of recognizing sameness in a world of differences is critical to our experience of routines as things that tend to stay on track.

But the question of *what* keeps routines on track is foremost a question about the psychological and sociological mechanisms that operate on the path of action that unfolds during normal routine execution.[10] What mechanisms operate there? Clearly, any such mechanisms need to connect the prior history of the path to its continuation, perhaps via signals and traces left behind, via memories and stories of participants, via structures and artifacts developed on prior passes through the routine, and so on. Action can stay on the normal routine track only if there are mechanisms in place that connect current action in some way to prior history. This means that action in routines is path-dependent. Continuation of the path of action during routine execution depends on things that happened on the way travelled so far. Prior actions have produced conditions (material, social, psychological, informational) that allow, and often force, continuation of work in a particular direction and preclude other directions. Often, the interactions between steps on a routine path are complex and produce rugged fitness landscapes (Siggelkow, 2001), meaning that variations of a path can have dramatic performance implications.

It is important to recognize here the difference between the current path and prior paths. Both form different histories. Both affect the course of action taken in a given situation. Both can conspire to keep routines on track. On the current path, earlier actions prepare the necessary conditions that enable and constrain (Ashforth and Fried, 1988; Pentland and Rueter, 1994) the next actions within the routine. From an abstract perspective, one could say that prior actions of a routine *select* (Luhmann, 1995) consecutive actions. 'Selection' here means that prior actions shape the availability and probability of next-step alternatives. Only after the wheels have been removed from a car (prior actions), do the brake components become accessible, and inspection and replacement of the brake pads (next steps) become possibilities with different probabilities.

Prior paths travelled through a routine in the past can create conditions that steer action in ways that align the current path with prior paths. For example, specific brake repair tools acquired in the past might demand a specific way of executing the brake job, the application of competencies developed during prior iterations might steer routine performance on specific tracks, and signs and instruction sheets created in the past might offer comfortable guidance.

Both types of paths affect the course of action taken within a routine. They interact in complex ways and thereby affect the degree to which action stays on track. Competencies, expectations, norms, rules, and so on, developed during prior iterations of the routine, need to be able to handle the diverse conditions lining the current path. Conversely, prior steps taken on the current path need to offer opportunities and signals that support and trigger things developed in prior iterations, such as rules, expectations, obedience, and neuronal connections to related steps. If the histories of the current and prior paths are misaligned, routines are likely to get thrown off track.[11] The two histories (of the current and prior path) are the primary referents for the selection of consecutive action during routine execution because the applicability (subjectively and objectively) of the routine to a given situation depends critically on the path travelled so far and on its match with prior paths. The match can easily be disrupted, as many might have discovered after finding themselves – on a Sunday morning – on the road to work instead of to the supermarket, the intended destination.

For action to stay on track the selection of consecutive action within routines needs to occur in ways that reproduce the 'normal' path of the routine.[12] For this to happen, prior actions taken within a routine need to facilitate (i.e., make available relevant conditions and increase the probability of) those next-step alternatives that lie on the normal path of execution of the routine. This means that routine-based selection mechanisms need to be in place that become active when actions taken so far on a path match those of the normal path. Such *routine reproduction mechanisms* keep action on track by selecting those next-step alternatives that lie on the normal path of the routine.

Routines thus stay on track by virtue of reproduction mechanisms that select consecutive action in ways that are related to both the history of the current path and the history of prior paths. The history of the current path produces the conditions necessary for action to stay on track, and the history of prior paths creates the conditions that orient action selection toward the normal path. Yet, because reproduction mechanisms keep action on track, they also help to create the normal path. Reproduction mechanisms thus coevolve with the routines that they help to stabilize.

If reproduction mechanisms shape the paths on which earlier actions select later actions and they are shaped by the history of prior passes through the same routine, how do they stabilize action, and how do the mechanisms themselves function and evolve? Although the literature on routines has not penetrated very deeply into this terrain, scattered discussions on such mechanisms can be found. In the following I will discuss a smattering of ideas on reproduction mechanisms gleaned from the sociological and psychological debates on routines and related phenomena, focusing in particular on the aspects of mechanisms that address how prior actions select consecutive action, and how the mechanisms coevolve with routines. The mechanisms are located on individual and collective levels and involve varying degrees of conscious attention to outcomes. Some mechanisms overlap partially with others, as thinking about routines has evolved in rather dispersed and sporadic ways.

Habitualization
Habitualization occurs usually on individual level, when actors develop expectations about themselves. The process is illuminated by Berger and Luckmann's story about 'solitary man', proverbially stranded on a desert island and building a canoe out of matchsticks, and who 'mumble(s) to himself, "There I go again", as he starts on step one of an operating procedure consisting of, say, ten steps' (Berger and Luckmann, 1967: 53). He becomes aware of the procedure, recognizing it as a separate entity that has stepped into his lonely island existence, bearing familiarity and friendship:

'even solitary man has at least the company of his operating procedures' (53). Each of his procedures has identity by virtue of the different activities it involves. It forms a distinct pattern 'which, *ipso facto*, is apprehended by its performer as that pattern' (53). It is an individual-level typification of action patterns which needs to be distinguished from more collective forms discussed below. The key to habitualization is an awareness of which actions belong to a routine and which do not. The selection of consecutive action is based on *familiarity* with things personally experienced in the past. At each step of the routine, solitary man selects those actions that fit into the familiar pattern of his routine. He is kept on track by a mental image (a private 'script': Schank and Abelson, 1977; 1995) that tells him which actions need to be taken next in order to complete his routine. An important aspect of habitualization is that it is often mindless, and can be knocked off track when unfamiliar situations arise, for example, when tools break, or materials become unavailable. Habitualization is closely related to notions of skill and 'knowing the job' in evolutionary economics (Nelson and Winter, 1982). Habitualization is strengthened by recurrent passes through the routine as this intensifies familiarity. Habitualization can also be accompanied and strengthened by pride. In his discussion on the relationship between bureaucratic structure and personality, Merton noted that bureaucrats develop a way of life and a 'pride of craft' which leads them to resist change of bureaucratic routines (Merton, 1968: 255). Pride of craft seems to play a significant role especially in professions where the craft is visible to customers. Just consider the pride of craft often displayed by doctors, TV chefs, referees in sports, and waiters of classy restaurants.

Priming
Habitualization within individuals is probably accompanied and facilitated by processes on the neuronal level. On that level, steps in a routine prime subsequent steps through spreading activation within neuronal networks (Collins and Loftus, 1975; Sheperd, 1979; Reggia and Sutton, 1988). Each step in a routine creates a situation with elements that remind the actor of the steps he took the last time he passed through the routine. Prior executions of the routine have left neuronal connections in the actor's mind. The actor recognizes the current situation as one that he has encountered before and that last time led to specific next steps. The path of action is driven forward by *attention spreading from activated areas to connected areas*. The mechanism is akin to singing a familiar song. The singer follows a well-practiced sequence of words and sounds. Consecutive syllables are linked fluidly together. The mechanism of selection is spreading activation. Familiarity of the melody and lyrics leads the singer from one phrase to the

next. The effect of priming is strong. It is well known, for example that stuttering is significantly reduced during singing, because of the subjects' familiarity of the melody and lyrics (Healey et al., 1976). Priming is strengthened by recurrent passes through the same routine because neuronal connections are strengthened (Gupta and Cohen, 2002). An interesting feature of priming is self-validation, where the actor interprets ambiguous stimuli in a manner consistent with an anticipated script (Ashforth and Fried, 1988), for example, when stock movements by insiders trigger sell-off routines, when overzealous 'experts' jump to conclusions, or when politicians filter (or even fabricate) evidence to justify military responses to difficult situations. Priming is also intriguing because it can be extended to multi-actor situations (Cohen and Bacdayan, 1994; see also the discussion on procedural memory below).

Reciprocal typification
This mechanism represents an extension of habitualization to relationships between participants. Reciprocal typification occurs when actors develop expectations about each other. In the solitary man scenario, typification starts when Robinson is joined by another person, Friday, who first observes, then recognizes Robinson's recurrent patterns of action as Robinson's routines. Friday might think 'Aha, there he goes again', recognizing a certain pattern of action as one of Robinson's routines, thus forming a typification of Robinson's behaviour. Moreover, the typification is reciprocal. Robinson and Friday form reciprocal typifications of each other's behaviour, and if they become involved in each other's projects or actions, they might say, 'There *we* go again'. As a result, outcomes of actions become predictable and a division of labour can be established between the actors (Berger and Luckmann, 1967: 56–9). In reciprocal typification, the selection of consecutive action is guided by *perceptions about the expectations and potential reactions of others*. Robinson is aware that Friday expects him to continue working on the canoe, not use it as a source of firewood, and that, if he burns the canoe, Friday might treat him as if he has lost his mind. Their joint history serves as the source of expectations that guide their action. Their expectations evolve and strengthen with recurrent passes through the routine. It appears that expectations developed through a shared history can make a relationship more efficient. For example, research on interorganizational routines has found that partner-specific experiences have positive effects on alliance performance (Zollo et al., 2002), while research on networks suggest that embedded ties generate economies of time (Uzzi, 1997). Departures from the typical path raise questions from the other party and can produce coordination problems and conflict – negotiation might ensue, agreement might be sought,

contracts and truces might be established (Nelson and Winter, 1982). Routine execution guided by reciprocal typification tends to be more pliable than that based on institutionalization (see below). It is a comparatively private social formation that allows things to be changed on an ad-hoc basis.

Institutionalization

This mechanism extends habitualization even further to the collective level. It starts when routines are passed down to new generations. For new generations, the origin of the routines is opaque as their history antedates their arrival. As a result, they accept the routines as the way of 'how these things are done', as 'historical and objective facticity'. The transmission of routines to large numbers of participants and generations can 'thicken and harden' the routines and may turn them into coercive norms (Berger and Luckmann, 1967: 59–60). Within the institutionalization mechanism, the selection of consecutive action is guided by *widely accepted and usually taken for granted conceptions of what the next step 'ought' to be*. After the groceries have been rung up by the cashier, the customer is expected to pay – little chance of negotiation there. Institutionalization is related to the ostensive side of routines, the 'abstract, generalized idea of the routine, or the routine in principle' (Feldman and Pentland, 2003: 101). Although institutionalization can provide strong guidance for selection of consecutive action, it is usually not monolithic. Degrees of institutionalization vary as different roles arise for different types of actors, meanings become misaligned and 'institutional segmentation' sets in (Berger and Luckmann, 1967: 84). Misalignment can weaken the degree of institutionalization of routines, while alignment can strengthen it: 'The ostensive aspect of organizational routines gains in apparent objectivity and concreteness as the views of different participants come into alignment' (Feldman and Pentland, 2003: 101). The degree of institutionalization of routines affects how closely routines stay on track. Weak institutionalization of routines will lead to more deviance while strong institutionalization will assure more faithful execution of the routines. Institutionalization blends into coercion when routines include mechanisms that enforce compliance (coercion is discussed below).

Value infusion

Value infusion is based on Selznick's view that institutionalization means 'infused with value beyond the technical requirements of the task at hand' (1957: 17). It captures those routine situations in which participants attach sentimental or symbolic value to the steps of the routine. It could be seen as similar to institutionalization insofar as the values come to be taken for granted and are shared among participants. The selection of consecutive action is guided by those *values* that actors hold about each step that should be taken along the path of action of a routine. In the case of symbolic values, the routine becomes a ritual, and steps are taken based on beliefs about the sacredness of the routine and its components. Value infusion is likely to intensify with repeated passes through a routine, as participants develop sentimental or superstitious attachments with the routine and its components. Often the presence of vestigial elements in rites can be traced back to value infusion.

Formalization

Routines can become encoded in rules, job descriptions, and structures (D'Adderio, 2003; March et al., 2000; Miner, 1987; Schulz and Jobe, 2001). Formalization can require extensive effort and might encounter considerable resistance from rule users (Conradi and Dybå, 2001). It nevertheless plays a critical role in popular management techniques, such as process mapping, TQM and re-engineering. Formalization establishes explicit directives that can provide guidance for action and facilitate monitoring and enforcement. Within formalized routines, action stays on track thanks to *compliance*. Compliance is not guaranteed, however, since actors often circumvent rules, often for good reasons. Rules are often incomplete and inconsistent, and they are usually rigid and quickly fall obsolete (Schulz, 1998b). It appears, however, that some types of formalization ('enabling bureaucracies', Adler and Borys, 1996) are more conducive to compliance. Drivers of formalization have found a bit of attention in prior research. Formalization tends to accelerate with organizational size and differentiation (Hage, 1980; Kralewski et al., 1985), but it decelerates with the number of rules in the system (i.e., rule birth rates decline with rule density; see Schulz, 1998a). Formalization is likely to intensify with recurrent passes through the routine because this produces recurrent exposure to the same problems ('problem sorting', Schulz, 1998a). A critical outcome of formalization is the enhanced capability to maintain and refine routines. This can be very important for power management and the cultivation of critical ties to outside parties (Staggenborg, 1988). Because formalization usually involves a considerable degree of analysis and articulation of informal arrangements and tacit knowledge, it can contribute significantly to knowledge production in organizations (Nonaka and Takeuchi, 1995).

Artifacts

Routine action is situated in a context that guides the selection of necessary steps of a routine. Ethnographic studies find that 'wall spaces and boards were plastered with pieces of paper containing checklists, diagrams, how-tos, company policies, flow charts, and various instructions' (Kogan and Muller, 2006: 762). Such routine artifacts help workers to get through their routines. They guide routine action from one stage to the next. Here, the selection of subsequent action is guided by *routine artifacts that enable and signal subsequent actions that need to be taken next*. The effect is likely to strengthen as artifacts become elaborated and entrained by recurrent passes through the routine. Artifacts can contribute to routine change if they diverge from the performative and ostensive aspect of routines (Pentland and Feldman, 2005). An important aspect of artifacts is that they are not unequivocal. The same artifact can be interpreted in different ways (Barley, 1986), and can play different roles in different routines. The meaning of artifacts is thus dependent on the routine within which they are used. An important artifact is technology which can be extremely effective in keeping action on track within a routine, but even they can be reinterpreted and used in ways that contradict the intentions of the technology's designers (DeSanctis and Poole, 1994). Tools are another type of artifact, and because of their prevalence in work settings play a tremendous role in keeping action on track. Normally, workers develop tool-specific skills through the repeated use of the tools, which contributes to keeping action on track (see the related discussion on competency traps below).

Concatenation of procedural memory

Because procedural memory is largely opaque to participants, routines reside partially in an 'organizational unconscious' (Cohen and Bacdayan, 1994: 556), and thereby tend to be taken for granted. Thus, procedural memory keeps routines on track in ways similar to institutionalization. However, one can identify a second line of argument in the procedural memory literature that is related to the way organizations connect individual-level routines to form organization-level routines: 'As individuals become skilled in their portions of a routine the actions become stored in their procedural memories and can later be triggered as substantial chunks of behaviour. The routine of a group can be viewed as the concatenation of such procedurally stored actions, each primed by and priming the actions of others (Tulving and Schacter, 1990)' (Cohen and Bacdayan, 1994: 557). The mechanism of selecting consecutive action is based on *reciprocal triggering*. Routines stay on track because each action is primed by and primes the actions of others. Patterns of concatenation are likely to evolve and strengthen by recurrent passes through the routine.

Calculation[13]

The mechanism of 'calculation' could be seen as an extension of habitualization into the realm of mindful behaviour. Returning to the image of solitary man, it is likely that he not only develops an awareness of routines as separate entities, but also an awareness of how individual actions taken within a routine contribute to the outcome of the routine. He uses the routine instrumentally to achieve his goals, and might reflect on the contribution of each step to his goals. His goals might include a close matching of the current path of routine execution with prior iterations of the routine, a situation that one could label 'routines as targets' (Nelson and Winter, 1982: 113). In calculation, the selection of subsequent action is guided by *awareness of action–outcome relationships*. At each step, he selects those actions that he considers to be *relevant* for specific outcomes of the routine. Calculation can involve various levels of cognitive effort, ranging from an 'inkling' to full-blown Weberian instrumental rationality. It might involve varying degrees of goal-seeking behaviour, and includes, as limiting cases, the painstaking adherence to a superstitious ritual and the meticulous performance of a drill (at this point, calculation blends into value infusion and habitualization).[14] Calculation is error-correcting and can repair routines when interruptions occur, for example, due to external shocks. Calculation thereby can also contribute to routine flexibility and adaptation (Feldman, 2000; Howard-Grenville, 2005). It is therefore an important ingredient in organizational capabilities development (Gavetti, 2005). Calculation is likely to become more accurate through recurrent passes through the routine as action–outcome relationships become better understood (Duncan and Weiss, 1979). The degree of calculation involved in a routine probably declines with the frequency of executing the routine and increases with the level and scope of the routine (Nelson and Winter, 1982: 83) – for example, an organizational product design routine usually involves more calculation (including political manoeuvre by different participants) than an individual-level skill. Calculation also increases in the presence of interruptions and operational and semantic ambiguity of the routine (Nelson and Winter, 1982: 83, 88). Furthermore, calculation can be affected by mood. Psychological research has shown that good mood leads to mindlessness (Bless et al., 1996). An interesting aspect of calculation is that it is often (if not always) complemented by less-mindful behaviour, such as when rational action draws on repertoires of automatic routines (Levinthal and Rerup, 2006).

Competency traps
Competency traps are closely related to calculation. One could even see them as a special case of calculation. 'A competency trap can occur when favourable performance with an inferior procedure leads an organization to accumulate more experience with it, thus keeping experience with a superior procedure inadequate to make it rewarding to use' (Levitt and March,

1988: 322). This mechanism applies not only to whole routines but also to their parts. Competencies developed in connection with a given action which is part of a routine make it more rewarding to re-use that action than to explore potential alternatives (March, 1991; Weiss and Ilgen, 1985). Competency traps operate to keep routines on track because they encourage actors to select those actions with which they have developed greater *competencies* during prior iterations of the routine. Competency traps are a special case of calculation insofar as competency traps involve a *consideration of how returns from competent action contribute to the outcomes* of the routine.

The type of calculation involved here is only limited rational. Competency traps imply a deliberate choice based on poorly formed estimates of potential returns from alternatives. It is important to note that competency traps deepen over time as recurrent passes through the routine increase competencies with the steps that currently are part of the routine. The reduction of cognitive effort that typically accompanies routines and that often serves as a source of efficiency can lock behaviour in potentially suboptimal channels.

Escalation of commitment
Action within a routine might continue on a prescribed path because of psychological investments made in prior stages. Actors might reason, 'we started on this path, we might as well continue'. It is often associated with behaviour that can be described as 'throwing good money after bad'. The underlying reasons for such escalation of commitment include psychological needs of actors to justify prior action and needs to satisfy social norms of consistency (Staw, 1981). In the extreme, actors might engage in wishful thinking and superstitiously assume that the intensity of clinging to their beliefs has a positive effect on the probability that their beliefs come true. Expression of commitment is then seen as critical for success. As a result, they engage in 'trying harder', 'praying harder', 'envisioning', 'staying the course' and 'positive thinking'. They abstain from action that would signal a weakening of their commitments. Their selection of subsequent action aims at maintaining consistency with prior beliefs. Routines are kept on track because actors take actions that *extend and re-affirm prior beliefs*. Escalation of commitment is likely to intensify the more 'staying the course' produces failures. The more failures are experienced in prior passes through the routine the more actions are taken that express steadfast commitment to the current course of action. Escalation of commitment is similar to institutionalization because it involves actors' conceptions of action patterns that give meaning to the current path and offer guidance for its completion. It can also be seen as a case of (flawed) calculation insofar

as it involves consideration of sunk costs as a reason for continuing the current path.

Coercion

Routines and rules are usually considered as modes of organizing that can substitute for hierarchical controls. Nevertheless, routines can include some form of coercion that constrains the range of actions that are selected by actors. Wide acceptance of routines can make them coercive (Berger and Luckmann, 1967); for example, the custom of displaying flags can turn into a coercive norm in patriotic countries. Research on self-managed work teams has found that the teams establish 'concertive controls' around their routines and team members exert peer pressure on each other to assure productivity and efficiency goals are met (Barker, 1993). Under coercion, routine execution is usually kept on track by an apparatus that monitors and enforces the faithful execution of some or all steps of a routine. Coercion involves imposition of *sanctions* for behaviour that departs from the prescribed course of the routine. Selection of consecutive action is driven by *avoidance of pain*. Insofar as the sanctions are considered by the routine's actors as a form of outcome to be avoided, coercion can be seen as a special case of calculation. Coercion can be strengthened when prior passes through the routine lead to the creation and elaboration of a power apparatus, however, coercion is far from fool-proof as intelligent agents tend to make efforts to evade the coercion mechanisms. Coercion is accompanied by a host of problems which make it a comparatively inferior mode of controlling operations (e.g., Gouldner, 1954; Martin and Freeman, 2003). To be effective for keeping routines on track, coercion needs to be accompanied with detailed commands, rules, or plans that can guide behaviour and that are effectively communicated to the users of the routine.

Leadership

This mechanism is similar to coercion as it involves a power relationship. However, for leadership, the power is typically based on voluntary submission to the leader and the order he has established. Followers adhere to routines because they consider them to be part of a legitimate order. The selection of subsequent action is based on *obedience*. Leadership is often facilitated by plans that prescribe the path that followers are supposed to take (e.g., House, 1996). Leadership is likely to become more efficient with recurrent passes through the routine as leaders and followers learn to accommodate and inspire each other. However, the lessons the leaders learn are often spurious because the world is complex and rapidly changing and produces ambiguous signals that can be interpreted in a number of ways (Cohen and March, 1986: 195–203).

Dimensions and typologies   The list of reproduction mechanisms presented above is most likely neither final nor exhaustive. Other types can be identified, and further research on this subject is likely to unearth additional candidates. Furthermore, there is a fair amount of overlap between the mechanisms. Mechanisms could be grouped and labelled in different ways. The list clearly reflects the conceptual choices of the scholars who introduced the mechanisms, and who often had totally different theoretical intentions in mind. Of course, the list also reflects the attention limits of this author and the idiosyncrasies of the search path followed. Therefore, the list should be treated as an invitation to think about routines in new ways, and not as a complete theory of routine reproduction mechanisms.

To organize the terrain and get a feeling for its shape, one could potentially develop a formal typology of mechanisms. To do so, one could start with the dimensions inherent in the current mechanisms. Several dimensions come to mind. One dimension is the degree of calculation (or mindfulness) involved. Another is the level of aggregation (individual, dyad, group, organization, society). A third is the degree of intrinsic or extrinsic motivation involved. Although one could probably develop a typology on the basis of these dimensions, it is not clear how constructive that would be. Many mechanisms occupy broad bands on these dimensions, and additional dimensions might emerge in future research. For these reasons, it might be wise to hold back on typology building efforts until the terrain has become more established.

Predictions   Reproduction mechanisms contribute to keeping action on track within routines. The discussion above suggests a few general predictions that are neither surprising nor complicated,[15] but can establish reasonable baselines for future research that might uncover interesting departures from them.

The first prediction is the most basic one, focusing on the presence of reproduction mechanisms in a given routine situation. The claim is that *the presence of a reproduction mechanism in a given routine situation will have a positive effect on the likelihood that action stays on track*. Clearly, some reproduction mechanisms might be stronger than others, and comparisons of their strength and the accommodating conditions that moderate their strength are important areas for future research.

More than one reproduction mechanism may be present in a given routine situation. It seems plausible to assume that their contributions might add up and produce a combined effect that increases with the number of mechanisms at work. Thus, the second prediction is that *the larger the number of reproduction mechanisms concurrently at work in a routine situation, the more likely that action will stay on track*. A similar prediction arises if one assumes that each mechanism can operate with some level of intensity, e.g., by being more or less dominant in a given situation. In that case, it seems likely that the likelihood of action staying on track is a positive function of the cumulated intensity of the reproduction mechanisms in place. The intensity of a reproduction mechanism can be conceptualized as its probability of guiding action in a given type of routine situation, and the cumulated intensity can be conceptualized as the sum of the intensities of the mechanisms operating in a given routine situation. Then the third prediction can be formulated as follows: *the larger the cumulated intensity of reproduction mechanisms in a given routine situation, the more likely that action will stay on track*. Clearly, the last two relationships might not be linear as different mechanisms might amplify each other or impede each other. But, unless combinations of mechanisms are mutually incompatible, one would expect a positive effect.

Reproduction mechanisms evolve and strengthen with use of the routine. The way this happens is quite underexplored at this point (a few initial explorations can be found in Espedal, 2006), but it seems likely that it happens in different ways for each mechanism. Habitualization is strengthened when recurrent passes through the routine intensify familiarity. Priming is strengthened by recurrent passes through the routine because this strengthens neuronal connections. Expectations and roles involved in typification evolve and strengthen with recurrent passes through the routine. Institutionalization is strengthened by recurrent transmissions of the routine to large numbers of participants. Formalization intensifies with recurrent exposure to problems in prior iterations of the routine. Artifacts become elaborated and entrained by recurrent passes through the routine. Patterns of concatenation are likely to evolve and strengthen with recurrent passes through the routine. Calculation is likely to become more accurate through recurrent passes through the routine as action–outcome relationships become better understood. Competency traps deepen as recurrent passes through the routine increase competencies with the steps that currently are part of the routine. Escalation of commitment is likely to intensify the more failures are experienced in prior passes through the routine and the more actions are taken that express steadfast commitment to the chosen course of action. Coercion can be strengthened when prior passes through the routine facilitate the elaboration of the power apparatus. Likewise, leadership is likely to become more efficient with recurrent passes through the routine as leaders and followers learn to accommodate each other.

Although more research, particularly empirical research, is needed to explore these relationships in further detail, it seems likely that prior passes through a routine strengthen the reproduction mechanisms in ways that produce a positive relationship between the number of prior iterations of the routine and the likelihood that action stays on track. The fourth prediction is thus: *the larger the number of prior passes through the routine, the more likely that action will stay on track during the current pass.* It is conceivable that this relationship is non-linear or even non-monotonic, for example, repeated passes through a routine can create burn-out (exemplified in Charlie Chaplin's *Modern Times*) or even give rise to forces that encourage straying off track when members figure out how to play the system or engage in conflict among themselves (e.g., Crozier, 1964; Espedal, 2006). The effects of such complications will have to be explored in future research.

Conclusion and outlook
Routines govern an astounding proportion of behaviour of individuals and organizations. Perhaps as a result, they also play an increasingly important role in theories of social and economic order. If routines are really a source of social order (as these theories seem to imply) then they should be equipped with internal mechanisms that stabilize them. If their stabilizing effect could be reduced to external forces, then we would not need a concept of routine. So, for routines to be able to explain social order, they need to be relatively independent from external forces.

My search for internal sources of stability has led me to a list of reproduction mechanisms that keep routines on track. Each of the mechanisms has its own way of shaping the selection of consecutive action. Each connects the selection of next steps to the prior history on the current path and the history of prior paths in ways that reproduce the routine. The reproduction mechanisms tend to strengthen over repeated passes through the routine, suggesting that they coevolve with the routines that they help to stabilize.

The list of reproduction mechanisms is not short, suggesting that routines are held in place by internal forces and that it would be difficult to reduce routines to 'grand' external forces such as rationality, power, and agency. Rather, routines are self-reinforcing phenomena that have an 'Eigendynamik' that can keep action on track and thereby produce stable patterns of order that guide and coordinate action in organizations and societies. In that view, routines do have a justifiable claim to be treated as central elements of theories of order.

Of course, this eigendynamic feature of routines merely offers an auspicious backdrop for deeper explorations of the relationship between routines and reproduction mechanisms. How do they coevolve? How do routines shed mechanisms and adopt new ones? How tolerant are routines with respect to disruptions of reproduction mechanisms? How can reproduction mechanisms contribute to routine adaptation? Clearly, there is much to do in this rapidly developing terrain, especially empirical work. But the path ahead looks promising.

Notes

1. The author wishes to thank Claus Rerup, James G. March, Brian Pentland, Martha Feldman, Laurie Barclay, Alfred Kieser, Christy Matsuba, Markus Becker and participants of the Third International Conference on Organizational Routines in Strasbourg for helpful comments and discussions on earlier drafts of this chapter. All remaining problems are the fault of the author only.
2. George Ivanovitch Gurdjieff, as quoted by P.D. Ouspensky in his book, *In Search of the Miraculous: Fragments of an Unknown Teaching*, first published by Routledge and Kegan Paul, 1949.
3. Thinking routines can be found in heuristics and pattern recognition 'habits of mind': (Louis and Sutton, 1991). Interestingly, feelings also involve routines, a notion inherent in the figure of 'habits of the heart'.
4. This does not mean that I assume that routines are inherently immutable. Of course, routines do change. But I think that the degree to which routines change is mainly an empirical matter, and cannot be decided on a priori grounds. The important issue here, however, is that routines possess an inherent degree of stability that is worth understanding and exploring. It is that aspect of routines that allows routines to exist. And, thus, the question of what stabilizes routines is logically anterior to the question of how routines change.
5. After all, the reliable fabrication of miracles is tricky business (outside Hollywood).
6. Weiss and Ilgen (1985: 57) refer to Langer (1978) at this point.
7. Some departures were caused by inaccuracies in the database, and others would 'contradict our normative sense, based on insights from the fieldwork, or what constitutes a complete, competent call' (Pentland and Rueter, 1994: 503).
8. By using the word 'manage' I do not intend to anthropomorphize routines. I do assume, however, that routines have capabilities comparable to the way that molecules, genes, cells, organs or insects have capabilities.
9. Our capacity to recognize sameness is curiously coupled with a universal preference for familiarity – humans seek out familiar situations.
10. By the way, there are some explanations that are popular but probably more speculative than helpful. For example, 'agency' is probably not a viable candidate for explaining how routines stay on track because it is too broad as a category and does not offer sufficient regularity to produce regular patterns. And the phases of the moon (unless amended by complex elaborations) are probably not a viable candidate either.
11. This is apparently a common problem for the replication of routines (and leveraging of knowledge assets) across different locations (Winter and Szulanski, 2000).
12. By 'normal path' I mean the path of action usually travelled within the routine (perhaps some weighted average of prior paths), and which often is perceived by participants as the normal course of action.
13. It seems the English term 'calculation' is similar to 'deliberation' insofar as both involve cognitive effort directed towards achievements of the intended outcomes of a routine. However, my sense is that most use of 'deliberation' implies a volitional component that is usually not included in 'calculation'.
14. The currently fashionable fascination with zombies, robots and meatpuppets might reflect the common mind's curiosity about this transition.
15. Nor are they tautological – note that the focus here is on routine situations (not routines) and the degree to which action stays on track in those situations.

References

Adler, Paul S. and Bryan Borys (1996), 'Two types of bureaucracy: enabling and coercive', *Administrative Science Quarterly*, **41**, 61–89.

Allison, Graham T. (1971), *Essence of Decisions: Explaining the Cuban Missile Crisis*, Boston, MA: Little, Brown.

Ashforth, Blake and Yitzhak Fried (1988), 'The mindlessness of organizational behaviors', *Human Relations*, **41**(4), 305–29.

Barker, James R. (1993), 'Tightening the iron cage: concertive control in self-managing teams', *Administrative Science Quarterly*, **38**, 408–37.

Barley, Stephen R. (1986), 'Technology as an occasion for structuring: evidence from observations of CT scanners and the social order of radiology departments', *Administrative Science Quarterly*, **31**(1), 78–108.

Beck, Nikolaus and Alfred Kieser (2003), 'The complexity of rule systems, experience and organizational learning', *Organization Studies*, **24**(5), 793–814.

Becker, Markus (2004), 'Organizational routines: a review of the literature', *Industrial and Corporate Change*, **13**, 643–77.

Berger, Peter L. and Thomas Luckmann (1967) (orig: 1966), *The Social Construction of Reality*, New York: Anchor Books

Birnholtz, Jeremy P., Michael D. Cohen and Susannah V. Hoch (2007), 'Organizational character: on the regeneration of Camp Poplar Grove', *Organization Science*, **18**, March–April, 315–32.

Bless, H., G.L. Clore, N. Schwarz and V. Golisano (1996), 'Mood and the use of scripts: does a happy mood really lead to mindlessness?', *Journal of Personality and Social Psychology*, **71**, 665–79.

Cohen, Michael D. (1991), 'Individual learning and organizational routine, Emerging Connections', *Organization Science*, **2**, 135–9.

Cohen, Michael D. and Paul Bacdayan (1994), 'Organizational routines are stored as procedural memory: evidence from a laboratory study', *Organization Science*, **5**, 554–68.

Cohen, Michael D., Roger Burkhart, Giovanni Dosi, Massimo Egidi, Luigi Marengo, Massimo Warglien and Sidney Winter (1996), 'Routines and other recurring action patterns of organizations: contemporary research issues', *Industrial and Corporate Change*, **5**(3), 653–98.

Cohen, Michael D. and James G. March (1986), *Leadership and Ambiguity*, 2nd edn, Boston, MA: Harvard Business School Press.

Collins, A.M. and E.F. Loftus (1975), 'A spreading activation theory of semantic processing', *Psychological Review*, **82**, 407–28.

Conradi, Reidar and Tore Dybå (2001), 'An empirical study on the utility of formal routines to transfer knowledge and experience', Proceedings of the European Software Engineering Conference 2001(ESEC 2001), New York: ACM Press, pp. 268–76.

Crozier, Michel (1964), *The Bureaucratic Phenomenon*, Chicago, IL: University of Chicago Press.

Cyert, R. and J.G. March (1963), *A Behavioral Theory of the Firm*, Englewood Cliffs, NJ: Prentice-Hall.

D'Adderio, Luciana (2003), 'Configuring software, reconfiguring memories: the influence of integrated systems on the reproduction of knowledge and routines', *Industrial and Corporate Change*, **12**(2), 321–50.

DeSanctis, Gerardine and Marshall Scott Poole (1994), 'Capturing the complexity in advanced technology use: adaptive structuration theory', *Organization Science*, **5**(2), 121–47.

Duncan, Robert and Andrew Weiss (1979), 'Organizational learning: implications for organizational design', *Research in Organizational Behavior*, **1**, 75–123.

Espedal, Bjarne (2006), 'Do organizational routines change as experience changes?', *Journal of Applied Behavioral Science*, **42**(4), 468–90.

Feldman, Martha S. (2000), 'Organizational routines as a source of continuous change', *Organization Science*, **11**(6), 611–29.

Feldman, Martha S. and Brian T. Pentland (2003), 'Reconceptualizing organizational routines as a source of flexibility and change', *Administrative Science Quarterly*, **48**, 94–118.

Gavetti, Giovanni (2005), 'Cognition and hierarchy: rethinking the microfoundations of capabilities development', *Organization Science*, **16**(6), 599–617.

Gersick, C.J. and J.R. Hackman (1990), 'Habitual routines in task performing groups', *Organization Behavior: Human Decision Processes*, **47**, 65–97.

Gouldner, Alvin W. (1954), *Patterns of Industrial Bureaucracy*, New York: The Free Press.

Grote, Gudela, Johann Weichbrodt and Hannes Günter (2007), 'Coordination in high-risk organizations: the need for flexible routines', Conference Paper for the Third International Conference on Organizational Routines, 'Empirical research and conceptual foundations', Strasbourg.

Gupta, Prahlad and Neal J. Cohen (2002), 'Theoretical and computational analysis of skill learning, repetition priming, and procedural memory', *Psychological Review*, **109**(2), April, 401–48.

Hage, Jerald (1980), *Theories of Organizations: Form, Process, and Transformation*, New York: John Wiley.

Healey, E.C., A.R. Mallard and M.R. Adams (1976), 'Factors contributing to the reduction of stuttering during singing', *Journal of Speech and Hearing Research*, **19**(3), 475–80.

House, Robert J. (1996), 'Path-goal theory of leadership: lessons, legacy, and a reformulated theory', *The Leadership Quarterly*, **7**(3), 323–52.

Howard-Grenville, Jennifer A. (2005), 'The persistence of flexible organizational routines: the role of agency and organizational context', *Organization Science*, **16**(6), 618–36.

Kieser, Alfred (1987), 'From asceticism to administration of wealth. Medieval monasteries and the pitfalls of rationalization', *Organization Studies*, **8**(2), 103–23.

Kogan, S.L. and M.J. Muller (2006), 'Ethnographic study of collaborative knowledge work', *IBM Systems Journal*, **45**(4), 759–71.

Kralewski, John E., Laura Pitt and Deborah Shatin (1985), 'Structural Characteristics of Medical Group Practices', *Administrative Science Quarterly*, **30**(1), 34–45.

Langer, E.J. (1978), 'Rethinking the role of thought in social interactions', in J.H. Harvey, W.J. Ickes and R.F. Kidd (eds), *New Directions in Attribution Theory*, vol 2, Hillsdale, NJ: Erlbaum.

Levinthal, Daniel and Claus Rerup (2006), 'Crossing an apparent chasm: bridging mindful and less-mindful perspectives on organizational learning', *Organization Science*, **17**(4), 502–13.

Levitt, B. and J.G. March (1988), 'Organizational learning', *Annual Review of Sociology*, **14**, 319–40.

Louis, M.R. and R.L. Sutton (1991), 'Switching cognitive gears: from habits of mind to active thinking', *Human Relations*, **44**, 55–76.

Luhmann, Niklas (1995), *Social Systems*, Stanford, CA: Stanford University Press.

Lyman, Stanford M. (1990), 'The drama in the routine: a prolegomenon to a praxiological sociology', *Sociological Theory*, **8**(2), 217–23.

March, J.G. (1991), 'Exploration and exploitation in organizational learning', *Organization Science*, **2**, 71–87.

March, J.G. and H.A. Simon (1958), *Organizations*, New York: John Wiley.

March, J.G., M. Schulz and X. Zhou (2000), *The Dynamics of Rules: Change in Written Organizational Codes*, Stanford, CA: Stanford University Press, 2000.

Martin, Kirsten and R. Edward Freeman (2003), 'Some problems with employee monitoring', *Journal of Business Ethics*, **43**(4), 353–61.

Merton, Robert K. (1968) (orig. 1957), *Social Theory and Social Structure*, New York: The Free Press.

Mills, C. Wright (1940), 'Situated actions and vocabularies of motive', *American Sociological Review*, **5**, 904–13.

Miner, A.S. (1987), 'Idiosyncratic jobs in formalized organizations', *Administrative Science Quarterly*, **32**, 327–51.

Miner, A.S. (1991), 'Organizational evolution and the social ecology of jobs', *American Sociological Review*, **56**, 772–85.

Nelson, Richard R. and Sidney G. Winter (1982), *An Evolutionary Theory of Economic Change*, Cambridge, MA: Belknap.

Nonaka, I. and H. Takeuchi (1995), *The Knowledge Creating Company*, Oxford: Oxford University Press.

Pentland, Brian T. and Martha S. Feldman (2005), 'Organizational routines as a unit of analysis', *Industrial and Corporate Change*, 14(5), 793–815.

Pentland, B.T. and H.H. Rueter (1994), 'Organizational routines as grammars of action', *Administrative Science Quarterly*, 39, 484–511.

Reggia, J.A. and G.G. Sutton (1988), 'Self-processing networks and their biomedical implications', III Proceedings of the IEEE, 76(6), 680–92.

Reynaud, B. (2005), 'The void and the heart of rules: routines in the context of rule-following, the case of the Paris Metro workshop', *Industrial and Corporate Change*, 14(5), 847–71.

Salancik, Gerald R. and Huseyin Leblebici (1988), 'Variety and form in organizing transactions: a generative grammar of organizations', in N. DiTomaso and S.B. Bacharach (eds), *Research in the Sociology of Organizations*, Greenwich, CT: JAI Press.

Sartre, Jean Paul (1965), *Nausea*, Harmondsworth: Penguin.

Schank, R.C. and R.P. Abelson (1977), *Scripts, Plans, Goals and Understanding: An Inquiry into Human Knowledge Structures*, Hillsdale, NJ: Lawrence Erlbaum Associates.

Schank, R.C. and R.P. Abelson (1995), 'Knowledge and memory: the real story', in R.S. Wyer (ed.), *Knowledge and Memory: The Real Story, Advances in Social Cognition*, 8, 1–85.

Schulz, Martin (1998a), 'Limits of bureaucratic growth: the density dependence of organizational rule births', *Administrative Science Quarterly*, 43(4), Winter.

Schulz, Martin (1998b), 'A model of obsolescence of organizational rules', *Journal of Computational and Mathematical Organization Theory*, 4(3) Fall, 241–66.

Schulz, Martin and Lloyd A. Jobe (2001), 'Codification and tacitness as knowledge management strategies: an empirical exploration', *Journal of High Technology Management Research*, 12, 139–65.

Schulz, Martin and Nikolaus Beck (2002), 'Die Entwicklung organisationaler Regeln im Zeitverlauf', *Kölner Zeitschrift für Soziologie und Sozialpsychologie*, 42, 119–50.

Scott, Marvin B. and Stanford M. Lyman (1968), 'Accounts', *American Sociological Review*, 33, 46–82.

Selznick P. (1957), *Leadership in Administration*, New York: Harper & Row.

Shanks, D.R. and P. Perruchet (2002), 'Dissociation between priming and recognition in the expression of sequential knowledge', *Psychonomic Bulletin & Review*, 9, 362–7.

Shepherd, G. (1979), *Synaptic Organization of the Brain*, London: Oxford University Press.

Siggelkow, Nicolai (2001), 'Change in the presence of fit: the rise, fall, and the renaissance of Liz Claiborne', *Academy of Management Journal*, 44, 838–57.

Staggenborg, Suzanne (1988), 'The consequences of professionalization and formalization in the pro-choice movement', *American Sociological Review*, 53(4), 585–605.

Staw, Barry M. (1981), 'The escalation of commitment to a course of action', *The Academy of Management Review*, 6(4), 577–87.

Tulving, E. and D.L. Schacter (1990), 'Priming and human memory systems', *Science*, 247, 301–6.

Uzzi, Brian (1997), 'Social structure and competition in interfirm networks: the paradox of embeddedness', *Administrative Science Quarterly*, 42, 35–67.

Weber, Max (1976), *Wirtschaft und Gesellschaft. Fünfte Auflag*, Tübingen: J.C.B. Mohr (Paul Siebeck).

Weiss, Howard M. and Daniel R. Ilgen (1985), 'Routinized behavior in organizations', *Journal of Behavioral Economics*, 14(1), Winter, 57–67.

Winter, Sidney G. (2003), 'Understanding dynamic capabilities', *Strategic Management Journal*, 24(10), 991–5.

Winter, S. and G. Szulanski (2000), 'Replication of organizational routines: conceptualizing the exploitation of knowledge assets', in N. Bontis and C.W. Choo (eds), *The Strategic Management of Intellectual Capital and Organizational Knowledge: A Collection of Readings*, New York: Oxford University Press.

Zander, Udo and Bruce Kogut (1995), 'Knowledge and the speed of the transfer and imitation of organizational capabilities: an empirical test', *Organization Science*, **6**(1) Jan–Feb. 76–92.

Zollo, Maurizio, Jeffrey J. Reuer and Harbir Singh (2002), 'Interorganizational routines and performance in strategic alliances', *Organization Science*, **13**, 701–13.

Zucker, Lynne G. (1977), 'The role of institutionalization in cultural persistence', *American Sociological Review*, **42**, 726–43.

12 The role of teams and communities in the emergence of organizational routines
Patrick Cohendet and Patrick Llerena

Routines and in particular 'organizational routines' are at the core of an evolutionary approach to the firm. However, as Felin and Foss (2004) write, 'While references abound to notions of organizational routines and capabilities, at present in evolutionary economics and strategy we have (1) no theory of their origin, (2) no agreed upon, clear definition, (3) no measurement and (4) no clear understanding of how exactly they relate to competitive advantage . . . the problem is to a considerable extent with the collectivist roots of routines and capabilities-based work, which sideline the individual, and scarcely allow for individual-level explanation' (Felin and Foss, 2004, p. 23). Our contribution is to explore the context of emergence of routines, their evolutions and the consequence of an evolutionary approach to the firm.

In their seminal contribution, Nelson and Winter (NW) (1982) underlined two main dimensions of routines. On the one side, there is a *cognitive and coordination dimension* when considering that routines encompass the organization's knowledge basis and they constitute the organizational memory ('organizations remember by doing', NW, 1982, p. 99). Routines guarantee the regularity and predictability of individual behaviour necessary for collective action, to 'guide or direct an unfolding action sequence that has been stored in some localized or distributed form' (Cohen et al., 1996, p. 683). As Paoli and Prencipe (2003) underlined, 'Routines embody the successful solutions to problems solved by the organization in the past. They are retrieved and executed whenever the organization faces a problem resembling one already solved' (p. 104). Thus memories of the members of the organization store much of the knowledge (both tacit and articulate) needed to perform organizational routines in repertoires of knowledge. However, for members of the organization, the required knowledge necessary for their coordination is much more than knowing what is in the repertoire, they must also know which routine to perform.[1] Attention and other cognitive resources being scarce, as a cognitive device, routines act as attention-focusing mechanisms economizing on scarce cognitive resources (Simon, 1947, 1977; March and Olsen, 1976) in order to 'free-up higher degrees of awareness, mental deliberation and decision making for the more complex decision' (Hodgson, 1997).[2]

On the other side, there is also a *motivational and incentive dimension* associated with the control of intra-organizational conflict: routines are truces among conflicting interests ('attempts to change routines often provoke a conflict which is destructive to the participants and to the organization as a whole' (NW, p. 134)). Coriat and Dosi (1998) consider routine 'as being a locus of conflict, governance, and a way of codifying microeconomic incentives and constraints' (p. 104).[3] According to the authors, the governance feature of routines is strictly dependent on the given mode of organization of production: 'The set of "Japanese" production routines does not only embody different channels of information processing but also distributes knowledge within the organisation in ways remarkably different from the Tayloristic/Chandlerian enterprise. And, at the same time, on the governance side, individuals' incentives to perform efficiently and learn are sustained (in the Japanese firm) by company-specific rank-hierarchies, de-linked from functional assignments, while in the Taylorian approach, the specific mechanism of incentive governance is twofold: on the one hand the design of a new pay system (the so called "differential piece rate system"), on the other hand, incentives had to be matched by direct visual control upon work-practices by foremen' (ibid., p. 105)

Therefore 'routines' can be viewed as a condensed way to remember by doing *what to do* and *how to do things* (cognition and coordination dimension) and *why to do* (motivation–incentive dimension). However the literature on routines has extensively examined the cognition and coordination dimension and somewhat neglected the motivation–incentive dimension, with some few significant exceptions (Coriat and Dosi, 1998). Our view is that this unbalanced treatment of the notion of routine is one of the explanations of some weaknesses of the concept which are underlined by many scholars (in particular Cohen et al., 1996). Despite a well-recognized central role in the modern theories of organization, the concept of routine still reveals ambiguities, inconsistencies and lack of empirical verifications, in particular in relation to the theories of the firm.

In this contribution, we propose to explore one of the neglected aspects of routine which results from this unbalanced treatment. The theoretical works on routines do insist on understanding 'what is a routine', but devote little attention to the nature of the group of agents 'who are involved in the routine'.[4] In other words, the members of the organization involved in a routine are generally considered as anonymous. For instance, the well-known definition of routine given by Cohen et al. (1996, p. 683), 'A routine is an executable capability for repeated performance in some context that has been learned by an organization in response to selection pressures', does not specify the type of groups of agents related to the routine. On the contrary, we consider that routines experienced in a functional group, in a project team, in a network of partners, in a community of different kinds, are all different in terms of power of replication, of degree of inertia, of potential of search. Thus, the establishment of a routine within an organization, its evolution, the testing of its problem-solving capacities, its reinforcement or its rejection, require a direct link between, on the one side, the coordination and cognitive dimension of the routine and, on the other side, the control-incentive and conflict-solving devices and the sharing mechanisms of the relational quasi-rent. The latter govern the relationships between individuals whose interests are not necessarily convergent. Such a perspective may entail considerable impacts on the understanding of the evolutionary theory of the firm. It suggests that the conditions of emergence of the routines drive to a large extent the modes of evolution of routines and the conditions of their replication for the organization. These considerations stand at the heart of the functioning of the knowledge-based firm.

We thus propose to examine carefully the organizational context from which the routine emerges. More precisely, we will select two different contexts of emergence of routines:

(1)   *teams*, which is a generic term used to define those hierarchical working groups in the firm (functional groups, project teams, task force, etc.) for which the context of work and coordination of specialized tasks is defined ex ante by the hierarchy; and

(2)   *knowing communities*, which is a generic term that defines different types of autonomous learning groups of individuals (communities of practice, epistemic communities, and other more or less informal learning groups) united by common beliefs and interests who voluntarily share their resources on a long-term basis in order to create and diffuse knowledge (Boland and Tenkasi, 1995).

The purpose of the contribution is to show that the process of formation of routines, the nature of the routine, the degree of replication of the routine, the modes of transmission of the routine to new members, the mode of selection of the routine, etc. differ significantly in these two types of contexts of emergence. Our view is consistent with one main result of the theoretical debates on routines: the fact that routines are essentially context-dependent. Execution of a routine can only be conceived in a given context that provides the natural locus of attention for collective action. As Nelson and Winter (1982, p. 105) emphasize, 'the context of the information possessed by an individual is established by the information possessed by all other members'. Hence the context is generative because the creation of shared languages and shared meanings stems from the interaction of organizational members. The relationship among organizational members is quintessential for the development and consequential execution of organizational patterned activities that embody the memory of the organization. However most of these approaches consider that the 'context' includes physical state of equipment, external memories, and work environment. We clearly suggest focusing on a specific type of context: the organizational context from which the routine emerges. 'The organizational context is both prone to active individuals' mnemonic processes and, more importantly, activate organizational mnemonic processes' (Paoli and Prencipe, 2003, p. 153).[5]

1   The initial organizational context of the formation of routines: teams and knowing communities

There is a large consensus in the literature that most contexts of production require bringing together complementary skills held by different agents who are committed to a common purpose, performance goals and approach for which they consider themselves mutually accountable. Thus, each elementary productive task in a given organization generally relies on the cooperative specialization process of a definite group of agents. Another point of agreement is that the superiority of groups over market mechanisms only emerges in conditions of joint production where the output yielded by a group is not the sum of the separable outputs of each of its members.

However, beyond this consensus, there are controversies over the nature of configuration of groups, and their economic efficiency. To be very schematic, two extreme positions can be distinguished: on the one hand, a tradition approach in terms of *teams* and, on the other, approaches grouping individuals in *knowing communities*.

1.1   Teams

The traditional economic approach following the seminal article by Alchian and Demsetz (1972) considers that *team* is the most appropriate and effective configuration of groups to accomplish a given task requiring complementary inputs held by heterogeneous agents. According to their view, team is a specific mode of cooperative specialization the efficiency of which comes from the existence of an internal mechanism to reduce any incentive of the members to shirk: the designation by the team members of a 'monitor' in charge of controlling and checking the performance of team members. In this perspective, the team is much more than an efficient mode of grouping of agents: according to Alchian and Demsetz, team is viewed as the elementary 'raison d'être' of organizations and the source of their superiority over market mechanisms. Following this seminal contribution, economists started considering teams as a generic concept to define those groups of agents *within* a firm who are *under the responsibility of the hierarchy of the firm*. In the present contribution we will adopt this broad definition of teams. There are many types of teams such as working groups of a functional department, project teams or task forces. Each of these groups reveals some distinct features (such as time and cost constraints in the case of a project team) that introduce some differences in the formation and reproduction of routines, but all these groups share the same fundamental traits.

In these cooperative devices:

(1)   the routine tends to emerge from an ex ante division of work: the tasks are allocated ex ante by the hierarchy to the members of the team;
(2)   the dominant learning mode that shapes the formation of routine is a learning-by-doing phenomenon that could be considered as a by-product of the existing division of work;
(3)   the scenario and the script of the routines are to a large extent under the responsibility and the supervision of the team leader (or the 'monitor' in the Alchian and Demsetz perspective) who has been chosen by the hierarchy. The team leader generally tunes the relative degree of exploration/exploitation of the collective process at stake; he has a specific hierarchical representation of the routine that will shape any endeavour to codify and replicate, and he has the power to pass in silence over what he considers to be of secondary importance.

As characterized in Cohendet and Llerena (2006), this is the classical representation of a Smithian division of labour.

More precisely, *teams* refer to a generic term that includes functional groups of employees who share a particular specialization corresponding to the classical division of labour (e.g. marketing or accounting). It also includes project teams of employees with heterogeneous skills and qualifications coordinated by a team leader and brought together to achieve a particular goal within a given period of time. For example:

a.   *Functional groups* are traditional groups of agents characterized by homogeneous agents sharing a disciplinary specialization (such as marketing, finance, accounting, etc . . .). They play the key role in the functional structures of the firm as described by Chandler (1977). They are also present in both divisional structures and matrix structures of the firm. In this type of group, the production of knowledge within the firm is unintended. The original knowledge is defined in the codebooks of the respective disciplines, and agents communicate with one another using codes and local jargons developed in their own disciplines. The dominant learning mode is learning-by-doing, and the recruitment procedure is based on the recognition of the mastering of the discipline (diploma) by the hierarchy of the firm. They are dominated by a vertical relationship to the hierarchy.

b.   *Project teams* refer to hierarchical groups. The main problem is certainly the capability to repatriate the knowledge created during the project in the existing structure of the firm and in the following projects. In other terms, there is an open question about the cumulativeness of such organization, i.e. the codification of new knowledge and the replication of the new routines.

1.2   Knowing communities

A recent growing literature (in particular through the notion of 'communities of practice', Lave and Wenger, 1990; Bowles and Gintis, 2000) has emphasized the functioning of *knowing communities* as an alternative efficient mode of coordination between agents. Based on Andriessen and Verburg's work (2004), we can adopt the following definition: *Knowing communities are inter- or intra-organizational, often geographically dispersed, groups of people that have a long-term orientation on knowledge-sharing or knowledge-creating activities. The groups have their own identities and focus their knowledge processes around a certain practice, i.e. a professional discipline, skill or topic.* A knowing community can thus be defined as a gathering within the organization (and sometimes across organizations) of individuals who agree to exchange *voluntarily* and on a *regular basis* views about a common interest or objective in a given domain of knowledge.

The interactions between members of the community are governed by a type of trust grounded in the respect for the common social norms of the community. 'Knowing communities' is a generic term for a large number of autonomous learning groups that encompass, among others, *epistemic communities* and *communities of practice*. These two main types of knowing communities can be differentiated according to the way they solve incentive problems and intra-organizational conflicts. Epistemic communities are rather oriented towards exploration and communities of practice towards exploitation. However, beyond these nuances, knowing communities have some fundamental common properties:

(1)   There is no hierarchy in charge of writing a given script or scenario.
(2)   As long as the community exists, there is no specific costly effort to be made in order to encapsulate and replicate the routines of the community; it is the natural product of the process of interactions between the members of the community.

(3)   The community does not in general emerge from an ex ante division of work: it emerges from the passion and commitment of its members vis-à-vis a given domain of knowledge

Knowing communities might sometimes be found in traditional work divisions and departments, but they usually cut across functional divisions, spill over into after-work or project-based teams, and straddle networks of cross-corporate and professional ties. Knowing communities can be of different natures in the way they deal with knowledge: some of them may focus on the accumulation and exploitation in a given field of knowledge (communities of practice), some of them on the exploration of a new field of knowledge (epistemic communities).

Epistemic communities can be defined as small groups of 'agents working on a commonly acknowledged subset of knowledge issues and who at the very least accept a commonly understood procedural authority as essential to the success of their knowledge activities' (Cowan et al., 2000, p. 234). Epistemic communities can thus be defined as a group of agents having a common goal of knowledge creation and a common framework allowing the shared understanding of this trend. Hence the goal of epistemic communities is simultaneously outside and above the community's members. Because of the heterogeneity of the agents, the objective of knowledge creation for the sake of knowledge, the first task of epistemic communities is to create a 'codebook'. Therefore knowledge circulating within epistemic communities is explicit (but not codified since it remains mainly internal to the community). Validation of the cognitive activity of an agent is made with respect to the procedural authority. What is evaluated is the contribution to the endeavour toward the goal to be reached, according to the criteria set within the procedural authority. Within an epistemic community, agents are bound together by their commitment to enhance a particular set of knowledge. The recruitment rule is thus defined with regard to the contribution an agent makes to fulfil this goal.

The concept of *communities of practice* was introduced by Lave and Wenger (1990) who, by focusing on individuals' practices, identified groups of persons engaged in the same practice, communicating regularly with one another about their activities. Members of a community of practice essentially seek to develop their competences in the practice considered. Communities of practice can then be seen as a means to enhance individual competencies (Lave and Wenger, 1990; Brown and Duguid, 1991). This goal is reached through the construction, exchange and sharing of a common repertoire of resources (Wenger, 1998). The self-consciousness is also visible in the mutual commitment of the community. It is built around activities commonly understood and continually renegotiated by its members. A community's member feeds it with his/her experience and, in turn, relies on the knowledge capitalized by the community to carry out his/her activity. They develop a jargon understandable by the members only. It is thus a mutual commitment that binds agents in a social entity and ensures cohesion of the community and recruitment of new members.

In addition, Lave and Wenger (1990) interpret the practice of these communities as the vector of learning that is, in turn, the building of an individual entity. Hence, the evaluation of an individual is made by the community of practice as a system and is focused both on the values adopted by the individual and on the progress made in his/her practice, the two being co-constitutive.

However, these two types of communities are just the principal components of a large spectrum of knowing groups of different kinds (for an extended analysis, see Bogenrieder and Nooteboom's paper on '*learning groups*', 2004). As informal groups, knowing communities exhibit specific characteristics that distinguish them from the traditional organized entities usually analysed in economics or business science:

a. Communities have no clear boundaries, and there is no visible or explicit hierarchy at the top of them that can control the quality of work or the respecting of any standard procedure.
b. What holds the community together is the passion and commitment of each of its members to a common goal, objective or practice in a given domain of knowledge. Thus, the notion of contract is meaningless within the members of the community, and in particular there is a priori no motive to think of any financial or contractual incentive devices to align the behaviours of the members of the community.
c. The interactions between members of the community are governed by a type of trust grounded in the respect for the common social norms of the community. Trust within the community can be measured when one can observe that the behaviours of the participants, exposed to an unexpected event, are guided, not by any form of contractual scheme, but by the respect of the social norm of the group.
d. Some of the specific motives that guide the behaviours of members of the community could have an economic interpretation. Frequency of interactions within the community considerably reduces opportunistic behaviours. With repeated interactions, hold-ups and moral hazard problems will be attenuated through the creation of norms of cooperation and routines[6] as well as the intensification of reputation mechanisms. Therefore, a large part of agency problems will be resolved spontaneously in the knowledge-based economy.

e.   The validation of the knowledge takes place first in analysis within a given community. In the same way, the interpretation of the knowledge provided by the outside (in particular by the hierarchy) is examined, criticized and reprocessed (to lead sometimes to creative adaptations) within communities.

This last characteristic is certainly one of the potential sources of conflicts between communities and hierarchies in the process of knowledge production and innovative design.

Knowing communities are thus repositories of useful knowledge, which is embedded in their daily practices and habits. The local daily interactions constitute an infrastructure that supports an organizationally instituted learning process that drives the generation and accumulation of knowledge by the community. Most of the time, the accumulation of knowledge by a given community is shaped by a dominant mode of learning (such as 'by circulation of best practices') adopted by the community, and can circulate through the existence of a local language understandable by the members only. As Wenger (1998) noted, 'a community drawing on interaction and participation to act, interpret and innovate, acts "as a locally negotiated regime of competence"'. The communal setting provides the context in which the collective beliefs and the representations structuring the individual choice are built. Communities allow the strengthening of individual commitments in an uncertain universe. Individuals remain attentive to the specific contexts and can therefore update the shapes of their cooperative engagements.

A key point about knowing communities that emerges from the above characteristics and that matters for the content of this contribution is that a 'knowing community' is not an umbrella term for any self-organized group. More precisely, if 'knowing community' implies to a large extent a self-organized process of coordination between members, all self-organized forms of coordination are not assimilable to knowing communities. As defined above, a knowing community refers to a group of individuals focusing on a given domain of knowledge, and intending to do so on a long-term basis. In this perspective a progressive cognitive construct (a 'codebook') is associated with the functioning of the community (which is not of course the case for all self-organized groups).

2   The role and evolution of routines: comparing teams and knowing communities

Our main point is to consider that the context in which routines emerge matters. The 'organizational' and knowledge environment has important consequences for our understanding of how routines work, along their three dimensions (cognition, coordination and motivation) and how they structure the firm. As a consequence of both the context-dependence and the capability design of routines, the localization of the routines in the organization is essential. The nature of the activities concerned (production, research development, finance . . .), the goals and motivations of the potential users and developers of the routines, contribute to shaping the speed and the inflexibilities and the different dimensions of the emerging and used routines.

Cognitive commonalities, that is, socially shared tacit knowledge including knowledge about social models of behaviour, may emerge spontaneously from intense communication as an unintended collective outcome and may, as such, be difficult to influence. Sometimes, however, the institutional set-up of the interactions assigns certain individuals a position in which they get a chance to shape the communication processes and thus to exert an influence on the collective outcome. The firm organization is a case in point. Indeed, the social-cognitive implications of bounded rationality are the key to understanding why firms, as organizations, are able to achieve internal consistency and coordination of individual efforts (Witt, 1998, p. 166).

Each type of groups (teams and knowing communities) has its own mechanisms of emergence of routines. The cognition, coordination and incentive being specific, with different properties in terms of knowledge production and allocation, the main task of the managerial area will be to define the relevant trade-offs according to the external selection mechanisms to which the firm is exposed: nature of the competition, specificities of the technology and products, etc.

All routines, independently of their origin, contribute to the cumulative process of knowledge creation and of allocation, to the searching processes and to the building of core competences, but in different ways:

a. Functional groups can then be viewed as the operators of the manager and the hierarchies to crystallize the know-how into codified rules and procedures.
b. Project teams as focused groups of individuals, having a common goal under hierarchical supervision, create specific knowledge to design an a priori defined artefact.
c. Epistemic communities are leading actors in the searching activities. They have an important capacity to replicate the relevant routines, to evaluate the new experiments and to capitalize them, creating new knowledge blocks. The hierarchies can try to monitor and control them, at least, but with some degree of freedom to leave them some dynamic flexibility.

d.   Communities of practice embed an important potential for the exploitation of existing routines, for increasing their efficiency, by exploiting the best practices. There is in this case a strong tendency for hierarchy to control these routines and to capture them, in particular their replication. One way to do so is to develop the codification process of the relevant know-how.

The balance between the different groups and communities will definitively shape the behaviour of the firm in terms of exploration and exploitation, i.e. the nature of its comparative advantages, and, *in fine*, its performance and comparative advantage.

It is possible to characterize the respective contributions of teams and communities to the nature of routines existing in a firm. Each of these two groups has its own process of creation of routines and each of them has cognitive, coordination and incentive characteristics. In addition, we should keep in mind that, if a routine usually ensures a main function, whether the routine deals mainly with activating a learning process, preventing an opportunistic behaviour or coordinating individual actions, it entails at the same time implications regarding the two other functions in addition to the main one. Any routine supports as well side (or related) functions. In other words any routine must be considered a priori as ambivalent, i.e. as a vehicle of several functions (Avadikyan et al., 2002). This characteristic implies important consequences in terms of organizational coherence.

2.1   *Cognitive processes*

As a capability, routine is the result of, and may be altered in the future by, a wide variety of learning processes. Learning implies a modification of routines, even if those are usually hard to change, and are responsible for inflexibility and inertia in organizational behaviours (NW, p. 400; Langlois and Robertson, 1995). Routines change in response to experience through two main mechanisms. The first is trial-and-error experimentation. 'The likelihood that a routine will be used is increased when it is associated with success in meeting a target, decreased when it is associated with failure' (Cyert and March, 1963). The second mechanism is organizational search: 'An organization draws from a pool of alternative routines, adopting better ones when they are discovered. Since the rate of discovery is a function both of the pool and of the intensity and direction of search, it depends on the history of success and failure of the organization' (Radner, 1986). According to March (1988), the importance of search is related to the hypothesis of bounded rationality: 'Since only a few alternatives, consequences, and goals can be considered simultaneously, actions are determined less by choices among alternatives than by decisions with respect to search'. As repeatedly argued (Nelson and Winter, 1982; Dosi and Egidi, 1991, Dosi et al., 2005), innovative activities involve a kind of learning quite different from Bayesian probability updating and regression estimation: it requires agents to build new representations of the environment they operate in (and which remains largely unknown) and to develop new skills which enable them both to explore and to exploit this world of ever-expanding opportunities. Such representations are embedded in the routines which characterize the organization.

The nature of their interactions contributes to shaping the balance between exploitation and exploration mechanisms of the firm. In addition, the shaping of the architecture of the firm (the interactions between hierarchical and autonomous communities) which determines the nature of the competences of the firm, underlines the specific role of the manager. With regard to routines, the manager acts as an internal selection mechanism. He focuses managerial attention towards specific capabilities and defines the 'core competences' of the organization. This argumentation will lead us to an additional justification of a dual theory of the firm (Cohendet et al., 1998, 2000; Cohendet and Llerena, 1999). This type of perspective allows us to integrate the 'motivational' dimensions of routines, currently missing in the literature.

2.2   Selection processes

Various processes of selection act as filters of evolution on routines. When an existing routine is a success, replication of that success is likely to be desired, but when a routine is a failure, Nelson and Winter (p. 121) raise the question of its 'contraction'. In a model of economic selection that operates on routines, many factors (the market being one selection mechanism amongst others) are involved in determining the consequences of 'sustained adversity' on the persistence or change of routines. Most of the selection mechanisms mentioned by the existing literature are external to the organization, and could thus be referred to as 'natural selection mechanisms' finding an appropriate role in the evolutionary vision of the firm. It must also be recalled that absence of action may lead to the elimination of a routine. As NW pointed out, the phenomenon of memory loss (due for instance to personnel turnover) will accelerate the decay of a routine.

2.3   Motivational aspects

In this conception, the new focus which is directed towards the mechanisms of governance comes from the fact that the creation and distribution of knowledge appear to be inherently and principally linked to the distribution of power and of conflicts of interests. Inequalities in the distribution of information are no longer so much considered to be the origin of the mechanisms of governance, but rather the stakes which the dynamics of the creation and distribution of knowledge reveals. In this context, for example, setting up incentive schemes results not so much from the need to correct asymmetries of information as from the need to control learning dynamics. In fact, the existence of shared knowledge reduces, a priori, the risks of moral hazard and of adverse selection as the risks of asymmetries of information become less acute. One can even put forward the hypothesis that, if one considers that all agents possess cognitive capacities, the divergence of preferences may lead to other effects than those generated by the strategic use of organizational asymmetries. Cohen (1984) thus showed that diversity with regard to preferences and objectives in a disrupted environment where learning and the creation of competences are the main elements for success can be a source of increased performances. In this way, he stressed that, where agents pursue objectives which are specific to their unit, and which might be contradictory, the resulting performances are higher compared to the situation where a group of members concentrate on the same objective. Such a situation can be explained by the effects of cross-fertilization in the solution-seeking process. The collective advantage of this type of diversity is also mentioned by Loasby (1989), for whom the differences in interpretation by individuals of the same group are the origin of organizational learning. The same reasoning is to be found in Schelling (1978) in the 'prisoner's dilemma' with N number of players. Whereas the traditional principal–agent theory is explained in a static context, a dynamic approach of learning in an evolutionary perspective leads to a thorough reconsideration of the setting up of incentive schemes. But how can one orientate learning towards desired directions while at the same time ensuring the 'repatriation' of different experiences? How can diversity be stimulated while maintaining coherence? How can individuals be incited to launch a process of error seeking, to implement new tasks and to evaluate their results and use them widely? And how can new incentive schemes be created which would make it possible to carry out, in the best conditions, processes for the creation and distribution of knowledge?

The origin of incentive schemes from an evolutionary perspective must therefore, according to us, aim to avoid, within the firm, a number of risks which are specific to a collective learning framework. Among these risks are the following:[7]

a.   The risk of a lack of incentive to improve an existing routine by 'locking oneself in' a given practice without ever seeking to change. This refers to the risk of overexploiting existing routines and causing practices to become inflexible without questioning them in the light of new experience and new information.

b.   The risk of a lack of incentive to explore new routines. As Nonaka (1994) stated, incentive schemes should influence an individual's commitment to create new knowledge. This commitment, which aims to avoid the risk of too great a conservatism, relies on the deep-rooted 'intention' of the individual to evolve in a learning context.

c.   The risk of 'conflicts' between individual learning and collective learning. This type of risk of a lack of incentive to combine individual and collective learning can take on many forms. Argyris and Schön (1978) noted that a major obstacle to the evolution of learning or of common knowledge stems from the gap which may exist between what individuals say ('espoused theory') and what they actually do ('theory in use', which actually controls agents' actions).

2.4   Distinctive features of routines: comparing teams and knowing communities

It is possible to characterize the contribution of the different communities to the nature of routines existing in a firm. Each community has its own process of creation of routines and each of them has cognitive, coordination and incentive characteristics (cf. Table 12.1).

Concerning the *cognitive processes*, the *nature* of the process strongly differs between, on the one hand, the teams and, on the other, the knowing communities (epistemic or practice). In the case of teams, most of the learning activity results from a *learning-by-doing* process. This means that the cognitive construct of the group (the jargon, common grammar and codes, social norms, etc.) is only a *by-product* of the 'main' objectives of the group which are essentially oriented towards coordination mechanisms or incentives (to ensure the task efficiently, to reach the goal of the project on time, etc.). This explains that, in the case of teams, specific efforts have to be undertaken by the hierarchy to delineate, capture, reproduce or replicate the routines that result from the learning-by-doing processes at stake. The cognitive construct that supports the routine is fragile in the sense that it has not been elaborated as the routine has been constructed. Most of the time, the hierarchy tries to absorb and replicate the routine of a given team with the global cognitive tools of the organization (common language and representations) which are necessarily somewhat 'distant' from the actual practice of the team.

In the case of knowing communities, the learning process is *intentional*. It is the *raison d'être* of the community that deliberately engages itself in a cognitive activity in which the cognitive understanding of the routine is inherent to and inseparable from the daily functioning of the group. For

Table 12.1 A typology of some communities within the firm

	Objectives	Agents	Cognitive activities	Recruitment rules	Dominant learning mode	Cohesion principles	Incentives
Teams (functional, project)	Ensure given tasks	Homogeneous	Disciplinary specialization	Hierarchical	Unintended learning by doing	Definition of the tasks	Meet given quantitative objective
Community of practice	Increase the skills in a given practice	Homogeneous	Articulation of knowledge about a given practice	Co-optation	Intended learning by doing and knowledge articulation	Common interest to the practice	Increased performance in a given practice
Epistemic community	Produce 'new' knowledge	Heterogeneous	Codification of knowledge (construction of languages and codes) and its circulation	By peers	Intended searching and codification	Respect of a procedural authority	Recognition by peers

instance, members of communities of practice by continuously circulating the best practice between them *simultaneously* work to improve their practised routines and build the common cognitive framework that holds the community together. The cognitive construct that supports the routine is thus built as the routine is formed. This explains the strong degree of encryption and replication of the routine, which, however, is supported by jargons and norms which are specific to the community. The replication for the hierarchy may be difficult, but for reasons and mechanisms that differ radically from the case of teams.[8]

In terms of *incentive mechanisms*, it is interesting to introduce a distinction between extrinsic incentive (adapted to the situations described by the theory of the agency) on the one hand and intrinsic motivation on the other (Kreps, 1997). The distinction relies on the intuition that some tasks, especially tasks undertaken by epistemic communities, cannot abide by standard incentive constraints. More generally, those are the tasks for which creativity and quality are essential dimensions. They are moreover multifaceted tasks, the more important aspects of which are difficult to measure. In such situations, it may be difficult to work out the proper incentives (Kreps, 1997, p. 361). More precisely:

a.   Either one considers that there are actual intrinsic motivations, such as pride in carrying out one's work as in the case of academic research and there is no 'disutility of effort', on the contrary. In this case extrinsic incentives should be as light as possible, for they are not necessary and could be counter-productive.
b.   Or one considers that intrinsic motivations are actually vague extrinsic incentives (e.g. respect of colleagues) and incentive mechanisms to be implemented must remain vague. In such a context of limited rationality where it is impossible to foresee everything, the use of rather vague evaluation criteria ex ante make it often easier to mobilize agents than criteria resting on rigid and precise formulas (Kreps, 1997, p. 361).

On the one hand, according to this classification, functional groups would develop rather extrinsic incentive schemes and, on the other, epistemic communities and communities of practice would have a tendency to adopt intrinsic motivations: the pride to do 'good work' or to be recognized as 'a peer among the peers'. The functional group will have a principal–agent type of incentive structure. In communities of practice, the 'best practice' implies both financial rewards and mutual recognition by the 'profession'. And, in epistemic communities, the endogenous evaluation process induces the recognition by the procedural authority, and finally ends with mere involvement in the procedural authority itself.

The coordination mechanisms are directly linked to the internal organization of these communities: the functional one, being vertically structured and coordinated; the two others being horizontally coordinated – among homogeneous practitioners in the former case, among peers in the latter.

But once the mere fact of a diversity of communities is accepted, then new questions arise:

a.   What can be said about the degree of 'compatibility' of the rules and routines emerging in those communities?
b.   What can be said about the 'coherence' of the communities, in terms of achieving the general goal of the firm, in addition or in opposition to the specific goal of the communities?
c.   What can be said about the frontier of the firm, knowing that communities such as the communities of practice and the epistemic ones very often cross the boundaries of existing firms?

These questions are items for further research. We just indicate in the final section some main properties, features and consequences of the organization of the firm resulting from the views presented in this chapter.

3   Some concluding remarks

The *distinction between teams and communities* that we propose clearly opens the door for an explicit recognition of the role of the hierarchy and the managerial component in the evolutionary approach of the firm.[9] Some authors (Loasby, 1991; Witt, 1998, 2000; Cohendet et al., 2000) already reappraised the role of entrepreneurs, and underlined the role of leadership as provision and enforcement frames in an evolutionary context. 'The way in which these cognitive frames emerge and change over time is influenced by communication processes with the social environment which endow people with tacit knowledge, socially shared interpretation of patterns, and social models of behaviour. In many cases, e.g. within neighbourhoods or circles of friends or peers, these communication processes develop spontaneously, i.e. without being shaped by any central guidance . . . Sometimes however, the institutional set-up of interactions assigns certain individuals a position in which they get a chance to shape the communication processes and thus exert an influence on the collective outcome. The firm is a case in point . . . this fact is an important reason why firms, as organizations, can achieve internal consistency and coordination of individual efforts' (Witt, 1998). In a way, the role of managers in an evolutionary approach is even richer than in a classical one. Beside the classical attributes of managers, the evolutionary approach allows them to shape cognitive commonalities and socially shared interpretation patterns and frames. They also influence (indirectly) the routines at all levels of the firm. They can orient the learning processes by focusing attention on certain characteristics of these processes (by rewarding, for instance, exploration instead of exploitation). They also play a significant role in the selection of the core competences of the firm, through the processes of acquisition and mergers to reinforce existing core competences or by allocating resources to accumulate new competitive knowledge in a specific and given core competence. In short, managers play the role of an internal selection mechanism that, beside other selection mechanisms (in particular external ones such as market forces), contributes to shaping the body of competences of the firm. All these attributes reinforce the assumption that managers, in an evolutionary context, do have to set up incentive mechanisms. Moreover, these additional characteristics of managers strongly plead for a richer design of incentives than in the pure transactions and incentive-oriented approaches.

In addition to the already mentioned mechanisms, organizational learning is also influenced by the 'structure' of the organization, which 'designates for each person in the organization what decisions that person makes, and the influences to which he is subject in making each of these decisions' (Simon, 1976, p. 37). The organizational structure therefore contributes to defining the context of any collective action within the firm: who is responsible for what, who should send what kind of information to whom, who has the authority to do so, and so on and so forth. In other words the organizational structure defines the rules of the games that individuals within an organization and parts of it (units, departments, services, and so on) repeatedly play and thus the frame within which organizational learning occurs.

What is crucial in this definition is that such rules of the games and routines should not be exogenously given but should emerge and evolve in the very process of interaction. The behaviour of a firm should also depend on the structure, which, by defining the way people interact within the organization, both among themselves and with the external environment, plays a crucial role in determining the outcome of the organizational decision-making process. In other words, beside the global evolutionary processes (diversity creation and selection) that the firm faces, there are similar processes taking place inside the firm to create, select and transform rules, routines and, more generally, the different mechanisms defining the organizational coherence of the firm.[10] Here again the entrepreneur/manager is too often neglected.

As Nelson stressed (1994), 'A firm can be understood in terms of hierarchy of practised organizational routines, which define lower-order organizational skills and how these skills are coordinated and higher-order decision procedures for choosing what is to be done at the lower level.' However, as argued in this chapter, the loci of emergence of routines may not be the hierarchically organized ones, but also (and mainly in a knowledge creative context) knowing communities. It then becomes a highly relevant issue for the management of innovative companies. The *distinction between teams and communities* and the mere fact that they are the loci of emergence and development of routines clearly opens the door for an explicit recognition of the role of the knowing communities and their boundaries.

Indeed, generally knowing communities are not confined within a given organization/teams or firm: they cross the boundaries even of firms. In and across organizations, there are many different kinds of communities, which vary in remit, organization and membership. Some of these communities emerge spontaneously from the hierarchical structures of the firm (some workshop staff may constitute a community of practice overlapping with the functional division of operations in the firm), while some communities may result from an adherence to a common passion of very dispersed individuals within the firm (for instance, a community of practice of people interested in computing in a given organization will not in general overlap with the staff of the computer department, but may comprise agents of the firm working in different positions, departments and even locations of the firm). Such communities, bound by relations of common interest, purpose or passion, and held together by routines and varying degrees of mutuality, are now being considered as key sites of knowledge formation and exchange, and learning. Communities thus defined seem to embody the pragmatic, situated, interactive and enacted knowledge routines that have been outlined above. These are characteristics that, as we have seen, cannot be captured by individual-centred or classical organization-centred approaches. Instead, they do seem to fit with the workings of project- or task-focused groupings caught up in daily processes of interaction and practices of knowing through the combination of conscious and unconscious rhythms of work. Through their dynamic interactions that cross the frontiers of any hierarchical structure, knowing communities are reservoirs of creative ideas that emerge from permanent horizontal interactions.[11]

Notes

1. 'There is much more to "knowing one's job" in an organization than merely having the appropriate routines in repertoire. There is also the matter of knowing what routines to perform. For the individual member, this entails the ability to receive and interpret a stream of incoming messages from other members and from the environment' (NW, 1982, p. 100).
2. As underlined by Becker (1999), 'To focus attention means to reduce the space of events that managers should scan in order to avoid bad surprises and take advantage of the good ones (Shapira, 1994). This is achieved by perceiving as noise and ignoring what

does not receive attention (Garud and Rappa, 1994) . . . Thus focusing has two sides: it has as much the meaning of "leaving something out of the window" as it does have the meaning of "being aware of something", or "drawing attention to something".' This focusing process being not only spontaneous but also intentional, opens the door to a specific role of managerial capabilities (and especially to dynamic capabilities (Teece and Pisano, 1994)).

3. The authors analyse this assumption by studying the archetypal forms of organization such as Taylorism, Fordism and Ohnism.
4. Among the few exceptions, there are Feldman and Rafaeli (2002) and Feldman and Pentland (2005).
5. See also Cohendet and Llerena (2003), a companion paper to this one.
6. The 'truce' hypothesis in Nelson and Winter's routine analysis.
7. This point was developed by Cohendet et al. (1998).
8. In these last two cases, the emergent routines constitute the so-called 'dynamic capabilities'. As defined by Zollo and Winter (2002), 'a dynamic capability is a learned and stable pattern of collective activity through which the organization systematically generates and modifies its operating routines in pursuit of improved effectiveness' (Zollo and Winter, p. 340).
9. In fact the role of managerial routines (or 'capabilities'), was fully recognized by Penrose (1959) in her seminal book. However, Penrose only focused on the functioning of managerial teams, without taking into account interactions at other levels of the firm.
10. Coherence refers to the coordination of distributed pieces of knowledge and involves the creation of commonly shared bodies of knowledge: sets of facts, notions, 'models of the world', organizational routines, rules, procedures which are – at least partly – known to all the members of the organization involved in a given interaction. In a sense this kind of coordination is a precondition for the coordination of actions which is examined by most current literature and which implicitly assumes that all these mechanisms for the coordination of dispersed knowledge are already in place. It seems in any case most unlikely that mere incentive mechanisms could alone be sufficient to promote this kind of coordination.
11. See Cohendet et al. (2006) for a more detailed development.

References

Alchian, A. and H. Demsetz (1972), 'Production, information costs, and economic organization', *American Economic Review*, **62**, 777–95.

Andriessen, J.H.E. and R.M. Verburg (2004), 'The development and application of the community assessment toolkit' (www.communities-research-group.tudelft.nl).

Argyris, C. and D. Schön (1978), *Organisational Learning: a Theory of Action Perspective*, Reading, MA: Addison-Wesley.

Avadikyan, A., P. Llerena, M. Matt, A. Rozan and S. Wolff (2002), 'Organisational rules, codification and knowledge creation in inter-organisation cooperative agreements', *Research Policy*, **30**, 1443–58.

Becker, M. (1999), 'The role of routines in organizations: a review of the literature and of empirical research on routines', *Working Paper*, Cambridge University, Judge Institute of Management.

Bogenrieder, I. and B. Nooteboom (2004), 'Learning groups: what types are there? A theoretical analysis and an empirical study in a consultancy firm', *Organization Studies*, **25**(2), 287–313.

Boland, R.J. and R.V. Tenkasi (1995), 'Perspective making and perspective taking in communities of knowing', *Organization Science*, **6**(4), 350–72.

Bowles, S. and H. Gintis (2000), 'Social capital and community governance', Working Paper 01-01-003, Santa Fe Institute (www.santafe.edu/sfi/publications/Working-Papers/01-01-003).

Brown, J.S. and P. Duguid (1991), 'Organizational learning and communities of practice: toward a unified view of working, learning and innovation', *Organization Science*, **2**(1), 40–57.

Chandler, A.D. (1977), *The Visible Hand: the Managerial Revolution in American Business*, Cambridge, MA: Harvard University Press.

Cohen, M.D. (1984), 'Conflict and complexity: goal diversity and organizational search effectiveness', *American Political Science Review*, **78**, 435–51.

Cohen, M.D., R. Burkhart, G. Dosi, M. Egidi, L. Marengo, M. Warglien and S. Winter (1996), 'Routines and other recurring action patterns of organizations: contemporary research issues', *Industrial and Corporate Change*, **5**(3), 653–98.

Cohendet, P. and P. Llerena (1999), 'La conception de la firme comme processeur de connaissances', *Revue d'Economie Industrielle*, **88**, 211–36.

Cohendet, P. and P. Llerena (2003), 'Routines and incentives: the role of communities in the firm', *Industrial and Corporate Change*, **12**(2), 271–97.

Cohendet, P. and P. Llerena (2006), 'Knowledge-based entrepreneur: an analysis from the division of knowledge perspective', International JA Schumpeter Society Conference: 'Innovation, Competition and Growth: Schumpeterian perspectives', Nice – Sophia Antipolis, 21–24 June.

Cohendet, P., P. Llerena and L. Marengo (1998), 'Theory of the firm in an evolutionary perspective: a critical assessment', DRUID Conference, Copenhagen, 9–11 June.

Cohendet, P., P. Llerena and L. Marengo (2000), 'Is there a pilot in the evolutionary firm?', in N. Foss and V. Mahnke (eds), *New Directions in Economic Strategy Research*, Oxford: Oxford University Press.

Cohendet, P., J.A. Héraud and P. Llerena (2006), 'Division of labour and division of knowledge in firms' innovative networks: an essay on Ehud Zuscovitch's theoretical perspectives', International JA Schumpeter Society Conference, 'Innovation, Competition and Growth: Schumpeterian perspectives', Nice–Sophia Antipolis, 21–24 June.

Cohendet, P., F. Kern, B. Mehmanpazir and F. Munier (1998), 'Routines, structure of governance and knowledge-creation processes', in J. Lesourne and A. Orleans (eds), *Advances in Self-organisation and Evolutionary Economics*, Paris: Economica.

Coriat B. and G. Dosi (1998), 'Learning how to govern and learning how to solve problems: on the coevolution of competences, conflicts and organizational routines', in A.D. Chandler, P. Hagström and Ö. Sölvell (eds), *The Dynamic Firm: the Role of Technology, Strategy, Organization and Regions*, Oxford: Oxford University Press, pp. 103–33.

Cowan, R., P.A. David and D. Foray (2000), 'The explicit economics of knowledge codification and tacitness', *Industrial and Corporate Change*, **9**(2), June, 211–53.

Cyert, R. and J. March (1963), *A Behavioural Theory of the Firm*, Englewood Cliffs, NJ: Prentice-Hall.

Dosi, G. and M. Egidi (1991), 'Substantive and procedural uncertainty: an exploration of economic behaviours in complex and changing environments', *Journal of Evolutionary Economics*, **1**, 145–68.

Dosi, G., L. Marengo and G. Fagiolo (2005), 'Learning in evolutionary environments', in K. Dopfer (ed.), *The Evolutionary Foundations of Economics*, Cambridge: Cambridge University Press.

Feldman, M.S. and B.T. Pentland (2005), 'Organizational routines as a unit of analysis', *Industrial and Corporate Change*, **14**(5), October, 793–816.

Feldman, M.S. and A. Rafaeli (2002), 'Organizational routines as sources of connections and understandings', *Journal of Management Studies*, **39**, 309–31.

Felin, T. and N. Foss (2004), 'Organizational routines: a skeptical look', DRUID *Working paper, 04–13*, October.

Garud, R. and M. Rappa (1994), 'A socio-cognitive model of technology evolution', *Organization Science*, **5**(3).

Hodgson, G.M. (1997), 'The ubiquity of habits and roles', *Cambridge Journal of Economics*, **21**(6), 663–84.

Kreps, D.M. (1997), 'The interaction between norms and economic incentives. Intrinsic motivation and extrinsic incentives', *American Economic Review*, **87**(2), 359–64.

Langlois, R. and P. Robertson (1995), *Firms, Markets and Economic Change*, London: Routledge.

Lave, J. and E.C. Wenger (1990), *Situated Learning: Legitimate Peripheral Participation*, New York: Cambridge University Press.

Loasby, B.J. (1989), *The Mind and the Method of the Economist*, Aldershot: Edward Elgar.
Loasby, B.J. (1991), *Equilibrium and Evolution: An Exploration of Connecting Principles in Economics*, Manchester: Manchester University Press.
March, J. (1988), 'Introduction: a chronicle of speculations about organizational decision making', in J. March (ed.), *Decisions and Organization*, Oxford: Basil Blackwell, pp. 1–24.
March, J. and J. Olsen (1976), *Ambiguity and Choice in Organizations*, Oslo: Universitetsforlaget.
Nelson, R.R. (1994), 'The co-evolution of technology, industrial structure and supporting institutions', *Industrial and Corporate Change*, **3**.
Nelson, R.R. and S. Winter (1982), *An Evolutionary Theory of Economic Change*, Cambridge, MA: Havard University Press.
Nonaka, I. (1994), 'A dynamic theory of organizational knowledge creation', *Organization Science*, **5**(1), 14–37.
Paoli, M. and A. Prencipe (2003), 'Memory of the organisation and memories within organisations', *Journal of Management and Governance*, **7**, 145–62.
Penrose, E. (1959), *The Theory of the Growth of the Firm*, Oxford: Oxford University Press.
Radner, R. (1986), 'The internal economy of large firms', *Economic Journal*, **96** (Supplement), 1–22.
Schelling, T. (1978), *Micromotives and Macrobehavior*, New York: W.W. Norton.
Shapira, Z. (1994), 'Evolution, externalities and managerial action', in J. Baum and J. Singh (eds), *Evolutionary Dynamics of Organizations*, Oxford: Oxford University Press, pp. 117–26.
Simon, H.A. (1947, 1977), *Administrative Behaviour*, 4th edn, London: The Free Press.
Simon, H.A. (1976), *Administrative Behaviour*, 3rd edn, New York, The Free Press.
Teece, D.J. and G. Pisano (1994), 'The dynamic capabilities of firms: an introduction', *Industrial and Corporate Change*, **3**, 537–56.
Wenger, E. (1998), 'Communities of practice; learning as a social system', *Systems Thinker*, June.
Witt, U. (1998), 'Imagination and leadership: the neglected dimensions of the evolutionary theory of the firm', *Journal of Economic Behaviour and Organization*, **35**, 161–77.
Witt, U. (2000), 'Changing cognitive frame – changing organizational forms: an entrepreneurial theory of organizational development', *Industrial and Corporate Change*, **9**(4), 733–55.
Zollo, M. and S.G. Winter (2002), 'Deliberate learning and the evolution of dynamic capabilities', *Organization Science*, Special issue on 'Knowledge, Knowing and Organization', **13**(3), May–June, 339–51.

PART IV

CONDUCTING EMPIRICAL RESEARCH ON ORGANIZATIONAL ROUTINES

13 Issues in empirical field studies of organizational routines[1]

Brian T. Pentland and Martha S. Feldman

Introduction

In organizational research, the most familiar units of analysis are individuals, groups, establishments and organizations. These units have relatively clear boundaries, which make them observable, distinguishable, comparable and countable. By comparison, organizational routines are difficult to observe, distinguish, compare and count. In this chapter, we draw on our own fieldwork experiences as a basis for reflecting on the issues of studying organizational routines through empirical field studies.[2] We focus on two very basic issues: identification (White, 1992) and comparison (Ragin, 1987). Identification involves recognizing empirical instances of a routine, the parts as well as the whole. Comparison can be cross-sectional (involving different routines), or longitudinal (involving changes in the same routine over time). Together, identification and comparison form the foundation for all empirical work on routines.

We begin with a 'confessional' (Van Maanen, 1988): a behind-the-scenes look at our own research process on routines. Our experiences and observations, and those of other field researchers, have led us to conceptualize organizational routines as generative systems rather than fixed things (Feldman and Pentland, 2003). With this conceptual framework as a guide, we discuss how identification and comparison apply to organizational routines. Issues such as point of view and concurrency can make identification and comparison particularly problematic when conducting field research on routines. Where appropriate, we draw upon examples of how these issues have been handled in existing empirical field research.

What is going on here?

In published research, one tries to create the impression of rigour and objectivity; a good design, well executed, with little error. Of course, field studies are usually not so clean or clear. To help readers appreciate our view of the issues, each of us will present some of the messy details from our own work.

Pentland's story

If you sit in a cubicle with a software hot line worker for a few hours, you will see them do a lot of different things. They will answer calls, make calls, answer questions, ask questions, look things up, write things down, fill out forms, and more. Once in a while, they may get up to go to a meeting or get a cup of coffee. But how do these activities connect? Is there a thread that ties these discrete actions into productive work?

I chose to study software support hot lines partly as a matter of convenience. It seemed like a very clear-cut and well-bounded kind of work: calls come in, answers go out. Everything happens in one place, within a fairly short time span. I reasoned that I could get a lot of data in a relatively short amount of time. Better yet, there were lots of software vendors in and around Cambridge, Massachusetts, easily accessible to a graduate student at MIT.

My first disappointment was that the work did not happen all in one place. In the sites I studied, calls were answered by switchboard operators who verified that the caller was entitled to support and then placed the call in a 'queue'. If I sat with the switchboard operator, as I did for several days at each site, I just observed the first bit. To find out what happened next, I had to follow the call.

Worse yet was the realization that a great deal of the 'work' happens on the other end of the phone. Most problems started long before the caller decided to call for help; by the time they called, they might have tried several different fixes and workarounds and gathered various kinds of evidence. In other cases, the support person asked the caller to do some investigating, run some tests, gather some information, and send it in before calling back. In any case, it was clear that the work happened in many different places and I could only observe one of them. In other words, the boundaries on this work process were not as clear or localized as I had thought.

It took me quite a while to realize that the boundaries were not the same in my two field sites, either. The sites were both 'software support hot lines', and the people working there were self-described 'support people'. These labels were accurate, but they masked important differences. In one site, the hot line staff would try to replicate problems and answer questions, but they did not even have access to the underlying code. If they thought they had found a bug, they would write it up and submit it to a separate group, housed in a separate building. Because of security precautions at the firm, I was not allowed access to that building. In the other site, the hotline people also tried to replicate problems and answer questions, but they did have access to the software code. They could edit code and create 'patches' that customers could use to fix bugs and even extend the basic product. Thus, the range of activities at the two sites was quite different.

Once these issues were clarified, the most challenging problem was how to figure out what happened when problems were not resolved in a single phone call (which they rarely were). Even for a very simple problem, there was often a round of phone tag (customer is at a meeting, out to lunch, etc.) When the support person got the customer on the phone, there was often a delay while the customer got more information or tried a workaround ('reinstall and let me know if you are still having the problem . . .'). In the meantime, the support person would move on to another call. The follow-up might not happen for a day or two (or longer), and it might not be handled by the same support person. These constant interruptions, trans-fers and delays made it almost impossible to observe entire performances from start to finish. I could collect a lot of data, but it was mostly frag-ments. My analysis of 'organizing moves' (Pentland, 1992) and 'interpre-tive moves' (Pentland, 1995) were based on these fragments.

Archival records from the field sites were a big help in dealing with this problem. Each site used a call-tracking database where hot line workers were supposed to enter significant steps taken on each problem. These records were less than perfect; they were typed in by busy hot line workers, and were usually just detailed enough to remind themselves what had hap-pened. Still, these databases allowed me to connect distinct actions into a sequential story for each problem, from beginning to end (opening, actions taken and closing). Without these records, it would have been impossible to examine the sequential structure of the hot line performances (Pentland and Reuter, 1994).

In addition to software support hot lines, I have observed a variety of other occupations: librarians, travel agents, bank investigators, financial auditors, and IRS revenue agents. In each of these cases, the work seemed to involve localized, repetitive, recognizable patterns. As with hotlines, however, it was easy to observe fragments, but hard to get whole perfor-mances. The work turns out to be more distributed than it seems at first, and the patterns are only recognizable and repetitive if you know what you are looking for.

Feldman's story

I have engaged in two longitudinal ethnographic field studies of organiza-tional routines. In one I saw the remarkable stability of an organizational routine that many who engaged in it thought made no sense. In the other, which I engaged in to understand this stability, I found change.

My first study took place in the US Department of Energy. In it I asked how the bureaucratic production of information was related to the policy process. Policy analysts spend much of their time writing reports. These reports are usually either required on a regular basis (e.g., an annual review of a programme) or as part of a particular policy decision. Regardless of why they are generated, they are seldom read by policy makers and appear to have no discernable relation to policy decisions. The title of the book I wrote, *Order Without Design* (Feldman, 1989), reflects the message that this routine made sense in ways that were not obvious to or created by the people who enacted the routine. My study identified regularity in the abstract pattern of report writing. Identifying this abstract pattern enabled me to connect particular features of the pattern to demands of the policy process. For instance, the concurrence process that was part of the report-writing routine required that a broad set of participants take part in any particular instance of the routine and that requirement ensured that there would be broad dissemination of information across the many organizations that were represented on the concurrence list. I argued that broad dissemination was one of the ways in which the report-writing routine had beneficial consequences for the policy process even though the participants in the routine were not aware of their contribution to these consequences.

I started my next study with the express goal of understanding how it is that you can have routines like the report-writing routine that are not intended by the people who enact them. This question took for granted that organizational routines are stable and inertial. I wanted to know how this stability was achieved. My assumption was that something about the way routines operated in organizations encouraged consistent behaviour and discouraged flexibility and innovation. I chose an organization, the housing division of a large state university, for two reasons. One, it had routines that dealt with the production of rooms and beds and things that are, in themselves, fairly stable. Two, I was assured by several people that the routines in this organization were mind-numbingly stable. I thought I was set. Alas, I had no idea what complexities this field site had in store for me.

Unlike the Department of Energy, in this organization the abstract patterns of routines were fairly easy to identify and before long I was happily following five routines that the participants had identified as important to what they do. The five were (1) budgeting for maintenance and renovation of the buildings and operations within the buildings, (2) hiring the student resident staff, (3) training them, (4) moving students into the residence halls at the beginning of the school year, and (5) closing the residence halls at the end of the school year. Within each of these routines there were multiple subroutines, and there was some variance in what was included in each of the routines, depending on who was describing them. Nonetheless, organizational participants had a good understanding of the rules and actions implied if one were to say, 'now we are doing budgeting' or 'now we are doing hiring'. Each of these routines had an annual cycle, which I followed for four years. Over those four years, four of the routines changed quite markedly. The one routine that changed only minimally was the budget routine. Ironically, it was the one that the supervisors in the organization wanted to change (Feldman, 2003).

It took me a long time to realize that what I needed to understand and explain was change. It took an even longer time for me to convince editors and reviewers. One of the difficulties was explaining what it was that was changing. At some level each of the routines stayed the same. Residence advisors applied for jobs, were screened, interviewed and hired. Parents brought their children to the university and moved them and their belongings into the residence halls.

Yet, in so many other ways, the routines had changed. The routines changed in the tasks that were undertaken to enact the routine, what one might call a change in scope. For the moving-in routine, the organization engaged in activities it had never undertaken before. They re-routed traffic, scheduled move-in times, made volunteers available to transport goods and set up a designated space for solicitors. For the hiring routine, the same actions were undertaken, but by different units in the organization. Rather than having the initial screening take place at each of the residence halls, it was centralized. The effect was quite substantial (Feldman, 2004).

Finally, one routine changed, not just in the tasks that were undertaken or by whom, but also in the meaning of the task itself, a change in signification. Damage assessment, part of the process of moving people out of the residence halls at the end of the year, had always been successful as a way of compensating the university for damage, but some thought it should also be a way of educating the students who caused the damage about the consequences of their actions. The routine was changed to accomplish this goal over the course of the four years of my observation (Feldman, 2000).

The housing study, unlike the Department of Energy study, forced me to focus on the different ways to identify an organizational routine. For the Department of Energy study I compared report-writing incidents in order to abstract the pattern. I used that pattern for the subsequent analyses. Because the focus of the housing study was always the internal dynamics of routines, the abstract patterns were the starting point and I compared the same routines over time. This strategy highlighted the performative aspect of routines and the difference that people and their performances in routines make (Feldman, 2000, 2003, 2004).

Our story
One theme that emerges from our field research is that, if you look closely, routines can be surprising. Pentland looked for repetition and found variety. Feldman looked for stability and found change. For the last several years, we have been working together to develop concepts and vocabulary

to describe and explain the range of phenomena we (and others[3]) have observed. All along, we have felt that, in spite of their obvious importance, organizational routines had been taken for granted and objectified. In response to this concern, we articulated the difference between ostensive and performative aspects of organizational routines as a means of explaining the enormous variation we observe, from great stability to tremendous change (Feldman and Pentland, 2003). In that paper, we did not talk much about artifacts, and the distinction between ostensive and artifact made only a cameo appearance.

We have subsequently realized that we needed to emphasize the distinction between the ostensive aspects of a routine from physical artifacts such as standard operating procedures, forms, computer systems and so forth (Pentland and Feldman, 2005). We continue that effort in the present chapter as part of our ongoing effort to understand and operationalize the ostensive. We sometimes conceptualize the ostensive as narrative – a story or stories about how work gets done (Feldman and Pentland, 2005; Pentland and Feldman, 2007). These stories imply *connections* between actors, actions and artifacts that enable us to recognize and reproduce the performances. Our understanding of this complex phenomenon continues to evolve through empirical study and our research conversation. The following discussion summarizes where we are to date and explores some of the research issues as they have emerged in our own and other people's field studies.

Conceptualizing organizational routines

Organizational routines are best conceptualized as generative systems that can produce a wide variety of performances depending on the circumstances. Figure 13.1 illustrates a simple way of visualizing the parts of an organizational routine. On one hand, routines consist of abstract, cognitive regularities and expectations that enable participants to guide, account for and refer to specific performances of a routine. We refer to these as the 'ostensive' aspects (Feldman and Pentland, 2003). On the other hand, routines consist of actual performances by specific people, at specific times, in specific places. We refer to this as the 'performative' aspect (Feldman and Pentland, 2003). These two aspects are mutually constitutive; without these two aspects, a routine cannot exist.

In any practical setting, these aspects of an organizational routine may be enabled and constrained, by various artifacts. Artifacts take many different forms, from written rules, procedures and forms to the general physical setting (e.g., a factory or an office). We call attention to artifacts here because they have been particularly prominent as a means of collecting data about routines. Artifacts such as rules and written procedures can

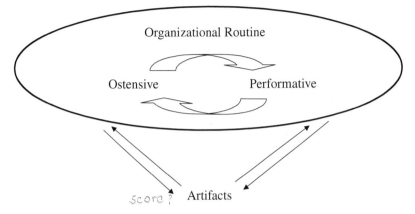

Figure 13.1 Organizational routines are generative systems

serve as a proxy for the ostensive aspect of a routine. Artifacts such as work logs and databases can also provide a convenient archival trace of the performative aspect (Pentland and Reuter, 1994). Artifacts can be 'enrolled' in the performance of a routine to varying degrees, at the discretion of the participants (Feldman and Pentland, 2005).

These aspects are distributed in time and space; different participants perform different parts of a routine. This simple fact forces us to choose a particular point of view when studying routines, because we cannot see the whole thing. Indeed, it is difficult to identify what a 'whole' routine is, an issue we explore in more detail below. In field studies of routines, point of view has a simple, basic sense of 'where one stands' while observing. For example, does one sit with the switch board operator? What if one cannot visit some parts of an organization where a routine is carried out? It also has a deeper sense of whether one adopts an etic or emic perspective (Headland, 1990). We use these concepts here to help clarify the ostensive and performative aspects of routines, and we return to them in more depth later.

Examining performances

Performances are actions taken by specific people in specific times and places. As such, they appear to be readily visible. Even so, performances are hard to see because, as Pentland discovered, they are usually distributed over time and space. Some events are visible and others are hidden from any particular point of view, and the boundaries are not given or self-evident. Thus, while a routine may generate a sequence of events, the particular events and sequences we observe are partly a result of our point of view on a process (Pentland, 1999a). Different understandings of a process result in looking for and seeing different performances. Point of view is equally important when considering the meaning of a performance: even though a customer and a service provider may agree on 'what happened' in a service interaction, they may have entirely divergent perspectives on its quality or acceptability.

When observing the performative aspect of a routine, researchers often choose a coding scheme to represent the observations. Point of view is obviously critical here. Unlike things, that usually have well-defined boundaries, events must be constructed and 'unitized' out of a stream of observation (Folger et al., 1984). In principle, actions can be broken down into arbitrarily fine-grained detail (Abell, 1987). In practice, much larger chunks are often more meaningful (Malone et al., 1999). Even if one is working inductively and defining codes based on participant categories, there is likely to be considerable discretion as to the number of codes actually used. For example, Sabherwal and Robey (1993) report that they started out with 25 codes, but found that it was difficult to distinguish them reliably. As a result, they reduced their lexicon to 15 codes. The specific coding scheme is a matter of researcher choice and judgment and reflects a basic choice between etic and emic perspectives.

Examining the ostensive
The ostensive aspects of organizational routines are the abstract patterns that participants use to guide, account for, and refer to specific performances of a routine. They are embodied understandings that are often communicated in a narrative form. The ostensive aspects are also distributed. They are distributed in two distinct, important ways. First, different people may understand different parts of the routine (e.g., a product development routine typically involves design, marketing, manufacturing and finance). Second, different people may have different, conflicting ideas about how a routine should be or is performed. While at times there may be a 'truce' (Nelson and Winter, 1982), both explicit and implicit conflict may often characterize the ostensive aspects of organizational routines. Thus, any particular rendering of the ostensive aspects of a routine is potentially contested.

Unlike performances, the ostensive is not directly visible. The ostensive aspects can be thought of as narratives about the routine, but the narratives need be neither coherent nor consensual. In addition, the ostensive aspects consist of tacit assumptions that must be true in order for the rest of the narrative to make sense (Cohen and Bacdayan, 1994). In any case, it seems clear that in most cases there is no singular, unified ostensive aspect of the routine that can be recovered. Instead, the ostensive aspects are more likely to be a collection of partial, overlapping narratives.

This poses challenges for the researcher who wants to pinpoint the ostensive aspect of a routine. Imagine trying to collect the story of 'little red riding hood' (or 'writing a policy statement') by interviewing each character about their role. One would get a different story from the point of view of each character, but they might not be able to explain how their parts fit together. At the same time, participants need to have *some* understanding of the ostensive aspect of the routine in order to see their actions as part of the routine. The challenge here is finding the thread – the narrative connection – that allows us to identify actions as part of a whole and to identify a diverse set of activities as a coherent flow.

One can cope with this potential variability in the ostensive aspects of a routine by suppressing it. The researcher creates a clear definition of the routine from an outsider's (etic, objective) point of view. This definition may draw on theory, artifacts, interviews or intuition, but the multiple and conflicting interpretations of the participants are not relevant. The primary pitfall of this approach is our tendency to mistake the definition for the routine (or the map for the terrain). Just because one defines something as the hiring routine, for instance, does not mean that this is the way hiring is accomplished.

Examining artifacts

Artifacts are physical manifestations of the organizational routine. Artifacts can reflect either the ostensive aspects of a routine (as in the case of a written procedure) or the performative aspect of a routine (as in the case of a transaction history or tracking database). The canonical artifact for an organizational routine is the standard operating procedure (SOP), the formal written rules that represent the routine. SOPs are often mistaken for the ostensive aspects of the routine or for the routine as a whole. Both mistakes undermine the agentic qualities of organizational routines. Mistaking the SOP for the ostensive aspects of the routine makes it difficult to see the individual and social processes of sense making that enable people to construct understandings of what they and others are doing. When researchers mistake SOPs for the routine as a whole, performances disappear and it is difficult to perceive their role in the ongoing production of organizational routines.

SOPs are not the only artifacts of routines that are important to consider. Artifacts also include, e.g., application forms, the physical layout of the workplace and the tools (e.g., telephones, files, assembly lines, etc.) used in performing the routine. Artifacts should be treated cautiously as indicators of the underlying ostensive or performative aspects. Participants have their own understandings of the artifact, and they have their own strategic reasons for enrolling a particular artifact (or not enrolling it) in their projects. We can discern only some of the significance of an artifact by inspecting it from our own (etic) point of view.

Our separation of artifact and understanding is consistent with Weber (1947, p. 93), who states that 'every artifact . . . can be understood only in terms of the meaning which its production and use have had or were intended to have . . . Without reference to this meaning such an object remains wholly unintelligible'. In the case of organizational routines, one also has to be cognizant of the meanings the object currently has from the perspective of the people using it and the way they use the artifact in their performances. Weber clearly distinguished artifacts from the meaning they have for participants, and that is the distinction we are recommending here.

Identification and comparison of routines

Because they are generative systems, distributed in time and space, and enacted by multiple participants, organizational routines are a challenging phenomenon to study. The complexity of organizational routines as a phenomenon requires us to take special care with respect to basic methodological issues that can be more safely skipped with other, more concrete, units of analysis. We will focus on two key questions that emerge, implicitly or explicitly, in any kind of empirical research: identification and comparison. These issues concern identifying the boundaries of the phenomenon, and establishing a way to compare one instance to another.

Identification

For most kinds of empirical research, the first concern is confirming the existence of the phenomenon or entity being investigated. We refer to this as 'identification'. As White explains (1992, p. 88), 'Identity is . . . the equation of distinct concrete instances as being truly equivalent.' In chemistry, for example, one typically identifies ('isolates') a particular chemical or compound in order to study its properties and its role in chemical reactions. In social science, it is equally important to establish the identity and boundaries of our units of analysis (Abbott, 1995). Yet, as White argues, boundaries are easily taken for granted:

> Choice of the kind of partition, as well as of particular boundaries, is all too easily taken for granted. Yet the aptness of measurement and modeling schemes, and thus proper training in methodology, will depend on this choice. We may obsess about numerical details of sampling and miss how important is the initial and perhaps unspoken split. (1992, p. 83)

For some aspects of organizational behaviour or organization theory, identification seems to pose no problem. At the individual level, we can easily identify and name specific individuals as the units of analysis. Our commonsense perception of the category 'person' makes identification appear trivial. In particular, it makes counting easy, but does not resolve questions about what it means to be a particular individual in a particular organization. There is an interpretive dimension to individual identity that is not easily reduced to numbers (Gergen, 1999; Rabinow and Sullivan, 1979; Taylor, 1971).

At the organization level, efforts to identify specific forms as the units of analysis is similar, though more problematic (Czarniawska, 1997). Problems arise, for instance, when attempting to define organizational 'births' and 'deaths' (Kaufman, 1976). In this case, the spatial boundary may be relatively clear, but the temporal boundary is not. Indeed, it is remarkably difficult to identify the boundaries of most kinds of complex social structures, such as social networks (Wasserman and Faust, 1994) or professions (Abbott, 1995). Our tendency to anthropomorphize organizations and other structures in everyday language helps produce a sense of concreteness and objectivity that spills over into our research methods.

Our experiences lead us to believe that, in the case of organizational routines, this sense of concreteness is particularly misleading. As we have noted, it is a mistake to equate artifacts with routines, even when the artifact's purpose is to represent the routine (Suchman, 1995). It is difficult to see entire performances and difficult to locate the boundaries that separate one routine from another (Lazaric, 2000; Lazaric and Denis, 2005). And of course, performances can display a lot of variability (Pentland and Reuter, 1994; Feldman, 2000; Howard-Grenville, 2005).

These features pose significant problems for identification (and also comparison). Using simulated data, Pentland (2003a) demonstrated that even small levels of random variation can mask the presence of two or more fixed patterns in a sample of sequences. Even with complete observations, a large sample of performances, and sophisticated mathematical tools (e.g., optimal string matching), it can be hard to tell if you are looking at one routine or two (or more). In real fieldwork, one is more likely to have only fragments of performances and a modest sample size. How can one identify particular routines?

Ironically, identification always starts with the *ostensive* aspects of a routine. For any kind of routine, the ostensive aspects are needed to answer the question: 'What kind of routine is this?' The ostensive aspects provide the abstract ideas that allow participants and researchers alike to recognize[4] particular actions as part of a coherent whole; it allows us to recognize patterns (and deviations). It allows us to interpret the significance of particular artifacts that may relate to a particular routine. Ostensive aspects that have been used in empirical research include model changeovers (Adler et al., 1999), creating a summer camp (Birnholtz et al., 2007), doing heart surgery (Edmondson et al., 2001), hiring, training and budgeting (Feldman, 2000, 2003, 2004), road mapping (Howard-Grenville, 2005), navigating (Hutchins, 1991), measuring quality (Lazaric and Denis, 2005), selling insurance and serving fast food (Leidner, 1993), doing a job (Miner, 1990, 1991), fixing air conditioners (Narduzzo, 1998), trouble-fixing and building a station (Narduzzo et al., 2000), software support (Pentland and Reuter, 1994) and converting a bank (Szulanski, 2000).

All of these routines involve actions that could be part of many different routines. The conversations, problem-solving efforts, selling, serving, fixing and so forth could often be classified as being part of a number of different projects or routines. Even actions that take place only in a specific domain such as the anesthesiology associated with heart surgery could be associated with many different medical procedures. Participants and researchers, nonetheless, identify specific routines as taking place.

Researchers appear to use two approaches to constructing the ostensive aspects of the routine. One approach is to identify the intended (or at least publicly intended) outcomes. The hiring routine is identified as a set of behaviours and the related narrative about the behaviours that one engages in when one wants (or wants to appear to want) to hire someone. Budgeting routines are similarly defined by the intention to produce a budget. This approach privileges the emic perspective of the people engaging in the routine. The routine is defined by what their answer might be if they were asked 'what are you doing now?'

Another approach to identifying the ostensive aspect focuses on particular events or actions. Different kinds of heart surgery, for instance, are identified by whether the breastplate is broken or not (Edmondson et al., 2001). Pentland and Reuter (1994) identified their routines by the call the customer made to the hotline. The call begins the routine, the moves that are taken in response to the call constitute the middle of the routine and the routine ends with a determination that the call is closed. While the intentions of the participants are clearly important to the execution of these routines, it is less important to the identification.

These two forms of identification exemplify the etic and emic approaches to research. Researchers taking an etic approach can make assessments that are independent of the assessments of the participants in the routines. A researcher might choose to explore an abstract, theory-driven category, such as 'strategy formation' (Van de Ven, 1992). These categories may or may not correspond to the labels or understandings of the participants, yet they are important theoretically. Thus, the researcher identifies the routine (or process), based on their own, theory-driven criteria.

Researchers taking an emic approach require the perspective of participants to identify intentions and understandings. The emic perspective focuses on ways in which routines are defined and energized by the subjective understanding of the participants. Because participants have different roles and different reasons for participating in a routine, they may have very different interpretations of what is (or should be) going on. Given this potential diversity of meaning, identifying the ostensive aspect of a routine involves two interpretive moves: first there are the interpretations of the multiple participants, and then there is the interpretation the researcher makes of these interpretations.

An emic approach enables the researcher to explore variation across participants more readily than an etic approach. This tends to support a view of organizational routines as ambiguous and variable rather than clearly defined and static. An etic approach can be used to impose boundaries on this shifting phenomenon. While this imposition of boundaries can artificially reduce ambiguity and variety, it can also allow researchers to identify patterns where there is enough ambiguity and variety for the participants not to see the patterns (e.g., Pentland and Reuter, 1994). Whether one adopts an etic or emic perspective, the creation of boundaries is what makes comparisons possible, because it creates identifiable units that can be compared.

Comparison
Distinguishing among routines and their performances leads to the second essential ingredient for empirical research, which is the ability to make comparisons. As Ragin (1987, p. 1) states, 'Virtually all empirical social research involves comparison of some sort.' Comparisons are critical to both cross-sectional (synchronic) and longitudinal (diachronic) studies, as described by Barley (1990). In a synchronic analysis, one makes comparisons at one point in time. One can compare different kinds of routines with one another. Are some routines more stable or changeable than others? Do some routines encourage more learning than others? Are some routines more effective? Darr et al. (1995) make synchronic comparisons in their study of pizza restaurants. In a diachronic analysis, one makes comparisons over time. How did participants in a particular routine respond when new technology was introduced (Barley, 1986; Orlikowski, 2000)? How does a routine at time 1 compare with a routine at time 2 and how do we understand the similarities and differences (Feldman, 2000)?

Cross-sectional studies can include both ostensive and performative definitions of routine, but the observation of performance is limited to short periods of time. The opportunity this form of research offers to compare one setting with another also brings with it a tendency to generalize rather than to focus on specific and situated performances. Studies of this sort have produced findings of variability at one point in time (synchronic variety) (Pentland and Reuter, 1994; Suchman, 1983), but, because they do not include observations over time, they cannot produce findings of variability over time (diachronic variety). In addition, because this method requires on site observation of people doing work, it is relatively costly in terms of access to data and data collection.

Longitudinal field studies are the most likely to encompass a performative as well as an ostensive perspective on routines. Because these studies involve a lengthy commitment to study one setting and the actions of the people in that setting, they confront the researcher with evidence of the impact of the mutual relationship between these aspects of routines. As a result, these studies have the potential to be the most complete with respect to change. It can also show both synchronic and diachronic variety (Barley, 1990; Burgelman, 1994; Feldman, 2000, 2003, 2004; Howard-Grenville, 2005; Hutchins, 1991; Miner, 1990, 1991; Miner and Estler, 1985; Orr, 1996). It is, however, expensive in terms of access to data and data gathering and observations are limited to one or a few sites.

Comparison can occur on any aspect of a routine: ostensive or performative. It can also be accomplished with artifacts. Table 13.1 shows that comparisons tend to be ostensive to ostensive, performative to performative and artifact to artifact. Leidner's (1993) study exemplifies the ostensive to ostensive comparison. While she observes the fast-food serving and insurance-selling routines, she does not so much compare them with each

Table 13.1   Comparison of routines

	Ostensive	Performative	Artifact
Ostensive	Adler et al. (1999) Feldman (2003) Leidner (1993)	Feldman (2003) Pentland (2003b) Howard-Grenville (2005) Birnholtz et al. (2007)	
Performative		Adler et al. (1999) Edmondson et al. (2001) Feldman (2000, 2004) Hutchins (1991) Narduzzo (1998) Pentland and Reuter (1994)	
Artifact	Lazaric and Denis (2005)	Narduzzo et al. (2000) Suchman (1983) Lazaric and Denis (2005)	Miner (1991) Rura-Polley and Miner (2000) March et al. (2000)

other as she compares them with some ideas, namely individuals as cogs in a machine and individuals as agents. Adler et al. (1999), fall into both the performative to performative and the ostensive to ostensive category. They compare the specific actions taken in the 1993 and 1995 Nummi model changeovers, and also at the more abstract level they compare Big-3 model changeovers with Nummi model changeovers. Many studies represent the performative to performative comparison. Miner (1991) and Rura-Polley and Miner (2000) with their emphasis on formalized job descriptions represent the artifact to artifact comparison.

Comparisons within a single cell are most common, but there are a few examples of off-diagonal comparisons. For example, Feldman (2003) compares the ostensive aspect of the budgeting routine from the supervisors' perspectives with the subordinates' performances in the budgeting routine. Another off-diagonal is the artifact to performance comparison. Suchman uses this comparison and describes the artifact as a template that guides without determining behaviour (1983). Narduzzo shows how the creation of artifacts helps to stabilize performances and institutionalize routines (1998). Lazaric and Denis (2005) relate artifacts to both the performative and ostensive aspects of organizational routines. They show how artifacts in the form of new rules help to guide new performances and also create new understandings of what constitute the organizational routine.

Off-diagonal comparisons are interesting because they enable us to explore divergence between different aspects of a routine. As we begin to explore these divergences, we can ask new questions about the internal structure and dynamics of routines. For example, under what circumstances do changes in the ostensive or in artifacts lead to predictable changes in performances? Or, perhaps more interesting, when are performances resistant to efforts to change the routine as a whole?

Point of view and concurrent activities
The difficulty of identifying and comparing organizational routines is compounded by the participation of multiple individuals, as well as the researcher, each of whom may have a different point of view on the routine. By selecting a particular point of view, we ensure that our observations will take the form of a temporally organized sequence of events. Point of view is especially important because, in a typical routine, many events may occur in parallel. In an assembly line, for example, all of the workstations are active more or less simultaneously. While assembly lines are a canonical example of routinized work, our ability to 'see' the sequence of actions depends on adopting the point of view of the work-in-process moving from one workstation to the next. If we observed a single workstation, we would probably see only a single event, repeated over and over. The overall

sequence would be invisible. And, of course, routines can be experienced and described quite differently by different individuals.

In any real organizational routine, it is likely that there are many activities occurring more or less concurrently. For example, in a full-service restaurant, there are people cooking, serving, arriving, eating, paying and cleaning up more or less all the time. By adopting the point of view of a patron, or cook, or a server, or perhaps a plate of food, we can linearize these activities into a discernable sequence. But any particular point of view is only a partial representation of the true scope and complexity of the routine, because it tends to reduce the pattern of activities to a linear sequence.

As Van de Ven (1992) notes, real processes can branch and recombine. If we attempt to draw a graph (such as a flow chart or an action network) that maps a process, simple linear sequences are probably not sufficient. A more complete representation would require a graph that allows branching and parallel activities. Pentland (1999b) describes the use of basic graph-theoretic techniques (Wasserman and Faust, 1994) to represent an organizational routine as a 'network of actions'. To represent a routine in this way, each action or event in the routine is a node in the graph. The nodes can be related by various kinds of relationships, such as temporal sequence, flows of materials or information, and so on. In graph-theoretic terms, all nodes in a linear sequence have in-degree and out-degree equal to one: one action follows after another, one at a time. To represent routines with concurrent activities, at least some nodes need to have out-degree greater than one (splitting into parallel paths) and in-degree greater than one (recombining into a single path). A full-service restaurant makes a good example. When a waiter takes the order from a table to the kitchen, that order may include salad, entrees, side-dishes, beverages, and so on, each of which can initiate a separate (but more or less concurrent) stream of activity. Then, when the order is delivered back to the customers, it is recombined. Any practical process mapping technique, such as flow charts, data flow diagrams, or Petri nets, allows for this kind of parallelism.

When mapping processes, it is easy to forget that the map typically does not represent the actual execution of the process or the routine (Suchman, 1995). At best, process maps are idealized artifacts. Any particular performance may diverge considerably from this ideal as the participants improvise and accommodate the details of their situation. Thus, for a given routine, each performance may generate a somewhat different graph – complete with branches, combinations, dead-ends, repetitions, temporal gaps, and so on. Pentland (1999b) suggests techniques for summarizing and comparing such graphs. The point here is simply that comparing performances that involve concurrent activities is a not a trivial matter.

Concurrency poses a further challenge because, in many organizational settings, there may be more than one of these patterns actively being executed at the same time (a waiter often serves more than one table at a time; a cook may be preparing several meals more or less at the same time). Thus, when the waiter goes to the kitchen to pick up a salad for one table, he may also pick up the dessert for another table. What may seem to be one action (going to the kitchen to pick up an order) is actually two actions in two active performances. Pentland (1992) observed the same thing in software support hot lines, where individual support engineers could have as many as 60 open calls in their queue at one time. Identifying a solution for one customer may solve a similar problem for other customers. Such concurrency is an everyday event in most organizations. Hiring routines overlap with training routines or with budgeting routines.

This kind of overlap of activities poses no problem for our ostensive understanding of the routine ('we close the call when we solve the problem' or 'we pick up orders and bring them to the tables'). But it can have a big impact on the performances themselves if participants are carrying out more than one performance at the same time. In the software support case, for example, one occasionally observes ten old calls that are suddenly closed without any apparent effort. The performances are, in effect, short-circuited because they are concurrent and interdependent.

Point of view and concurrence are examples of concepts that affect the ostensive and performative aspects of routines and the artifacts that support organizational routines differently. These kinds of considerations lead us to emphasize the importance of distinguishing between these three (ostensive, performative and artifact) and, to some extent, studying them independently.

Conclusion

Field studies complicate our understandings of organizational routines because they confront us with the messiness of the real world. This messiness is both the strength and the weakness of field studies. As our confessional stories show, the messiness of the real world poses many challenges for the identification and comparison of organizational routines. At the same time, this complexity enables field researchers to confront the inadequacies of any system of concepts and to develop new concepts that allow us to see new things. This process opens up new worlds of both understandings and questions.

Much current fieldwork has taken up questions of stability and change in organizational routines. We are just beginning to examine the internal structure and dynamics of routines: the interaction between ostensive, performative and related artifacts. While these internal structures pose some challenging problems for field researchers, they also move us to the next level. They allow us to open up the black box of organizational routines and look inside to examine how this ubiquitous organizational phenomenon operates.

Notes

1. This chapter is an equal collaboration.
2. By 'empirical', we mean 'based on, concerned with, or verifiable by observation or experiment' (Concise OED, 2004: 467); we do not limit ourselves to numeric or statistical methods. We have chosen to exclude laboratory experiments and computer simulations, which are treated elsewhere in this volume.
3. Adler et al. (1999), Cohen et al. (1996), Hodgson (2003), Hutchins (1991), Lazaric (2000), Lazaric and Denis (2001; 2005).
4. The ostensive aspect also allows us to misrecognize (Latour, 1986).

References

Abbott, Andrew (1995), 'Things of boundaries', *Social Research*, **62**, 857–82.
Abell, P. (1987), *The Syntax of Social Life: the Theory and Method of Comparative Narratives*, New York: Clarendon Press.
Adler, P.S., B. Goldoftas and D.I. Levine (1999), 'Flexibility versus efficiency? A case study of model changeovers in the Toyota Production System', *Organization Science*, **10**(1), 43–68.
Barley, Stephen, R. (1986), 'Technology as an occasion for structuring: evidence from observations of CT scanners and the social order of radiology departments', *Administrative Science Quarterly*, **31**, 78–108.
Barley, S.R. (1990), 'Images of imaging: notes on doing longitudinal fieldwork', *Organization Science*, **1**(3), 220–47.
Birnholtz, J.P., M.D. Cohen and S.V. Hoch (2007), 'Organization character: on the regeneration of Camp Poplar Grove', *Organization Science*, **18**, 315–32.
Burgelman, Robert A. (1994), 'Fading memories: a process theory of strategic business exit in dynamic environments', *Administrative Science Quarterly*, **39**, 24–56.
Cohen, Michael and P. Bacdayan (1994), 'Organizational routines are stored as procedural memory: evidence from a laboratory study', *Organization Science*, **5**(4), 554–68.
Cohen, Michael D., Roger Burkhart, Giovanni Dosi, Massimo Egidi, Luigi Marengo, Massimo Warglien and Sidney Winter (1996), 'Routines and other recurring action patterns of organizations: contemporary research issues', *Industrial and Corporate Change*, **5**(3), 653–98.
Concise Oxford English Dictionary (2004), Catherine Soanes and Angus Stevenson (eds), 11th edn, Oxford: Oxford University Press.
Czarniawska, B. (1997), *Narrating the Organization: Dramas of Institutional Identity*, Chicago, IL: University of Chicago Press.
Darr, E., L. Argote and D. Epple (1995), 'The acquisition, transfer, and depreciation of knowledge in service organizations: productivity in franchises', *Management Science*, **41**(11), 1750–62.
Edmondson, A.C., R.M. Bohmer and G.P. Pisano (2001), 'Disrupted routines: team learning and new technology implementation in hospitals', *Administrative Science Quarterly*, **46**, 685–716.
Feldman, Martha S. (1989), *Order without Design*, Stanford, CA: Stanford University Press.
Feldman, Martha (2000), 'Organizational routines as a source of continuous change', *Organization Science*, **11**(6), 611–29.
Feldman, Martha S. (2003), 'A performative perspective on stability and change in organizational routines', *Industrial and Corporate Change*, **12**(4), 727–52.
Feldman, Martha S. (2004), 'Resources in emerging structures and processes of change', *Organization Science*, May–June, **15**(3), 295–309.

Feldman, M.S. and B.T. Pentland (2003), 'Reconceptualizing organizational routines as a source of flexibility and change', *Administrative Science Quarterly*, **48**(1), 94–118.

Feldman, M.S. and B.T. Pentland (2005), 'Organizational routines and the macro-actor', in Barbara Czarniawska and Tor Hernes (eds), *Actor Network Theory and Organizing*, Koege, Denmark: Liber and Copenhagen Business School Press.

Folger, J.P., D.E. Hewes and M.S. Poole (1984), 'Coding social interaction', in B. Dervin and M.J. Voight (eds), *Progress in Communication Science, Volume IV*, Norwood, NJ: Ablex, pp. 115–61.

Gergen, K.J. (1999), *An Invitation to Social Construction*, London: Sage.

Headland, Thomas N. (1990), 'Introduction: a dialogue between Kenneth Pike and Marvin Harris on emics and etics', in Thomas N. Headland, Kenneth L. Pike and Marvin Harris (eds), *Emics and Etics: The Insider/Outsider Debates*, Newbury Park, CA: Sage, pp. 13–27.

Hodgson, Geoffrey M. (2003), 'The mystery of the routine: the Darwinian destiny of *An Evolutionary Theory of Economic Change*', *Revue Économique*, **54**(2), March, 355–84.

Howard-Grenville, J. (2005), 'The persistence of flexible organizational routines: the role of agency and organizational context', *Organization Science*, **16**(6), 618–36.

Hutchins, E. (1991), 'Organizing work by adaptation', *Organization Science*, **2**(1), 14–39.

Kaufman, H. (1976), *Are Government Organizations Immortal?*, Washington, DC: Brookings.

Latour, Bruno (1986), 'The powers of association', in John Law (ed.), *Power, Action and Belief*, London: Routledge and Kegan Paul.

Lazaric, Nathalie (2000), 'The role of routines, rules and habits in collective learning: some epistemological and ontological considerations', *European Journal of Economic and Social Systems*, **14**(2), 157–71.

Lazaric, Nathalie and Blandine Denis (2001), 'How and why routines change: some lessons from the articulation of knowledge with ISO 9002 implementation in the food industry', *Économies et Sociétés*, Série *Dynamique technologique et organisation*, **6**(4), 585–611.

Lazaric, Nathalie and Blandine Denis (2005), 'Routinisation and memorisation of tasks inside a workshop: an illustration through a case study', *Industrial and Corporate Change*, **14**(5), 873–96.

Leidner, R. (1993), *Fast Food, Fast Talk: Service Work and the Routinization of Everyday Life*, Berkeley, CA: University of California Press.

Malone, T.W., K. Crowston, J. Lee, B.T. Pentland, C. Dellarocas, G. Wyner, J. Quimby, C. Osborne, A. Bernstein, G. Herman, M. Klein and E. O'Donnell (1999), 'Tools for inventing organizations: toward a handbook of organizational processes', *Management Science*, **45**(3) (March), 425–43.

March, J.M., M. Schulz and X. Zhou (2000), *The Dynamics of Rules: Change in Written Organizational Codes*, Stanford, CA: Stanford University Press.

Miner, Anne (1990), 'Structural evolution through idiosyncratic jobs: the potential for unplanned learning', *Organization Science*, **1**, 195–210.

Miner, Anne (1991), 'Organizational evolution and the social ecology of jobs', *American Sociological Review*, **56**, 772–85.

Miner, A.S. and S.E. Estler (1985), 'Accrual mobility: job mobility in higher education through responsibility accrual', *Journal of Higher Education*, **56**(1), 121–43.

Narduzzo, A. (1998), 'Organizational memory, cognitive artifacts and routinization: suggestions for a field-study', *Revue Internationale de Système*, **12**(1), 51–62.

Narduzzo, Alessandro, Elena Rocco and Massimo Warglien (2000), 'Talking about routines in the field', in Giovanni Dosi, Richard Nelson and Sidney Winter (eds), *The Nature and Dynamics of Organizational Capabilities*, New York: Oxford University Press.

Nelson, R.R. and S.G. Winter (1982), *An Evolutionary Theory of Economic Change*, Cambridge, MA: Harvard University Press.

Orlikowski, Wanda (2000), 'Using technology and constituting structures: a practice lens for studying technology in organizations', *Organization Science*, **11**(4), 404–28.

Orr, J.E. (1996), *Talking about Machines: An Ethnography of a Modern Job*, Ithaca, NY: Cornell University Press.

Pentland, B.T. (1992), 'Organizing moves in software support hot lines', *Administrative Science Quarterly*, **37**(4), 527–48.

Pentland, B.T. (1995), 'Read me what it says on your screen: the interpretative problem in technical service work', *Technology Studies*, **2**(1), 50–79.

Pentland, B.T. (1999a), 'Building process theory with narrative: from description to explanation', *Academy of Management Review*, **24**(4), 711–24.

Pentland, B.T. (1999b), 'Organizations as networks of action' in J. Baum and W. McKelvey (eds), *Variations in Organization Science: Essays in Honor of Donald T. Campbell*, Thousand Oaks, CA: Sage.

Pentland, B.T. (2003a), 'Conceptualizing and measuring variety in organizational work processes', *Management Science*, **49**(7), 857–70.

Pentland, B.T. (2003b), 'Sequential variety in work processes', *Organization Science*, **14**(5), 528–40.

Pentland, B.T. and M.S. Feldman (2005), 'Organizational routines as a unit of analysis', *Industrial and Corporate Change*, **14**(5), 793–815.

Pentland, B.T. and M.S. Feldman (2007), 'Narrative networks: patterns of technology and organization', *Organization Science*, **18**(5), 781–95.

Pentland, B.T. and H.H. Reuter (1994), 'Organizational routines as grammars of action', *Administrative Science Quarterly*, **39**(3), 484–510.

Rabinow, P. and W.M. Sullivan (1979), 'The interpretive turn: emergence of an approach' in P. Rabinow and W.M. Sullivan (eds), *Interpretive Social Science: A Reader*, Berkeley, CA: University of California Press.

Ragin, Charles C. (1987), *The Comparative Method*, Berkeley, CA: University of California Press.

Rura-Polley, T. and Anne Miner (2000), 'The relative standing of routines: some jobs are more equal than others', in Mie Augier and James G. March (eds), *The Economics of Choice, Change and Organization: Essays In Memory of Richard M. Cyert*, Cheltenham, UK and Northampton, MA, USA: Edward Elgar.

Sabherwal, R. and D. Robey (1993), 'An empirical taxonomy of implementation processes based on sequences of events in information system development', *Organization Science*, **4**(4), 548–76.

Suchman, L.A. (1983), 'Office procedure as practical action: models of work and system design', *ACM Transactions on Office Systems*, **1**, 320–28.

Suchman, L. (1995), 'Making work visible', *Communications of the ACM*, **38**(9), 56–64.

Szulanski, G. (2000), 'Appropriability and the challenge of scope', in Giovanni Dosi, Richard R. Nelson and Sidney G. Winter (eds), *The Nature and Dynamics of Organizational Capabilities*, Oxford: Oxford University Press.

Taylor, C. (1971), 'Interpretation and the sciences of man', *The Review of Metaphysics*, **25**(1), 3–51.

Van de Ven, A.H. (1992), 'Suggestions for studying strategy process: a research note', *Strategic Management Journal*, **13**, 169–88.

Van Maanen, J. (1988), *Tales of the Field*, Chicago, IL: University of Chicago Press.

Wasserman, S. and K. Faust (1994), *Social Network Analysis: Methods and Applications*, New York: Cambridge University Press.

Weber, Max (1947), *The Theory of Social and Economic Organization*, New York: Free Press.

White, Harrison C. (1992), 'Cases are for identity, for explanation, or for control', in Charles C. Ragin and Howard S. Becker (eds), *What is a Case? Exploring the Foundations of Social Inquiry*, New York: Cambridge University Press, pp. 83–104.

14 Conducting experimental research on organizational routines

Alessandro Narduzzo and Massimo Warglien

1 Introduction

Despite the rapid popularity gained by the concept of routines after the publication of Nelson and Winter's (1982) book, experimental research directly inspired by their framework is still rather limited, the most important exception being the research project initiated by Michael Cohen and Paul Bacdayan (1994) at the University of Michigan in the early 1990s and further developed in subsequent years by researchers gravitating around the Trento Experimental Lab. Still, there is a very large body of research in experimental psychology that provides building blocks for in-depth examination of key features of routinization both at the individual and the group level. Furthermore, recent developments in behavioural game theory and experimental economics, mostly related to the problem of learning in games, promise new opportunities of interaction between students of routines and behavioural, experimentally-oriented game theorists. This chapter attempts a broad recognition of the experimental work more directly related to the concepts of routine and routinization, and explores some opportunities of dialogue with the recent work in experimental economics and behavioural game theory.

The chapter starts by reviewing the roots of the routine concept in the tradition of experimental psychology, a prominent role being played by Luchins' '*Einstellung* effect', although some important themes can be traced back to the work of Thorndike in the early 20th century. We reconstruct how implicit learning has been experimentally analysed, present a first discussion of individual v. group level of analysis, and we shortly reconsider the behavioural v. cognitive opposition. In the subsequent section, we discuss some features of organizational routines that are amenable to experimental inquiry, focusing on procedural memory issues, how routines are retrieved, the implications of routinization for information search, suboptimality and path dependency. We finally come back to the individual v. group behaviour comparison. In the last section, we discuss recent developments in behavioural game theory (and the related experimental work) that show important complementarities with research on routines. Finally, we discuss some experimental avenues that might bring closer to the spirit of research on routines the experimentation on learning in games.

2   History: experimental psychology and the roots of routines

Einstellung effect and the 'mechanization' of problem solving: routine as blindness
One of the earlier and most prominent experimental studies on routinized behaviour is due to Abraham Luchins (1942), who, for over a decade, has analysed the mechanization effect that arises when individuals repeatedly solve the same class of problems. After experimental subjects have been exposed to the same type of problem a few times, they stop dealing with a new instance of the problem as if it was a novel one, and instead develop some habit, or mechanical reasoning, that is applied even when it is not efficient. When this mechanical mind set (*Einstellung*) is reached it tends to be reinforced over time and it becomes extremely hard to escape from it. Subjects act as if they were blind to the evidence of the novel situation.

The basic experiment that Luchins designed to study the *Einstellung* effect is a volume-measuring problem. Subjects are given three jars of various capacity and they have to use them to measure a certain volume of liquid (e.g. water or milk). The capacity of the jars and the volume of the liquid to be isolated change in each problem, but the best solution of the first five problems implies the same procedure: fill the biggest jar and eliminate from it one middle-sized jar and two small-sized jars (Big-Medium-2xSmall). The seven subsequent problems are different, in the sense that they admit more efficient solutions that differ from the one learned and applied to the first problems. Nevertheless, the large majority of subjects mechanically repeat what they have learned early on and do not find any better solution. The situation does not change even when some experimental factors (e.g. incentives to reward the efficiency or more concrete experimental conditions meant to increase subjects' thoughtfulness) are introduced (Luchins and Luchins, 1950). The magnitude and the persistence of the *Einstellung* effect in problem-solving tasks are quite impressive and such effect encompasses most of the issues that dominate the later research on individual routinized behaviour.

Implicit learning and cognitive efficiency: from Thorndike to Reber
While the experimental research about implicit learning has been developed during the 1960s, mainly thanks to the contribution of Arthur Reber and his colleagues, the first studies on incidental learning and learning without awareness began much earlier (Jenkins, 1933; Thorndike, 1911; Thorndike and Rock, 1934). Implicit learning, in fact, refers to situations

where individuals apparently learn rules or contingencies, without being aware that a learning process takes place. As a consequence of this form of learning, subjects do not develop any explicit memory; that is, they are not able consciously to recollect recently acquired information by means of memory tests such as free recall or recognition. According to Holyoak and Spellman (1993: 278) knowledge that is acquired through an implicit process of learning can be characterized in the following way: 'It is (a) knowledge about covariations in the environment, (b) learned by exposures to stimuli exhibiting the covariations, (c) obtainable without intention or awareness (although in some cases similar knowledge might be obtained explicitly), and (d) demonstrated by improved performance on tasks that seem to require thinking (e.g. generalization and prediction); but it is knowledge that does not have a fully explicit representation in that (e) it is not fully verbalizable and (f) it is not manipulable in the sense that it cannot be re-presented explicitly to serve as input to other procedures.'

Among various explanations that have been proposed to give an account for the existence of implicit mechanisms for memory and learning (see, for instance, Schacter, 1987), Reber (1993) suggested an evolutionary argument. According to Reber, in fact, unconscious processes are the oldest and most essential cognitive structures (*'the primacy of the implicit'*); they were developed earlier on and they worked as bases for the further development of more sophisticated conscious mechanisms. Therefore, according to this evolutionary perspective, implicit learning is not regarded as a residual activity of a cognitive system dominated by consciousness, but rather the opposite, as the most relevant and fundamental process. In Reber's (1993) view, some classic clinical studies on patients who suffer various disorders in their conscious activity (e.g. amnesia, blindness) and are able to perform effectively some task in the absence of awareness support the hypothesis that unconscious and conscious processes are functionally separated and that the former are older and more robust than the latter.

The most extensive experimental research programme on implicit learning has been conducted by Reber and his associates and is based on artificial grammars. After a training session where subjects are shown a list of string generated according to an unknown grammar (i.e. system of rules), subjects are presented with other, different, strings and they have to judge whether they are 'grammatically correct' or not. According to experimental results, subjects learn to identify grammatically correct strings, even though they are not able to express any rule. Other situations that have been extensively used to study implicit learning are the dynamic systems tasks where subjects control a rule-based system by making decisions upon a small number of variables. For this purpose, an experimental design has been introduced that simulates a working sugar plant (see, for instance,

Berry and Broadbent, 1984). Subjects are asked to keep under control the level of plant production that they can manipulate by deciding how many workers the company should employ. The results are consistent with those produced by experiments based on artificial grammars: subjects learn how to control a plant, but they are hardly able to explain their decisions or to provide a representation model of the system.

Individual and group behaviour

The experimental research on routines has been mainly developed at the individual level and has investigated automatic behaviour of individuals. Nevertheless, the concept of routines has been implicitly extended to group behaviour at least since Nelson and Winter (1982) introduced this concept as a metaphor to analyse behaviour in organizations. A comparison between the two conditions was posed a long time ago by Floyd Henry Allport (1919; 1920) who proved experimentally how isolated individuals behave differently from individuals acting in the presence of others. From this standpoint a deep analysis of individual behaviour in groups has been initiated and expanded on to provide the basis for a comparison of individual and group behaviour. For instance, an experimental study on productions of norms has been used to assess the effect of social interaction, communication patterns and group atmosphere on individual behaviour (Shaw, 1932). The experimental setting for these studies are typically based on autokinetic effects, that is an experiment on visual perception. Since this effect is reliable it has been used as an experimental context to study the impact of social influence on individual judgment (Rohrer et al., 1954).

A related stream of research on individual and group behaviour aims at comparing the individuals and groups in terms of performance. In a survey published at the end of the 1950s, Lorge et al. (1958) claimed that experimental research did not reach any definitive conclusion: the overall result of individual interactions that characterize group behaviour is not necessarily positive. The typical explanations that are reported to explain the disappointing group performance are mainly due to conformity, conflict avoidance (e.g. groupthinking effect) or social pressure. On the other hand, groups exhibit some advantage when tasks consist of the discovery of some best solutions as well as of repeated tasks where specific information processing is involved. It is apparent that performance supremacy is not independent of the nature of the task. Some studies found that groups perform better than individuals on average (Kocher and Sutter, 2005), but the best individuals outperform the best groups. Recently, these findings have been confirmed by Alan Blinder and John Morgan (2000), who ran two experiments. The first experiment is based on an urn problem and subjects were asked to guess the composition of the urn. In the second experiment subjects were asked to act as central bankers and make decisions on the level of the interest rate. The results of these two experiments are consistent. Moreover, they collected some experimental evidence against the beliefs that individuals make decisions faster than groups. Further, groups that make decisions by unanimity are not slower than those acting according to a majority rule.

In the case of automatic behaviour, like routine, it is particularly important to understand and to compare how behaviour becomes automatic in individuals and in groups; in other words, to understand the differences between automatic behaviour at the individual and at the group level, we may compare how implicit learning takes place in individuals and in groups.

Behavioural v. cognitive perspectives
One of the open debates about organizational routines is the perspective that scholars take when they analyse the phenomenon (Cohen et al., 1996). According to a behavioural perspective, investigators emphasize patterns of action and the degree of automaticity of these patterns. On the other hand, along with the cognitive perspective, students are more concerned with stable representations that subjects develop in the face of repeated situations (classes of problems). Both these perspectives have been unfolded through experimental research; to assess the formation of routines from a behavioural perspective, researchers look at the reaction time that subjects exhibit when they have to take an action or make a decision. To detect the presence of routines from a cognitive perspective, researchers usually look for the existence of a rule-based system and one typical strategy to prove it is to study how subjects deal with structurally equivalent problems.

In order to assess the presence of organizational routinization in an experimental setting, Cohen and Bacdayan (1994) identified and analysed four major measurable dimensions: reliability in performance improvement, increased speed in making a decision, repeated action sequences that are activated when a situation occurs and occasional suboptimality, that indicate the cost of utilizing an existing routine that does not fit perfectly the actual situation. To analyse organizational routines, Cohen and Bacdayan created an ad hoc problem-solving environment, based on a card game played by two subjects, *Target the Two*. While in typical card games players act against each other, in *Target the Two* they play together and in order to solve the problem they need to coordinate their action. Subjects cannot communicate during the experiment. To collect all the data about players' behaviour (moves, speed, errors) a computer version of the game has been developed and used in all the experiments reported here. Subjects are asked to play the game 40 times, but the initial position of the card changes from one hand to the next one, so the sequence of moves to solve the problem is not fixed. Cohen and Bacdayan (1994) observe that subjects learn how to play and they develop some routines that they apply faster and faster during the experiment. In particular, most of the pairs of subjects discover and apply a sequence of moves that is a solution for a large number of cases (even though it is not always the most efficient).

Using the same experimental design, *Target the Two*, Egidi (1996) extended the experimental analysis to study the formation of stable systems of rules that subjects learn and apply routinely to solve the problems. He actually hypothesized that organizations learn to decompose the original problem in a sequence of sub-problems and they develop a coordinated system or rules that they implicitly implement. Further, a computational model of routinization as an effect of a system of rules that are learned through the game has been developed by Pereira and Patelli (1996). This computational model is an application of the problem decomposition proposed by Egidi, and the repertoire of rules derives from subjects' behaviour registered during the experiments on *Target the Two*.

3   Features of routines amenable to experimental inquiry

Memory and routines: declarative v. procedural essence
Forms of automatic behaviour being stored as tacit knowledge, routines rely heavily on individual long-term memory. Thus, features of human memory should be expected to be mirrored in routinized behaviour. The psychology of long-term memory distinguishes two forms of memory, corresponding to different storage and retrieval modalities. On the one hand, declarative memory stores data and knowledge structures in explicit, symbolic, verbalizable form (Squire, 1986; Squire et al., 1993). For example, when Mary tries explicitly to describe the rules of chess playing, she searches in her declarative memory. On the other hand, procedural memory stores skills and procedures in a more implicit, often non-verbalizable, way: 'It is memory for how things are done that is relatively automatic and inarticulate' (Cohen and Bacdayan, 1994: 554). The two memories are quite independent: for example, you can play chess correctly without remembering explicitly its rules, like certain brain-impaired patients. Furthermore, they work in different ways: they exhibit different reaction times and different decay rates. Procedural memory usually implies faster, semi-automatic retrieval, and decays at much slower rates than the declarative one. Furthermore, procedural skills are less transferable to new tasks than declarative knowledge (see below). Clearly, routines both at the individual and the group level should be expected to be stored as procedural memories (Cohen and Bacdayan, 1994). At the individual level, Singley and Anderson (1989) provide impressive evidence of the

procedural nature of the acquisition of even intellectual skills such as computer programming, text editing and calculus. Their experimental studies confirm that procedural and declarative knowledge differ with regard to the degree of awareness and its persistency in the individual memory. In the experiments based on calculus (namely, differentiation problems), for instance, Singley and Anderson distinguished two main tasks: the selection of the appropriate operator to solve the problem and the application of an operator to get the final solution to the problem. The experiment consists of two sessions that take place on two consecutive days. In the first session, each subject undertakes one of the following treatments: (a) operator selection only, (b) operator application only, (c) the whole process (operator selection and its application) and, finally, (d) they simply repeat the selection and application actions that an experimenter performs and shows to the subject. The following day all subjects are assigned the same experimental condition, that consists of the whole task (operator selection and application) and the performances are compared. Not surprisingly, subjects exposed to treatment (a) and (b) significantly improve their performance in the task they practised the day before. It is less predictable to guess which is the effect of one task over the other one. Singley and Anderson found a strong transfer effect from the application to the selection and a negligible transfer effect from the selection to the application tasks. They explain this asymmetric transfer effect as a consequence of the difference between declarative and procedural knowledge. In fact, subjects that were exposed to the treatment (b) on the first day had developed some declarative representation of the various operators and they used this general knowledge to perform the selection task the next day. On the other hand, subjects that practised on selection task did not develop any declarative representation that might become decisive for the subsequent application of the operator.

Cohen and Bacdayan (1994) showed how properties of procedural memory can help to interpret also the nature of collective routines. As we mentioned, they experimentally analyse the learning behaviour of pairs of subjects that have to learn a collective pattern of problem solving in a card game, *Target the Two*, that implies asymmetric roles and the coordinated chaining of moves from both players. The basic task is repeated in similar but not identical versions, so that learning the problem solutions requires some generalization and some flexibility of behaviour (in this regard, see for instance Feldman and Pentland, 2003). Two important measures of routinization are used: the shrinking of reaction time over learning, and the decay rate of memory when the task is repeated after two weeks. A third indicator is the ability to transfer acquired skills when the game is modified in some significant component (e.g. the role of the players is swapped).

Experimental data fully support the hypothesis that routines are stored as procedural memory, projecting at the group level the basic features found at the individual one by Singley and Anderson (1989). Cohen and Bacdayan's experimental design consists of two subsequent sessions. In one experimental condition the delay between the two sessions is short (a few hours), while in the other the delay is much longer (one to two weeks). Their findings show that the performance does not decay with time; this result is consistent with the assumption that procedural memory is less sensitive than declarative memory to the time decay.

Nelson and Winter's (1982: 72) analogy between individual skills and organizational routines thus finds a substantial empirical corroboration from laboratory experimentation. They also refer to the conceptualization developed by Michael Polanyi (1958) which is heavily inspired and supported by experimental study on animal behaviour. The identification of a *domain of ineffability* where knowledge is not articulated and its content is mainly instrumental, and where latent learning is substantially an unaware process, are tightly related to the acquisition of tacit knowledge.

Retrieval of appropriate routines

To some extent, being able to retrieve appropriate routines from individual or organizational memory encompasses the access and the use of implicit knowledge (Cohen, 1991). According to the behavioural approach, what triggers the automatic execution of a specific action as a reaction to a situation is a function of relative frequency of past behaviour and performance (*repetition priming*). By repetition, actions become automatic reactions, that is, habits, and a pointer that past behaviour is a predictor of future behaviour. Within this perspective the activation of the appropriate routine is not mediated by intentions, attitudes or by any conscious process, but it is affected by typical biases and heuristics, such as availability and the base rate fallacy. Availability strongly restricts the individual ability to retrieve experience and rules from her memory and to recall the appropriate routine. In fact, it is more likely that individuals recall a routine when (i) it refers to personally experienced events, (ii) it comes from the experience of someone with whom the decision makers share an identity, (iii) it is tied to a vivid experience or a story, rather than to abstract, statistical information (March, 1994). In general, the selection of the appropriate alternative to solve a problem at hand has been conceptualized by James March as a particular form of rational behaviour that he called 'logic of appropriateness' and that differs from the typical means–end rationality. Within this logic of appropriateness, decision making is essentially rule-based and, when decision makers recall a routine to solve a problem, they implicitly recognize the situation they are facing; they restate their identity and who they are and then they apply the appropriate rule. A special case of retrieval of the appropriate routine is related to situations where individuals and organizations transfer their implicit knowledge and try to apply it in a new domain that does not correspond to the original one. As we mentioned, Singley and Anderson's (1989) findings suggest that procedural knowledge incorporated in the repertoire of routines is extremely sensitive to the context of learning and it may hardly transfer to a different domain.

While routine retrieval has been mainly elaborated from a behavioural perspective, a cognitive-based understanding of this process has been proposed and experimentally tested. According to a cognitive approach, in fact, routines are mentally represented as links between goals and instrumental actions. In order to activate the appropriate goal-directed action, individuals go through a cognitive process that allows them to recognize some cues that characterize the present situation and to retrieve the appropriate routine from their memory. After repetition, such a cognitive process eventually becomes automatic; a link between goal and action is eventually established, but what triggers the action is a goal-oriented cognitive representation of the situation. Aarts and Dijksterhuis (2000) compared the reaction of two groups of subjects requested to select a habitual action (e.g., biking); one group was provided with the goal of carrying out a particular action (e.g., to attend a lecture at the university, or to go shopping at the mall). They proved that the automatic recall of a habitual action when a goal is mentioned is faster than the case where the goal is not evoked at all.

Information search
Because of its automaticity, routinized behaviour is often regarded as a unified and continuous process, even though it is also possible to single out a sequence of steps (Betsch et al., 2002). Information search takes place immediately after decision makers identify a selection problem and before they actually make a choice. Moreover, information search is quite a limited activity, since decision makers mainly limit their exploration to their memory or to some alternatives that are made available through the experience. For this reason information search is largely biased by past behaviour. As we have seen when discussing the *Einstellung* effect, when individuals frame a decision as an already-known situation they tend to neglect some distinct properties of a novel situation and they directly apply some effective solutions that they have previously learned. Tilmann Betsch and his colleagues (2001) have explored and deeply analysed these phenomena, in particular by examining under which conditions individuals activate the information search phase while dealing with routinized situations. In their study Betsch et al. (2001) show that both confirmation bias and search for

information depend on routinization strength. Their experimental design is based on a micro-world computer simulation, involving a number of steps and decisions and it controls for the strength of the routines that subjects learn during the experiment. After the training phase, the experiment introduces a situation in which past experience (i.e. prior beliefs) and new information are conflicting. Subjects that are exposed to the training phase that favours strong routinization are more reluctant to give up the routine, even though new information suggests leaving it; this result is moderated by a context effect, like, for instance, a time pressure. The same study also allows assessing the persistency of the confirmation bias effect. Strongly routinized subjects are affected by a confirmation bias, but this effect tends to disappear and they avoid confirmatory search when it is announced that they are facing a new situation. These findings are consistent with the hypothesis that 'people are inductively sensitive to bases rates if this knowledge is based on directly made experiences' (Betsch et al., 2001: 47). In a way, these experimental results also confirm that information search is not a random process: 'the space is a frame within which the agent brings knowledge to bear to search for the desired object' (Newell, 1990: 98). In particular, with regard to routinized behaviour, the depth of information search is negatively correlated with routine strength, as some experimental analysis has proved (Aarts and Dijksterhuis, 2000). Likewise, the search strategies are more elaborated when the routines are weak and they tend to become simpler when the routines' strength increases (Verplanken et al., 1997). In this case, the experimental setting takes into account subjects' habits in real life. The experiments present a decision-making problem about a transportation mode and they assess to what extent individual behaviour is sensitive to habits, to environmental conditions (e.g. time pressure) and to a clear identification of goals.

Routines transfer, suboptimality and path dependence
Knowledge that individuals and organizations develop and store as a repertoire of routines directly refers to the specific contexts that have been experienced. One major issue under investigation is the extent to which such knowledge can be generalized and transferred to other situations (Reimer et al., 2005). Scholars' approach to this issue changed over time. Field experiments done by Lave (1988) suggested that there is no substantial skills transfer across domains. She analysed the arithmetic routines and the calculations that a group of subjects accomplish to do grocery shopping and they evaluate various alternatives to identify the best-buy. She also analysed the behaviour of the same group when they were asked to solve comparable problems in class. For instance, in order to choose the best-buy, subjects needed to compare two different ratios expressed by price and

quantity. Subjects' behaviour in the two situations, the real shopping and the simulated one, largely differ and people fail to apply in class the sophisticated routines that they use to compare the product at the store.

At the beginning of the 20th century, associationists like Thorndike firmly conceived learning as a form of memorization of connections between stimulus–response elements; under this perspective transfer could take place only between pairs of *identical elements*: 'addition improves multiplication because multiplication is largely addition; knowledge of Latin gives increased ability to learn French because many of the facts learned in the one case are needed in the other' (Thorndike, 1906: 243). Against this conceptualization of rote learning, other alternative approaches have been formulated. Gestalt psychologists, for instance, affirmed that learning involves, not simple associations, but a representation and an understanding (*meaningful learning*) of a larger structure of relations that qualify a problem or a situation. Singley and Anderson's (1989) distinction between procedural and declarative knowledge helps to characterize these processes and to predict to what extent routines may be transferred to other domains. As we mentioned above, their experimental evidence supports the conclusion that procedural knowledge is strongly tied to the experiential context and cannot be easily generalized. Cohen and Bacdayan's (1994) experimental analysis on organizational routines was also addressed to assess the degree of transferability of the knowledge incorporated in routines. For this purpose, Cohen and Bacdayan compared the behaviour of a group of subjects that played a second session of the original *Target the Two* game with the behaviour of another group that was asked to play a different version of the game. The performance of the group of subjects that faced the 'novel' treatment of the problems was significantly worse than the performance of the other group, meaning that there was not any relevant transfer effect of knowledge. Along with Singley and Andersons's conclusions, Cohen and Bacdayan's data confirm that subjects undergo a limited transfer of their skills when a major change in the problem structure is introduced. In other words, subjects were able to learn how to play the original card game and they developed some routines, but they failed to adapt their routines to a novel, structurally equivalent problem.

Finally, another feature that qualifies individual and organizational routines is suboptimality (Cohen and Bacdayan, 1994). In other words, routines are applied even in situations where better alternatives do exist, but they are unknown; rather than starting a search process, decision makers deploy suboptimal routines. Such circumstances have been clearly assessed at the individual level by Luchins in the jar experiments reported above. Cohen and Bacdayan (1994) found that suboptimality occurs also in organizational routines. Since the knowledge incorporated by routines largely depends on individual and organizational experience it is plausible to believe that routines and their content of knowledge are path-dependent. Using Cohen and Bacdayan's *Target the Two* experimental design, Egidi and Narduzzo (1997) found that procedural knowledge acquired through experience is affected by strong path-dependency. The strength of a routine is positively correlated to its use; when a problem solution is practised over time, it is eventually applied in an automatic fashion. Therefore, the routine that is learned to solve the first problems is subsequently and systematically recalled by a significant number of subjects, no matter its suboptimality. This path-dependency effect is strengthened by environmental conditions like time pressure that reward speed and quick reactions (Garapin and Hollard, 1999).

Individual v. group
Organizational routines typically involve some degree of coordination among multiple actors or organizational units. Even though organizations reach a clear division of labour, routinized behaviour in organizations may be exposed to situations of coordination failure that have no equivalent at the individual level. Reimer et al. (2002) experimentally analysed and compared problem-solving routines in individuals and groups. In this study the problem to solve is the Tower of Hanoi game; after the training session and a couple of games, subjects are exposed to a different version of the game, in order to assess and compare the ability of individuals and groups to transfer the acquired skills to a novel situation. The findings show that groups are more heavily exposed to a negative transfer effect than individuals; the subjects who play the game in the group condition face some difficulties in adapting their routinized behaviour to the new situation and they perform badly. At the same time, it is worthwhile to notice that such a negative transfer effect disappears when subjects are taught and trained to solve the game following a goal recursion scheme rather than a move-pattern procedure. In other words, when subjects are trained to solve the game by decomposing the problem into a hierachy of sub problems in a recursive way, they do not suffer any negative transfer effect when later they play in groups to solve a novel situation.

Since routines are a repertoire of solutions repeatedly applied to a known class of problems, they help individuals to deal with typical tasks in an automatic way (for a review, see Betsch et al., 2002). Nevertheless, routines seem to play an important role, not only at the individual level but also at the group level. Group routines consist of a repertoire of patterns of activities automatically activated by stimuli, and performed by the group members to solve a problem. Such a pattern of activities assumes that some coordinated division of labour among the group members has been acquired by the group during a phase of routinization. As a positive consequence, individual as well as group routines improve the performance in speed and predictability. While a great deal of experimental research has been developed upon the effect of routines on individuals, some important lines of experimental research have explored organizational routines, too.

What seems to qualify the experimental research on routinized group behaviour is the emphasis given to the coordination. Coordination (and coordination failures) concerns (i) the selection of the appropriate routine to perform, and (ii) an agreement upon who accomplishes what, to avoid overlaps and oversights. With regard to the first point, it is necessary so that the group coordinates the identification of the routine to activate: what triggers the beginning of the automatic answer, or who is in charge for selecting the appropriate routine in a given situation. With regard to the second point, the group coordination on who should perform each single sub-task is particularly critical when the sub-tasks are highly interdependent.

A typical situation where individuals and groups' behaviour may diverge is when they face a novel problem. Both types of coordination failures may take place when groups try to apply a routine to a novel problem. As we have seen in the *Einstellung* effect, routines may be problematic when applied to novel problems that present a superficial similarity to old situations, even though they are not structurally equivalent. In group routines this negative transfer effect becomes even more relevant because of the coordination problem.

In an experimental study on group routines, Reimer et al. (2002) compared the behaviour of individuals and groups (i.e. dyads) dealing with the same problem, the Tower of Hanoi problem. In this experimental study, subjects who were taught to solve the problem by applying a pattern of moves worsen their performance when they have to solve a modified version of the problem. More precisely, this study compares the individual and the dyads' performance and it shows that dyads are more exposed to the negative transfer effect. While subjects playing alone eventually understand that the previous routine may not be appropriate to solve the novel problem, dyads persist in their routine even when it is clearly inefficient. At the same time, it is important to note that this particular stickiness in the routinized behaviour helps the dyads to perform better than the single individuals in a novel problem equivalent to the original one (positive transfer effect) when the subjects are trained to solve it through a goal-recursion procedure. In other words, it matters if routines are conceived and conveyed as patterns of actions (e.g. series of moves to solve the game) rather than as a pattern of nested sub-goals to apply to solve the problem.

4   Behavioural game theory, and the theory of routines: how far apart are they really?

While behavioural game theory does not deal explicitly with the notion of routine, many experimental game settings clearly provide interesting ground for the emergence of routinized behaviour. Game experiments often concern behaviour in repeated interactive situations, and phenomena observed in such laboratory experiences are familiar to students of routines. For example, persistence of out-of-equilibrium behaviour often happens in even very long series of iterations (up to many hundreds); furthermore, such behaviour persists despite being substantially suboptimal. Moreover, such out-of-equilibrium behaviour is far from being the result of random errors, but on the contrary displays high stability and predictability. Transfer of learning is sometimes observed across similar games, and rule-based, conditional behaviour is the case when different games are played in the same session.

Consequently, despite the scarcity of dialogue between studies of routines and behavioural game theory, it is non-trivial to ask how really far apart they are. In what follows, we will try to capture some potential convergence between the two fields, and suggest how experimental practices on games might be oriented to further their dialogue.

Rote learning

While repeated games have been the object of experimental research since the 1950s, explicit attention to the nature of the interactive learning processes associated with such games is more recent, and finds its hallmark in the studies by Erev and Roth on learning in both strategic and extensive form games (Roth and Erev, 1995; Erev and Roth, 1998). Especially noteworthy is their study on learning in repeated games with unique mixed strategies equilibria. This study is significant for many reasons. First, it tries to deal with a large dataset of 13 experiments in which subjects play at least 100 times a same stage game: thus, learning processes have plenty of time to unfold. Such experiments are all focusing on the same class of games, those with unique mixed strategies equilibria. Such games are interesting for many reasons: they have unique equilibria, thus, an unequivocal 'rational' benchmark to evaluate human behaviour, but such equilibria are non-trivial, since they involve some degree of randomizing behaviour, and are anything but obvious to naïve subjects. Furthermore, in such experimental games the Nash equilibrium proves to be a quite modest predictor (often worse than random behaviour) and, consequently, the search for alternative explanations of behaviour is well justified. Finally, Erev and Roth use only experiments designed and performed by other researchers as a test-bed for learning models, avoiding the potential pitfalls of using experiments designed to confirm their own theories.

For students of routines, the most striking result from Erev and Roth is that a simple behavioural rule of rote learning turns out to be surprisingly good at fitting and predicting experimental data. Such a rule is the venerable reinforcement learning, which assumes that individuals reinforce only the actions they actually try, proportionally to the outcomes of the action, and with decreasing effects of new experiences over time.

In particular, the low-cognition reinforcement learning clearly outperforms the high-cognition Nash equilibrium; attempts by the authors to enrich the reinforcement model with some explicit belief formation process do not improve its performance, while making it cumbersome, with a large number of parameters to estimate. It is important to stress that reinforcement learning is not implying any strategic reasoning by its very nature (others' moves are taken into account only indirectly, through their effect on experienced payoffs) and it is very 'cheap' informationally, since it does not use any information concerning the others' payoffs: even one's own payoffs are considered only once an action is tried. What is more, players do not consider each time even the outcomes they might get from moves other than the one they tried (no counterfactual thinking). All this is even more remarkable since, in almost all experiments considered by Erev and Roth, subjects have full information on the payoff matrix of the game.

Some cognition is needed
Furthermore, what makes Erev and Roth's results more striking is also a source of weakness, as revealed by subsequent research. In particular, individuals do consider others' payoffs, as revealed by many experiments, and rote learning turns out to be unrealistically slow in experiments where there is a large range of available actions, and observations of others' actions can be exploited to achieve faster convergence (see Camerer, 2003, for a synthesis of criticism). A good example is that of coordination games. In a coordination game, the payoff each agent can achieve is conditional on his ability to converge with other players' behaviour. Furthermore, in such games there may be a pretty large number of available actions. In such games, reinforcement learning is often exceedingly slow because, if actions corresponding to coordination points are not initially tried by a player, it might take a long time before they are attempted, since players do not observe directly others' behaviour. Of course, the larger the action space, the lower the probability to try the 'coordinated' action, and thus the lower convergence. Belief learning models provide an alternative that takes explicitly into consideration how experience shapes players' beliefs about others' behaviour (in the simplified form of probability distributions over others' actions). The best-known example is fictitious play, in which a

player updates expectations on the grounds of the cumulated empirical frequencies of play by the other players.

However, the success of pure belief learning models in predicting behaviour has been limited, and attempts to track the evolution of beliefs through repeated play have shown considerable divergence from what was predicted by fictitious play models (Nyarko and Schotter, 2002). A more successful strategy has been to create hybrid models that blend features of both reinforcement and belief learning. The most prominent example of this family is EWA (Experience Weighted Attraction), by Camerer and Ho (1999). The basic idea in EWA is to have a model that 'assembles' belief learning, reinforcement learning and their main variants (e.g. fictitious play v. Cournot dynamics, which is a 'memory-less' fictitious play) and have parameters regulating the relative weight of such different learning models. Thus, an interesting feature of EWA is that it allows keeping multiple learning styles in one model. As data from different games are used to estimate such parameters, differences in ways agents adapt to the game are suggested by differences in parameter values. In fact, data from different games show a considerable variance in parameters. While this may be seen as a weakness of the theory, Camerer and colleagues address the problem in a way that may be an important source of insight also for students of routines. In a subsequent version of the model (Ho et al., 2007), they introduce a process of self-tuning of the learning parameters, through which different values of such parameters can be generated as a response to the specific experience in each game. Factors such as surprise and post-decision regret govern the way the rate of forgetting and the scope of attention are tuned: in rather stable contexts, behaviour is highly inertial and attention is restricted to own payoffs, while in more changing environments lessons of the past tend to go unlearned and attention scope is broadened. Self-tuning implies a strong downsizing of free parameters in the model, but, despite this, its predictive and descriptive performances remain quite unaltered, showing that there might be a bright future for the notion of 'learning to learn' and of hierarchically embedded adaptive processes (a point that was already at the heart of the routine/metaroutine distinction).

Learning as ex-post rationalization

An alternative view of learning in repeated games emphasizes the role of ex-post rationalization (Selten et al., 2005). Starting from experiments such as a laboratory replication of the 'market for lemons', in which reinforcement learning converges towards the Nash equilibrium, but human behaviour seems to stabilize out of equilibrium, Selten and co-authors show that the actual long-run behaviour is better explained by a process of ex-post rationalization driven by regret. In particular, they suggest that individuals adjust each time in the direction of what might have been the best move, given what the other player actually did last round. The theory in fact is articulated in a 'zero-parameters', qualitative theory predicting only the direction of adjustment (the 'learning direction theory' and an associated parametric stationary concept (the 'impulse balance equilibrium') which basically predicts that behaviours will stabilize around a point in which the 'impulses' to move in a different direction due to regret balance each other. Imagine an archer trying to hit the centre of a target: after each attempt, he will adjust his shot in the direction of the centre of the target (this is the 'learning direction' prediction). However, in games, each archer deals with a moving target, where the position of the target is determined by the other's move. The process will reach a stationary distribution in which, on average, the impulse to adjust the shot in different directions will be null. Both the learning direction theory and the impulse balance equilibrium have so far shown a remarkable predictive success in games as diverse as asymmetric information games, guessing games, zero-sum games, repeated prisoner's dilemmas etc. (see Selten et al., 2005 for a review). For students of routines, there are elements of potential interest in this view of experimentally observed interactive learning. First, the accent on rationalization is compatible with bounded rationality: computing ex-post what would have been optimal is much simpler than considering ex-ante all alternatives and computing the equilibrium behaviour. Second, the learning direction theory is clearly based on simple feedback mechanisms that we observe currently in the acquisition of simple abilities such as motor skills. Finally, the impulse balance equilibrium provides an interesting example of a behavioural alternative to standard equilibrium concepts.

Conditional behaviour and rule-based adaptation

The prevailing game experimental paradigm is that one of repeated experiments: a stage game is repeated N times, always with the same structure of actions and payoffs. Indeed, this is a quite unnatural framework for studying human learning. Only recently have issues of the way individuals learn to play similar but not identical games been experimentally addressed within the behavioural game theory tradition, with very interesting results. For example, Stahl and Van Huyck (2002) have studied groups of subjects that learn to play a sequence of different 'stag hunt' coordination games. In a stag hunt game, there are two equilibria: the first one is payoff-dominant but risky: if players fail to coordinate they may experience low payoffs; the second one is payoff-dominated but safe – no matter what the other does, a player risks no significant losses as compared to the safe equilibrium outcomes. Their experiment used stag hunt games in which the riskiness of the payoff-dominant solution differed from round to round: the result is that groups of subjects tended to develop conditional behaviour, i.e. different coordinated responses to different values of the parameter determining the riskiness of the payoff-dominant solution. Clearly, this conditional behaviour cannot be easily expressed by models such as reinforcement learning or EWA in which an agent unconditionally learns which strategy to play. In order to have effective coordinated conditional behaviour, some classification process must be part of the learning process, and there must be some convergence between agents' categories. Thus, Stahl et al. have advocated on the grounds of these results rule-based models of learning that can properly handle different responses to different contexts. Beyond the specific model they propose, Stahl and Van Huyck's experiment pioneers the exploration of more realistic learning processes in which experience is not merely repetitive but instead implies a variable set of conditions individuals have to simplify by categorization. Interactive learning gives rise to behaviour that is stable within categories but changes when category boundaries are crossed. It is important to emphasize that categories are emerging in their experiments as social conventions instead of mere individual processes: different groups may develop this different classification of their decision-making environment.

5   Behavioural game theory, and the theory of routines: making the experimental dialogue more fruitful

We hope to have shown that there is considerable (and underexploited) room for a dialogue between students of routines and the burgeoning field of research on learning in experimental games. Still, making such dialogue more fruitful requires not only recognizing converging themes, but also a more careful consideration of the experimental framework within which observations are generated and theory development can be supported. From this point of view, the classical paradigm within which experiments on learning in games are developed seems too narrow for understanding the development of routines. In what follows, we suggest a few critical points.

As already noted, the dominant paradigm of experimental games is one of repeated games. A same 'stage game' is repeated many times, sometimes even many hundreds, without ever varying the structure of interactions. Usually subjects are paired randomly at each round, to prevent the development of reputation phenomena (although sometimes fixed pairing is also exploited). This seems an inappropriate environment to cultivate routines. The most important aspect is probably that routines are better understood as the result of acting in similar, but not identical, situations. In other words, routines are the result of both repetition and generalization from experience (this is what contributes to their flexibility: Cohen et al., 1996). This point was central in the seminal experiment by Cohen and

Bacdayan (1994) on organizational routines, in which pairs played similar but not identical games of coordination (and Egidi and Narduzzo, 1997, have exploited the similarity structure of the experiment to detect path-depedence in the acquisition of routines). The development of experimental settings such as Stahl and others' will help to generate data on learning in environments which are more likely to improve our understanding of routinized behaviour. Also, more emphasis on fixed pairing might greatly contribute to taking into account the social nature of interactive learning and the development of routines, by letting subjects develop a shared history of play.

A related, important problem is how learning is transferred between agents (Narduzzo and Warglien, 1996). The role of vicarious learning (how to learn from the experience of others) has received minor interest in the behavioural game literature, but is of obvious relevance for routines, where transfer of learning between agents within the development of specific routines and the replication of pre-existing routines are central themes. The problem is complicated by the role of implicit knowledge in routinized behaviour, which constrains in relevant ways what can be transferred, and how it can be transferred. Designing experiments in which the relative effectiveness of different modalities of knowledge transfer can be assessed (possibly conditionally on the task type) might greatly improve our understanding of routine replication, but also enrich the way we consider some classical structure of interaction in game theory, as for example in the case of coordination games. The paper by Weber and Camerer (2003) on organizational cultures and codes is an important step in this direction, extending to the emergence of common codes the study of coordination games, and exploring the difficulties of transferring idiosyncratic codes after they have been stabilized. Incidentally, the paper by Camerer and Weber shows the fruitfulness of designing experiments in which response times (a crude indicator of automatization) can be part of the incentive structure of the game – a point well known to the experimental literature on routines.

A second feature of economic experiments on learning in games is that in general most of the complexity is in the underlying equilibrium concept: actions, on the other side, are given as single moves or at best as ready-made sequences of moves. This is not the case of routines, which may be more complex assemblies of elementary steps (maybe organized in modules which have to be recombined 'generatively': Pentland and Reuter, 1994). It might be interesting to look more at learning in interactive contexts in which sequences of elementary moves have to be discovered and tried without being obviously available. This gives rise to complications which are interesting both in terms of ecological validity (learning how to assemble steps is an important part of developing a routine: Narduzzo et al.,

2000) and in theoretical terms (e.g.: how is credit for success assigned to single steps when only long sequences of steps can be evaluated in terms of outcomes?).

This last remark raises an important problem of experimental method. How complex should the experimental task be? Clearly, there are important trade-offs to consider here. On the one hand, aspirations to ecological validity push towards 'semi-realistic' task complexity, but usually this comes at the price of some fundamental problems. A first problem is the difficulty of defining benchmarks: is there any kind of normative solution offering a benchmark against which to evaluate actual behaviour? The whole history of behavioural decision making and behavioural game theory is there to show how such benchmarks can make the evaluation and the analysis of observed behaviour easier and more crisp. This is due not only to the advantage of having a clear target for refutation or empirical support, but also to the fact that a well-defined normative benchmark may help to define clearly what behaviours constitute mistakes, and a typology of such mistakes. In turn, this is a precious source of constraints for behavioural theories: a theory that has to explain both (occasional) 'correct' behaviour and the variety of observed mistakes has much fewer degrees of freedom available (see Singley and Anderson (1989) for a remarkable theoretical exploitation of the variety of mistake types in learning). The very definition of testable hypotheses in highly complex tasks may be hindered by the excessive complexity of the task, that may make it difficult to discriminate among alternative behavioural paths. So, it should be recommended that experiments on routines explore larger task complexity than standard game-theoretic ones, but should still maintain complexity within the boundaries of analysability and the definability of normative benchmarks.

An almost completely overlooked issue in behavioural game learning theories is the role of affordances in learning. While the literature on 'situated learning' has extensively demonstrated how humans can exploit the structure of the environment (in particular of the artifacts surrounding them) in the process of learning (Hutchins, 1995), nothing has been done in this direction in the study of learning in games. Little indeed has been done in this direction by students of routines either, at least in the domain of experimental research. This offers very attractive common fields for adventure to both behavioural game theorists and research on routines. An interesting underexploited connection is the notion of focal point (Schelling, 1960). Focal points are in fact kinds of affordances that allow individuals to coordinate with each other even when there are potentially infinitely many possible coordination solutions available. While experimental economics has extensively explored the role of focal points in one-shot coordination games (Mehta et al., 1994), issues of how focal points may address learning have never been explored (see, however, Devetag, 2003) for an early experimental study of dynamic focal points). Studying affordances as focal points for learning might open a fruitful dialogue between research on routines and behavioural game theory.

Language is both a vehicle of the generation of routines and a by-product of routinization (in the form of idiosyncratic code). Routines are created, maintained and replicated through interactions in which linguistic communication (*lato sensu*, including different forms of visual and gestural language) often plays a fundamental role. Yet linguistic communication between subjects is carefully kept out of most experiments on learning in games. This is very much an effect of the 'repeated game with randomly matched anonymous players' syndrome: no way to identify each other and develop a reputation should be left to experimental subjects. But it also reflects a genuine embarrassment of game theory with communication. Most experimental studies of communication in games have been dominated by the 'cheap talk' paradigm, looking mostly at the credibility of communication in a one-shot non-cooperative game (Crawford, 1998). Recently, however, there has been a small but growing stream of experimental research looking at more dynamical issues of how individuals use or create language to solve coordination problems unfolding over time (Weber and Camerer, 2003; Selten and Warglien, 2007). In those experiments, a communication code emerges as the outcome of repeated attempts at reaching coordinated action under constraints of communication cost. Selten and Warglien in particular analyse how the structure of such experimentally grown languages reflect the underlying decomposition of the task and the degree of flexibility needed when the environment is non-repetitive. Efficient but 'idiomatic' codes flourish in stationary environments where the same situations are recurrent. Such idiosyncratic codes could only be transferred by case-by-case demonstration, since they have no generative rule producing them. However, more abstract, combinatorial, grammar-like languages prevail when individuals have to coordinate over never-repeating tasks. This suggests a critical threshold of variety beyond which the typical features of idiosyncratic codes become dysfunctional and give way to more abstract codes of coordination, that could be more easily transferred by general rules. Transferred out of the laboratory, these results suggest that the language observed in the performance of coordinated action should be an important source of information on the nature of the underlying patterns of action.

Summing up: a productive interaction between research on routines and behavioural game theory (especially behavioural theories of learning in games) seems ripe. Still, this interaction would greatly benefit from the exploration of experimental paradigms in which repetition gives way to similarity of experiences, anonymity is replaced by social identifiability, vicarious learning interacts with personal experience, actions need to be chained in complex patterns, and both language and environmental affordances matter. While not all these features could be simultaneously present in an experiment without killing the need to control experimental conditions, all of them are amenable to separate analysis and might bring new useful insights for both research communities.

Conclusions

A final comment for those readers who may consider studying organizations and organizational routines in a laboratory setting. This chapter shows that organizational routines may be thoughtfully studied in the laboratory. Some better understanding of routines and routinization process have been reached, but it is also true that studies may be further explored and developed. In this chapter we did not explicitly mention all the peculiarities that characterize experimental research in a laboratory. Some comprehensive handbooks on experimental economics have been written and they provide useful references and guidelines. Besides them, it is worthwhile mentioning the chapter on organizational research in the laboratory written by Karl Weick (1965) a long time ago. He took into account both methodological and substantive themes that are still relevant in the organizational field; he discussed the possibility of studying organizations in a laboratory by means of experiments and he carefully analysed the three main components that are always present in an experimental environment: settings, tasks and subjects. It is still a great reference.

References

Aarts, H. and A. Dijksterhuis (2000), 'Habits as knowledge structure: automaticity in goal-directed behavior', *Journal of Personality and Social Psychology*, **78**(1), 53–63.

Allport, F.H. (1919), 'Behavior and experiment in social psychology', *Journal of Abnormal Psychology*, **14**, 297–306.

Allport, F.H. (1920), 'The influence of the group upon association and thought', *Journal of Experimental Psychology*, **3**, 159–82.

Arrow, K.J. (1963), *Social Choice and Individual Values*, Wiley.

Berry, D.C. and D.E. Broadbent (1984), 'On the relationship between task performance and associated verbalizable knowledge', *Quarterly Journal of Experimental Psychology*, **36**, 209–31.

Betsch, T. and S. Haberstroh (eds) (2005), *The Routines of Decision Making*, Lawrence Erlbaum Associates.

Betsch, T., K. Fiedler and J. Brinkmann (1998), 'Behavioral routines in decision making: the effects of novelty in task presentation and time pressure on routine maintenance and deviation', *European Journal of Social Psychology*, **28**, 861–78.

Betsch, T., S. Haberstroh and C. Höhle (2002), 'Explaining routinized decision making, a review of theories and models', *Theory and Psychology*, **12**(4), 453–88.

Betsch, T., S. Haberstroh, A. Glöckner, T. Haar, and K. Fielder (2001), 'The effects of routine strength on adaptation and information search in recurrent decision making', *Organizational Behavior and Human Decision Processes*, **84**(1), 23–53.

Blinder, A.S. and J. Morgan (2000), 'Are two heads better than one? An experimental analysis of group vs. individual decisionmaking', NBER Working Paper, 7909.

Camerer, C. (2003), *Behavioral Game Theory: Experiments in Strategic Interaction*, Princeton University Press.

Camerer, C. and T-H. Ho (1999), 'Experience-weighted attraction learning in normal form games', *Econometrica*, **67**, 837–74.

Cohen, M.D. (1991), 'Individual learning and organizational routine: emerging connections', *Organization Science*, **2**(1), 135–9.

Cohen, M.D. and P. Bacdayan (1994), 'Organizational routines are stored as procedural memory: evidence from a laboratory study', *Organization Science*, **5**(4), 554–68.

Cohen, M.D., R. Burkhart, G. Dosi, M. Egidi, L. Marengo, M. Warglien and S. Winter (1996), 'Routines and other recurring action patterns of organizations: contemporary research issues', *Industrial and Corporate Change*, **5**, 653–98.

Crawford, V. (1998), 'A survey of experiments on communication via cheap talk', *Journal of Economic Theory*, **78**, 286–98.

Devetag, G. (2003), 'Coordination and information in critical mass games: an experimental study', *Experimental Economics*, **6**(1), 53–73.

Egidi, M. (1996), 'Routines, hierarchies of problems, procedural behavior: some evidence from experiments', in K. Arrow et al. (eds), *The Rational Foundations of Economic Behavior*, Macmillan, pp. 303–33.

Egidi, M. and A. Narduzzo (1997), 'The emergence of path-dependent behaviors in cooperative contexts', *International Journal of Industrial Organization*, **15**, 677–709.

Erev, I. and A.E. Roth (1998), 'Predicting how people play games: reinforcement learning in experimental games with unique, mixed strategy equilibria', *The American Economic Review*, **88**(4), 848–81.

Feldman, M.S. and B.T. Pentland (2003), 'Reconceptualizing organizational routines as a source of flexibility and change', *Administrative Science Quarterly*, **48**(1), 94–118.

Garapin, A. and M. Hollard (1999), 'Routines and incentives in group tasks', *Journal of Evolutionary Economics*, **9**, 465–86.

Ho, T-H., C. Camerer and J-K. Chong (2007), 'Self-tuning experience-weighted attraction learning in games', *Journal of Economic Theory*, **133**(1), 177–98.

Holyoak, K.J. and B.A. Spellman (1993), 'Thinking', *Annual Review of Psychology*, **44**, 265–315.

Hutchins, E. (1995), *Cognition in the Wild*, The MIT Press.

Jenkins, J.G. (1933), 'Instruction as a factor in incidental learning', *American Journal of Psychology*, **45**, 471–7.

Kocher, M.G. and M. Sutter (2005), 'The decision maker matters: individual versus group behavior in experimental beauty-contest games', *The Economic Journal*, **115**, 200–223.

Lave, J. (1988), *Cognition in Practice*, Cambridge University Press.

Lorge, I., D. Fox, J. Davitz and M. Brenner (1958), 'A survey of studies contrasting the quality of group performance and individual performance, 1920–1957', *Psychological Bulletin*, **55**(6), 337–72.

Luchins, A.S. (1942), 'Mechanization in problem solving', *Psychological Monographs*, **54** (248), 1–95.

Luchins, A.S. and E.H. Luchins (1950), 'New experimental attempts at preventing mechanization in problem solving', *Journal of General Psychology*, **42**, 279–97.

March, J.G. (1994), *Primer on Decision Making: How Decisions Happen*, Free Press.

Mehta, J., C. Starmer and R. Sugden (1994), 'The nature of salience: an experimental investigation of pure coordination games', *The American Economic Review*, **84**(3), 658–73.

Narduzzo, A. and M. Warglien (1996), 'Learning from the experience of others', *Industrial and Corporate Change*, **5**(1), 113–26.

Narduzzo, A., E. Rocco and M. Warglien (2000), 'Talking about routines in the field: the emergence of organizational capabilities in a new cellular phone network company, in G. Dosi, R.R. Nelson and S.G Winter (eds), *The Nature and Dynamics of Organizational Capabilities*, Oxford University Press.

Nelson, R.R. and S.G. Winter (1982), *An Evolutionary Theory of Economic Change*, Belknap Press.

Newell, A. (1990), *Unified Theories of Cognition*, Harvard University Press.

Nyarko, Y. and A. Schotter (2002), 'An experimental study of belief learning using elicited beliefs', *Econometrica*, **70**(3), 971–1005.

Pentland, B.T. and H.H Reuter (1994), 'Organizational routines as grammars of action', *Administrative Science Quarterly*, **39**(3), 484–510.

Pereira, R.A.M. and P. Patelli (1996), 'The emergence of cooperative playing routines: optimality and learning', WP-96-22, IIASA Laxenburg (Austria).

Polanyi, M. (1958), *Personal Knowledge*, The University of Chicago Press.

Reber, A.S. (1993), *Implicit Learning and Tacit Knowledge*, Oxford University Press.

Reimer, T., A.-L. Bornstein and K. Opwis (2005), 'Positive and negative transfer effects in groups', in T. Betsch and S. Haberstroh (eds), *The Routine of Decision Making*, Lawrence Erlbaum Associates, 175–92.

Reimer, T., K. Opwis and A.-L. Bornstein (2002), 'Routine problem solving in groups', in W. Gray and C. Schunn (eds), *Proceedings of the Twenty-Fourth Annual Conference of the Cognitive Science Society*, Lawrence, Erlbaum Associates, 780–85.

Roth, A. and I. Erev (1995), 'Learning in extensive-form games: experimental data and simple dynamic models in the intermediate term', *Games and Economic Behavior*, **8**, 164–212.

Rohrer, J.H., S.H. Baron, E.L. Hoffman and D.V. Swander (1954), 'The stability of autokinetic judgments', *Journal of Abnormal and Social Psychology*, **49**, 595–7.

Schacter, D.L. (1987), 'Implicit memory: history and current status', *Journal of Experimental Psychology: Learning, Memory and Cognition*, **13**(3), 501–18.

Schelling, T.C. (1960), *The Strategy of Conflict*, Harvard University Press.

Selten, R. and M. Warglien (2007), 'The emergence of simple languages in an experimental coordination game', *Proceedings of the National Academy of Science*, **104**(18), 7361–6.

Selten, R., K. Abbink and R. Cox (2005), 'Learning direction theory and the winner's curse', *Experimental Economics*, **8**(1), 5–20.

Shaw, M.E. (1932), 'A comparison of individuals and small groups in the rational solution of complex problems', *The American Journal of Psychology*, **44**(3), 491–504.

Shaw, M.E. (1971), 'Group dynamics', *Annual Review of Psychology*, **12**, 129–56.

Singley, M.K. and J.R. Anderson (1989), *The Transfer of Cognitive Skill*, Cambridge: Harvard University Press.

Squire, L. (1986), 'Mechanisms of memory', *Science*, **232**, 1612–19.

Squire, L., B. Knowlton and G. Musen (1993), 'The structure and organization of memory', *Annual Review of Psychology*, **44**, 453–95.

Stahl, D.O. and J. Van Huyck (2002), 'Learning conditional behavior in similar stag hunt games', WP, Texas A&M University.

Thorndike, E.L. (1906), *The Principle of Teaching: Based on Psychology*, Seiler.

Thorndike, E.L. (1911), *Animal Intelligence*, Macmillan.

Thorndike, E.L. and R.T. Rock (1934), 'Learning without awareness of what is being learned or intent to learn it', *Journal of Experimental Psychology*, **17**, 1–19.

Verplanken, B., H. Aarts and A. van Knippenberg (1997), 'Habit, information acquisition, and the process of making travel mode choice', *European Journal of Social Psychology*, **27**, 539–60.

Weber, R.A. and C.F. Camerer (2003), 'Cultural conflict and merger failure: an experimental approach', *Management Science*, **49**(4), 400–415.

Weick, K.E. (1965), 'Laboratory experimentation with organizations', in J.G. March (ed.), *Handbook of Organizations*, Rand McNally.

Index

11 September 2001 terrorist attack 37–8

Aarts, Henk 127, 128, 309, 310
Abbott, Andrew 73
Abelson, R.P. 231, 240
accidents 39, 41, 194, 210–11, 233
accounting 88–9
  see also accounting change; accounting systems; institutional perspective on management accounting routines; management accounting
accounting change 99–103
accounting systems 88, 100–101
Acharya, A. 44–5
action 23, 91–3, 94, 109, 156, 211, 212, 235, 237–9, 292
  see also action networks; collective action; line of action; performance feedback theory; performative aspect of routines
action networks 296
adaptation
  and calculation 245
  in capability-based view of the firm 117–18
  in loosely-coupled systems 56
  and negative feedback 141, 142
  and organizational learning 175
  and organizational routines in evolutionary economics 68–9
  and organizations as going concerns 55, 56, 69
  and revision of organizational routines 127
Adaptive Control of Thought (ACT) theory 208
Adler, P.S. 294, 295
administration 65–6
affordances 320–21
aggregation, as dimension of reproduction mechanisms 248

aircraft accidents 210–11, 233
Alchian, A. 259, 260
Aldrich, Howard E. 125, 126, 142–3
Allison, Graham T. 35–6, 40, 41, 168, 234
Allport, Floyd Henry 304
Anderson, J.R. 206–7, 208–9, 210, 213, 306–7, 308, 309, 311
Anderson, P. 162, 171–2, 173
Andriessen, J.H.E. 261
Aoki, M. 111
appreciative theory 68, 71, 74, 75
appropriateness 6, 45, 169, 308–9
arenas see social worlds/arenas
Argote, L. 153, 159, 161, 163, 169, 171, 293
Argyris, C. 269
Aristotle 19–20
artifacts
  and change in organizational routines 244
  comparison of organizational routines 294, 295
  in concept of organizational routines 286–7, 288, 289–90
  described 236, 244
  in empirical field studies of organizational routines 283–4
  and identification of organizational routines 291
  as reproduction mechanism 243–4, 249
  see also codebooks; rules; standard operating procedures
artificial intelligence 206, 207–8, 231–2
Ashford, Blake 233
aspiration level, in performance feedback theory 188, 189–91, 195–6, 197–8, 199, 200
assumptions, taken-for-granted, in management accounting 93, 94, 100, 101, 102
Atkinson, R.C. 209

attention 209, 212, 256, 258
authority 66, 73, 78–9, 110
    see also charismatic authority;
        control; formal authority;
        power; procedural authority
automatisms 128, 130, 245, 305,
    312–13
    see also cognitive automatisms;
        motor-sensory automatisms;
        visual automatisms

Bacdayan, Paul 11, 22, 23, 97, 139,
    155, 161, 171, 194, 206, 208, 217,
    234, 244, 288, 305–6, 307–8,
    311–12, 319
bankruptcy 126, 136, 137, 144
bargaining 36, 38, 41, 172
Barker, James R. 247
Barley, Stephen R. 73, 74, 244, 293
Bartlett, J. 216–17
Beamish, Thomas D. 60
Becker, Howard S. 56, 60–61
Becker, Markus C. 58, 94, 95, 97
Beckman, C.M. 162, 166, 173
'behavioral theory of the firm' 156–7,
    158, 188–9, 190, 230
    see also performance feedback
        theory
behaviour perspective, in experimental
    psychology 305–6
behavioural cues 131, 132, 139
behavioural game theory and theory of
    routines
    critique and future directions
        318–22
    current research 314–18
behaviours
    in concept of habits 16, 17, 127, 128,
        129, 130
    in concept of organizational routines
        18, 19, 20, 132
belief learning models 315–16
Bendor, J. 42, 43
Benner, M.J. 175
Berger, Peter L. 154, 231, 239–40, 241,
    242, 247
Bergson, H. 211–13
best practices 264, 266, 271
Betsch, Tilmann 309–10
Biggart, Nicole W. 60

biological factors *see* body; brain;
    neuronal networks; 'routines as
    genes'
Blinder, Alan S. 304
body 212–13, 215
Boekle, Henning 45, 47
Bohmer, R.M. 164
Boland, R.J. 258
Bornstein, A.-L. 313
Boulding, K. 214
boundaries 274, 282, 288, 290–93
bounded rationality
    and coordination 265
    in evolutionary economics 67–8, 70,
        71
    and game theory 317
    in performance feedback theory 188
    in problem-solving 38–9, 112
    and ready-made solutions 134
    and search 266–7
brain 213–14, 215
bricolage 161, 163, 165–6
British artillery case study 23, 156,
    234
Brooks, D. 161, 171
bureaucracies 64–6, 72–3, 74, 165
bureaucratic politics 35–41
Burgelman, R.A. 161, 165, 168
Burns, John 89, 90, 91, 92, 94, 98, 99,
    101–3
Burns, Tom 73–4

calculation 244–5, 248, 249
Camerer, C.F. 316, 319, 321
Camus, J.F. 209
capabilities 18, 21, 35–6, 69, 179–80,
    256
    see also capability-based view of the
        firm; capacities; competency
        traps; dynamic capabilities;
        skills
capability-based view of the firm
    change in organizational routines
        118
    cognitive dimension 117, 265, 266–7
    described 108
    and organizational routines 108–9,
        117–18
    problem-solving capability and
        governance structure 109–11

towards a formal representation
111–17
capacities 19–21, 23, 24, 25, 109, 153
see also capabilities; competency
traps; developmental capacity;
generative capacity; skills
capitalism 64–7, 71, 78–9
card playing 155, 161, 217, 305–6,
307–8, 311, 312
Carnegie School 62, 230
centralization 114, 220–21
ceremonial accounting routines 98–9
Chandler, A.D. 260
change 96–7
see also accounting change; change
in organizational routines;
cultural change; economic
change; environmental change;
evolutionary theories;
organizational change;
resistance to change; social
change; technological change
change in organizational routines
in accounting 99–103
artefacts, role of 244
in capability-based view of the firm
118
and economic change 58
in empirical field study research
285–6
in evolutionary economics 68–9,
141–2
incremental and radical changes 9,
195, 197
limited capacity 24
and organizational learning 175–8,
194, 195
and organizational structure 194,
195
and performance feedback theory
192, 193, 194, 195–8, 199–200
in political science 40, 41
quality standards *see* quality
standards
and social change 235–6, 285
and technological change 118
charisma 229, 230
charismatic authority 66, 78, 230
Clarke, Adele E. 56
Clarke, Lee 46

clusters of conventions 56, 58, 62,
71
codebooks 260–61, 262, 264
codes 288, 319, 321
codification
effect on innovation 218, 219
in knowing communities 262, 266
and organizational learning 177
and organizational memory 154–5,
156
and pre-planned retention 170
and replication of organizational
routines 24
resistance by individuals 219
in Tayloristic organizations 110
in teams 260, 261, 265
codified rules 265
coding schemes 288
coercion 242, 247, 249
cognitive acts 112
cognitive automatisms 208, 209–11,
212, 222, 223, 233
cognitive commonalities 177, 265, 269,
271, 272–3
cognitive dimension 117, 153, 230,
234–5, 256, 257, 266–8, 269–71
see also learning; memorization;
ostensive aspect of routines
cognitive efficiency 302–4
cognitive effort 215, 246
cognitive perspective versus
behavioural perspective on
organizational routines 305–6
Cohen, Michael D. 11, 21, 22, 23, 57,
97, 101, 109, 112, 127, 139, 155,
161, 171, 194, 206, 208, 217, 234,
244, 247, 256, 257, 268, 288,
305–6, 307–8, 311–12, 318–19
Cohendet, Patrick 260, 267
coherence 272, 273, 275
collective action 55, 58, 59, 60, 69, 77
commitment 246–7, 249, 263, 264,
270
communication 260–61, 272
communities of practice 262–3, 266,
269, 270, 271, 272, 274
comparison of routines, in empirical
field studies 293–5
competency traps 231, 233, 245–6, 249
competition 69, 175

complexity 192, 211, 281–6
compliance 242, 243
computer programs 18, 20, 21
    see also artificial intelligence
concatenation of procedural memory
    23, 244, 249
concept of organizational routines
    and concept of habits 15–17, 131–2
    coordination 153, 256, 257
    dimensions 256–7
    dispositions 4, 5, 18, 20, 21, 25, 131
    in empirical field studies of
        organizational routines 286–90
    information transmission 21–5
    order 6–7, 118
    'routines as capacities' (*see*
        capacities)
    'routines as computer programs' 18,
        20, 21
    'routines as genes' 5, 10, 18–19, 20,
        21, 142, 143, 144, 145, 232
    rules (*see* rules)
concurrency 296–7
conditioned behaviour 317–18
confirmation bias 309–10
conflicting norms 43–4, 45–6, 47
conflicts of interest
    and accounting change 102–3
    in capability-based view of the firm
        116
    in concept of organizational routines
        257
    in evolution of organizational
        routines 268, 269
    in knowing communities 264
    in ostensive aspects of routines 288
    and problem-solving in capability-
        based view of the firm 109–10
    and reciprocal typification 241–2
conscious processes 303
consequences 169
constraints 17, 37, 38, 41, 44, 95,
    129–31
context 21, 109, 211, 212, 257, 258–9
    see also context; external
        environment; knowing
        communities; physical
        environment; social
        environment; teams; uncertain
        task environment

contextual cues 127, 128–9, 130
control 117, 209
conventions, social *see* social
    conventions
cooperative strategies 42
coordination
    and bounded rationality 265
    bureaucratic politics and
        organizational routines 35
    in concept of organizational routines
        153, 256, 257
    in group problem solving 312–13
    institutional perspective on
        management accounting
        routines 93–4
    and managers 272–3
    and replication of organizational
        routines 126
    teams versus knowing communities
        272
    and transactive memory 217
    and uncertain task environments 132
coordination games 315–16, 317–18,
    319, 320–21
copying fidelity 138
core competences 273
Coriat, B. 110, 116, 257
creative destruction 58
creativity 164, 165, 180, 218, 219
    see also imagination; innovation
cross-sectional studies 293–4
Crozier, Michel 74
Cuban missile crisis 35, 38, 40, 168
cues 21, 22–3, 25–6, 127
    see also behavioural cues; contextual
        cues
cultural change 62
cultural stability 62
culture 60–61, 62
current paths 238, 239
custom 16
customary law 42, 43–4
Cyert, Richard M. 38–9, 72, 95, 97, 98,
    156–7, 158, 188, 190, 230, 266

Dalton, Melville 72
Damasio, A. 214–15
dance band study 60–61
Darr, E.D. 159, 164, 170, 293
Darwin, Charles R. 23

de Ruyter, K. 218–19
decentralization 114, 115
decision making
    appropriateness, logic of 45, 169,
        308–9
    and bounded rationality in problem
        solving 38–9
    bureaucratic politics and
        organizational routines 36, 38
    and institutional perspective on
        management accounting
        routines 98
    learning routines and politics 179
    in performance feedback theory 188,
        189, 190, 192, 201
    and problem-solving in capability-
        based view of the firm 117
    top management and organizational
        memory 156
declarative knowledge
    context 211
    in ISO certification case study 222
    versus non-declarative knowledge
        213–14
    and organizational learning 172
    and organizational memory 155
    versus procedural knowledge 206–9,
        306–8, 311
declarative memory
    in content of organizational memory
        218
    in experimental research on
        organizational routines 306
    role 207, 208, 213, 214
    and tacit learning 303
    in theories of organizational
        routines 234
decomposition, in problem-solving
    114–15, 116, 117
definitions of organizational routines
    as capability/capacity 18, 21, 25, 109
    cognitive dimension 25, 153
    as dispositions 21, 25, 131–2
    in evolutionary economics 18, 21,
        58, 109, 187, 217
    general 18, 191
    in organizational economics 18, 58
    in organizational learning 21, 257
    as procedural knowledge 206, 208
    'routines as genes' 18–19

Demsetz, H. 259, 260
Denis, Blandine 118, 177, 220–23, 291,
    294, 295
depreciation from organizational
    memory 170
developmental capacity 139, 140, 141
Dewey, John 6, 16
differential replication 126, 138–41,
    142, 144
diffusion 126, 134, 136, 137, 138, 142,
    144, 164, 166
Dijksterhuis, Ap 127, 128, 309, 310
disequilibrium 58
dispositions
    in concept of habits 16, 25, 127–9,
        130
    in concept of organizational routines
        4, 5, 18, 20, 21, 25, 131
dissociated memory 208, 303, 306
distributed processes 283, 287, 288
division of cognitive labour 111, 117
division of labour 57, 221, 260, 312–13
Divry, C. 217
Dosi, Giovanni 107–8, 109, 110, 112,
    114–15, 116, 117, 118, 257, 267
Douglas, Y. 162, 169
Drezner, Daniel W. 46
dyads 241–2, 305–6, 313, 319
Dyer, J.H. 170
dynamic capabilities 69, 118, 232

ecological validity 319
economic change 58
economics, research routines 76–7
Edmondson, A.C. 164
effectiveness 232
efficiency 241–2
effort 216, 223, 224, 243
Egidi, M. 306, 312
Eichenbaum, H. 208, 213–14
Einstellung 302
elimination 134, 142
emergent processes
    retention 161–2, 171–2
    selection 161–3, 168–9
    variation 161–3, 165–6
    see also knowing communities
emic perspective 288, 292–3
emotions 16, 61, 171, 213, 214–15, 224,
    233–4

empirical field studies of
    organizational routines
    comparison of routines 293–5
    conceptualizing routines 286–90
    concurrency 296–7
    identification of routines 290–93
    point of view 287–8, 289, 295–6
empirical research 71, 74–5, 290–91
    see also empirical field studies of
        organizational routines
enabling routines 95
enforcement 34, 35, 42, 242, 247
environmental change 233
environmental feedback 143
environmental interaction 126, 140,
    142
environments *see* context;
    environmental change;
    environmental feedback;
    environmental interaction;
    external environment; physical
    environment; social environment;
    uncertain task environment
epistemic communities 262, 265, 269,
    270, 271, 272
Epple, D. 159, 293
equilibrium 42, 43–4, 46, 314, 315,
    316–17, 319
equivocality, and sensemaking 62
Erev, I. 314–15
ethnography 79
    see also empirical field studies of
        organizational routines;
        organizational ethnographies
etic perspective 288, 289, 292, 293
European integration 34
evaluation, in performance feedback
    theory 189
events 208, 211, 212, 213, 214
evolutionary economic sociology
    67–75
evolutionary economics 18, 21, 58–9,
    60, 65–6, 67–70, 71, 141–2, 267
evolutionary game theory 42–4
evolutionary system philosophy 24–5
evolutionary theories
    incentive systems 268–9
    leadership and managers 272–3
    memory and learning 303
    principles

information transfer 125, 126,
    135, 136, 137, 139–40
    selection 125–6, 135, 136–42,
        143–4
    variation 125, 135–6, 138, 140, 158
    purpose 125, 135
    replication of habits and
        organizational routines 138–41
    theories of organizational routines
        141–3, 232
    types 135–6
    see also evolutionary economic
        sociology; evolutionary
        economics; evolutionary game
        theory; evolutionary system
        philosophy
EWA (Experience Weighted
    Attraction) 316
ex-post rationalization 316–17
exit 126, 136, 137, 144
expectations 240, 241, 249
    see also ostensive aspect of routines
experience 17, 154–5, 158, 263
experimental psychology and
    organizational routines 302–6
experimental research on
    organizational routines
    behavioural game theory and theory
        of routines
    critique and future directions
        318–22
    current research 314–18
    features amenable to experimental
        inquiry
    individuals versus groups 312–14
    information search 309–10
    memory 306–8
    retrieval of appropriate routines
        308–9
    routine transfer, suboptimality
        and path dependence 306,
        307, 309, 310–12, 313, 319
    history 302–6
experimentation 159, 164, 175, 178–9,
    192, 266
explicit memory *see* declarative
    memory
expressive aspect of routines *see*
    performative aspect of routines
external environment 72

external sources
  retention 160, 162, 170–71, 171–2
  selection 160, 162–3, 167–8, 169
  variation 160, 162–3, 164–5, 166

facts, memorization of 208, 211, 212, 213, 214
Faillo, Marco 108, 109
failure of organizational routines 37–8, 41
familiarity 240
Farrell, T. 45–6
Feldman, Martha S. 9, 62, 72, 93, 100, 153–4, 175–6, 179, 211, 216, 219, 235–6, 242, 244, 245, 284, 285, 286, 287, 291, 294, 295
Felin, T. 256
financial accounting 88
firms, as replicators 138–9
fitness 56, 113–14, 136–7
flexibility 214, 245
focal points 320–21
forgetting of routines 163, 169, 220
  see also unlearning of routines
formal authority 62, 66, 110, 177, 223, 224
formal rationality 66, 71
formal rules 34
formal structure, going concerns 70–71, 72
formal theory, in evolutionary economics and evolutionary economic sociology 68, 71, 74
formalization 243, 249
  see also codebooks; codification; rules
Foss, N. 256
free will 211, 212
Freeman, John 24, 142, 197
Fried, Yitzhak 233
functional teams 260–61, 265, 269, 270, 271
functionality, of institutions 64, 65

game theory *see* behavioural game theory and theory of routines; evolutionary game theory; prisoner's dilemma
Garud, R. 158, 159, 167
generative bricolage 161, 166

generative capacity 68–9
generative processes, routines in capability-based view of the firm 117–18
generative selection 126, 134, 136, 137–41, 142, 143, 144
generative structure 19, 21, 25
genes, routines as 5, 10, 18–19, 20, 21, 142, 143, 144, 145, 232
George, Alexander L. 39
Gersick, Connie J.G. 194, 210–11, 233–4
goals
  hierarchical structures 194–5, 198, 199
  in performance feedback theory 188, 190, 191, 192, 193, 198–9, 200
  in retrieval of routines 309
Goertz, Gary 41, 47
going concerns 55–6, 57–8, 69, 70–71, 72
Goldsmith, J.L. 42, 43
Gong, Yan 161, 163, 166, 172, 180
Gouldner, Alvin W. 72–3
governance 109–11, 115–17, 118, 257, 267–8
governmental politics
  analytical studies of international law 33–4
  bureaucratic studies 35–8, 39–41
  and international norms 41–7
grammars 235, 303–4
graphical representation 296
Greve, Henrich R. 159, 167, 188–90, 191, 196, 197–8
grounded theories 68, 71, 75
groups
  and distribution of organizational memory 217
  experimental research on organizational routines 304–5, 312–13
  in performance feedback theory 188, 190–91, 192, 196, 198, 199–200
  see also occupational groups; self-organized groups; teams

habit-memory 212
habits
  changes 192, 195
  concept 5–6, 15–17, 25, 127–9, 132

and concept of organizational
    routines 15–17, 131–2
definitions 15–16, 127–9, 191
development 129–31
in performance feedback theory
    191–3, 195, 198, 199
and procedural memory 22–3
properties 133–4
replication and generative selection
    138–41
replication through imitation 17, 24,
    126
as replicators 126, 138, 139, 140,
    141
strength 129
habitualization 231, 239–40, 249
Hackman, J. Richard 194, 210–11,
    233–4
Halperin, Morton H. 36
Hannan, Michael T. 24, 142, 197
'hard' law 34–5
Hargadon, A.B. 162, 169, 171
Hatch, N.W. 170
Haunschild, P.R. 160, 162, 165, 166,
    173
Henderson, A.D. 159, 160, 167–8, 172
Herrmann, Richard K. 47
hierarchies
    of goals 194–5, 198, 199
    of management 72, 74
    of organizational structures 194,
        195, 200
    see also bureaucracies; high-level
        officials; levels of routines;
        lower-level officials; lower-level
        units; top management
high-level officials 33, 35, 36, 39–40
Ho, C.-H. 316
Hodgson, Geoffrey M. 25, 94, 125,
    126, 128, 131–2, 136, 138, 139,
    143, 153, 191, 256
Holyoak, K.J. 303
Howard-Grenville, Jennifer A. 177,
    178, 245, 291
Hughes, Everett C. 55–6, 61–2, 67, 69
Hull, David L. 25, 138, 139, 140
Humphrey, C. 98–9
Hutchins, Edwin 155, 162, 166, 194,
    320
hypocrisy 43, 178

identification of routines 290–93
images, memorization 211, 213, 214
imagination 212
    see also creativity
imitation 17, 24, 99–100, 126, 131
implicit learning 17, 302–4, 305, 306–8
implicit memory *see* non-declarative
    memory
improvization 161, 165–6, 179, 180
incentive-based view of the firm 107–8
incentives
    in capability-based view of the firm
        110, 116, 117
    in concept of organizational routines
        257
    in evolution of organizational
        routines 268–9
    for habits 17, 130–31
    for knowledge creation 269
    and organizational learning 177
    for organizational routines 133
    and resistance to change 224
    teams versus knowing communities
        270, 271
incremental change in routines 9, 195
individual routines *see* habits
individuals
    and distribution of organizational
        memory 217
    experimental research on
        organizational routines 304–5,
        312, 313
    identification in empirical research
        290–91
    in performance feedback theory 190,
        191–2, 195, 198, 199, 200
inertia
    bureaucratic politics and
        organizational routines 35, 36
    and capability-based view of the
        firm 118
    and cognitive automatisms 210–11
    and performance feedback theory
        196, 197, 198
    and persistence of organizational
        routines 133
    and population ecology 142
    from tacit and procedural
        knowledge 234
informal norms 46

informal organizational structure
70–71, 72
informal rules 34
informal standard operating
procedures 154–5
information collection 192, 193
information overload 220, 222, 224, 225
information processing 209
see also cognitive automatisms
information transfer
in concept of organizational routines
21–5
in evolutionary theories 125, 126,
135, 136, 137, 139–40
in institutional perspective on
management accounting
routines 94–5, 97
international norms 41–7
innovation 68–9, 73–4, 218, 219
see also creativity; new job creation;
new knowledge; new product
development; new routines; new
technology; research and
development
instinctive imitation 17
institutional perspective on
management accounting routines
accounting change 99–103
accounting routines: properties 93–9
accounting rules and routines 90–91
actions and institutions 91–3, 94
overview 89–90
institutional perspective on
organizational routines 231
institutionalization 154, 155, 242, 249
institutionalized search 187
institutions 64–7
intentions 16–17, 128, 130, 290
inter-organization transfer of
organizational routines 132–3
inter-organizational search 187–8
inter-organizational transmission of
rules 41–7
interaction
and organizations as going concerns
55
and selection in evolutionary
theories 126, 138–9, 140, 141,
142, 144
and social conventions 58, 61

see also knowing communities;
teams
interactive learning 317, 319
interactors 24–5, 126, 138–9, 140, 141
internal sources
retention 159, 161, 170, 171
selection 159, 161, 167, 168–9
variation 158–60, 161–2, 164, 165–6
international law 34–5, 42, 43–4
international norms 41–7
international regimes, defined 31
intuition 17
Ireland 45–6
iron triangles 40
ISO certification 175, 177, 218, 219,
220–23
Israeli government 39

Jagd, S. 96–7
James, William 16, 213
Japanese Ohnistic organization
110–11, 257
Jobe, L.A. 170
jobs 161, 165, 168, 169, 170
see also occupational groups
Johnson, H. 99
Jones, Dorothy V. 43
Jordan, Andrew 34

Kaghan, William N. 72
Kahneman, D.A. 209
Kanter, Arnold 36
Kaplan, R. 99
Kauffman, S.A. 9, 113–14
know how *see* procedural knowledge
know why *see* declarative knowledge
knowing communities 258, 261–2,
263–4, 265–6, 269–72, 274
knowledge
in concept of organizational routines
15, 25, 256, 257
creation 218, 219, 222, 223, 243, 261,
262, 265–6, 269
and habits 17
in knowing communities 261, 262,
263, 264
in teams 260–61
see also declarative knowledge;
procedural knowledge; tacit
knowledge

knowledge brokers 170–71
Knudsen, Thorbjørn 8, 17, 25, 95, 125,
    126, 128, 132, 136, 138, 139, 143,
    153
Krasner, Stephen D. 31, 39
Kreps, D.M. 271
Kuhn, Thomas S. 76
Kuperman, Ranan D. 39
Kyriakopoulos, K. 218–19

labour mobility 23–4
languages 234–5, 321
    see also grammars; shared languages
Lant, Theresa K. 167, 191, 196, 200
Latham, Gary P. 191, 192, 200
Lave, J. 262, 263, 310–11
law 24, 34–5, 42, 43–4, 164–5
Lazaric, Nathalie 118, 177, 217,
    220–23, 291, 294, 295
leadership 247, 249, 260, 272
    see also management; managers; top
        management
learning 17, 46–7, 109, 178–81, 264,
    314, 315–18, 319, 320–21
    see also experimentation; implicit
        learning; learning-by-doing;
        organizational learning;
        organizational learning and
        organizational routines;
        population-level learning;
        reinforcement learning; rote
        learning; trial-and-error
        learning; unlearning of
        routines; vicarious learning
learning-by-doing 260, 269, 270, 271
legitimacy 160, 170
Leibenstein, H. 223, 224
Leidner, R. 294–5
level of aggregation, as dimension of
    reproduction mechanisms 248
levels of routines
    and organizational learning 173,
        175, 176, 177
    and performance feedback theory
        195–8, 199, 200, 201
    and search 118
Levinthal, Daniel 107–8, 116, 117, 118,
    127, 175, 245
Levitt, Barbara 21, 167, 230–31, 233,
    245–6

Levy, Jack S. 37, 40
Liang, D.W. 217
line of action 55, 77
Llerena, Patrick 260, 267
Loasby, B.J. 268
localization, and international norms
    45
localized routines 165
lock-in 162, 169, 210–11, 231, 246,
    268–9
Locke, Edwin A. 191, 192
long-term memory 209, 214, 306
longitudinal studies 293
loosely coupled systems 56–8, 62,
    78
Lorge, I. 304
lower-level officials 33, 36
lower-level units 165, 168
Luchins, Abraham S. 302
Luckmann, Thomas 154, 231, 239–40,
    241, 242, 247

Macintosh, N. 89, 95
macro-level routines 195–8, 199, 200,
    201
Maitlis, S. 171
management 65, 72, 73–4
    see also management accounting;
        managers; professional
        management; strategic
        management approach; top
        management
management accounting 88, 89–90,
    103
    see also institutional perspective on
        management accounting
        routines
managers 190, 191, 200, 272–3
mapping processes 296
March, James M. 6, 21, 38–9, 57, 72,
    95, 97, 98, 141, 156–7, 158, 167,
    169, 173, 175, 179, 188, 190, 194,
    230–31, 233, 245–6, 247, 256,
    266–7, 308–9
Marengo, Luigi 107–8, 109, 112,
    114–15, 116, 117, 267
market selection 142, 160, 167
McDougall, William 16
McKeown, Timothy J. 38, 40
meanings 96–7, 258–9

measurement of organizational
routines 41
see also Tayloristic organization
mechanical mindset 302
memorization
cognitive automatisms 208, 209–11,
212, 222, 223, 233
declarative versus non-declarative
knowledge 213–14
dissociated memory 208, 303, 306
and emotions 213, 214–15
procedural versus declarative
knowledge 206–9, 306–8
representations versus memorization
in action 211–13
see also declarative memory;
depreciation from
organizational memory;
forgetting of routines; long-
term memory; non-declarative
memory; organizational
memory; procedural memory;
transactive memory; working
memory
Merton, Robert K. 240
meso-level routines 198, 199, 200,
201
meta-routines 118, 175, 179
metastability 117–18, 119
methodologies 12–13, 47, 68, 71–5,
76–7, 320
see also cross-sectional studies;
empirical field studies of
organizational routines;
empirical research;
experimental research on
organizational routines;
longitudinal studies;
organizational ethnographies
micro-level routines 195, 196, 199, 200,
201
military planning 37, 40–41, 45–6
Miller, P. 95, 99
mindfulness *see* calculation
mindlessness 233, 240, 245
see also automatisms
Miner, Anne S. 153, 154, 156, 159, 160,
161, 163, 164, 165–6, 167, 168,
169, 170, 172, 173, 174, 179, 193,
194, 218, 294, 295

mistakes 194, 233
see also accidents
mixed methods of research 68, 71, 75
mood 245
Moorman, C. 218
Morgan, John 304
Morison, Elting E. 23, 156, 234
motivation 223, 248, 257, 263, 267–9,
270, 271
see also incentives; payoffs; rewards
motor-sensory automatisms 209
multiplication 133–4
Murray, F. 159, 164

Narduzzo, A. 161, 162, 165, 176–7,
294, 295, 312, 319–20
narratives 288–9
Neal, D.T. 127, 128, 129, 130, 133
negative feedback 141–2
negotiation 241–2
Nelson, Richard R. 5, 10, 18–19, 21,
67–9, 71, 74, 75, 87, 93, 94, 95, 97,
100, 101, 109, 110, 118, 126, 136,
137, 139, 141–2, 144, 175, 217,
232, 240, 242, 245, 256, 258, 267,
273–4, 288, 304, 308
neoclassical economics 67, 68, 88, 98–9
networks 62–3, 163, 166, 241–2, 296
neuronal networks 240–41, 249
new entrants 126, 136, 137
new job creation 161, 165
new knowledge 218, 219, 222, 223, 243,
261, 262, 265–6, 269
new product development 159, 160,
161, 164, 165, 168, 179, 218
new routines 40, 127, 134, 141–2, 157,
261
new technology 158, 159, 164, 220,
221
NK-model (Kauffman) 113–14
non-declarative memory 213, 214, 303
see also procedural memory
Nonaka, I. 243, 269
norms 7, 16, 41–7, 261, 263, 271
nuclear weapons, accidents with 39, 41

obsolete routines 23, 156
occupational groups 65, 73
see also jobs
off-diagonal comparisons 295

Ohnistic (Japanese) organization
110–11, 257
Olsen, Johan P. 56, 72, 167, 169, 256
Olson, C.A. 173
Olson, O. 98–9
one-shot games 320–21
opaqueness 112
optimization 88, 114, 115, 232
see also sub-optimality
Opwis, K. 313
order 6–7, 118
organizational behaviour 107–8
organizational change 62, 101
organizational culture 62
organizational ecology 60
organizational economics 69
organizational ethnographies 71–4,
79
organizational forgetting 220
see also unlearning of routines
organizational learning 21, 152–3,
231
see also forgetting of routines;
organizational learning and
organizational routines;
unlearning of routines
organizational learning and
organizational routines
change in mix of stable routines
156–75
challenges and future research
172–5
retention 157, 159–63, 170–72,
174–5
selection 157, 159–63, 166–9,
174–5
variation 157, 158–66, 174–5
experimentation 159, 164, 175, 266
and organizational memory 154–6,
161, 171, 172, 177
and organizational structure 273–4
routines for learning 178–81
theory overview 141, 230–31
transformational change in
organizational routines 175–8,
194, 195
see also performance feedback
theory; search
organizational memory 18, 97–8,
154–6, 170, 216–23, 256

organizational routines
change (*see* change in organizational
routines)
concept (*see* concept of
organizational routines)
definitions (*see* definitions of
organizational routines)
importance 15, 25
properties 133–4
recognition 237
as replicators 126–7, 138, 139, 140,
141
theory overview 229–36
organizational sociology and
organizational routines
organizational routines, managerial
work and macrosociology of
capitalism 63–7
organizations as going concerns and
loosely coupled systems 55–8
research routines 76–7
social conventions and
mesosociology 62–3
social conventions and
microsociology 58–62
towards an evolutionary economic
sociology 67–75
organizational structure
and change in organizational
routines 194, 195
and firm entry and exit 137
going concerns 70–71, 72
and organizational learning 273–4
and performance feedback theory
198–9
organizations 7, 55–8, 291
see also firms, as replicators; going
concerns
ostensive aspect of routines
comparison of organizational
routines 293, 294–5
in concept of organizational routines
153, 175, 176, 177, 178, 219,
236, 242, 286, 287, 288–9
and identification of organizational
routines 291–2
and institutionalization 242
outcomes 19, 20, 159, 167, 169, 245
see also performance standard
Ozcelik, H. 171

Paoli, M. 217, 256, 259
Park, Robert E. 56
Parker, C.F. 37–8
past performance 167, 188, 189, 190
path dependency 101, 114, 231, 237–9, 312
payoffs 315, 317–18
peer groups 188, 190–91
Peirce, Charles Sanders 6, 16
Pentland, Brian T. 9, 41, 62, 127, 129, 153–4, 175–6, 219, 234–5, 236, 242, 244, 283, 286, 287, 288, 291, 292, 293, 294, 296, 297, 319
perceptual rigidity 37
performance feedback theory
    described 188–91
    individual habits and group routines 191–3, 195, 198, 199–200
    integrated model 198–9
    intraorganizational routines 193–5, 198, 199
    levels of organizational routines 195–8, 199, 200, 201
    and pre-planned selection 159, 167
    unanswered questions 199–200
performance gaps 157, 167
performance standard 116, 117, 217, 304–5
    see also past performance; performance feedback theory; performance gaps
performative aspect of routines
    comparison of organizational routines 293–4, 295
    in concept of organizational routines 153–4, 175–6, 177, 178, 219, 286, 287–8
    concurrency 296–7
    described 236
    empirical field studies 285
    grammatical structure 235
    identification of organizational routines 291
    see also action; performance feedback theory
Perrow, C. 211
Perruchet, P. 210
persistence 20–21, 23, 24, 130, 133, 137, 138
Phillips, D.J. 163, 166

physical environment 22–3
Pisano, Gary P. 69, 118, 164
planning, military 37, 40–41, 45–6
plans 37, 38
point of view 287–8, 289, 295–6
Polanyi, Michael 17, 308
policy analysis 33–4, 283–4, 285
political science 31, 32–3
political science and organizational routines
    analytical studies in international law 34–5, 42
    bureaucratic politics 35–41
    historical trajectory of studies 32–4
    international norms and interorganizational transmission of rules 41–7
political stability 41
politics 179, 219
population ecology 142–3
population-level learning 162, 171–2
positive feedback 131–2, 142
Posner, Eric A. 42, 43
Postrel, Steven 129, 130
potentialities, in concept of organizational routines 20
power 47, 110, 116, 243, 247, 268
    see also authority; control
pre-planning
    retention 159–60, 170–71
    selection 159–60, 167–8
    variation 158–60, 164–5
    see also teams
predictability 18, 20
Prencipe, A. 217, 256, 259
Price, George R. 125, 136, 137
pride 191, 240, 271
priming 23, 240–41, 249
principal-agent model 117, 263, 269, 271
prior paths 238, 239
    see also repetition
prior performance *see* past performance
prior routines 173–4
prisoner's dilemma 268
problem representation 116, 117
problem-solving
    and automatisms 312–13

behavioural versus cognitive
perspectives 305–6
and bounded rationality in decision
making 38–9
and evolutionary theories 141
experimental research on
organizational routines 305–6,
312–13
and governance structure in
capability-based view of the
firm 109–11
and intentions 130
in theories of organizational
routines 230
towards a formal representation of a
capability-based view of the
firm 111–15, 116–17, 118
see also performance feedback
theory
problemistic search
and confirmation bias 309–10
defined 187, 309
and organizational routines
117–18
in performance feedback theory 188,
189, 196, 197, 200
and satisficing 130, 230
search effort 116
towards formal representation in
capability-based view of the
firm 111, 112, 114, 116
procedural authority 262, 271
procedural knowledge
and cognitive automatisms 210–11
in content of organizational memory
218–19
context 211
versus declarative knowledge 206–9,
306–8, 311
in definitions of organizational
routines 206, 208
institutional perspective on
management accounting
routines 94–5, 97–8
in ISO certification case study 221,
222, 223
and organizational memory 155
transfer failures 211
procedural memory
concatenation 23, 244, 249

experimental research on
organizational routines 306–8
and information transmission 22–3,
25–6
in organizational learning 161, 171,
172, 177
role 208
in theories of organizational
routines 234
production memory 207
production rules 208
professional conduct 46
professional management 62, 65, 66,
71
professionals 65
professions 73
project teams 261, 265, 269, 270
propensities 16, 20
see also dispositions
prospect theory 196–8
psychology 16, 17, 128, 133, 302–6
see also cognitive dimension;
memorization; organizational
learning
public administration 32–3, 34

quality management 118
see also ISO certification; TQM
(total quality management)

radical change in routines 195, 197
Ragin, Charles C. 293
rational authority 66, 78–9
rational choice 42–5, 59, 71
rationality 64, 65, 66, 67, 88, 107–8,
112
see also behavioural game theory
and theory of routines;
bounded rationality; formal
rationality
rationalization 16, 230
ready-made solutions 132, 134, 256
Reagans, R. 161, 171
Reber, Arthur S. 17, 302, 303
reciprocal typification 241–2, 249
recognition 191, 237, 270, 271
recurrent collective activity 58, 69
redundant routines 23, 156
refinement 127, 134, 243
regret 317

Reimer, T. 312, 313
reinforcement learning 130, 131, 133,
    315, 316–17
repeated games 42, 314–18, 321
repetition
    and cognitive automatisms 208, 212
    and concept of organizational
        routines 4
    in definitions of organizational
        routines 153, 232, 237, 256
    habits 16, 128, 129, 130
    and strength of reproduction
        mechanisms 240, 241, 245, 246,
        249–50
replication 17, 21–5, 99–100, 126–7,
    138–41, 142, 144
replicators 24–5, 126–7, 138, 139, 140,
    141
report-writing empirical field study
    283–4, 285
representations 116, 117, 211, 212, 213,
    296
representative aspect of routines *see*
    ostensive aspect of routines
reproduction mechanisms
    dimensions and typologies 248
    examples
        artifacts 243–4, 249
        calculation 244–5, 248, 249
        coercion 242, 247, 249
        competency traps 245–6, 249
        concatenation of procedural
            memory 244, 249
        escalation of commitment 246–7,
            249
        formalization 243, 249
        habitualization 239–40, 249
        institutionalization 242, 249
        leadership 247, 249
        priming 240–41, 249
        reciprocal typification 241–2,
            249
        value infusion 242–3
    predictions 248–50
reputation 44, 263
research and development 178–80,
    187
research routines 76–7
resistance to change 101–3, 197, 219,
    222, 223, 224, 240, 243

resource-based view of the firm 69
resource dependence theory 60
retaliatory strategies 42, 43
retention
    in evolutionary economic sociology
        70
    in evolutionary economics 70
    and formalization 243
    habits and organizational routines
        134
    organizational learning and
        organizational routines 157,
        159–63, 170–72
        emergent from external sources
            162, 171–2
        emergent from internal sources
            161, 171
        implications of prior research
            174–5
        pre-planned from external sources
            160, 170–71
        pre-planned from internal sources
            159, 170
        research frontiers 172, 173
retrieval 256, 308–9
Reuter, H.H. 127, 234–5, 283, 287, 291,
    292, 293, 294, 319
rewards 116, 130–31, 191
    see also incentives; payoffs
Reynaud, B. 177
Rhodes, E. 39
rigidity 37, 40–41, 193
risk 69, 189–90, 196–8, 201, 268–9
Rittberger, Volker 45, 47
Roberts, J. 92, 97
Robey, D. 288
Rocco, E. 161, 162, 165, 319–20
rote learning 311, 314–15
Roth, A.E. 314–15
'routines as genes' 5, 10, 18–19, 20, 21,
    142, 143, 144, 145, 232
routinization 154, 155–6, 220–23
rules
    in analytical studies in international
        law 34
    and behavioural game theory 318
    bureaucratic politics and
        organizational routines 39
    and concept of organizational
        routines 4, 18, 19, 20, 21, 153

and formalization 243
institutional perspective on
    management accounting
    routines 90–95
in problem-solving experimental
    studies 306
and replication of organizational
    routines 24
in teams 265
see also codification; norms;
    production rules; standard
    operating procedures
Rumelt, Richard P. 129, 130
Rura-Polley, T. 154, 156, 161, 168–9,
    294, 295

Sabherwal, R. 288
Sagan, Scott D. 39, 41
satisficing 130, 230
Scapens, Robert W. 88, 89, 90, 91, 92,
    95, 97, 98, 99, 103
Schacter, Daniel L. 22, 244
Schank, R.C. 231, 240
Schelling, T.C. 268, 320
Schmidt, R.A. 209
Schneider, W. 206, 209
Schön, D. 269
Schulz, Martin 154, 159, 170, 243
Schumpeter, Joseph A. 58, 118
Schwab, A. 173
scripts 231–2, 233, 240, 241
search 187–8
    see also performance feedback
        theory; problemistic search
selection
    and concept of organizational
        routines 21
    in definitions of organizational
        routines 109, 256
    in evolutionary economic sociology
        70
    in evolutionary economics 68, 70,
        71, 142, 267
    in evolutionary system philosophy
        24–5
    ·and habits 17, 134
    by managers 273
    organizational learning and

        organizational routines 157,
            159–63, 166–9
        emergent from external sources
            162–3, 169
        emergent from internal sources
            161, 168–9
        implications of prior research
            174–5
        pre-planned from external sources
            160, 167–8
        pre-planned from internal sources
            159, 167
        research frontiers 172, 173
    and path dependency 238–9
self-organized groups 264
self-tuning 316
self-validation 241
Selten, R. 316–17, 321
Selznick, P. 242–3
sensemaking 62, 71
sequential responses 21, 25, 139
Shannon, Vaughn P. 47
shared cognitive bundles 153
shared languages 258–9, 263, 264, 270,
    271
shared meanings 258–9
shared understandings 176, 262–3
Shiffrin, R.C. 206, 209
Shuen, Amy 69, 118
Simon, Herbert A. 7, 32, 70, 78, 95,
    111–12, 114, 115, 130, 188, 194,
    206–7, 230, 256, 273
Sine, W.D. 160, 170
Singley, M.K. 306–7, 308, 309, 311
skills 17, 25, 232, 240
    see also capabilities; capacities
slack search 187, 189
social change 61–2, 72, 235–6, 285
social cognition 231–2
social conventions 55, 56, 58–63, 71
social environment 22–3
social factors, and habits 16, 17
social movements, and emergent
    selection 163, 169
social networks 62–3, 163, 166
social worlds/arenas 56, 61–2, 74, 77–8
socialization 45–6, 61
sociology 76–7
    see also evolutionary economic
        sociology; organizational

sociology and organizational
routines; structural-functional
sociology
sociotechnical systems 65–6, 73–4
'soft' law 34–5
software support hot line empirical
field study 281–3, 296
somatic markers 215
Sorenson, O. 167, 172
specialization, and transactive memory
217
Spellman, B.A. 303
Squire, L.R. 211, 213, 306
stability
and habits 127, 128, 130, 131
institutional perspective on
management accounting
routines 94
in organizational routines 133
organizational routines in capability-
based view of the firm 117–18
and organizations as going concerns
55, 56
path dependency 237–9
reproduction mechanism (*see*
reproduction mechanisms)
and social conventions 61, 62
see also cultural stability;
metastability; political stability
Stahl, D.O. 317–18
Stalker, G.M. 73–4
standard operating procedures 35,
37–8, 39–40, 41–2, 153, 154–5,
156–7, 158, 230, 288
Staw, Barry M. 246
Stern, E.K. 37–8
Stern, I. 159, 160, 167–8, 172
stimulus-response theory 233–4
strategic change 196–8, 200, 201
strategic management approach 59
strategy 38, 39, 42–3, 107–8
Strauss, Anselm L. 56, 73
strength 129, 240, 241, 245, 246,
249–50, 310
structural-functional sociology 65, 68
student housing empirical field study
235–6, 284–5
sub-optimality 115, 231, 232, 246, 305,
311–12
sub-problems 114–15, 116, 117

sub-routines 58, 175, 176
sub-units 39
subset selection 125–6, 134, 136, 137,
138, 142, 144
subsets, of habits 127, 128, 129
substantive rationality 66
Suchman, L.A. 73, 288, 291, 294, 295,
296
Swaine, Edward T. 43–4
Swistak, P. 42, 43
Szulanski, G. 112, 138, 140, 155

tacit knowledge
and accounting rules and routines
90, 97–8
in concept of organizational routines
256
and evolutionary economics 67–8,
232
and formalization 243
and implicit learning 308
and long-term memory 306
and pre-planned retention 170
and procedural memory 22, 23,
234
in theories of organizational
routines 234
tacit learning *see* implicit learning
taken-for-granted assumptions 93, 94,
100, 101, 102
Takeuchi, H. 243
task complexity 192
Tayloristic organization 110, 111,
257
team leaders 260
teams 258, 259–61, 265, 269, 270, 271
technocracies 66
technological change 118
technological complexity 211
technology 244
see also new technology;
technocracies; technological
change; technological
complexity; technology lock-in
technology lock-in 162, 169
Teece, David J. 69, 118
Tenski, R.V. 258
terrorist attacks 39
Thomas, William 16
Thompson, James C. 40–41

Thorndyke, E.L. 302, 311
thoughts 16, 17, 127, 128, 129, 130,
    132
tightly-coupled systems 57, 58, 62, 78
time-dependence 61
time factors, in empirical field studies
    of organizational routines 282,
    283, 284–5, 287, 293–4
    see also persistence
tools 244
top management 156, 200
TQM (total quality management) 155,
    179, 243
traditional authority 66, 78
transactive memory 161, 171, 217
transfer of routines 132–3, 306, 307,
    309, 310–11, 313, 319
trial-and-error learning 175, 176, 180,
    266
    see also experimentation
Tripsas, M. 159, 164
truces 94, 110, 118, 242, 288
trust 163, 217
Tulving, Endel 22, 244
Tushman, M.L. 175

uncertain task environment 132
uncertainty reduction 232
unconscious processes 16, 17, 303
    see also automatisms; mechanical
    mindset
Ungson, G.R. 154
unlearning of routines 222, 223
    see also forgetting of routines
urban ecology 56

validation of knowledge, in knowing
    communities 264
value infusion 242–3
Van de Ven, A.H. 158, 159, 167, 292,
    296
Van Huyck, J. 317–18
variation
    and capability-based view of the
        firm 118
    empirical field studies of
        organizational routines 282–3,
        285, 289, 291, 292, 293–4
    in evolutionary economic sociology
        70

in evolutionary economics 68, 70
in evolutionary theories 125, 135–6,
    138, 140, 158
organizational learning and
    organizational routines 157,
    158–66, 172–4
    emergent from external sources
        162–3, 166
    emergent from internal sources
        161–2, 165–6
    implications of prior research
        174–5
    pre-planned from external sources
        160, 164–5
    pre-planned from internal sources
        158–60, 164
    research frontiers 172, 173–4
social conventions 60–61
Veblen, Thorstein B. 16, 20
Verburg, R.M. 261
veto power 116
vicarious learning 153, 319
visual automatisms 209
voluntary attention 212

Wagner, Wolfgang 45, 47
Waldo, Dwight 33
Walsh, J.P. 154
war planning 37, 40–41
Warglien, M. 161, 162, 165, 319, 320,
    321
Weber, R.A. 319, 321
Weberian theories 6, 64–5, 66–7, 69,
    72, 74, 78–9, 229–30, 290
Weeks, John R. 73
Weick, Karl E. 6, 56–7, 62, 71, 194,
    322
Wenger, E.C. 262, 263, 264
White, Harrison C. 290
Wilson, Woodrow 32–3
Winograd, T. 206, 207
Winter, Sidney G. 5, 10, 18–19, 21, 57,
    67–9, 71, 74, 75, 87, 93, 94, 95, 97,
    100, 101, 109, 110, 112, 118, 126,
    127, 136, 137, 138, 139, 140,
    141–2, 143, 144, 155, 175, 187,
    217, 232, 240, 242, 245, 256, 258,
    267, 288, 304, 308
Witt, U. 265, 272
Wood, W. 127, 128, 129, 130, 133

working memory 207, 208, 209
World War II artillery case study 23,
    156, 234

Zelikow, Philip 35, 36
Znaniecki, Florian 16
Zollo, Maurizio 57, 69, 127